Signature Seasons

Signature Seasons

*Fifteen Baseball Legends
at Their Most Memorable,
1908–1949*

PAUL WARBURTON

McFarland & Company, Inc., Publishers

Jefferson, North Carolina, and London

All of the photographs were provided by
Transcendental Graphics/theruckerarchive.com

LIBRARY OF CONGRESS CATALOGUING-IN-PUBLICATION DATA

Warburton, Paul, 1953–
    Signature seasons : fifteen baseball legends at their most
memorable, 1908–1949 / Paul Warburton.
        p.   cm.
    Includes bibliographical references and index.

    ISBN 978-0-7864-4655-1
    softcover : 50# alkaline paper ∞

    1. Baseball players — United States.   2. Baseball — United
States — History.   I. Title.
    GV863.A1W368   2010
    796.3570922 — dc22 [B]   2010024636

British Library cataloguing data are available

Cover image: Lou Gehrig (Transcendental Graphics)

Manufactured in the United States of America

*McFarland & Company, Inc., Publishers
    Box 611, Jefferson, North Carolina 28640
    www.mcfarlandpub.com*

To my parents, Ralph and Rosemary,
who inspired my passion for baseball.

Contents

Acknowledgments ix

Preface 1

1. Matty Was Master of Them All: Christy Mathewson
in 1908 5

2. Detroit's Wildcat at His Peak: Ty Cobb in 1911 25

3. The Babe at His Best: Babe Ruth in 1921 40

4. The Mighty Rajah: Rogers Hornsby in 1922 56

5. The Sizzler and His Browns: George Sisler in 1922 68

6. How to Drive in 191 Runs: Hack Wilson in 1930 81

7. The Beast of the White Elephants: Jimmie Foxx in 1932 97

8. Mr. Dean at His Dizziest: Dizzy Dean in 1934 112

9. Larrupin' Lou and McCarthy's Bombers: Lou Gehrig
in 1936 128

10. The Motor City's Big RBI Man: Hank Greenberg
in 1937 144

11. Boston's Kid Bats .406: Ted Williams in 1941 157

12. Rapid Robert's Triumphant Return: Bob Feller in 1946 172

13. The Pride of the Redbirds: Stan Musial in 1948 184

14. The Great DiMag: Joe DiMaggio in 1948 199

15. Jackie's MVP Season: Jackie Robinson in 1949 214

Chapter Notes 231

Bibliography 239

Index 243

Acknowledgments

So many people were helpful to me in writing this book. First, I would like to thank my parents Ralph and Rosemary Warburton, who I dedicate the book to. They believed in me, inspired my love of baseball, and were so supportive of my efforts. My mom taught me how to read and work with numbers by using the back of baseball cards. She attended the World Series in Milwaukee in 1957, 1958, and 1982, and was a big Milwaukee Braves and Brewers fan. She died in October 2009. After her death I thought about giving up the book project but I knew she would have wanted me to finish it. My father played baseball at Dartmouth College under coach Jeff Tesreau, the former star pitcher for John McGraw's New York Giants, and follows the game closely today at age 85. He also played on the 1948 USA Olympic hockey team at St. Moritz and inspired my respect for good sportsmanship.

I thank the late Jack Kavanagh of SABR, who taught me so much about writing and baseball. I would also like to thank SABR's Len Levin and Bill Reynolds of the *Providence Journal*, who critiqued my work and helped me improve it. I must thank SABR's Mark Rucker of Transcendental Graphics for working with me on the photos used in the book. I thank my brother-in-law John Brough for helping me organize the book on a disc and my sister Martha Brough for her support on the project. I also thank George Milkaitis and Mike Buffi, who served as my designated readers.

Preface

This book is a tribute to the stars of old-time baseball in their most interesting if not best single season. It is an attempt to take the reader back to those days long ago when baseball was the unchallenged king of sports in America. The 15 players showcased in this book are stars your father or grandfather might have told you about. Hopefully my writing will make them come alive again at their very best.

Many people say today's major league ballplayers are better than those from previous generations. They are bigger, stronger and faster. They have the benefit of better training, better equipment and better dietary information. Many use performance-enhancing supplements. If you believe the testimony of many around the game, modern-day ballplayers made extensive use of amphetamines (greenies) for a period of at least 30 years and steroids for at least a decade. The widespread use of illegal drugs and steroids has tainted the sport.

The Mitchell report in December of 2007 sadly revealed just how prevalent the use of steroids and human growth hormones has been in major league baseball. But this book is not an attempt to tear down modern-day baseball. Before 1947, African American ballplayers were not allowed in the major leagues. For that reason alone one has to say that modern-day major league baseball is superior to the game that preceded it.

Yet I believe there is a lot to be said for the old-time ballplayer. The guys that played in flannel uniforms with four-fingered gloves created the foundation for which the millionaires who now excel in the sport benefit. Prior to 1961, there were only 16 major league teams while today there are 30. There were also more than twice as many minor league teams. The competition to reach the major leagues was fierce. Baseball was the only sport in which a significant amount of money could be made unless an athlete wanted to take a chance of getting his brains beaten out as a prize-fighter. Pro football, basketball and ice hockey were in their infancy. Pro soccer was non-existent. Golf and tennis were almost exclusively for the elite upper class. Just about all the best athletes in America went into baseball.

In the early 1900s every town or village in America had a semi-pro or amateur adult baseball team. Kids filled the sandlots playing baseball for hours. Young boys were in love with playing baseball and for many the days weren't long enough. A kid might get to bat more than 50 times a day. They did not spend long hours watching television, surfing the Internet, or playing video games. Baseball was the king of America's youth and skills were honed each year in the summer sun on the sandlots. The population in the United States has doubled since, but it may be true that more Americans actually played baseball back then. And they played the game more often, almost to the point where baseball was like a religion.

The old-time major leaguers did not have the luxury of five-year multi-million-dollar contracts. When Hank Greenberg missed most of the 1936 season due to a broken wrist, Detroit had him sign a one-dollar contract until he proved in spring training of 1937 that he could still play the game as well as before. Then and only then did big Hank receive the same $25,000 salary he was paid in 1936. Major leaguers had to prove themselves over and over again every spring. Cardinals star Enos Slaughter recalled that every spring there was a different outfielder who had batted .350 or .375 in the minors and was given the opportunity to challenge for a starting job. Baseball was a ticket out of the hard labor of the mills, mines, factories or farm fields.

Yet most major league players were not any better off financially than the average Joe. Some of today's stars earn more money for a few games than a policeman or teacher makes in a year. That was not the case then. Most players had to work a job in the offseason to make ends meet. As late as 1950, Mickey Mantle, the Yankees' premier prospect, worked in the mines back home in Oklahoma in the offseason before joining the team for spring training in 1951.

The old-time ballplayers also were eligible for the military draft and many served their country in time of war. In World War I, three stars showcased in this book — Christy Mathewson, Ty Cobb and George Sisler — volunteered for the Chemical Warfare Division, considered one of the most hazardous of all units. Mathewson became exposed to deadly poison gas and thereafter suffered from tuberculosis, which led to his death at age 45. Grover Cleveland Alexander, then arguably the best pitcher in the game, served at the front in the 342nd Field Artillery. The firing was incessant in his seven weeks of action in charge of a battery. He returned permanently deaf in one ear with an even worse affliction, epilepsy, to be discovered.[1]

World War II was even worse. By the time the hostilities ceased in 1945, more than 1,000 major leaguers were in the armed forces.[2] Six players featured in this book — Hank Greenberg, Ted Williams, Joe DiMaggio, Stan Musial, Jackie Robinson and Bob Feller — served in the war. Greenberg served in India, Burma, and China, spending 11 months in war zones and participating in the first land-based bombing of Japan. Williams trained fighter pilots for three years in World War II. Later in the Korean War, he flew 39 combat missions, and once crash-landed his plane before emerging from the flaming wreckage fortunate to be alive. DiMaggio did not see action in the war but he did volunteer and spend three years in the armed forces, instead of patrolling center field in Yankee Stadium for good money. Musial spent a year assigned to ship repair duty at Pearl Harbor. Robinson served first as a cavalry officer and then in a tank division. The best pitcher in the game, Bob Feller, joined the navy two days after the attack on Pearl Harbor and saw combat action in the Pacific on the USS *Alabama* in charge of an anti-aircraft gun. He was not eligible for the draft because he was the sole support for his family. His father was ill with cancer and would die in 1943. But Feller volunteered anyway. He traded in a $50,000-a-year income for military pay of $80 a month. He, like many, wanted to do his part, and he did not feel special. In an interview with author John Sickels on October 18, 2002, Feller declared, "I'm no hero. Get this straight. The heroes didn't come back. Only the survivors did."[3]

The fact that African American ballplayers were not allowed in the major leagues until Jackie Robinson broke the color barrier with a season of extraordinary courage in 1947 is an American tragedy. It was simply wrong and inexcusable. Many great black ballplayers were denied the right to compete on baseball's biggest stage. Certainly many white ballplayers who played before 1947 wouldn't have reached the major leagues if the black ballplayers had been allowed in. Some may argue that many white ballplayers became legends at the expense of the excluded black ballplayers; they have a point. Yet I believe these same white ballplayers would have been in the major leagues then if black ballplayers WERE included AND there were 30 teams (as there are now) instead of only 16 teams in existence before 1961. The point I am trying to make is that the skill level in the major leagues was very high back then, just as it is today.

Frank Robinson, the first black manager in the major leagues, spent most of his adult life in baseball and knows as much about the game as anyone. When asked to compare Barry Bonds with Babe Ruth and the eras they played, Robinson was quoted in the April 5–11, 2006, edition of *USA Today Sports Weekly*, opining, "You have to take each era on its own merits. How can anyone say, 'So-and-so would have hit this many home runs in this year?' You can't. No one knows."[4] I agree with Mr. Robinson about the eras and the home runs.

In my final chapter on Jackie Robinson, I include a high appraisal of the talent in the so-called Negro Leagues, particularly their two greatest stars, Satchel Paige and Josh Gibson. As Paige said, "If you want to know the truth, I wasn't the onliest one who could pitch in the Negro Leagues. I told them at Cooperstown we had a lot of Satchels. There were a lot of Joshes. We had top pitchers. We had quite a few men who could hit the ball like Babe and Josh. Wasn't any mebbe so."[5]

Chapter 1

Matty Was Master of Them All: Christy Mathewson in 1908

Christy Mathewson was the player most responsible for the popularity explosion of major league baseball at the start of the twentieth century. Fans admired baseball stars for their athletic prowess, but ballplayers were thought to be low class, irresponsible, and dumb. Most possessed little education and were crude in speech and manner. They drank liquor in excess, chased women, and were stereotyped as a ruffian breed too lazy to work for a living. Mathewson was different.

Mathewson rarely drank or smoked. When he did it was in moderation. He was president of his class at Bucknell College, where he was also a member of two literary societies and a three-sport star. The ace pitcher of the baseball team, he played center in basketball and fullback in football. He was the best kicker in the nation in an era when field goals counted as much as touchdowns. Bucknell played such football powers as Army and Navy. Walter Camp, the originator of college football's All-America team, called Christy "the best all-around football player I ever saw."[1] Mathewson majored in forestry and possessed a sharp mind. He sometimes played ten checker or chess opponents simultaneously and defeated them all. He also shot in the mid–70s in golf.

Mathewson came from a devout Methodist family and refused to play ball on Sundays due to a promise he made to his mother. He earned a reputation of being impeccably honest and a true Christian gentleman. He stood 6'2" and weighed 195 pounds. He was a good-looking man with big shoulders, short blond hair and blue eyes. He played for the New York Giants, the most glamorous team of his era. He was known to be toughest with the game on the line, and he even authored a book entitled *Pitching in a Pinch*.

At the turn of the century major league baseball was not a sport attended by ladies or children. Gamblers frequented the games, and heavy betting was commonplace. Umpires were verbally and physically abused by unruly managers, players and spectators. The arbiters often worked a game alone and seemed like the only sane man in the ballpark.

Matty gave the game a new look. Historian Alexander Scourby wrote, "All at once the game received a new respectability. Young ladies could now ask their escorts to take them to the Polo Grounds to see a college boy play."[2] When Mathewson pitched, the size of crowds doubled.

Author Jonathan Yardley likened Mathewson to the fictional hero of boys sports books, Frank Merriwell. Yardley wrote, "Matty had what we now call charisma, and that along with his remarkable performances made him into a legend. Few if any Americans of his day were so widely and deeply loved.... Matty was worshipped. Men and women of all classes held him up as a model for their children, and no doubt secretly regarded him as one for themselves."[3]

In 17 years Mathewson won 373 games while losing 188 with a 2.13 ERA in 4,780 innings. In 101⅔ innings of World Series pitching, Mathewson's ERA was 1.15. Matty possessed four pitches — a blurring fastball, a wicked curve, a deceptive change of pace and a mystifying reverse curve, which he called his fadeaway. The fadeaway is known nowadays as a screwball. For the right-handed-throwing Mathewson, the pitch broke in on right-handed hitters. He threw it only about 12 times per game because he said it wore down his arm. Opposing batters found it unhittable. Matty had good stuff, but his best asset was astonishing control. He averaged 1.6 walks per nine innings and fanned 2,502 batters. In 1913 he went 68 straight innings without issuing a walk. He once won a nine-inning game with 67 pitches.

The 1908 season was Mathewson's best. In 56 appearances and 390 innings he won 37 games against 11 defeats with a 1.43 ERA. He fanned 259 batters and walked 42. He led the league with 34 complete games, 11 shutouts and five saves. In an incredible pennant race with the Cubs and Pirates, Matty got the ball more than ever. The pennant race that year caught the imagination of Americans like no race before it. The Giants drew 910,000 fans to the Polo Grounds, the most any team would attract until Babe Ruth and the Yankees drew 1,289,422 to an enlarged Polo Grounds in 1920. Mathewson's Giants would have won the pennant if they had not been denied a victory over the Cubs by a technicality in the Merkle incident, which will be described later.

Matty was regarded with awe at the Polo Grounds. His rival, Mordecai Brown of the Chicago Cubs, recalled, "I can still see Christy Mathewson making his lordly entrance. He'd always wait until about ten minutes before game time, then he'd come from the clubhouse across the field in a long linen duster like auto drivers wore in those days, and at every step the crowd would yell louder and louder."[4]

Mathewson's manager, John McGraw, was nicknamed "Little Napoleon" because of his determination to control every aspect of his team's play. McGraw

The ace of the Polo Grounds in 1908, Christy Mathewson won 37 games against 11 defeats with 11 shutouts, 5 saves and a 1.43 ERA in 390 innings. He fanned 259 batters and walked only 42. The last line on his plaque at the Baseball Hall of Fame reads "Matty was master of them all."

called pitches from the dugout but never messed with Matty's repertoire. The two lived together with their wives in an apartment for a while in New York and discussed baseball strategy often. McGraw was the chief tactical genius of the Dead Ball era.

Matty would coast when he had a big lead, a situation that didn't occur often. Most of his duels were 1–0, 2–1 or 3–2 games, with the margin for error small. There were some high batting averages by an elite circle of hitters in some Dead Ball seasons, but 1908 was not one of them. In 1908 the NL's batting average was .239 and the league ERA was 2.35. Home runs were rare occurrences. In 1906 the Chicago White Sox won the world championship despite clubbing just seven homers. Stolen bases, bunting, and hit-and-run plays dominated baseball strategy.

Up until the 1920s a ball usually was not replaced until it was knocked into the stands. The ball was doctored with foreign substances by pitchers affecting its flight and adding weight to it. In 1920 the spitball and shine ball were outlawed except for a few designated hurlers who were allowed to continue throwing the pitch. The spheroid then ricocheted off bats like never before.

Mathewson was born in 1880 in Factoryville, Pennsylvania, the oldest of six children of Gilbert and Minerva Mathewson. His father was a post office worker and gentleman farmer. The family was considered wealthy. Matty began pitching with the Giants in 1900, when they were the doormat of the league. After McGraw was hired as manager, the team improved steadily.

The 1904 and 1905 Giants were two of the best teams ever assembled in the Dead Ball era. In 1904 McGraw's bunch won 106 games and copped the pennant. Led by Mathewson (33–12, 368 innings, 2.03 ERA), Joe McGinnity (35–8, 408 innings, 1.61 ERA) and a deaf mute, Luther "Dummy" Taylor (21–15, 296 innings, 2.34 ERA), the Giants compiled a 2.17 team ERA. On offense, McGraw's speedsters swiped 283 bases and led the NL with 744 runs.

In 1905 the Giants won 105 games and then bested Connie Mack's Philadelphia A's in the World Series in five games. Mathewson posted a 32–8 record with a 1.27 ERA in 339 innings before whitewashing the A's three times in six days in the Series. McGinnity and newcomer Leon Ames won 22 games apiece. The Giants swiped 291 bases and topped the league again with 780 runs.

In 1906 the Giants won 96 games yet finished 20 games behind the new power of the league, Frank Chance's Chicago Cubs. Chicago won a record 116 games while losing 36. Their team ERA was 1.75. In 1907 the Cubs ERA dropped even lower, to 1.73, and they topped the Tigers in the World Series. From 1906 to 1910 Chance's ball club won four pennants in five years and averaged 106 wins per season by combining incredible pitching with speed, defense, and clutch hitting.

The Giants started 1907 in fine fashion, winning 17 straight games early. But they fell out of first place and finished a disappointing fourth with an 82–71 record, 25½ games behind the Cubs. Matty (24–13, 315 innings, 2.00 ERA) was in good form but McGinnity (18–18, 310 innings, 3.18 ERA) had slipped. In addition the Giants had aged, covering less ground in the field, stealing fewer bases (205) and scoring fewer runs (574). A major shakeup was needed if they were to compete with Chance's Cubs.

In December, McGraw made a blockbuster trade by swapping starters Dan McGann, Bill Dahlen, and George Browne, catcher Frank Bowerman, and pitcher George Ferguson to the Boston Doves. In return McGraw received Fred Tenney, Al Bridwell, and Tom Needham. Tenney was Boston's player-manager in 1907 and McGraw liked his flawless glove work. He would play first base, bat leadoff, and lead the NL in runs scored in 1908 with 101. Bridwell gave the Giants better range at shortstop and added a pesty bat, averaging .285. Needham replaced the 39-year-old Bowerman as the Giants back-up catcher, giving Roger Bresnahan his days off.

Bresnahan introduced shin guards to the backstop position in 1907, and by 1909 they were commonplace. Once the victim of a bad beaning, he also pioneered a crude batting helmet in 1908. He caught a career-high 140 games, batted .283, and coaxed a league-leading 83 walks. Art Devlin was a fixture at third base for the Giants, leading the league in putouts, assists, and fielding percentage. Two youngsters, Larry Doyle and Buck Herzog, batted .308 and .300, respectively, and provided good defense while sharing time at second base. Cy Seymour patrolled center field, batting .267 with 92 RBIs. During the season McGraw acquired outfielder "Moose" McCormick from the Phils; "Moose" hit .302 in 73 games.

The big addition to the Giants offense was the return of outfielder "Turkey Mike" Donlin. In 1905 Donlin batted .356 and led the league with 124 runs. A broken leg limited him to 37 games in 1906. He quit baseball in 1907 to pursue a career in vaudeville. He married actress Mabel Hite and thought he could earn more money in vaudeville. He returned to the Giants in 1908, batting .334 with 106 RBIs, before Donlin quit the diamond again for an acting career. After two years he returned to baseball. In all or part of 12 seasons, Donlin batted .333. He received his nickname because he strutted like a turkey when he walked.

The Giants opened the season in Philadelphia. Spinning a four-hitter, Mathewson outpitched Phillie ace George McQuillan, 3–1, and drove in the deciding runs with a single in the sixth inning. Four days later Matty pitched against Brooklyn in the home opener at Washington Park. He blanked the Superbas, 4–0, fanning 12. On April 22, Matty pitched his third home opener in a row, this time at the Polo Grounds before 25,000 fans. The New York

Tribune reported: "It was the opening game of the season under Coogan's Bluff, and the biggest crowd which ever saw a game in this city filled every stand, circled the field and lined the viaduct and surrounding points of vantage."[5]

The contest was stopped while McGraw and Brooklyn manager Patsy Donovan met to discuss what to do about the overflow crowd, which was moving closer and closer to the playing field. They decided nothing could be done and play continued. Brooklyn led, 2–1, into the ninth inning when rookie Fred Merkle pinch-hit for Matty and swatted a ground-rule double into the overflow crowd. Spike Shannon bunted Merkle to third. Tenney banged a hard grounder that was fielded crisply and Merkle was tagged out in a rundown between third and home. Donlin ran the count to 2-and-2 and brought the house down with a game-winning belt into the right-field bleachers. Fans mobbed the field and Donlin had to battle his way through the crowd to circle the bases. The New York *Evening Journal* reported that his wife, Mabel, clapped her gloved hands wildly as tears of joy streamed down her cheeks.[6] Mabel was starring in the hit comedy show "Merry-Go-Round" at the time. Theater critics called her the funniest lady on stage. Sadly, she died at age 27 of intestinal cancer.

Matty took the mound five days later at the South End Grounds in Boston and tossed a one-hitter, blanking the Doves, 2–0. He was not as fortunate on April 29. He appeared in relief of George Wiltse and allowed the Doves to tie the game with two runs in the fifth. Boston went on to win in 11 innings, 7–6. Back in New York on May 4, Matty shut out the Phils for six innings while the Giants opened up a 9–0 lead. McGraw rested Mathewson for the final three innings, and the Giants romped, 12–2. Boston came into the Polo Grounds on May 9 and touched up Matty for two runs in the first inning, but the Giants responded with five runs in the bottom of the frame. Matty coasted the rest of the way to a 7–3 win and improved his record to a perfect 6–0. The Giants were two games behind the Cubs with an 11–7 mark.

It was apparent McGinnity's arm had seen its best days. In June the Giants put him on waivers in a failed attempt to rid themselves of Joe's $4,000 salary. They tried again on August 22 but found no takers. As a spot starter and reliever, Joe managed an 11–7 record. Five of his wins were shutouts, and his five saves and 2.27 ERA in 187 innings helped the Giants' cause. McGraw gave the ball to rookie Otis Crandall for 24 starts and he broke even at 12–12. Injury-riddled Red Ames (7–4) and Dummy Taylor (8–5) were spot starters. The biggest boost to the Giants' hopes was the hurling of George "Hooks" Wiltse, who enjoyed a career season while going 23–14 with a 2.24 ERA in 330 innings.

Just when it seemed Christy Mathewson was invincible, he proved he was human. He suffered his first loss on May 13 in Pittsburgh. The Pirates knocked him out in the fifth frame with four runs on the way to a 5–1 win. Howie Camnitz, nicknamed "the Kentucky Rosebud," silenced the Giant bats. The red-headed steel city boxman put together quite a season, going 16–9 in 237 innings with a 1.56 ERA.

The Bucs were led by Honus Wagner. Wagner had threatened to retire in the offseason at age 34, but he changed his mind and joined the Bucs shortly after Opening Day, when his salary was doubled to $10,000. That made him the highest-paid player in the game. In 1908 he led the league in hits (201), doubles (39), triples (19), RBIs (109), stolen bases (53), batting (.354) and slugging (.542). Known as "the Flying Dutchman," the Pittsburgh shortstop topped the league in batting average eight times, socked 3,418 hits, and batted .327 through 21 seasons. No powder-puff hitter, he led the league in slugging percentage six times. Wagner whirled his arms like a crazed sprint swimmer as he dug for extra-base hits and swiped 722 bags.

In addition to Camnitz, the Bucs had a stingy pitching rotation that included Vic Willis (23–11, 2.07 ERA), a workhorse nicknamed "the Delaware Peach" who hurled more than 300 innings in eight seasons. Also on the hill for the Bucs were Nick Maddox (23–8, 2.28 ERA), Sam Leever (15–7, 2.10 ERA), and Lefty Leifield (15–14, 2.10 ERA). Pittsburgh's team ERA of 2.12 was better than the 2.14 ERA of the Giant and Cub staffs. Managed by outfielder Fred Clarke, the Bucs won 98 games and stayed in the race until the end. Clarke was nearing the conclusion of his playing career in 1908 (.265, 24 steals, 83 runs). In 21 seasons he batted .315 with 2,708 hits and 506 steals.

The Giants visited Cincinnati next and Mathewson was clubbed for three runs in the first two innings, prompting McGraw to pinch-hit for him in the third. New York lost, 3–1. Matty asked McGraw for a chance to redeem himself two days later and the Reds hammered him, pounding 15 hits and netting nine runs in seven innings. New York lost, 9–5. On May 25, Matty was hit hard in Chicago for the fourth game in a row. The Cubs tagged him for seven hits and five runs in two innings, although the Giants fought back to tie the score before losing in the tenth inning, 8–7. Over a span of four games Matty had been routed for 33 hits and 22 runs in 16 innings. It was the worst slump of his career.

Members of the Giant team reportedly attributed Matty's slump to too much checker playing. When the Giants were on the road, local checker champions came from near and far to challenge Matty at checkers and he accommodated them all.[7] The majority of sports scribes criticized McGraw for his trade the previous winter, and now they were predicting Matty had seen his best days. But on May 30, the bold headlines in the *New York Times* shouted

"MATTY COMES TO LIFE IN BROOKLYN." Mathewson out dueled Brooklyn's Napoleon Rucker, 1–0, with a four-hitter.

Now back on track, Mathewson held the Doves to three singles on June 3, struck out 11, and allowed just one walk in a 3–0 whitewash. On June 6, he stopped St. Louis, 3–2, Matty's 20th consecutive victory over the Cardinals. In the eighth inning the Cards loaded the bases. A medium fly ball to Seymour in center scored Billy Gilbert from third. Seymour's throw sailed over catcher Tom Needham's head, and Bill Ludwig tried to score the tying run from second. But Matty alertly backed up his catcher, retrieved the errant toss, and threw Ludwig out at the plate. The victory was Mathewson's ninth against three losses, but the Giants were in fifth place with a mediocre 21–20 record. McGraw no longer seemed the wizard of past campaigns and only Matty's arm was keeping his ballclub's nose above water.

Clarke's Pirates came into New York on June 10 for a four-game series. Crandall beat them in the opener, 8–2. Wiltse lost a heart-breaker to Leever, 1–0, the next day when Clarke dashed home on an infield grounder in the fourth inning, arriving an eyelash ahead of Tenney's throw. Matty pitched game three but was a victim of crucial errors by Bridwell, Doyle, and Devlin while losing to Willis, 5–2. Wagner smashed a homer. In game four Maddox outpitched McGinnity, 4–0, and the Giants' record fell back to 23–23.

It was then McGraw's team finally caught fire and began its drive into the pennant race. The Reds rambled into town and McGraw's gang beat them three straight. Crandall won the opener, 3–2. Matty and McGinnity then combined to win a doubleheader, 2–1 and 4–2, respectively. Matty scattered seven hits, fanned seven Reds, and didn't walk a batter. Chance's first-place Cubs entered the Big Apple next. Joe Vila of the *Sporting News* wrote: "McGraw and his men have absolutely no chance to finish near the top. If the Cubs win the series this week, it will be all over."[8]

But the Giants had a surprise for Chance. After dropping the opener, 7–5, the Gothamites whipped the Windy City boys three straight. Crandall outhurled Jack Pfiester, 6–3. Matty spun a three-hit shutout next before a standing-room-only crowd of 25,000, winning, 4–0, and prompting W.W. Aulick to write in the *New York Times*, "Our esteemed Matty was all there. He threw 'em in fast and savage and plentiful, and every now and then Roger Bresnahan had to walk away from the plate or stoop down and pick up a little gravel, or stall in some other equally genteel way so's Matty wouldn't be so fast. But even at that, Christy was the Lightning Kid and struck out six Cubs."[9]

When Wiltse finished off the Chicagoans on June 22, 7–1, William F. Kirk penned gleefully in the *New York American*, "The Chicago invaders came here with bells on, growling awful threats. They went away peaceably, pathetically, like nice, well behaved little Cubs."[10]

The Cubs were not discouraged. The ace of their staff, Mordecai "Three Finger" Brown, was almost the equal of Mathewson. At age seven Brown had his right hand get caught in a corn grinder. Doctors had to amputate almost all of his forefinger. His middle finger was saved but it had been mangled, leaving a permanent crook. Brown started pro ball as an infielder but learned he could add remarkable spin to the sphere by releasing it off the stub of his mangled finger. In 1906 he won 26 games, including nine shutouts, and posted a 1.04 ERA in 277 innings. In 1908 he won 29 games against nine defeats, completed 27 of 31 starts, added 13 relief appearances, and his ERA was 1.47 in 312 innings.

The number-two Cub starter, "Big Ed" Reulbach, was almost as tough. From 1906 to 1908 his record was 60–15. In 1906 opposing batsmen hit just .175 against the 6'1" fireballing right-hander in 218 innings. Reulbach's eyesight was so poor Cub catchers used white-painted mitts so he could see his target. In 1908 he compiled a 24–7 record with a 2.03 ERA in 297 innings. In September he hurled shutouts in both ends of a doubleheader against Brooklyn.

Others on the staff included 6'2", 214-pound right-hander Orval "Jumbo" Overall (15–11, 1.92 ERA in 225 innings), and Jack "the Giant Killer" Pfiester (12–10, 2.00 ERA in 252 innings). Pfiester's 15–5 lifetime record against McGraw's club included seven shutouts.

The Cubs boasted the best defensive infield in the game. The 6'1" Chance provided a good target at first base for second baseman Johnny Evers, shortstop Joe Tinker and third baseman Harry Steinfeldt. He also hit a respectable .272 and stole 27 bases. Evers, who stood 5'9" and weighed just 125 pounds batted .300 and stole 36 bases.. Tinker batted .266 with 30 steals and hit Matty like he owned him. Steinfeldt was a solid fielder but slumped to .241 at the plate. Cub catcher Johnny Kling was regarded to be superior defensively to Bresnahan. Kling hit .276 in 1908 and then won the world pocket billiard championship. He quit baseball to concentrate on billiards in 1909 before returning after losing the world title.

On June 23, Matty pitched twice in relief with mixed results during a doubleheader against Boston. He relieved McGinnity in the ninth inning of the opener with two on and no out and preserved a 6–3 win. In the second game, he relieved Taylor with the score tied but dropped his fifth game of the year, 9–7, when the Doves tallied twice in the ninth. The following afternoon the Giants swept the Doves, 4–0 and 7–1. Wiltse fired a two-hit shutout in the opener. Matty was breezing along with a 7–0 lead after seven innings of the second game when McGraw rested him due to the sweltering heat.

On June 27 in Brooklyn, the Giants swept another doubleheader, 4–3 and 5–2. In the opener, Matty relieved Wiltse in the ninth and fanned three consecutive batters to nail down the victory. He took the mound for the second contest and went the route for his 13th win.

On July 2, Matty beat the Phils at the Polo Grounds, 4–3, despite five errors made behind him. On the nation's birthday, the Giants swept the Phils, 1–0 and 9–3. Wiltse tossed a masterpiece in the opener. The game was scoreless into the ninth with Wiltse throwing a perfect game. In the top of the inning he believed he had caught Phillie pitcher George McQuillan gazing at a third strike, but umpire Charles Rigler called the pitch a ball. Wiltse's next offering plunked McQuillan, and the Phils had their only baserunner of the contest. The Giants rallied to win in the tenth inning, 1–0, with Wiltse recording a no-hitter. Wiltse was a left-hander who chose baseball over a career selling carpets in the family business. His nickname of "Hooks" came from his ability to field his position well; he was said to hook in everything that came close to the him. The Giants had won 18 of their last 23 games and climbed to third place, just 1½ games behind front-running Pittsburgh. Chicago was just a half-game back in second place.

On July 6 the Giants visited Cincinnati for a four-game series. The New Yorkers managed to get a split thanks to Matty. Mathewson ran his record to 16–5 with a pair of 2–1 victories, outdueling Bob Ewing and Andy Coakley. In both games he threw a four-hitter and did not issue a single free pass. The two victories were part of a 22-game win streak Matty enjoyed against Cincinnati, which ran into 1911.

On July 10 McGraw's gang started a four-game series with the Buccaneers at Exposition Park. The Black Flaggers won the opener, 7–6, on Tommy Leach's ninth-inning inside-the-park home run. The Bucs also took the second game when Willis outpitched Dummy Taylor, 6–2. But on July 13 the Giants rebounded to sweep the Pirates in a doubleheader, 7–0 and 7–4. Mathewson threw a sparkling three-hit shutout in the opener. For the third straight game he did not walk a man. McGinnity won the second game. The double win pulled the Giants within one game of first-place Chicago, with Pittsburgh a half-game back.

The next stop on the western tour was Chicago. The Giants shocked the Cubs by tearing apart Brown, 11–0, in the first of four. In game two, Crandall took a 4–1 lead into the ninth but the Cubs loaded the bases with one out. Mathewson had been giving his arm some work in deep center field prior to the inning before going into the clubhouse for a shower. With Crandall in trouble, McGraw yelled for his players to summon Matty from the clubhouse. The Giants stalled while Matty dried off, but Chance protested the delay and action resumed. The Cubs tallied another run and the bases remained loaded when Matty took the mound. He was allowed five warm-up pitches but elected to take only two.[11] He retired the first man he faced on an easy ground ball while another run scored, cutting the Giant lead to 4–3, before Matty saved the day by striking out the last Cub to end the game.

The third game of the series featured a classic pitching duel between Mathewson and Brown. Brown won, 1–0, on Tinker's inside-the-park homer in the fifth inning. As Tinker reached third, the Giants Devlin slowed the runner's advance by stepping in front of him, a common trick in those days. Third-base coach Heinie Zimmerman attempted to grab Tinker to prevent him from trying to stretch the hit for a homer. But Tinker ran through Zimmerman and beat Bridwell's relay to the plate by a millisecond. Tinker was the hero of the final game also. He tripled in the first Cub run in the sixth frame and then settled the argument with a two-run double in the ninth. The Cubs won, 5–4.

Matty exhibited his endurance by beating the Cards in 12 innings, 4–2, on July 21 in St. Louis. Back at the Polo Grounds after the long road trip, the Giants hosted first-place Pittsburgh for four games. It was a chance for New York to take the lead in the standings. Wiltse bested Willis in the curtain raiser, 2–1, and the Pirate lead shrank to a single game. With Matty scheduled to pitch game two of the series, more than 30,000 fans traveled to the Polo Grounds. The overflow of spectators stood on the field and New York officials feared a forfeit might take place if the throng could not be pushed back. Wagner stole the show.

Honus banged five hits, including two doubles, as the Bucs battered Mathewson for a 7–2 win. Wagner was locked in a close duel with Donlin for the batting crown. On July 4 Donlin lead the Dutchman, .342 to .336. Wagner's 5-for-5 day, however, put him ahead of Donlin, .340 to .328. Each time Honus hit safely after the second hit, he hollered out to Donlin in right field, "That's three!" "That's four! That's five!"[12]

The Bucs increased their lead to three games over New York with a 4–3 win in game three. Wagner was the Bucs big gun again with two key doubles. Owen "Chief" Wilson drove in Wagner twice by smacking a double and a triple. The final game was called because of darkness after 16 innings with the two teams tied, 2–2. Wiltse and Willis both hurled all 16 innings and not a single runner crossed home plate after the sixth inning.

New York seemed unshaken by the tough Pirate series. They righted themselves by sweeping the Cards four straight. On July 29, Matty out dueled Harry Sallee, 1–0, with the lone run scoring on a passed ball. Matty surrendered just three hits and one walk. On August 4, the Giants swept the Reds in a doubleheader, 4–3 and 4–1, running a winning streak to seven games. Matty was the winning pitcher in both games. In the opener he relieved McGinnity in the ninth and pitched 3⅔ innings of scoreless ball before the Giants won in 12 innings. McGraw handed the ball to Matty to start the second game and "Big Six" came through by firing a four-hitter. Seymour slugged two home runs. Matty's record stood at 21–7. The Giants sported a 57–37 record and were back within a half-game of Pittsburgh.

The Cubs were struggling when they came into New York on August 8. Their woes continued when Wiltse bested Brown in the opener, 4–1, before another crowd of 30,000. The Cubs started the month with an embarrassing 14–0 loss to Boston and lost eight of their first 11 August contests to drop 5½ games out on August 15. News of a clubhouse brawl that took place in July involving outfielder Jimmy Sheckard, utiltyman Heinie Zimmerman, and Chance surfaced.

In the second game Matty beat Overall, 3–2. The Giants jumped on Overall for three runs in the first inning. Herzog coaxed a one-out walk and Bresnahan slammed the ball into another overflow crowd in left for a ground-rule double. Herzog scored with a terrific slide on a Baltimore chop single by Donlin. Bresnahan raced to third. Donlin then purposely got caught in a pickle between first and second. At the opportune time Bresnahan broke for the plate and made it when Evers' throw sailed wild. Donlin galloped to third and scored on Seymour's hoist to center. That was all Matty needed. Chicago scored single runs in the eighth and ninth but couldn't tie the game. Tinker's success continued against Matty as he went 3-for-3, including an eighth-inning triple. A doubleheader was scheduled for August 11 but the opener was called after six innings because of rain. Pfiester prevented a Giant sweep by tossing a 4–0 shutout in the shortened contest.

The Giants still trailed the Pirates. Mathewson surprised newspapermen by saying he considered the Cubs the team to beat. On August 13, he relieved Ames after two innings with the Giants trailing Brooklyn, 3–2, and put up goose eggs for the next seven frames. The Giants rallied to win, 5–3. Seymour homered and Donlin doubled and tripled. Afterward the Polo Grounders headed west for their last road trip of the season.

In St. Louis on August 17, Mathewson fired his eighth shutout of the season, blanking the Cards in a rain-shortened, six-inning contest, 3–0. In the bottom of the fifth a loud thunderclap was heard in the darkening skies. McGraw ordered Seymour to make an attempt to steal home and get tagged out on purpose, which Cy did. The next batter, Chad Barry, followed McGraw's orders and swung and missed wildly at the first three pitches. The Giants sprinted to their positions. Three more outs were needed for the game to be official. Amidst thunderous booms Matty retired three of the four batters he faced and registered his 23rd consecutive victory over St. Louis.

Three days later in Cincinnati, the Giants ascended into a first-place tie with the Pirates as Matty mowed down the Reds, 2–0. Meanwhile, construction work was going on at the Polo Grounds, where workers built seating accommodations for 5,000 additional spectators in the bleachers and grandstand.

After sweeping the Reds three straight, the Giants invaded Pittsburgh for a head-to-head battle for first place. On August 24 at packed Exposition Park, the McGraw nine beat the Bucs twice, 4–1 and 5–1. Wiltse won the opener on a four-hitter and Matty went the distance in the second game, backed by Doyle's single, double and triple. New York trailed, 1–0, into the eighth round of the opener before Bresnahan bashed a two-run triple off Willis and Donlin followed with a two-run homer. The Giants also won game three, 5–3, as Crandall bested Maddox. The fabulous Wagner was thrown out twice at the plate. The Giants completed the sweep when the combination of Taylor, McGinnity, and Mathewson outpitched Irving Young, 4–3. Matty hurled a scoreless ninth and got credit for the win when the Giants came from behind with two runs in their final at-bat. Doyle singled, Bresnahan was hit by a pitch, Donlin delivered an RBI single, and Seymour won the game with a sacrifice fly.

While the Giants were sweeping the Bucs in Pittsburgh, thousands viewed the progress of the games on electrical bulletin boards at Madison Square Garden and Gotham Theatre back in New York. The action was simulated with each player's position lit by incandescent bulbs.

Following the big wins, the Giants hopped a train for their final visit to Chicago. They now led the standings by 3½ games over both the Pirates and Cubs. Things were looking rosy, but there had been a revival in Chicago. The Cubs, given up for dead two weeks earlier, had swept Brooklyn five straight.

Pfiester won the opener over Wiltse, 5–1. More than 27,000 fans jammed into the West Side Grounds to see Mathewson go up against Brown in the second game. Thousands had to be turned away. The field was so dense with fans, police had to clear lanes so Matty and Brown could take their warmups. Brown won, 3–2. The Cubs tore into Matty with a five-hit fusillade in the fourth stanza, scoring all three of their runs. That proved enough for the "Three-Fingered Man." Chicago was just as baseball mad as New York. In the Windy City's downtown bulletin boards, the contest was reproduced by lights as a crowd of 50,000 viewed the action.

In the third game, Pfiester continued his mastery over New York, beating Crandall, 2–1. At month's end the Giants hung onto first place at 69–45. Chicago, which had won nine straight, was three percentage points back at 71–47. Like the biblical Lazarus, the Cubs had risen from the dead. Pittsburgh was seven percentage points back at 70–47. The Giants were being given the edge by most experts to cop the flag because they were scheduled to play their last 20 games at home.

Larry Doyle was swinging a hot bat, socking 18 hits in the recent series against Pittsburgh and Chicago. Doyle told writer Jack Sher in 1948, "We were a rough lot, we Giants in those days. All except for Matty. He was no namby-pamby. He'd gamble at cards and take a drink now and then, but he was always quiet and had a lot of dignity. I remember how baseball bugs would rush up to him and pester him with questions. Matty hated it. But he was always courteous. I never saw a man who could shake those bugs so slick, without hurting their feelings."[13]

McGraw had a Dr. Jekyll-and-Mr. Hyde personality toward his players. He could praise them to the heavens but cut them to pieces with vicious sarcasm. Sher wrote of Mathewson: "The big pitcher was, as the years went on, sort of liaison man between the irascible, Napoleonic McGraw and the other players. Whenever the fiery-tempered manager lit into a player too harshly, Matty was always on hand to soothe injured feelings and to patch things up between McGraw and his players. He was like a rock. He was as dependable emotionally as he was as a pitcher."[14]

The Giants caught fire at the beginning of September and won 16 of their first 17 games. On September 1, Wiltse and Mathewson beat the Doves in a doubleheader in Beantown, 4–1 and 8–0, respectively. Devlin whacked six hits, including a triple. After a day of rain, the Giants swept the Doves again, 3–0 and 8–5. McGinnity tossed a shutout in the first game and Mathewson bailed out Ames in the second win.

On to Philadelphia, the Giants took three of four from the Quakers. Matty won the second game of the series over McQuillan, 5–1, yielding six hits while not walking a batter. The 1908 season was one of four campaigns that Mathewson pitched more than 300 innings and walked less than a batter a game. Three days later he outlasted Brooklyn's Rucker in 11 innings at the Polo Grounds, 1–0. With the sun setting and the game in danger of being called because of darkness, Bridwell singled sharply to left to drive in Seymour. It was Mathewson's 30th win of the season.

The Giants swept five straight from Brooklyn. On September 12, Matty beat the Superbas, 6–3. With his team trailing, 3–2, in the eighth, Matty creamed a triple to dead center, driving in the tying and go-ahead runs. Doubles by Donlin and Devlin and a triple by McCormick were featured in the rally. The Cards visited the Polo Grounds next and the Giants swept them four straight. Matty saved Ames in the opener by getting the victory in relief, 5–4, when Tenney doubled in Bridwell. The New Yorkers' hot streak kept them in first place, but their schedule would get tougher. The Pirates and Cubs were due in town.

On September 18, New York's police commissioner sent 200 extra policemen to the Polo Grounds. More than 35,000 fans somehow squeezed into the Harlem Meadow, with thousands more turned away. Again the Polo

Grounds was the scene of the largest crowd ever to see a baseball game up until that time. The Giants swept both games of the doubleheader from Pittsburgh, 7–0 and 12–7. Matty tossed his 11th shutout in the opener. He also torched a fifth-inning rally with a double. Out in the outfield Donlin opened a gash under an abusive fan's eye with a haymaker. "Turkey Mike" also swatted a three-run homer in game one and added a key double in game two. He was just as tough with his bat as he was with his fists. The Giants ripped 18 hits, including four by rookie Buck Herzog and three by Wiltse in the 12–7 win. They had won 18 of 19 contests.

The Pirates, who won 25 of 33 games in September, recovered to take the third and fourth games of the series, 6–2 and 2–1. In the fourth game Willis bested Matty with a two-hitter. Matty allowed just three hits, but they all came in the third inning when Pittsburgh scored twice. Clarke's two-run single was the key blow.

On the eve of the big Chicago series, the Giants were still atop the standings at 87–48. The Cubs' record stood at 87–53 (2½ games back). Pittsburgh was three games back at 87–54. On September 22, the Cubs pennant hopes brightened when they swept a doubleheader from New York by 4–3 and 3–1 scores. Brown saved Overall in the seventh inning of the opener then retook the mound and went the route in the second game.

The Giants sent Mathewson to the mound in game three. The Cubs opposed him with Pfiester. At stake was first place. Matty's nemesis, Tinker, gave the Cubs a 1–0 lead with a homer, but the Giants tied it in the sixth on Donlin's RBI single. With one out in the bottom of the ninth, Devlin slapped a base hit but was forced at second on McCormick's infield bouncer. Fred Merkle singled to right, moving McCormick to third. Bridwell then seemingly ended the game with a clean hit to center. Jubilant Giant fans mobbed the field to congratulate their heroes.

But instead of touching second, Merkle veered off to the center-field clubhouse. It was a common practice then. Cub second baseman Johnny Evers noticed and screamed for the ball. The throw from center fielder Solly Hofman slipped by Evers and entangled in the crowd on the field. McGinnity saw what Evers was up to and some accounts say he outwrestled Tinker for the ball and tossed it into the stands. But another ball appeared. Many believe it came from the Cubs ball bag. Evers stood atop second clutching the new ball and shouted to base umpire Bob Emslie, "That run don't count!" Emslie said he did not see the play and refused to make the call. He asked home plate umpire Hank O'Day, who said he saw Merkle's action, granted Evers' appeal, and called the Giants rookie out on a force play. Because the crowd had covered the field and the Giants were already celebrating in their clubhouse, O'Day declared the game a 1–1 tie.

NL president Harry Pulliam stood by O'Day's call and declared the contest a 1–1 tie. His decision was appealed by the Giants. Eventually McGraw's team was told it would have to replay the game on October 8. The Cubs initially wanted the Merkle game to be declared a forfeit win for them because fans had swarmed the field and made play impossible. They relented from that position and demanded the game be made up in a doubleheader the next day. The Giants refused to play a doubleheader but won the final game of the heated series, 5–4. Mathewson was the hero, coming on in relief of Wiltse in the seventh inning and holding the fort the rest of the way. He was credited with his 34th win. Donlin keyed a two-run rally in the first inning with a double and a three-run rally in the fifth with a triple.

McGraw never blamed Merkle for losing the pennant, declaring instead that his team should have won 12 other games during the season that it lost. Merkle spent 16 years in the majors, batting a respectable .273. He was known to be a heads-up player, yet was haunted by the catcalls of "Bonehead" from spectators. The Giants were shaken in disbelief by Pulliam's ruling. A second catastrophe followed on September 25 when they dropped a doubleheader to lowly Cincinnati, 7–1 and 5–2. Rookie Rube Marquard started the first game and was cuffed for seven hits and five runs. Afterward he admitted to Mathewson he was petrified by the presence of the thousands of fans packed into the Polo Grounds.

The next day the Giants revived to beat the Reds twice, 6–2 and 3–1. Matty went the distance in the opener for victory number 35. He had hurled 365 innings and his arm was feeling the strain. The Phils arrived next for a string of eight straight games at the Polo Grounds. New York closed out September by taking three of the first four. On September 30, Matty went the route again for a 6–2 win. He was not as sharp as in the past, yielding nine hits. At month's end the Giants clung to first place by the narrowest of margins with a 93–53 record. The Pirates had won nine of their last ten and were four percentage points behind at 95–55. Chance's hated Cubs were in third at 94–55, a half-game off the pace.

The Giants played their fourth doubleheader in seven days on October 1. With just one day's rest, Matty beat the Phils in the opener, 4–3, although he was tagged for ten hits. Devlin scored what proved to be the winning run in the sixth inning when Sherry Magee muffed a drive by Needham. Phils rookie Harry Coveleski topped Wiltse in the second game, 6–3. The Cubs' Reulbach, somewhat rested after his doubleheader shutout of Brooklyn on September 26, blanked the Reds on a two-hitter. It was "Big Ed's" fourth straight whitewash.

The next day the Pirates took over first place by sweeping St. Louis in a doubleheader, 7–4 and 2–1. Wagner won the second game with a home run in the ninth inning. The Giants exploded for seven runs in the first inning and beat Philadelphia, 7–1, behind Ames. The Cubs' Brown blanked the Reds, 5–0.

On October 3, the Pirates kept their grip on first place by nipping the Cards again, 3–2, as Wagner socked two more key hits. In New York, Matty, working on just one day's rest again, was beaten by the upstart rookie, Coveleski, 3–2. The rookie had gone to his manager and volunteered to pitch the game. It was Coveleski's third victory over the Giants in five days, yet he would never defeat the Giants again in his career. The Cubs shellacked the Reds, 16–2.

The Pirates led the league with a 98–55 record. Chicago was a half-game behind at 97–55 and the Giants were 1½ games back at 95–55. The Giants were idle on October 4, while the Pirates and Cubs squared off for a showdown before 30,247 fans in Chicago. A Pirate win would eliminate the Cubs. Brown opposed Willis. Cub outfielder Frank "Wildfire" Schulte socked RBI singles in the first and fifth innings to give Chicago a 2–0 lead. The Bucs tied it at 2–2 in the sixth as Wagner doubled in a run and scored on a single by Ed Abbatichio. Brown helped himself with an RBI single in the bottom of the sixth. An error by Wagner led to another Cubs run in the seventh. In the eighth Brown smacked a two-out single and scored on Evers' double to put the Cubs up, 5–2.

Wagner led off the Pirate ninth with a single. Abbatichio belted a shot down the right-field line that was ruled foul by ump O'Day. Pittsburgh bitterly protested the call, causing O'Day to ask his base partner, Cy Rigler, for help. Rigler backed O'Day and Abbatichio struck out. A story has been handed down through the years that Abbatichio's drive would have been a game-winning grand slam if ruled fair. The story claims that a woman, who was struck by the ball, sued for damages and swore in court that she sat in fair territory. In fact, Wagner was the only runner on base at the time, and while O'Day's call might have choked a Pirate rally, it did not nullify a grand slam. Brown retired the side on two ground balls and the Cubs took over first place.

A multiple of scenarios were now possible. For the Giants to tie the Cubs, they would have to win their three remaining games with Boston. McGraw's team had appealed Pulliam's ruling on the Merkle game, and Pulliam was meeting with the NL board of directors to discuss this appeal. New York could win the pennant if the team swept Boston and the Merkle game was declared a Giants victory. If the Giants won two of three from Boston and the Merkle game was ruled in their favor, the race would end in a three-way tie. Likewise, if the Giants won two of three from the Doves and beat Chicago in a replayed Merkle contest, the race would also end in a three-way tie. If the Giants could only win one from Boston and the Merkle game was ruled a Giants win, then the Pirates and Cubs would finish in a two-way tie for the flag. Also, if New York won just one from the Doves but beat the Cubs in a replayed Merkle game, Chicago and Pittsburgh would be deadlocked at the top. The drama was unreal.

The Giants swept the Doves by 8–1, 4–1 and 7–2 scores. McGraw figured his team could take Boston and rested Matty. The Giants' appeal was then denied and the Merkle game remained a 1–1 tie. Pittsburgh was finally mathematically eliminated. The Merkle game was ordered to be replayed on October 8 at the Polo Grounds, with the winner taking the pennant. Pulliam would be vilified in the New York press. He suffered a nervous breakdown and committed suicide in 1909.

The replayed Merkle showdown is one of the most discussed games in history. The Cubs sent Pfiester to oppose Mathewson. The *New York Tribune* estimated that more than 50,000 fans saw the game. There were 35,000 people in the ballpark, and the eyes of another 15,000 people perched on Coogan's Bluff and the tops of surrounding buildings viewed the action from afar.

The Giants discussed beforehand whether they should refuse to play the game, believing they were competing for something they had already won fair. They decided to play. The game was started 15 minutes early, at 2:45 P.M., allowing the Cubs only five minutes of batting practice. When McGinnity appeared at the plate 15 minutes early to hit pre-game grounders to the Giant infield, Chance protested. His Cubs had traveled 1,000 miles by train and needed time to limber up. McGinnity raised his bat threateningly. Chance backed off.

Mordecai Brown said of the contest in an interview for *My Greatest Day in Baseball*: "I never heard anybody or any set of men called as many foul names as the Giant fans called us that day from the time we showed up till it was over."[15] Given the hostile atmosphere, Chance instructed his players not to respond to taunts.

Matty made his lordly entrance ten minutes before game time. In the first inning he fanned Sheckard, retired Evers on a grounder, and fanned Schulte to a chorus of roars. Pfiester seemed nervous by the hostile setting. He plunked the Giants leadoff hitter, Tenney, with a pitch and walked Herzog on four pitches. Bresnahan was next to bat. Writers in the New York press were critical of McGraw for not having Bresnahan bunt the runners along. McGraw thought that his number-three hitter could bust the game open. Instead, Bresnahan struck out and Kling caught Herzog breaking foolishly for second with a quick throw. Two were out. The prospects of a big inning seemed ruined.

But Donlin ripped a double down the first-base line to score Tenney. Matty remembered in *Pitching in a Pinch*: "For the first time in almost a month, Merkle smiled. He was drawn up in the corner of the bench, pulling away from the rest of us as if he had some contagious disease and was quarantined."[16]

Pfiester walked Seymour next. Chance called for Brown. "The Three-Fingered Man" had either started or relieved in 11 of the last 14 Cub games. He had received death threats in the mail warning him not to pitch in New York. Brown fanned Devlin and the Cubs escaped a knock-out punch.

Chance began the Cub second with a base hit to left, but Matty picked him off first base. Chance protested the call for five minutes. Matty then fanned Steinfeldt and Del Howard. Schulte helped Brown with two superb catches in the bottom of the second, including a grab of Bridwell's drive that bordered on the spectacular. Despite Matty's good start, he was not feeling strong. His wife, Jane, remembered her husband saying to her prior to the game, "I'm not fit to pitch today. I'm dog tired."[17] Mrs. Mathewson added that it was the first time she had ever heard him express any doubt about a ballgame he started.

Tinker, who was poison to Mathewson, started the Cub third. The New York press reported that Mathewson and Donlin gestured to center fielder Seymour to back up. The writers added that Seymour ignored the instructions. The result decided the pennant. Tinker drove the ball over Seymour, just out of reach of his grasp, and motored into third with a triple. Had Seymour backed up, he would have easily caught Tinker's drive and Matty might have pitched a shutout. Instead, Kling singled in Tinker. Brown moved Kling to second with a sacrifice bunt. Sheckard flied to Seymour, who was now standing deeper in center. It could have been the third out of the inning with no runs scored but it wasn't. Evers walked and Schulte and Chance followed with doubles, giving the Cubs a 4–1 lead.

The score stayed the same until the Giant seventh. Devlin and McCormick started the inning with singles and Brown appeared rattled as he walked Bridwell to fill the bases. Matty was scheduled up next but McGraw sent Doyle in to pinch-hit. Doyle had been out of the lineup with a spiked heel. He had not faced an opposing pitcher in two weeks. Matty was a good-hitting pitcher and probably hugely disappointed that he would not get a chance to help win the game. Doyle fouled out to Kling. Tenney brought in one run with a sacrifice fly, but Brown got Herzog on a bouncer to Tinker to escape with a two-run lead.

Brown retired the Giants in the eighth and ninth and the Cubs won their third consecutive pennant. But they still had to get out of the ballpark alive. Brown recalled,

> As the ninth ended with the Giants going out, one-two-three, we all ran for our lives, straight for the clubhouse with the pack at our heels. Some of the

boys got caught by the mob and beaten up some. Tinker, Howard and Sheckard were struck. Chance was hurt most of all. A Giant fan hit him in the throat and Husk's voice was gone for a day or two in the World Series that followed. Pfiester got slashed on the shoulder by a knife.... We made it to the dressing room and barricaded the door. Outside wild men were yelling for our blood — really. As the mob got bigger, the police came up and formed a line across the door. We read the next day that the cops had to pull their revolvers to hold them back. I couldn't say as to that. We weren't sticking our heads out to see.[18]

The Cubs left the ballpark with a police escort.

The *New York American* said, "Probably no member of the Giants took the defeat as keenly as did Christy Mathewson. Long after the other players had donned their street clothes and made for home Matty sat down disconsolate in the dressing room. Folks that lingered tried to cheer the peerless pitcher, but he could not speak. He seemed loath to go out and face the people."[19]

Matty pitched for the Giants until 1916 and hurled in three more World Series before being traded to Cincinnati. He took over as manager of the Reds in the middle of 1916. In 1918 he left Cincinnati to join the army during World War I. He volunteered for the "Gas and Flame" Division. While in France an accident occurred that later cost him his life. His job was to instruct soldiers on the proper use of gas masks. Real poison gas was used in the drills and somehow he got exposed to the gas. One account says he breathed in the fumes during a drill. Another account says he inhaled the fumes while touring empty trenches that had not been purged of gas. When he returned to America, tuberculosis had set in.

Matty served as a coach for the Giants in 1919, 1920, and 1921. He was diagnosed with tuberculosis in 1921 and spent the next two years in a sanitarium in Saranac Lakes, New York. By 1923 he had recovered some of his strength. Against instructions of his doctors, he took on the position as president of the Boston Braves. He suffered a relapse and died in 1925 at age 45. The last line on his plaque at the Baseball Hall of Fame in Cooperstown reads "Matty was master of them all."

Chapter 2

Detroit's Wildcat at His Peak: Ty Cobb in 1911

Sport magazine scribe Jack Sher wrote in 1948

> This is the story of the greatest ballplayer of all time. He made his first appearance in a major-league ball park on August 30, 1905, at Bennett Field in the city of Detroit. His name was not even on the score card. He arrived at the plate unknown, a pinch-hitter, an angry-faced, jut-jawed, mean-eyed 18-year-old kid who held his bat like a club, left hand high, right hand low. Facing him was Jack Chesbro, New York's great spitballer, winner of 41 games the previous season. The rookie batter twisted his mouth scornfully, taunted Chesbro with a few derisive words, then whacked out a double, driving in two runs.[1]

Sher continued: "That hit began the career of baseball's most fabulous performer, the player of the century, the 'Georgia Peach,' the tyrant of the Tigers, Tyrus Raymond Cobb. Twenty-three years later, when Ty Cobb finally hung up his spikes, he had played in more ball games, scored more runs, made more hits, stolen more bases, held more records than any other man in baseball history. He was, in truth, a colossus."[2]

Sher made a good case for Cobb as the best player of all time. In the first vote for the Baseball Hall of Fame in 1936, Cobb finished on top with 222 points; Babe Ruth and Honus Wagner tied for second with 215 points. Time has changed things. The majority of fans now rate many sluggers ahead of Cobb, whose low home run numbers have contributed to his fall.

Cobb no longer holds the record for the most games played. His lifetime hit total of 4,191 was broken by Pete Rose (4,256), although Rose went to bat 2,624 more times. His lifetime runs total of 2,245 was broken by Rickey Henderson. Henderson has also topped Cobb's single-season and lifetime stolen base marks. Yet one record of Cobb's records seems untouchable. He maintained a .367 lifetime batting average through 11,429 career at-bats, and captured 12 batting titles in 13 seasons.

Ty Cobb played the game at 200 percent and believed the base paths belonged to the runner. In 1911 he was at his peak, batting .420 with 248 hits, 144 RBIs, 147 runs scored, and 83 stolen bases. Some say his ferociousness on the field was his way of refighting the Civil War.

One must give the old terror his due. Cobb was the top offensive player of the Dead Ball era. His play was geared to that era. He adopted a place-hitting style that was not equaled. In a span of 10 years, from 1910 to 1919, he hit .387. After Ruth revolutionized the game with his slugging in 1920, Cobb's offensive production could not match the Babe's. But in the Dead Ball era he led the league in slugging eight times and won a Triple Crown in 1909.

Although Rickey Henderson and Lou Brock have topped Cobb's stolen base marks, they didn't do the things that Cobb did on the bases. He would sometimes advance two bases on infield ground outs, fly ball outs, and even on bunts. He would fly home from first base on singles. Other baserunners have performed these feats but not to the extent of Cobb. He is commonly credited with a record 35 steals of home, but the Society of Baseball Research's ad hoc committee on steals of home (Larry Amman, Craig Carter, and Bob Davids) after much research put Cobb's real number at 54.[3]

Cobb had blurring speed. He was timed at 10 seconds for a 100-yard dash while in full uniform and baseball spikes. The world record holder at the time, Dave Kelley, ran the hundred in 9.6 seconds in track shoes. Cobb was a master of every elusive sliding technique imaginable. He could run over infielders and kick the ball out of their gloves with the toughest of baserunners. Because he played the outfield, he was free from being a target for retaliation by opposing baserunners. Legend has it that the "Dixie Demon" sharpened his spikes by using a file on his steel.

Cobb was at his terrifying best in 1911. He led the league in hits (248), doubles (47), triples (24), runs (147), RBIs (144), stolen bases (83), batting average (.420), and slugging (.621). He finished second to Philadelphia's Frank Baker in home runs with eight. In the field he led flychasers with 376 putouts and had 24 assists.

Cobb was born in the backwoods village of Narrows, Georgia, in 1886. The closest town was Royston. His father, William Hershel Cobb, was a schoolteacher who rose to become a state senator. Ty was a pretty good student but seemed to lack the mental discipline to become a lawyer or doctor, which would have pleased his father greatly. Ty loved baseball and played in the minors at Augusta. Just a week before he was called up to the Detroit Tigers, Ty learned that his mother, Amanda, had killed his father with a shotgun. She said she mistook him for a burglar.

Ty's father left home that night because he said he had to go out of town on business. Around midnight, he arrived back home and climbed onto the second-story porch armed with a revolver. Amanda said she heard a scratching at her bedroom window and saw a large figure trying to break loose the lock. She grabbed a shotgun and fired two blasts. The first blast blew her husband's intestines apart. The second blew his head off. Gossipers believed William suspected his wife of being unfaithful. What Ty believed was never known. He kept the whole situation bottled up inside him, never allowing it to be mentioned in his presence.

Ty grew up idolizing the lost cause of the Confederacy. More than 258,000 Confederate soldiers had died in the Civil War, and Ty saw the South as an oppressed underdog society. Apparently it never occurred to him that the Confederacy, which was fighting to preserve an economic system that relied heavily on the enslavement of African Americans, was itself oppressive. According to his biographer, Al Stump, Ty's public language included the use of "the scurrility of 'nigger' or 'nigra'" and privately he used "shine," "coon" and "Sambo."[4] In an Associated Press story dated January 29, 1952, however, Cobb came out in favor of integration in baseball, saying, "Certainly it is O.K. for them to play. I see no reason in the world why we shouldn't compete with colored athletes as long as they conduct themselves with politeness and gentility."[5] This remark begs the question: Was Cobb polite and gentlemanly on the field of play?

When Ty reached the Tigers, he found that his teammates considered the Confederates lousy traitors. He alienated many with his southern ways and some Tigers banded together to run him off the team. They conspired to keep Ty from getting batting practice. He found his glove's stitching ripped apart. His specially made ash bats were shattered at the handles. The hazing got to Ty in his second season and the Tiger management sent him to a sanitarium outside Detroit for 44 days.[6] When Ty returned, he finished the season at .320. The next year, 1907, he was thoroughly thrashed in two fistfights with Tiger catcher Charles Schmidt. Schmidt outweighed Ty by 42 pounds and once fought an exhibition boxing match against future world heavyweight champ Jack Johnson.

But winning has a way of muffling clubhouse disputes. Cobb led the Tigers to pennants in 1907, 1908, and 1909. He topped the league in batting and RBIs all three seasons and stole an average of 55 bases per season. His manager, Hughie Jennings, said Cobb performed a "miracle a day" on the base paths.

In 1910 Hugh Chalmers announced he would give a Chalmers "30" automobile to the winner of the AL batting crown. Cobb was locked in a race for the title with Cleveland's Napoleon Lajoie. In a doubleheader on the last day of the season, St. Louis manager Jack O'Connor ordered rookie third baseman John Corriden to play deep whenever Lajoie came to the plate. Lajoie belted a triple and then beat out a ridiculous seven bunts to go 8-for-8. After the game Cobb's teammates sent a congratulatory telegram to Lajoie. AL president Ban Johnson allowed Lajoie's eight hits to stand but said there would be no more prizes awarded to batting champs. When the final stats were calculated, Cobb still edged Lajoie .384944 to .384084. Years later further research found an error that revealed Lajoie had the top average. At any rate, Hugh Chalmers gave an automobile to both players.   •

The 1911 season opened at Bennett Park amidst snow flurries. The Tigers beat the White Sox, 4–2, before a chilled crowd of 5,500. Cobb belted a homer into the left-field bleachers off spitballer Ed Walsh in the third inning. Walsh hurled 368 innings with his salivator pitch and won 27 games with a 2.22 ERA and 255 strikeouts. Also known as the "moist shoot," "cuspidor ball," "eel ball" and "mystery vapor float," the spitter was the most devastating pitch of the Dead Ball era. Walsh was its true master. In his career total of 2,964 innings, Walsh yielded just 23 homers and posted the best lifetime ERA ever at 1.82. He would stop a 40-game hitting streak by Cobb on July 4.

The next day Detroit bested Chicago again, 6–0, as Cobb singled, doubled, stole a base, and made two sparkling catches in center field. A snow storm halted Detroit's third game of the year in the eighth inning with the Tigers ahead, 2–0. Cobb socked two singles and scored the game-winner in the seventh frame. He singled to open the inning and reached second on an error by shortstop Rollie Zeider. Ty then raced home when second baseman Andy McConnell muffed a ground ball. In the field Ty made another fine running catch, hauling in a drive by Tex Jones amidst blizzard-like conditions.

The Tigers (some newspapers referred to them as the "Tygers") went on to win 12 of their first 13 games. Cobb's play was immense during the hot streak. In Chicago's opener on April 20, Ty slashed two singles and a double as Detroit touched up Walsh again, 6–3. In a 6–3 triumph in Cleveland on April 27, Cobb smashed a home run over rookie "Shoeless Joe" Jackson's head in the sixth and then ignited a three-run, game-winning rally in the ninth with a double. He came up big the next day, too, singling, doubling, and tripling in a 5–3 win over the Indians. His triple came in the ninth frame, but he was thrown out trying to it stretch to a homer by Jackson.

Jackson was Cobb's main rival for the batting race in 1911. "Shoeless Joe" went to work in a textile mill at age six and never learned to read or write. But he could hit. By age 13 he was playing for the mill's baseball team, and in 1908 he reached the minor leagues. The Philadelphia A's Connie Mack purchased him but gave up on him and traded Jackson to Cleveland. In his true rookie year of 1911 with Cleveland, Jackson swatted 233 hits, with 45 doubles, 19 triples, 126 runs, 83 RBIs, and 41 stolen bases, and batted .408.

Jackson's RBI single on April 29 sent the Tigers down to their second defeat of the season, 2–1. But the striped cats reeled off another nine straight wins to reside on top with an amazing 21–2 record on May 9. On April 30, Cobb's blistering drive through Cleveland first baseman George Stovall's hands plated the deciding run of a 5–4 win. On May 1, Ty gave a display of daredevil baserunning in a 14–5 win over Cleveland. He reached on a Lajoie error in the fifth inning, promptly stole second and third, and scored on Sam Crawford's single. The next inning he tripled in Davy "Kangaroo" Jones. When the Cleveland infield relaxed, he broke for the plate and made it after dancing around in a rundown amidst four Cleveland infielders before avoiding catcher Grover Land's tag with a clever slide. Cobb was able to change directions with uncanny bursts of speed in rundowns and often escaped from them safely.

On May 6 in St. Louis, Ty singled sharply in the first inning and dashed into second on center fielder Danny Hoffman's bobble. Catcher Nig Clarke tried to pick Cobb off second but his throw sailed into center field. Cobb took off for third and then sprinted home. In the third inning he tripled in two runs as Detroit won, 8–4.

The Tigers topped Guy "Doc" White and the Chisox, 5–4, in 10 innings on May 7 thanks to Cobb. White had long been a nemesis for Cobb and the Tigers. In Ty's first year, White struck him out three times in one game, but in this contest Cobb singled four times in five at-bats. He singled in a run in the opening inning, tied the game at 4–4 with his eighth-inning single, then decided it with an RBI single in the tenth frame. In 1911 Ty would bang 10 hits in 17 at-bats against the pitching dentist, Doc White.

On May 9 the Tigers reached their high-water mark of the season with their 21st win in 23 games, a 10–0 rout of the Highlanders. Cobb singled, doubled, and scored twice but "Wahoo" Sam Crawford was the top gun with a single, double, and homer. Like Cobb, Crawford was enjoying a great start. He began the season with two singles, three doubles, and a triple in his first seven at-bats. The all-time triples leader with 311 (Cobb is second with 297), Crawford's 1911 season included 217 hits, 109 runs, 115 RBIs, 37 steals, and a .378 batting average. The *Sporting News* observed, "Sam Crawford has been showing more speed and greater hitting ability than ever before in his career. He is lighter than Detroit has ever seen him and his work on the bases has been a frequent subject for remark."[7] In 19 seasons "Wahoo" Sam smacked 2,964 hits and batted .309.

Crawford had been the established star on the Tigers when Cobb broke into the majors. Ty always resented that Crawford did not do anything to try to stop the hazing that Cobb received then. Crawford defended himself by telling writer Lawrence Ritter in *The Glory of Their Times*, "He (Cobb) came up from the South, you know, and he was still fighting the Civil War. As far as he was concerned, we were all damn Yankees before he even met us." Crawford added, "We weren't cannibals or heathens. We were all ballplayers together, trying to get along. Every rookie gets a little hazing, but most of them just take it and laugh. Cobb took it the wrong way."[8] Cobb did campaign for Crawford's induction into the Baseball Hall of Fame in 1957.

The *Sporting News'* 1911 early-season comments on Cobb included: "Western critics, after seeing Ty Cobb play, agreed unanimously that the reports from the South that Ty had slowed up were such stuff as dreams are made of. He is still the only Ty."[9] "Cobb is as frisky as ever on the bases. He is an immense portion of the Detroit team, all right."[10] "Tyrus Cobb simply forces his name into the sporting pages by some sensational feat in batting, fielding or base-running almost daily."[11] "Cobb has been playing fine ball and the entire outfield has been pulling down line drives in a manner to send the fans fairly frantic."[12]

On May 12 the Tigers topped the Highlanders, 6–5, as Cobb singled, doubled, walked twice, knocked in two runs, and scored three. In the first inning he scored from first on Crawford's single. In the sixth he scored from second base on a wild pitch. In the seventh he doubled in two runs. While a group of Highlanders were protesting a safe call on Bush at the plate, Ty caught them sleeping. He stealthily made his way around third and snuck through the group of argumentative New Yorkers into home. The Highlanders had neglected to call time. Catcher Ed Sweeney was not aware of Cobb's advance until the last instant, and his tag attempt was too late.

The next day against Boston, Cobb crushed a grand slam in the third inning and tied the game at 11–11 with an RBI double in the ninth inning, but the Red Sox prevailed, 13–11, in 10 innings. Some writers said Cobb's blast was the longest ever seen at Bennett Park. Two days later Cobb began his 40-game hitting streak by socking a single and double against Joe Wood in a 10-inning, 5–4 win over the Bosox.

And there were adventures for Ty off the field as well. On May 22, his new Chalmers "30" was parked outside a hotel in Cadillac Square in Detroit when 19-year-old John Miles tried to steal it. Cobb was sitting in a nearby car when he noticed the thief. The *Sporting News* described Cobb's quick reaction: "A few moments later the chase was on and after a sprint of over 100 yards, Cobb, disregarding consequences, leaped into the front seat and hurled the youth into the street."[13] But Ty seemed to have a sympathetic side at times. The *Sporting News* further reported, "Cobb did not desire in court this morning to prosecute John Miles for driving off with his world championship automobile last night.... The bride of the young man talked to Cobb this morning and then Cobb decided that he did not want to prosecute. 'They have been married only a little while and things have not been breaking well for them,' he said in court."[14]

Back on the diamond Cobb led the Bengals to a 9–8 win over Washington on May 23. Ty singled twice, doubled, scored twice, and swiped three bases, bringing his batting average over .420. Cobb ignited Detroit's five-run eighth inning with a double, stole third, and scored on an error. Later in the inning he drew a walk with the bases loaded off Walter Johnson to force in the winning run. At the end of May, Detroit had won 33 games against just 11 defeats and led the defending champion A's by seven games. But Detroit suffered a bad setback when rookie first baseman Del Gainor, who was hitting around .350, had his wrist broken by a fastball from the Athletics' Jack Coombs on May 20. Gainor appeared in 70 games in 1911.

On the first day of June, President William H. Taft was in attendance as the Tigers took on the Senators in Washington. Taft greeted Cobb, Jennings, and pitcher Bill Donovan at his box prior to the game. Cobb had met Taft while Taft was vacationing in Augusta. Taft was said to be a Cobb fan. The Tigers bested the Senators in 10 innings, 8–7, and Tyrus did not disappoint. He singled twice, doubled, and pilfered three bases. A couple of days later Ty singled once, tripled twice, and scored twice as the Tigers routed Walter Johnson, 7–2.

Cobb enjoyed good success against Johnson, knocking out a .335 average in 245 at-bats. Ty said his success was due to the fact that Johnson was too good of a soul for his own good. Johnson possessed the best fastball in the game but feared his smokeball would someday bring permanent injury to a batsman. Ty hung his head over the plate and scared "the Big Train" from pitching inside to him. With only half a plate to cover, Ty hit Johnson like few others.

The Tigers visited Philadelphia to take on the second-place A's next. With the new cork-centered ball in play in 1911, the Tiger team was batting .297. The A's were even better, sporting a .318 average. In the opener Ty singled in a run in the fifth frame and then unloaded an RBI triple in the seventh. When third baseman Frank Baker mishandled the throw from the outfield, Ty alertly took off for the plate and made it amidst a geyser of flying dust. Despite his performance, the A's won, 4–3.

The Tigers rebounded to win game two, 8–3, as Cobb put together a 3-for-3 day against Eddie Plank. In the fourth he singled, stole second and continued home when catcher Ira Thomas' throw flew into center field. In the fifth he made an acrobatic catch of Bris Lord's liner before doubling up Plank with a quick toss to first base. He beat out a bunt in the sixth, stole second but was thrown out trying to steal third. He singled again and scored in the eighth as the Tigers poured it on.

But Philadelphia fielded a superior team to Detroit. Stuffy McInnis, Eddie Collins, Jack Barry, and Frank Baker became known as "the $100,000 infield" during Philly's run of four pennants in five years, from 1910 to 1914. They were the game's best infield offensively and defensively. Mack's 1911 pitching staff included 28-game winner Jack Coombs as well as Hall-of-Famers Eddie Plank and "Chief " Bender. The A's outhit the Tigers in 1911, .296 to .292, and outscored them, 861 runs to 831. The A's far outclassed the Tigers in pitching, boasting a 3.01 team ERA to Detroit's 3.73 ERA.

The A's won the rubber game of the series, 5–4, when Jack Barry stole home in the eighth inning. With two men on in the Tiger ninth, A's second baseman Eddie Collins made a brilliant backhand stab of a scorching grounder off Cobb's bat and threw out the sprinting "Peach" at first base to end the game.

On June 12 in Boston, Ty went 4-for-4, including two doubles, as the Tigers edged the scarlet hose, 5–4. On June 18 in Chicago he lashed five hits in six trips to the dish as the Tigers came back from a 13–1 deficit to overtake the White Sox, 16–15. Ty tripled in two runs in the fifth, singled in a run in the sixth, and singled in another run with his 100th hit of the year in the eighth. In the ninth he beat out an infield single with a fierce slide into first base as the tying run scored. Crawford's long drive over Ping Bodie's head drove in Cobb and completed the amazing comeback win. Cobb was batting .443 and predicting that he would get 300 hits.

Cobb's second child, whom he named Shirley Marion, was born in June. At the time Ty was the highest-paid player in the game at $9,000 per season. Ty was not satisfied with that. He became busy in the stock market. He bought cotton futures and United (later General) Motors stock and also fared well in copper-mining investments. He made his biggest killing on Wall Street when he bought Coca-Cola stock at dirt-cheap prices. When he died in 1961, he was worth $12 million.

On June 21 against Cleveland, Cobb struck a weird two-run homer in the first inning of a 5–3 win. He laced a laser shot that rebounded off the first base bag and ricocheted into the stands. In those days balls that bounced into the stands from fair territory were homers. On July 2 against Cleveland again, Cobb ran his consecutive-game hitting streak to 40 with a pair of singles and a triple during a 14–6 victory. But it was his baserunning that stood out. In the first frame he stole second and third but did not score. In the second he scored from first base on Crawford's single upon seeing Jackson's juggle of the ball in right. In the sixth he tripled and then pranced halfway toward the plate, drawing a throw to third that went astray. Tyrus easily jogged home. In the seventh he scored from first on Crawford's double while avoiding a tag at the plate with one of his patented slides. His batting average stood at .432, and the *Sporting News* observed: "Although it is rumored that Cobb is in bad with some of his teammates, it doesn't seem to worry Ty any. He goes along in his conquering way just the same as ever."[15]

Cobb's hitting streak came to a halt on the Fourth of July in the morning game of a doubleheader when Chicago's Ed Walsh collared Ty in four trips to the plate. The Chisox won the morning game, 7–3, but Detroit took the afternoon tilt in 11 innings, 11–10. Cobb singled and doubled in game two but mysteriously took himself out of the game in the eighth frame when fans in the Detroit bleachers began insulting him.[16]

According to Marc Okkonen's chronicled highlights of Cobb's career, entitled *The Ty Cobb Scrapbook,* Ty batted .456 during his 40-game streak.[17] A story entitled "Cobb on a Rampage," written by Larry Amman and published in *The Baseball Research Journal* in 1991, put Cobb's batting average during the streak at .467.[18] Whatever the number, it was an incredible display of hitting and the longest streak since "Wee Willie" Keeler's 44-game streak in 1897. The 5'4" 140-pound Keeler popularized the place-hitting science when he told Abe Yager of the *Brooklyn Daily Eagle* that the secret of his success was "I hit em' where they ain't."

Cobb was a bigger, stronger, and faster version of Keeler. Tyrus once declared, "If a player can really place his hits, he has a long advantage over the man who cannot. He can cross up the opposing pitcher and outfielders almost at will. It's difficult, if not impossible, to work any combination against him. But the ability to do this thing is the most difficult problem a batter ever has to conquer. It is a problem so difficult and so important that he is justified in devoting not only one game but his entire career to its mastery. That is exactly what I have done."[19]

The A's overtook Detroit for first place on July 4 by sweeping two from the Highlanders, but the Bengals regained the top spot by routing the Chisox, 8–1, on the following day. Cobb ripped two triples and two singles and drove in four runs. The Tigers then took three of four from Washington. In a 7–5 win over the Nationals on July 11, Cobb slashed two doubles and a triple and scored two runs, one from second base on an infield ground out. He also threw out two runners from center field. Cobb's 392 lifetime outfield assists rank second only to Tris Speaker's 448.

The A's came into Detroit on July 11 trailing the Tigers by 1½ games. The Tigers exploded for seven runs in the eighth inning to take the opener, 14–8. The hitting star was Jim Delahanty with four hits, including a homer. Jim was one of five Delahanty brothers to play major league ball. The oldest of the five, "Big Ed" Delahanty was one of the premier sluggers of nineteenth-century play. He ripped 2,597 hits with a .346 batting average. Jim Delahanty had the best season of his 13-year career in 1911. After being switched from second to first base because of Gainor's injury, Jim batted .339 with 94 RBIs. He was the second best of the Delahantys, finishing his career with 1,159 hits at .283.

The Tigers took the second game, 9–0, behind Bill Donovan's four-hitter. Cobb gave another dazzling exhibition of baserunning. He walked in the first inning then stole second, third, and home on three successive pitches. He later swiped a fourth base and scored twice more. In the seventh inning he charged home from second base on a flyout, forcing the ball loose from catcher Paddy Livingston's grasp in a ferocious football-like collision. In recalling

Ty in later years, Casey Stengel offered, "Ya got to remember that he went for the plate like a freight train. Ooooooo, he was scary!"[20]

The Jenningsmen knocked off the A's again the next day, 8–7. Cobb went 3-for-5 and drove in three runs with a third-inning double. With the score tied at 7–7 in the ninth, Ty singled and tallied the winning run from first on Delahanty's single. Jennings, who was coaching third, tried to put the brakes on Cobb but Ty pushed him aside. The throw to the plate had Cobb beat but it was high. Ty slid wide around Ira Thomas's tag attempt but missed the plate. He then jumped back to touch the plate in a flash just ahead of a second tag attempt.

The Tigers won game four, too, by a 5–1 score to push the A's 5½ games back. Cobb went 2-for-3 with a double and a sacrifice. There seemed to be no stopping the Tigers as they went on to sweep the Red Sox four straight. In the opener with Boston, Ty singled, doubled, stole three bases and scored twice to pace a 9–4 win over Wood. In the final game he laced three singles as Jennings' wildcats routed the Bostonians, 14–7. Cobb was batting .438 with 146 hits in 333 at-bats. Joe Jackson was second in the league at .400, while Crawford checked in at .384.

Cobb admired Jennings, later writing that Hughie "kept us eager to conquer at all times, maintaining our spirit and fight and imparting a tremendous urgency into what can easily become a dull task. On the coaching line, Hughie's wild cry of 'Ee-Yah!' and his shrill whistles let us know he was with us and on top of every play. He'd dance with glee at a good play and tear up grass."[21] Jennings managed Cobb and the Tigers from 1907 to 1920, winning 1,131 games and losing 972.

Just when the season looked like a cake walk for Detroit, the Tigers hit the skids near the end of July. The Highlanders came into Bennett Park on July 20 and swept Detroit four straight. When the Tigers entered Philadelphia for a five-game series on July 28, their lead had shrunk to 3½ games. With a crowd of more than 32,000 on hand, the A's opened the series by sweeping the Tigers in a doubleheader. In the sixth inning of the first game, Cobb made two of the most remarkable catches of his career, fighting his way through the rowdy standing crowd in center field to snare drives off the bats of Eddie Collins and Danny Murphy. The A's prevailed, however, 1–0. Collins singled off Ed Summers, sending in winning pitcher Chief Bender in the eleventh inning with the game's only run. The A's won the second game, 6–5, cutting the Tiger lead to 1½ games. Cobb went 3-for-9 on the day with a stolen base and a run scored. When facing Cobb, legend has it that Mack told his A's, "Let him sleep, if he will. If you get him riled up, he will annihilate us."[22]

Eddie Collins, who was on his way to a .365 season, went 5-for-5 in game three as the A's routed the Tigers, 11–3. In 1910 Collins had set a record with 81 stolen bases. Cobb broke that with 83 steals in 1911 and then broke his own record with 96 steals in 1915. Detroit rebounded to take games four and five. Cobb socked a key single in a three-run tenth-inning rally that decided game four, 6–3. In the final game, Ty tripled in Bush and tallied on Crawford's single in the first inning. In the second, Ty's three-run homer just inside the right-field foul pole highlighted a seven-run Tiger uprising. Ty singled in Bush in the third frame as the wildcats opened up a 10–0 lead. In the fifth he walked, swiped second and third, and scored on Delahanty's single. He retired in the fifth with his team up, 12–3. The final was 13–6. The Tigers left Philly on August 1 with a 2½-game lead.

Detroit's season turned downhill fast. They dropped four straight to the Red Sox. On August 4, the A's took over first place for keeps with a sweep of the Browns. Philly's record was 63–34; the Tigers were at 63–36. From there Mack's A's would win 38 and lose 16 to finish on top with a 101–50 record. The Tigers would win 26 and lose 29 to finish in second place, 13½ games back at 89–65.

Cobb was troubled by a persistent cough and a bad case of bronchitis, which in those days brought fears of tuberculosis. His fast-stepping pace slowed at the plate and on the bases. The *Sporting Life*, which estimated Ty's value to the Tigers at $100,000, described Cobb as being "in bad shape physically."[23] On August 3 his average dipped to .419.

A split with the Highlanders followed. Cobb tied the first game of the series at 6–6 by driving in three runs with a frozen-rope double to the left-field fence in the seventh inning off Ray Caldwell. He then scored the deciding run on Delahanty's single. The next day a capacity crowd turned up at Hilltop Park to see the Highlanders sweep a doubleheader, 6–4 and 2–1. Cobb went 3-for-7 before being ejected in the third inning of the second game. New York first baseman Hal Chase saved the first game by spearing a liner off the bat of Cobb in the ninth inning and converting it into a double play. Cobb started the second game by turning a routine single in the first inning into a double with sheer speed and scoring from the midway on an infield error. He was ejected two innings later for protesting in rage that he had been struck by a pitch. The Tigers won the getaway game of the series, 8–3. Cobb tripled in Jones with Detroit's first run and singled and scored in the seventh frame, riding home on Crawford's double.

Cobb's health problems worsened and he took himself out of the lineup on August 13 for four days. On August 18 Cobb was back with two singles, a triple and a first-inning steal of home, but the Tigers lost to Boston, 9–3. They beat the Bosox, 6–3, the following afternoon thanks to Ty, who singled twice and doubled off Wood to net two RBIs. Dissension was forming in the Tiger ranks, however. Team captain George Moriarty and Jennings exchanged angry words during one defeat. Most of the Tigers were complaining of Jennings' mishandling of pitchers, biting sarcasm, and special treatment for Cobb.

Detroit managed to beat the A's, 9–8, in 11 innings in an incredible game on August 29, but such victories were too few and far between. In that game the A's scored twice in the top of the eleventh only to have Detroit come back with three in the bottom of the inning. Cobb doubled, stole third and scored in the fourth inning. He keyed a five-run rally in the fifth with a two-run double. Crawford's base-loaded single in the eleventh settled the matter.

Cobb enjoyed a good Labor Day doubleheader, socking six singles and swiping three bases, but Detroit only managed a split with the Browns. With the A's opening up a big lead in the standings, the fans' interest shifted to the batting race between Cobb and Jackson.

At mid-season Cobb was flirting with .450 while Jackson was 70 points behind. From July 11 to August 26, Jackson hit safely in 36 of 37 games, raising his average into contention at .405. Pitchers tried to stop "Shoeless" Joe by throwing at him. Tiger pitcher George Mullin predicted Joe would run away from the plate and never come back if pitchers starting throwing at him. Joe was hit eight times but dug in and hit at an even better pace. Pitchers eventually got the message that the illiterate kid did not scare easily. More than 30 years later, Jackson declared with pride, "I never pulled away from the plate as long as I was in baseball."[24]

The new "rabbit ball" helped both batsmen. The cork-centered ball, introduced in 1911, was wound tighter than the old balls, and batting averages jumped 30 points. The pitchers would get the upper hand by the end of the decade and some baseball historians believe the balls used for the remainder of the Dead Ball era lacked the hardness of the 1911 ball. On September 1, Jackson's average stood at .400, but Cobb still held a substantial lead at .421. Actually, "Shoeless" Joe never got within nine points of Cobb all season. But he did make Cobb play harder. Remembering the shenanigans on the last day of the 1910 season, Ty was determined that no one would be in a position to deny him the title in 1911.

In the last game ever played at Detroit's Bennett Park, the Tigers topped Cleveland in 13 innings, 2–1. Cobb stole second and third in the opening inning but was left stranded. In the eighth he legged out an infield bouncer and continued toward second when shortstop Ivy Olson's throw went astray. Ty didn't stop there. As the recovery throw came into second, Cobb turned on the burners and headed toward third. A bad throw to third encouraged Cobb to shoot for the plate. Catcher Ted Easterly had the ball ahead of Ty but Cobb evaded the tag with an elusive slide, tying the game at 1–1. Cobb's third hit of the day contributed to the Bengals' winning rally in the thirteenth.

Two days later the same teams played another 13-inning game, this time in Cleveland. Cobb slashed three hits and stole three bases as the Tigers triumphed, 9–6. His triple in the thirteenth chased home the go-ahead run. Cobb also made two circus catches. In this three-game series, the last time Cobb and Jackson went head-to-head, Ty outhit the shoeless wonder, .411 to .272, to widen his lead in the race.

And Cobb wasn't finished. On September 19 at Boston's Huntington Avenue Grounds, he was 3-for-4 with a stolen base and a homer into the left-field bleachers. But the Bosox won, 2–1, pushing the Tigers closer to mathematical elimination.

With the batting race still hot, Cobb closed the season with two banner days. On September 27 in Washington, he collected four singles and a sacrifice and stole another base. The Tigers won, 7–5. Two days later in the nation's capital, Cobb unloaded two doubles and a triple, scored three times and drove in two runs as the Tigers won, 9–5. With his lead in the batting race secure, Cobb chose to sit out the season-ending series in St. Louis.

Later in life Cobb would fabricate a story in his 1961 autobiography about how he psychologically manipulated the simple-minded Jackson into losing the 1911 batting title. Ty explained he gave Jackson the cold shoulder during a season-ending six-game series with Cleveland. When Jackson supposedly asked Cobb, "Gosh, Ty, what's the matter with you?" Cobb supposedly snarled back, "Get away from me!" As Ty tells it, Jackson reacted with puzzlement and hurt in his eyes, while Cobb proceeded to outhit and overtake him in the series to win the batting crown.[25] The fact was there was no six-game season-ending series between the two teams and Jackson never came within nine points of Cobb at any time.

After the 1918 season Cobb served as a captain in the Gas and Flame Chemical Warfare Division during the war but didn't see combat action. He was player-manager of the Tigers from 1921 to 1926. In those six years Babe Ruth's Yankees hit 111 homers a year while Detroit hit 46 homers per season. But the Tigers outhit the Yankees, .302 to .288, and outscored them 848 runs to 813 runs per season. Cobb's judgment in handling pitchers was criticized, but he could teach hitting. One of his pupils, lifetime .330 hitter Heinie Manush, said, "Ty Cobb was always on my ass. If I went without a hit on Friday, he wouldn't speak to me on Saturday. I couldn't like him as a man, no way. He ran things like a dictator. But as a teacher — well, he was the best."[26]

Cobb teammate Fred Haney painted a gloomy picture of Cobb as manager. "We thought that Cobb would crack up any day. One day he would be riding high and working well with his lineup, next day he'd go around with the whites of his eyes flared and be the meanest guy you ever saw. He had spells, fits. Unimportant things made him blow. Some of the boys thought it was a case of brain fever."[27]

Cobb married twice and both marriages ended in divorce. He had many brawls in his lifetime, including some with black people. Ty's short fuse seemed even shorter in disputes with blacks. His unpopularity with his peers was exhibited when only four baseball people attended his funeral. But he was capable of acts of kindness. He built a top-flight hospital for poor people in Royston. He donated a lot of his money to create the Cobb Educational Fund, which paid the way of hundreds of poor kids, both black and white, through college. He cared for his crippled sister, Florence, until she died.

When Ty died of cancer at age 74 in an Atlanta hospital in 1961, beside his bed lay a million dollars in negotiable securities stuffed inside a paper bag. On top of the bag was a Luger pistol. A Hollywood movie depicted Cobb as a crazed old man near the end of his life when he was taking morphine to battle cancer pain and drinking alcohol in excess. No one can deny Ty Cobb's greatness as a ballplayer. But Cobb was from an era that died a long time before he did. The old Confederacy was long gone with the wind by 1961. The Dead Ball days were history. The home run ruled. Many of the game's top players were black. The world had changed a lot since Cobb burned up the AL in 1911, but old Ty at times had trouble accepting it.

Chapter 3

The Babe at His Best: Babe Ruth in 1921

The day after Christmas 1919, Red Sox owner Harry Frazee finished a deal with New York Yankee co-owners Jacob Ruppert and Cap Huston in which he sold Babe Ruth's contract for $100,000 in cash plus a loan of $300,000 against a mortgage on Fenway Park. The deal changed baseball. Ruth's booming bat revolutionized the sport as titanic home runs flew from his club to distances never seen before. In the post-war prosperity of New York City in the Roaring Twenties, the Babe became the most famous athlete this nation ever produced. Baseball needed a lift after the Black Sox Scandal, and Ruth provided it. Few questioned the integrity of the 400-foot homers he sent flying out of ballparks.

Ruth came out of St. Mary's Industrial School in Baltimore in 1914 to become the best left-handed pitcher in baseball. He won 18 games his rookie year with the Red Sox, 23 his second year, and 24 his third year before being moved to the outfield on a part-time basis. He pitched 29⅔ consecutive scoreless innings in World Series play, but Boston manager Edward Barrow saw that the Babe's future lie in hitting a baseball.

In 1919 Ruth won nine games as a pitcher and slammed a record 29 home runs while playing 111 games in the outfield and four at first base. After moving to the Big Apple in 1920, Ruth belted an unheard-of 54 home runs while nearly carrying the Yankees to a pennant. No other batter in the league hit more than 19 homers and only one team hit as many as 50. Pitchers walked him 148 times. His slugging average was .847, which represented the record until Barry Bonds slugged .863 in 2001. Babe reached base 53 percent of the time and scored 158 runs.

As great as Ruth's numbers were in 1920, they were better in 1921. Ruth enjoyed the greatest season of the twentieth century when he led the Yankees to their first pennant. He batted .378, whacked 204 hits, 44 doubles, and 16 triples, and walloped 59 home runs. He scored 177 runs. Nobody has ever scored more in a season. He drove home 171 runs. He walked 144 times, including 50-plus intentional passes. His slugging percentage was one point behind his 1920 mark at .846, and he amassed 457 bases, the all-time record.

Still young and slender, he was a complete player, stealing 17 bases and throwing out 17 runners from left field. Newspaper accounts described him taking an extra base because of an outfielder's momentary bobble. It wasn't rare to see him make a tumbling catch on the dead run.

A record 1,289,422 fans passed through the turnstiles at the Polo Grounds to see Ruth hit in 1920. Another 1,230,696 fans showed up in 1921. It took the Yankees until 1946 to draw more fans despite moving to Yankee Stadium in 1923. Ruth was a more powerful hitter at the Polo Grounds than he was at Yankee Stadium. In 1920 he hit .397 with 29 homers and a .985 slugging percentage at the Harlem meadow. In 1921 he hit .404 with 32 homers and a .929 slugging percentage there. The Babe's highest slugging mark ever at Yankee Stadium was .805. After swatting 41 home runs while batting .393 in his first year at Yankee Stadium, Ruth declared he would have hit 80 home runs had he still played at the Polo Grounds.

In 1921 Babe Ruth, shown here at Sportsman's Park, put together perhaps the greatest offensive season of all time, batting .378 with 59 homers, 171 RBIs, a still-record 177 runs scored, and 457 total bases. Still young and relatively slender, he legged out 16 triples, stole 17 bases, and threw out 17 runners from left field.

The newspapermen tried to outdo each other describing Ruth. They called him "the Sultan of Swat," "Behemoth of Bust" and "Wizard of Wallop," among other monikers. People showed up at ballparks to see him put on a show during batting practice. Some left the game after his last at-bat regardless of the score. The Babe's power was viewed as so remarkable that he was sought by medical research for testing. A Columbia University Medical School test assessed him "one man in a million."[1]

In 1921 the Yankees needed all they could get from Ruth to outdistance Tris Speaker's defending world-champion Cleveland Indians. But the 1921 Yankees were not a one-man team. First baseman Wally Pipp hit .297 with 97 RBIs. At second base Aaron Ward batted .306. Shortstop Roger Peckinpaugh put up a .380 on-base percentage and scored 128 runs. Frank Baker and Mike McNally produced 95 RBIs at third base. Baker, who missed the entire 1920 season due to the illness and death of his wife, was especially effective, driving in 71 runs in 330 at-bats. Switch-hitting catcher Wally Schang socked 30 doubles and batted .316.

In right field the Yankees possessed another slugger, Bob Meusel. Meusel hit .318 with 40 doubles, 16 triples, 24 homers and 135 RBIs. At 6'3", Meusel cut an imposing figure in right field with a strong arm. He led the league with 28 assists. In center field significant time was shared by Braggo Roth, Chick Fewster, and Elmer Miller. In 592 at-bats, the platoon combined to hit .292, with 37 doubles and 114 runs.

The ace of the New York pitching staff was Carl Mays. Mays, who had a submarine motion and a reputation as a beanball pitcher, was notorious for throwing the pitch that killed Cleveland shortstop Ray Chapman in 1920. The Indians won the 1920 pennant and wore black armbands in memory of Chapman while beating Brooklyn in the World Series. Mays pitched a shutout one week after the beaning but did not accompany the Yankees in their last series in Cleveland. Yankee co-owner Cap Huston explained Mays's absence: "Not because we think there is danger of any trouble, but out of respect to the feeling of the people there. We don't want to offend them. It is largely a matter of sentiment."[2]

A group of Indians, meeting without player-manager Tris Speaker, circulated a petition calling for AL teams to refuse to play the Yankees whenever Mays pitched. Boston, Detroit, St. Louis and Washington supported the petition. The A's and White Sox did not. Eventually nothing came of it.

An unnamed pitcher once summed up the bad feeling against Mays by asking F.C. Lane of *Baseball Magazine*, "Mays is a low ball pitcher. How does it happen that when he puts the ball on the inside, it generally comes near the batter's head?"[3]

Mays told Jack Murphy of the *San Diego Union*, "Chapman was the fastest base-runner in the league; he could fly. He liked to push the ball toward second or down the first-base line and run. I had to guard against this of course. I knew Chapman had to shift his feet in order to get into position to push the ball. I saw him doing this — I was an underhand pitcher, my hand almost scraped the ground — and I threw my fastball high and tight so he would pop up. Chapman ran into the ball. If he had stayed in the batter's box, it would have missed him by a foot."[4]

Mays added, "I fooled them. I went out and pitched the rest of the year. Why should I let it ruin the rest of my life? I had a wife and two children, and they had to eat. I had to provide for them."[5]

Mays was at his peak in 1920 (26–11, 312 innings, 3.06 ERA) and 1921 (27–9, 337 innings, 3.04 ERA). In 1921 he hit .343 with 22 RBIs. The other two workhorses on the staff were Waite Hoyt (19–13, 282 innings, 3.10 ERA) and Bob Shawkey (18–12, 245 innings, 4.08 ERA). Hoyt, known as the "Brooklyn Schoolboy," was signed by the Giants when he was 16. He pitched one inning for New York before being shipped to Boston. His record was nothing to brag about there except for one game against the Yankees in which he pitched nine consecutive perfect innings in between hits in a 13-inning game he lost, 2–1. This impressed the New York brass. The Yankees acquired him in 1921. Hoyt was at home in New York. He sang at the Palace Theater, appeared in vaudeville acts, dabbled in painting and writing, and once declared, "Wives of ball players, when they teach their children their prayers, should instruct them to say: 'God bless mommy, God bless daddy, God bless Babe Ruth! Babe has upped daddy's pay check by 15 to 40 percent!"[6]

The manager of the Yankees, Miller Huggins, stood 5'6" and weighed 140 pounds. He played 13 seasons as a second baseman with Cincinnati and St. Louis. His lifetime batting average was .265, but he led the league in walks four times, stole 30 bases a year, and scored more than 100 runs three times. He was nicknamed "the Mighty Mite." It is odd that Huggins benefited from the home run as a manager because as a player he hit only nine homers, all inside-the-parkers. That was not unusual in the Dead Ball era. Detroit's Sam Crawford hit a record 51 inside-the-parkers.

A crowd of 37,000 turned out in sunny weather for Opening Day at the Polo Grounds to see the Yankees rout the A's, 11–1. Mays was brilliant with his grass-clipping deliveries, tossing a three-hitter. Ruth ripped three singles and two doubles.

The much-awaited initial home runs for Ruth and Meusel came three days later in a 3–1 win over the A's. Ruth's blast crashed into the right-field upper deck in the sixth inning. The crowd of 25,000 at the Polo Grounds gave him a rousing ovation as he made his pigeon-toed trot around the paths. The Red Sox entered the Polo Grounds next and Mays whitewashed them, 4–0. Ruth, Mays, Hoyt, and Schang were all former Red Sox. Star pitchers

Joe Bush, Sam Jones, and Herb Pennock as well as shortstop Everett Scott and third baseman Joe Dugan would follow to New York over the next two years, fueling the Yankee powerhouse. Owner Harry Frazee's Red Sox finished in fifth place in 1921 with a 75–79 record. Their leading home run hitter was Del Pratt with five. As a team the Red Sox poled 17 homers.

The next afternoon Ruth broke up a 1–1 tie in the seventh inning with a shot off the facade of the right-field grandstand for a two-run homer. Meusel added a three-run homer in the eighth and the Yanks bested Boston again, 8–4. Frazee used the money he got from the Yankees to finance theatrical flops until finally hitting it big on Broadway with *No! No! Nanette.*

On April 21 in Philadelphia, Ruth answered a razzing with a first-inning RBI double. Later he put the frosting on the cake of the 6–1 win with a ninth-inning home run that smashed a window on 20th Street. On April 25 back in New York, Ruth blasted one of flame-thrower Walter Johnson's speed shots a couple of feet from the right-field roof. Mays had a no-hitter going into the eighth that day but Yankee errors sabotaged his effort. The Senators came back to win, 4–3. In the Yankees' last game of the month, a fight almost started between Ruth and Washington catcher Patsy Gharrity. Ruth dropped his bat and was ready to duke it out during a balls-and-strikes argument with Gharrity. Both benches emptied but the dispute never got beyond the bounds of conversation. Ruth ended April hitting .439.

In his first appearance of the season, at Fenway, Ruth was greeted by cheers. The Babe homered off Jones in the ninth inning to tie the contest at 2–2, but the Bosox gained a rare victory, 3–2, in the tenth inning. On May 6 in Washington, Ruth sent his seventh homer disappearing over the scoreboard in right-center as the Yanks won, 9–2. The next day the Yanks prevailed in the nation's capital, 6–5, in a game witnessed by former President Woodrow Wilson. Wilson had suffered a stroke in 1919 while touring the country at a blistering pace, trying to get support for his League of Nations plan. An invalid for months, he clung to his executive power while his wife and doctor shielded him from business that tired him. The Senate ultimately rejected his League of Nations idea and Wilson died in 1924 a disappointed man.

The game Wilson saw that day was a dandy. With the Senators leading, 4–2, in the eighth, Ruth timed one of Johnson's blazers and sent it skyrocketing beyond the center-field barrier, which was 421 feet from home plate. The newspapermen called it the longest homer ever hit in Washington. Doubles by Meusel and Ward followed to tie the score at 4–4. Meusel handed the Senators a 5–4 lead in the top of the ninth frame with a wild throw that skidded past third base. In the bottom of the ninth "Long Bob" redeemed himself. Having already singled, doubled, and homered in the contest, this time he slashed a game-deciding two-run triple.

When the Yankees went to Washington, Ruth often stopped at Baltimore to hit a few for the gang at St. Mary's. Although he lived the high life during the Roaring Twenties, Ruth seemed most comfortable when surrounded by a crowd of kids. He possessed a genuine love for the underdog. Teammate Lou Gehrig remembered a time in Chicago when he was supposed to meet Ruth at an agreed-upon spot. When Ruth failed to show after a long period of time, Gehrig walked off to find him. He found Babe in an alleyway teaching a crippled black kid how to hit. Ruth was photographed at hospitals and orphanages promising to hit homers for kids who were down on their luck. Cynical people might suggest the photo shoots were publicity ploys. Yet according to Bill Slocum, a popular writer for the *New York American,* for every occasion Ruth was photographed with kids, he made 50 other appearances that went unpublicized.[7] Ruth loved kids and enjoyed spending time with them. Sometimes he was moved to tears by the sick kids he encountered. Sportswriter Paul Gallico offered, "His generosity and his affections were just as Gargantuan as his appetites."[8]

Ruth admitted he drank liquor, stole, and chewed tobacco at an early age. His parents sent him to St. Mary's Industrial School, a training school for orphans, incorrigibles, and children of poor parents who had no other means of providing an education for them. His mother died when he was 13 years old. Ruth stayed at the school for most of the years from 1902 to 1914. There he learned to be a shirtmaker and play baseball.

While at St. Mary's, Ruth came under the guidance of Brother Matthias. The Babe wrote:

> I think I was born as a hitter the first day I ever saw him hit a baseball. I can remember it as if it were yesterday. It was during the summer of 1902, my first year in St. Mary's. The baseball of that time was a lump of mush, and by the time St. Mary's got hold of one it was considerably less. But Brother Matthias would stand at the end of the yard, a finger mitt on his left hand and a bat in his right, toss the ball up with his left hand and give it a terrific belt with the bat he held in his right hand. When he felt like it he could hit it a little harder and make the ball clear the fence in center field. ... I would just stand there and watch him, bug-eyed.[9]

While at St. Mary's, Ruth played two or three baseball games a day. He was discovered by Jack Dunn, owner of the Baltimore Orioles of the International League. Ruth was released from St. Mary's in 1914 to play for Baltimore for a salary of $600.

On Mother's Day 1921 at the Polo Grounds, Fewster stole home in the ninth inning to tie the score at 3–3 with the A's. Hats and scorecards sailed onto the field celebrating Fewster's spectacular dash. Chick was popular with the fans. In 1920 he was hit in the head with a pitch and so badly injured that he was unable to speak for a month. He was sent to Baltimore for surgery to remove a blood clot and returned bravely to assist the Yankee cause in 1921. Ruth copied Fewster's idea and tried to steal home in the tenth inning but was tagged out in a close play. Ruth whacked three singles, but Eddie Rommel pitched the A's to a 5–4 win in 14 innings.

Ty Cobb's Tigers entered New York on May 10. Cobb was given the job of player-manager for Detroit in 1921. Tiger management hoped he could duplicate what Speaker had accomplished in his first year as Cleveland's player-manager. Under Cobb the Tigers hit .316 in 1921 (the AL record) but finished in sixth place.

In the series opener Ruth slugged a two-run first-inning homer and Mays made it stand up with his subway slants in the 2–1 victory. In the second game Ruth tried to steal home in the third inning. The Bambino thought that he had made it this time but was called out. Babe was enraged as he pleaded his case vehemently before leaving the field in disgust. Detroit won, 2–1, when Donie Bush stole home in the eighth inning for the deciding tally. In game three Ruth banged a two-run homer in the first inning and delivered an RBI single in the third inning. Still, the Tigers led, 10–9, into the ninth. Peckinpaugh led off with a walk and Ruth slammed the sphere over Cobb's head for a game-tying triple. He tagged up and jogged home with the winner on Pipp's fly ball. The Yanks also won game four, 6–4. Ruth loomed big in the victory again. The Tigers chose not to pitch to him most of the afternoon by giving him three walks. But with the bases loaded in the second inning, there was no place to put Babe and he lashed a three-run triple to the fence.

Miller Huggins' team invaded Cleveland for the first time on May 14. The Indians were leading the league with a 16–9 record, two games ahead of New York. Speaker's club had scored ten or more runs in six of its wins, including a 23-hit, 18–5 thrashing of the Tigers and a 20-hit, 17–3 slaughter of the White Sox. The only pitcher Cleveland wasn't hitting was Chicago's Red Faber, who tossed a pair of two-hit shutouts at the Tribe.

In the opener the Yanks trailed, 4–2, in the eighth inning. Roth then started the Pinstripers' winning rally by getting hit with a pitch. Peckinpaugh dumped a Texas-League single and Ruth clobbered Jim Bagby's second pitch into the center-field bleachers. It was the first ball ever hit over the center field wall at League Park, which was 420 feet from home plate. The next day, a crowd of 28,000 that was expecting to see Mays pitch required roped-off accommodations. Hoyt threw instead and beat the Indians, 8–2. Mays won the third game, 6–3, powered by Meusel's three-run inside-the-park homer.

Cleveland won the final game, 4–2, behind the hurling of George Uhle. Ruth's baserunning adventures continued as he was picked off second base twice. In his attempt to get back into second base the second time, he slammed into

Cleveland's tiny shortstop, Joe Sewell. Sewell retired briefly to the clubhouse to take care of a bloody nose. When Sewell reentered the field, Ruth trotted out of the dugout to offer his apologies. This angered Speaker, who raced in from center field with some choice words. A shouting match began. Both teams gathered around second base before Babe retreated into the Yankee dugout. In the ninth inning he hit a homer over the 45-foot-high right-field screen.

Despite the early setback, Cleveland proved to be a game foe. Speaker hit .362 with 52 doubles (42 at League Park) and juggled his lineup to produce what was then a record 355 doubles, a .308 team batting average, and 925 runs scored — just 23 fewer than the Yankees. Among the Tribe's talented batsmen were Sewell (.318), Larry Gardner (.319), Steve O'Neill (.322), George Burns (.361), Riggs Stephenson (.330), Charlie Jamieson (.310), Elmer Smith (.290 with a team-leading 16 homers), and former pitcher Joe Wood (.366, 60 RBIs in 194 at-bats). Speaker, Gardner, and Wood were all former Red Sox.

On May 25, Ruth crushed the longest home run to date at Sportsman Park in St. Louis, a rocket that sailed more than 500 feet into the summer sky. He wasn't juiced; he was just plain strong. In early June the Indians came into the Polo Grounds sporting a 2½-game lead. The Yankees won the first two games, 9–2 and 4–3. Ruth missed most of the second game because he was arrested for speeding in his sports car and spent part of the afternoon in a Manhattan station house. Ruth had his uniform brought to him and put it on in his cell. At four o'clock a police motorcycle escort led him from downtown Manhattan through city traffic to the Polo Grounds in 18 minutes.[10] Word had spread regarding his whereabouts. When he reached the Polo Grounds, Ruth ran through the center-field gate to a huge ovation. The Yanks proceeded to win on Braggo Roth's ninth-inning RBI single.

The Indians regrouped to pound the Yankees in game three, 14–4. In the fourth game Cleveland knocked out Mays with three runs in the ninth inning to tie the score, and won in the eleventh, 8–6, on Gardner's homer.

Cobb's Tigers followed the Indians into the Big Apple sporting a 29–25 record and entertaining hopes of getting into the pennant race. Ruth destroyed those aspirations. In the curtain raiser, Ruth's three-run homer in the seventh tied the game and Peckinpaugh's ninth-inning RBI single won it, 7–6. In the second game Ruth doubled twice and pumped his 19th homer into the upper deck to pace a 21-hit New York attack in a 12–8 win.

In the third game, Ruth went both ways in a 13–8 triumph. He pitched one-hit ball through the first four innings and fanned Cobb before being relieved by Mays in the sixth with the Hugmen up, 10–4. He also homered twice more, one of his wallops being the first ball ever hit into the center-field bleachers at the Polo Grounds, a distance of 433 feet from home plate. On June 14 the Yankees completed the sweep, 9–6, with Ruth bombing two more homers — one of them again landing in the center-field bleachers. This clout was reported to have outdistanced the shot from the day before and brought an amazed gasp from the crowd. Angry about losing the series, Cobb smashed chairs and windows in the visitors' clubhouse with a bat.

Cobb finished the season at .389, and his star pupil, Harry Heilmann, led the league at .394. Ruth finished third in the batting race at .378. Cobb boasted he could hit a lot of home runs if he tried. After one boast he hit a record five homers in two consecutive games in May 1925. Yet Cobb's claims were not true. If Cobb could have rivaled Ruth by hitting 40 or 50 home runs while keeping his average up, he would have done it. The truth was he had adopted a punch-and-slash style during the Dead Ball days. He never mastered the art of slugging and was angry that the game was passing him by. Ruth boasted if he went for "dinky singles" he could have batted .600.

Ruth and Cobb nearly had a physical altercation in August 1921. During a hard-fought Yankee-Tiger game, Cobb rode Ruth with some vulgar bench-jockeying. After the game Ruth barged into the Tiger clubhouse looking for Cobb. Upon seeing the enraged Bambino, Cobb asked Ruth, "What's the matter, big stuff? Can't you take it?"[11] Ruth charged toward Cobb but several Tigers intercepted him and tossed him out the door.

Cobb believed it was an advantage for Ruth to start his career as a pitcher. He said Ruth had the luxury of experimenting with his hitting because he did not have to worry about losing his position as an everyday player. Ruth once said, "I copied my swing after Joe Jackson's. ... Joe aims his right shoulder square at the pitcher, with his feet about 20 inches apart. But I close my stance to about eight and a half inches or less. I find I pivot better with it closed ... once my swing starts, though, I can't change it or pull up. It's all or nothing."[12]

The completion of Ruth's violent swing twisted the Babe into a corkscrew shape whenever he missed, bringing ooohs and aaahs from the fans. With his huge stride and swing, it took super-human coordination for Ruth to club 714 career homers while maintaining a .342 lifetime batting average.

On June 20 in Boston, Ruth singled, doubled and then led off the tenth inning by tagging Elmer Myers's first pitch over the left-field wall to get the Yanks a 7–6 win. On July 2, the Babe homered in both ends of a doubleheader as New York swept Boston, 5–3 and 5–1. That gave him 30 homers and put him 17 days ahead of his 1920 pace. He had homered 14 times in the last 22 games. Ruth's feats didn't go unnoticed that day, although boxing great Jack Dempsey grabbed the headlines by knocking out European champ Georges Carpentier in the fourth round before 90,000 in Jersey City. The Parisians were stunned by the news.

The Yanks celebrated the Fourth of July by whacking the A's, 6–4 and 14–4, before a capacity crowd at the Polo Grounds. Baker homered twice.

Meanwhile in Cleveland, the Indians swept the White Sox, 6–4 and 11–10, winning the second game after falling behind, 10–0. The Indians led the league at 46–26. New York owned a 45–28 record.

On July 5, Ruth walked twice, doubled, and homered as the Yanks completed their sweep of the A's, 7–5. In the seventh inning he was walked intentionally. Baker responded with a three-run double. On July 12 in St. Louis, the Babe powered a 6–4 win over the Browns with two homers and a double. At the next whistle stop in Detroit, he smashed a homer during a 10–1 victory that groundskeepers measured at 560 feet. He then doubled, stole third, and scored the go-ahead run as the Yankees completed a four-game sweep in Detroit, 6–5.

Sam Jones, who pitched from 1914 to 1935, including nine seasons as Ruth's teammate, told author Lawrence Ritter, "Babe Ruth could hit a ball so hard, and so far, that it was sometimes impossible to believe your eyes. We used to absolutely marvel at his hits. Tremendous wallops. You can't imagine the balls he hit. And before that he was a great pitcher, too. Really great.... It was hard to believe the natural ability that man had."[13]

The Pinstripers rode into Cleveland next with an eight-game win streak. The two leaders split a hard-fought four-game series. The wire services reported there was much bitterness displayed by the contending teams. One of the Indians' wins was especially sweet as they drove Mays from the box with seven runs in the third inning in a 17–8 rout.

Cleveland was getting solid pitching from Stan Coveleski. Baseball got "Covey" out of the coal mines, where he worked for five cents an hour, 72 hours a week. The spitball helped get him to the majors at age 27. In 1921 he won 23 games with a 3.36 ERA in 316 innings. George Uhle was Cleveland's second-best hurler, winning 16 games. A boost to the Indians's pitching came with the acquisition of Allan Sothoron from Boston. Sothoron was a flop in St. Louis and Boston, but won 12 of 16 decisions for Cleveland. When the Indians did not get good pitching, their hitters bailed them out. In a series against George Sisler's Browns, Cleveland swept four straight by scores of 12–6, 11–9, 10–8, and 12–5.

When the Indians came into New York for another big series on July 30, they still held a two-game lead with a 61–34 record. They arrived at the Polo Grounds with a bang, embarrassing the Yankees, 16–1. Coveleski's shutout was spoiled by Ruth's 37th homer. The next day the Yanks rebounded. Mays threw a two-hitter and whacked a bases-loaded double in a 12–2 win. Ruth singled, tripled, swiped a base, and homered again. The rubber game saw Hoyt stymie the Tribe, 5–2.

The Yankees arrived in Cleveland for the last time on August 23. Ruth hammered a pair of two-run homers in New York's 6–1 triumph in the first of three. Hoyt outdueled Coveleski, 3–2, in the second game. A near-riot took place in the final game when Yankee hurler Harry Harper hit three consecutive Cleveland batters with pitches. The third batter to get plunked, O'Neill, fired the ball back at Harper. Mounted police came out on the field when the game ended to protect New York players from a threatening crowd. The Indians won the game, 15–1, to retake the league lead.

As September opened, the Yankees swept six straight from the Senators. Mays won the final game, 9–3, with Ruth swatting his 50th homer. The Babe tied his 1920 mark of 54 homers during a three-game set in Philadelphia a week later. In the final game of the series Ruth singled, doubled, and tripled as the New Yorkers socked 24 hits in shellacking the Mackmen, 19–3. The Yanks showed no mercy while scoring nine runs in the ninth inning.

On September 15, the Yankees swept a doubleheader from the Browns, 10–6 and 13–5, in New York. Ruth broke his record with homerun number 55 but hurt his leg sliding into third base with a triple. He retired in favor of Fewster in the second game. Cleveland swept two in Philly that day by 17–3 and 6–0 scores. Charlie Jamieson enjoyed a banner afternoon with two singles, two doubles, a triple, and a homer.

The next day the Indians passed the Yanks and moved back into first place by a .631 to .629 percentage point margin. Uhle tossed a two-hitter at the Senators and Joe Wood's triple in the eighth inning broke a scoreless tie. In New York, Sisler's grand slam in the ninth inning punctuated a 10–3 Browns rout. Ruth hit his 56th homer, but St. Louis ace Urban Shocker struck him out three times.

The ultimate showdown took place at the Polo Grounds from September 23–26. The Indians arrived in town after besting the Red Sox, 9–8, in 12 innings at Fenway. New York had won 20 of its previous 28 games since last meeting Cleveland in the Lake City in August. The Indians, who played their last home game on September 8, had won 19 of 27 games since meeting the Yanks.

Hoyt bested Coveleski in the opener, 4–2, as Ruth ripped three doubles and scored three times. Uhle came back to blank New York, 9–0, in the second game with a four-hitter, silencing the standing-room-only crowd of 40,000.

On September 25 the grandstand was sold out two hours before the game. The park was closed one hour prior to gametime, turning back thousands of would-be spectators trying to see the hottest show in town. It was estimated that 100,000 people tried to get into the game. The Hugmen rose to the occasion by rolling up a 15–4 lead after four innings and coasting to a 21–7 romp. Meusel singled, tripled, and homered. Mays gave up 13 hits and seven runs but went the distance.

The final game was a thriller. Speaker tried Coveleski on two days' rest. He was gone by the third inning. New York started Jack Quinn, who was knocked out with three runs in the first. Ruth crashed a solo homer in the first inning and shot a two-run missile over the roof in right in the fifth. Hoyt relieved Quinn and pitched until the seventh, when he injured his hand trying to stop a line drive off the bat of Speaker. Mays came to the rescue.

Yankee center fielder Elmer Miller played a major role in the game. In the seventh he threw out Sewell at third base, killing an Indian rally. In the eighth, his diving grab of a blooper off Speaker's bat with runners on second and third saved two runs. Mays finally nailed down an 8–7 Yankee win by fanning O'Neill with two on and two out in the ninth. Yankee co-owner Jacob Ruppert became so worked up with the tension of the contest that he left the press box and missed the dramatic ending.

The Yankees never relinquished first place thereafter. They clinched the pennant when Mays gained his 27th victory, 5–3, in the first game of a doubleheader on October 1 against the A's. Ruth came in to pitch in the eighth inning of the second game with the Yankees leading, 6–0. The A's scored six runs, but Huggins left him in and Ruth got the win after pitching shutout ball in the ninth, tenth, and eleventh. Ruth pitched twice more, in 1930 and in 1933, both times to boost attendance at the end of the season. Both times he won, making his pitching record 5–0 with the Yanks.

In the final game of the year, Ruth hit homer number 59 with two men on as New York topped Boston, 7–6. In 1921 the Yanks won 98 games, hit .300, scored 948 runs, and led the league in pitching (3.79 ERA). Ruppert, who said his idea of a perfect game was a 10–0 Yankee victory, had won his first of many pennants. He proceeded to buy Huston out, build Yankee Stadium, and accumulate a fortune of $70 million. A four-time congressman and owner of a brewery that he inherited from his father, Ruppert remained a resolute bachelor. He enjoyed the company of women but never married. He lived in a 15-room Fifth Avenue apartment as well as a 25-room mansion in Garrison, New York, where he kept monkeys, peacocks, and prize-winning St. Bernards.

The Yankees's opponents in the World Series, the New York Giants, won 94 games and drew a then–NL record 973,477 fans to the Polo Grounds. The Yankees were the tenants of the Giants at the Polo Grounds. The fact that the Pinstripers outdrew the Giants angered John McGraw.

The Giants trailed Pittsburgh by 7½ games on August 23 but defeated the Pirates in their last 10 meetings to take first place. The Giants lineup featured first baseman George "Highpockets" Kelley (.308, 122 RBIs and a league-leading 23 homers), shortstop Dave Bancroft (.318, 121 runs), third baseman Frankie Frisch (.341, 100 RBIs, 121 runs and 49 stolen bases) and outfielders Ross Youngs (.327, 102 RBIs), George Burns (.299, 111 runs and a league-leading 80 walks) and Bob Meusel's brother, Emil Meusel (.343, 96 runs). The Giants led the majors in pitching with a 3.56 ERA.

Ruth hit the first pitch thrown to him in the Series for a ground-ball single up the middle to score Miller. That was the all the offense Mays needed as he tossed a five-hit shutout to beat Phil Douglas, 3–0. In Game 2 Hoyt allowed only two singles to outpitch Art Nehf, 3–0. Ruth walked the first three times up. In the fifth inning he excited the crowd, which was split evenly in its loyalty to the Yankees and Giants, by stealing second and third base. He did not score, however. The Yanks led, 1–0, in the eighth when Frisch muffed a short fly by Peckinpaugh. Ruth forced Peckinpaugh out at second but Meusel followed with a single. Pipp drove in Ruth with an RBI ground ball and Meusel stole home for the final run.

In Game 3 the Yanks took a 4–0 lead. It looked as if a rout of McGraw's Giants was on. But after 20 scoreless innings, the Giants awoke to tie the score with four runs in the third and then exploded for eight runs in the seventh. They socked 20 hits in winning, 13–5. Ruth struck out twice, walked, and drove in two runs with a single. He left in the eighth inning for a pinch-runner. Fans who knew baseball recognized something was ailing him. Others jeered. He tipped his cap to his antagonists.

It was learned then that Ruth was hurt. He scraped his left elbow on the rough infield with his steal of third in Game 2 and the arm was infected. Reports circulated that Babe would be out for the Series. He arrived at the ballpark for Game 4 with his arm in a sling. A surgeon lanced his left forearm below the elbow and advised him not to play. After sitting on the bench throughout batting practice, Ruth emerged from the dugout and jogged to left field when the Yankees ran out to their positions. An exultant roar rose from the crowd. He hit a home run in the ninth inning but the Giants evened the Series with a 4–2 win.

Ruth also played Game 5. His elbow was rigged with a tube to drain the wound, and his left wrist was heavily bandaged. His legs were taped their full length. He limped to bat in the first inning and struck out, one of his three whiffs on the day. His face expressed pain every time he swung. Nevertheless, he still figured big in a 3–1 Yankee win. In the fourth, with the score tied, 1–1, he shocked the Giants by beating out a bunt. He then scored all the way from first base on Meusel's double. He slid across the plate, got up, and stumbled into the dugout. Huggins had to call time at the end of the inning so the Bambino could collect himself. Babe then surfaced from the dugout, and the crowd roared as he jogged to left field.

After the game physicians examined him. The wound was draining more and the swelling in his arm increased. Rumors of blood poisoning and possible amputation arose. Ruth was told that under no condition should he attempt to play ball again in the Series.[14]

Ruth sat in a box seat for Game 6. In the press box sat *New York Sun* columnist Joe Vila. Vila wrote a story after Ruth's appearance in Game 4 including the following:

> Ruth possibly enjoyed the trick he played on the fans by going into the game after the report had been spread that he had been forced out of the series by an operation on his "infected elbow." On numerous occasions during the pennant race the public was informed that Ruth had been disabled and couldn't play, yet the Home Run King invariably bobbed up to battle for the Yankees. According to official information on Saturday, The Babe had been seriously injured and the Hugmen would have to worry along without him. But Ruth, with a bandage around his elbow, surprised everybody in the stands by taking his place in left field and by hammering the ball for a single and a four-bagger. Further reports of the Bambino's indispositions will be taken with plenty of salt.[15]

Ruth spotted Vila and started to make his way over to the press box. Vila saw Ruth and thought Babe was going to tear him apart. He raised his typewriter to ward off an attack. Instead, Ruth rolled up his sleeve, showed his wound, and shouted, "Why don't you take a picture of this and put it in your paper?"[16]

Without Ruth the Yankees lost the next two games, 8–5 and 2–1. In the final game of the best-of-nine Series, Huggins sent Ruth up to pinch-hit in the ninth inning with his team trailing, 1–0. Ruth grounded out to Kelley at first base, a sad way for his greatest season to end. McGraw's Giants had beaten the upstart Yankees, five games to three.

Ruth was suspended five times and missed 44 games in 1922. The Yanks won the pennant but lost to the Giants again in the World Series. On Opening Day at new Yankee Stadium in 1923, Ruth christened the baseball palace with a home run as his Yanks beat Boston before 70,000 fans. He did not break his home run record in 1923, but he reached base 375 times on 205 hits and 170 walks, batted .393, and led the league in homers (41), runs (153) and RBIs (130). He belted three homers and batted .368 as the Yanks finally defeated McGraw's Giants in a World Series, four games to two. His success continued in 1924 when he led the league in homers (46) and won the batting title (.378). But the team slumped resulting in a second-place finish, two games behind Washington.

During the winter of 1924 Ruth lived it up. He reported to spring training in 1925 weighing a hefty 256 pounds. Huggins worked him hard in the southern sun. In twenty days he dropped twenty-one pounds and incredibly was batting .449. Then on the morning of April 8, he collapsed while passing through a train station in Asheville, North Carolina. On April 17 it was reported that Ruth underwent surgery to remove an "intestinal abscess."

He returned to the Yankee lineup on June 1 and struggled (.290, 25 homers, 66 RBIs in 98 games). The team dropped to seventh place. At one point Ruth was suspended and fined $5,000 by Huggins. During Ruth's illness, his wife, Helen, was hospitalized for a nervous breakdown. She soon moved to Boston. Ruth sold their house in Sudbury. After the spring of 1925, Ruth rarely saw Helen and their adopted daughter, Dorothy. Neither sued for divorce. When they did meet it was on friendly terms, but their life together was essentially over.

Helen was an attractive if not glamorous women. Ruth met her while she was a waitress in Boston. She died in a house fire in January 1929. Ruth attended her funeral. He then married actress Claire Hodgson in April 1929. Ruth had known Claire since 1923 and visited her often in New York. She had a daughter named Julia by her first marriage, which ended in divorce. The Babe and Claire were a good match, and they remained together until Babe's death in 1948.

In 1926 sportswriters unanimously predicted Ruth wouldn't regain his previous form. The Babe shocked them. He toned down his excesses. He worked hard to recapture and maintain his strength and coordination. He put himself in the hands of Arthur McGovern, a trainer who ran a gym on Madison Avenue. By Opening Day each April, from 1926 to 1932, the Babe was in condition to play hard. In those seven seasons he hit .353 in 3,579 at-bats, and averaged 180 hits, 49 homers, 143 runs, 151 RBIs and 126 walks per season. In 1927 he stunned the baseball planet by launching 60 round trippers. His salary reached its peak at $80,000 in 1930. When told he had been paid more than the president of the United States, the Babe quipped, "I had a better year."

The most popular story involving Ruth and sick boys came about during the 1926 World Series. The boy's name was Johnny Sylvester, the son of the vice president of National City Bank. Johnny was seriously ill but he still followed the World Series on radio from his home in New Jersey. He kept a scrapbook on Ruth and asked his father for a ball signed by Ruth. His father wired Ruth in St. Louis. Two baseballs signed by the stars of Ruth's Yankees and Rogers Hornsby's Cardinals arrived by airmail to Johnny's house on the day of the fourth game with a kind note. Contrary to legend there was no promise by Ruth to hit a homer for Johnny. That was the day Ruth powered a 10–5 win over the Cards by belting three homers. Each clout traveled farther than the one before. The first two completely cleared the right-field grandstand, and the final blast landed in the deepest part of the center-field bleachers at Sportsman's Park. Johnny was cheered up immensely by the three homers.

A radio announcer heard of the sick boy and the baseballs and invented the story of a Ruthian promise of a home run delivered in triplicate. Johnny's health began to improve after the game. The legend grew that Ruth cured the boy. After the Series and just five days after the three-homer game, Babe made a surprise visit to Johnny and talked baseball with the child.

The legend grew that Ruth could do anything he wanted on a baseball diamond simply by willing it. The clearest evidence of this was the story of Ruth's "called shot" home run in the 1932 World Series against the Cubs. At the time Ruth was 37 years old. This was his last World Series. The Yanks won the first two games in New York, and the scene shifted to Chicago. A crowd of 49,986 fans filled Wrigley Field. Some nasty bench-jockeying had been going on during the Series. Ruth blasted a three-run homer off Charlie Root in the first inning, but in the fourth he missed a shoestring catch, allowing the Cubs to tie the game, 4–4. When Ruth came to bat in the fifth against Root, the Chicago crowd was hurling a barrage of verbal abuse at Babe. He held up his hand, acknowledging the first pitch whizzed by for called strike one. Two balls followed before Root fired in a second called strike. Again Ruth raised his hand in acknowledgment. The jeers heightened. What occurred next has been disputed for seventy years. Some say Babe pointed his bat toward the center-field bleachers. Others say he was pointing toward Root. Another view is that he was sweeping the bat toward the Cub bench jockeys, indicating he still had one strike left. Whatever the case he clobbered the next pitch to the flagpole in center field, giving the Yanks a 5–4 lead and breaking the Cubs' spirit. The Yanks went on to win, 7–5, and sweep the Series.

The truth is that Ruth's career needs no embellishment. The combination of his career stats — 714 homers, 2,211 RBIs, 2,174 runs, 2,056 walks, a record .690 slugging percentage, a .342 batting average, a 94–46 record as a pitcher with a 2.28 ERA in 1,221 innings — has never been matched.

It is not surprising that many thought Babe to be supernatural. Yankee teammate Joe Dugan once stated, "To understand him, you had to understand this: He wasn't human. No human could have done the things he did and lived the way he lived and been a ballplayer. Cobb? Could he pitch? Speaker? The rest? I saw them. I was there. There was never anybody else. When you figure the things he did and the way he played, you got to figure he was more than animal even. There never was anyone like him. He was a god."[17]

Chapter 4

The Mighty Rajah:
Rogers Hornsby in 1922

While Babe Ruth thrilled fans with skyscraping home runs in the American League during the 1920s, the St. Louis Cardinals' Rogers Hornsby terrorized National League pitchers with screaming line drives. Unlike the free-living Ruth, Hornsby took care of himself. He was not a smoker or drinker. He would not attend movies for fear they would damage his eyesight. He also avoided reading to any extent. He believed religiously in the benefits of a good sirloin steak. The formula seemed to work. In the five years from 1921 to 1925, the amazing hitter who grew up playing ball against grown men in the stockyards of Fort Worth, Texas, went to bat 2,679 times and stroked 1,078 hits for an average of .402.

No other batter ever put up a better record of sustained hitting. It is doubtful anyone ever will. Of the five years, 1922 was Hornsby's most productive, although he hit for the modern-day record .424 in 1924. Ty Cobb had a higher lifetime batting average and Ruth was more of a home run threat, but Hornsby combined the ability to hit for a stratospheric average with the ability to drive the ball over the fence better than anyone who ever played.

In 1922, Hornsby won the Triple Crown with 42 homers, 152 RBIs and a .401 batting average. No other batter in history has hit 40 homers while batting .400 in a season. He led the league in hits (250), runs scored (141), doubles (46), on-base percentage (.459), slugging percentage (.722), and total bases (450). The "Mighty Rajah's" 450 total bases is second all-time to Ruth's 457 in 1921.

Rogers was a selective hitter, much like Ted Williams. He once said, "The secret of good batting, in my opinion, is to hit only good balls. That is what I would tell any young batter. Let the bad ones alone. The pitcher must put the ball over the plate or pass you. You can afford to wait. Don't be led by impatience to go after bad balls. That's exactly what the pitcher is trying to make you do. The batter should never do what the pitcher wants him to do. When the pitcher gives you a ball to your liking, then is the time to hit it and hit it hard."[1]

The walloping Texan was not a waiter who liked to walk. He walked 11 percent of his plate appearances, compared to 21 percent for Ted Williams. Hornsby wanted to get his cuts and never got cheated at the plate. He stated, "Take your swings, all three of them. Have your cut at the ball. Don't let them call you out on strikes or get you in the hole. Have your three swings and you will hit."[2]

Hornsby was born in Winters, Texas, Ed and Mary Hornsby's fifth child and the last of four boys. His father died when he was four years old and the family soon moved to Fort Worth. Rogers got an after-school job in the meat-packing yards, and at 113 pounds, began playing shortstop for any of the three stockyard teams that needed him.

At 14, Hornsby was a tireless, skinny kid who played baseball some days from dawn until sundown. He remembered, "My mother was wonderful about understanding how much I wanted to be a ballplayer. She never nagged me about playing even when I'd come in long after meals were over. She never saw a game of professional baseball in her life, but she understood what the game meant to me."[3]

Bob Connery, a scout for the Cardinals, discovered Hornsby while Rogers was playing shortstop for a minor league team in Denison, Texas. Connery was impressed with Hornsby's fielding and speed and signed him for $500. In 1915, Hornsby was brought up to the Cardinals at age 19. He stood 5'11" and weighed 135 pounds. He choked the bat high and hit .246 in 57 at-bats.

His manager at St. Louis, Miller Huggins, told him at season's end, "You're a good ballplayer, son, but you're not big enough. I think we're going to have to farm you out."[5]

Legend says the naive Hornsby, thinking the Cardinals were going to send him to a farm to bulk up, decided to get the jump on them. Instead of going home to Fort Worth, he spent the offseason on his uncle's farm in Lockhart, Texas, eating wholesome food and doing farm chores. When he returned to the Cardinals spring training camp in 1916, he packed a solid 160 pounds into his frame. In the first pre-season game, he picked the heaviest bat off the rack, held it at the end of the handle, and whacked the first pitch for a triple off the center-field wall.

In the next four years Hornsby hit .311 while playing all four infield positions. He finally settled in at second base. In 1920 Hornsby won his first of seven batting titles with a .370 average. In 1921 he was batting over .400 until he went hitless in his last two games to finish the season at .397, easily good enough for

In the five years from 1921 to 1925, Rogers Hornsby had 1,078 hits in 2,679 at-bat for an average of .402. In 1922 he became the only player ever to hit 40 homers and bat .400 in the same season and amassed 450 total basses, a National League record that still stands.

his second batting title. Before the 1921 World Series between the Giants and Yankees, John McGraw was asked if his Giants were worried about Ruth's bat. McGraw replied, "Why should I worry about Ruth? My pitchers have been throwing to a better hitter all summer."[5] He was referring to Hornsby.

McGraw coveted Hornsby's hitting ability. In 1921 the Giants offered $200,000 plus four players to get him. The previous season they had offered a straight cash deal for $250,000. Hornsby said he didn't want to play in New York. Branch Rickey declared that Hornsby wouldn't leave St. Louis as long as he was the Redbirds' manager. Huggins had taken the Yankee job in 1918, and Rickey became Hornsby's manager in 1919. The *Sporting News* invented a name for the Hornsby trade rumors that popped up each spring: "hornsbyitis."

Hornsby kept his batting eye sharp after the 1921 season by playing in a four-team league in California. The teams played a 10-week autumn schedule. Hornsby played for the Los Angeles entry while Ty Cobb, Harry Heilmann, and George Sisler were the stars on the three other teams. Cobb led the league in batting average, but Hornsby hit .390 in 61 games and led in home runs with 13.

Cobb later said of Hornsby, "The greatest natural hitter I ever saw was Rogers Hornsby. Hornsby has the best stance at the plate of any of them. His position is as near perfect as I have seen. I would call it bomb-proof. He stands well back from the plate and steps into the ball. You can't fool him on a thing."[6]

Pitcher Grover Cleveland Alexander also sang the praises of Hornsby: "Hornsby is the perfect hitter. He can hit anything and hit it hard. There's none of this bunting, rapping out little grounders and that kind of stuff about Hornsby. He hits curves, slow balls, fast balls, any old kind of balls for good, solid smashes. He's the most dangerous batter I ever faced."[7]

Hornsby batted from the right side. He stood at the far rear corner of the batter's box, feet close together, but pitchers who thought they could get him out by pitching to the outside corner discovered he had tremendous power to the opposite field. He said that he never tried for home runs but did attempt to hit every pitch as hard as he could. He was renown among opposing catchers as one of the two hitters of his era who would not shorten their grip with two strikes. The other was Ruth.

Hornsby wielded a 35-inch bat to slash his line drives. His swing was a thing of beauty to fans and players alike — perfectly balanced, powerful, and smooth. But Hornsby was not a popular ballplayer. Ruth was an affable, hedonistic showman who was at home at a party. Hornsby was aloof, austere, and tactless. He had no respect for the baseball opinions of those who had never played the game and told them so. His diversions from baseball were sitting in hotel lobbies and betting on horses. When he was told that the public didn't consider him a colorful ballplayer, Hornsby responded, "I am told that

I lack color. I don't fight with umpires and I'm not going to. I don't run wild on the base paths spiking other players. If I had to play dirty baseball, I would rather not play at all. Color, in the popular eye, seems to consist of just these things. I'll go along doing my best, letting my work speak for me."[8]

On Opening Day at Sportsman's Park in 1922, 17,000 fans saw the Cards humble the Pirates, 10–1, as Hornsby socked a single and belted a homer. A then-franchise record 536,998 fans saw the Cardinals at home in 1922. They battled the Giants for the lead before falling in mid–August and September into a tie for third place, eight games off the pace. The Cardinals hit .301, ranked seventh in the league in pitching with a 4.44 ERA, and finished last in fielding with 239 errors.

The Cardinals had a standout young hitter named Austin McHenry, whose stats in 1921 (.350, 201 hits, 17 homers, 102 RBIs) signaled future super-stardom. The favorite of "Knot Hole Gang" kids who sat in the bleachers free of charge at Sportsman's Park on Fridays, McHenry became ill early in the 1922 season. At first doctors thought he had a bad case of the flu, but surgery revealed a tumor wrapped almost entirely around his brain. He left the team after 64 games with a .303 batting average and died the following November at age 27. With McHenry healthy, the Cards might have outdistanced McGraw's ballclub.

Hornsby hit safely through his first eight games, tagging two homers and four doubles along the way. His streak was stopped in Cincinnati when he was walked four times and dropped down a sacrifice bunt in a 6–3 win. On April 28 in Chicago, Hornsby crushed a three-run homer in the first inning and smashed a titanic solo shot over the dead-center-field fence in the ninth inning. The second blast was reported to be the longest ball hit at Wrigley Field. The Cards won the game, 11–3, and were banging the ball consistently, but their 8–7 record at the end of April was nothing to get excited about.

Hornsby was hitting .389. Unlike most .400 hitters in history, he would stay under .400 most of the season before ripping three hits on the final day to finish at .401. In 1924, when Hornsby hit for the modern-day record .424, he batted .469 at Sportsman's Park and .370 on the road. Yet in 1922, Hornsby was almost equally dangerous at home (.402) and on the road (.400).

On May 15, the Cards routed the Phils, 19–7, knocking out 23 hits. Hornsby contributed two singles and a triple to the fray. Young shortstop George "Specs" Torporcer, one of the first major leaguers to wear eyeglasses, enjoyed a career day with two triples and a homer.

On May 17, the Cardinals shelled Brooklyn spitballer Burleigh Grimes, 11–0, as Hornsby singled twice, homered, and swiped two bases. He stole 17 bases in 1922, matching his total in each of his three previous seasons. It was his top mark. He wasn't known as a base stealer, but like DiMaggio, he went from first to third like an impala. Christy Mathewson, picking his all-time team, called Hornsby "the fastest man in baseball."[9]

Les Bell, a teammate of Hornsby for four years in St. Louis, said, "Hornsby was the greatest right-handed hitter that ever lived, I can guarantee you that. Maybe even the greatest hitter, period. He had the finest coordination I ever saw. And confidence. He had that by the ton. There was another thing that Hornsby could do that a lot of people don't realize — he could run. When he was stretching out on a triple, he was a sight to see. If he had hit left-handed he probably would have hit .450. He was a streak going down the line."[10]

On May 19, during a 10–6 win over Brooklyn, Hornsby lined a rocket into the center-field bleachers at Sportsman's Park that newspapermen said was the longest drive ever hit in St. Louis. On May 22, his seventh-inning three-run homer against Boston tied the score at 6–6, but the Braves went on to win in 13 innings, 8–6. The next day Hornsby hit another three-run homer in the seventh inning, but the Braves won again by the same score. Boston and Cincinnati were the only teams that held Hornsby under .400 in 1922; he hit .348 against the Braves.

Old-timers told a story about Hornsby's 1928 season with the Braves. A decade after that season, one of the Braves came into the dugout complaining to manager Casey Stengel about the configuration of and the prevailing winds at Braves Field. "How the hell can they expect anybody to hit up there. The wind is always with the pitcher. Nobody can hit up there." Stengel answered mildly, "All I know is that Hornsby played here one whole season and batted .387."[11] (During that season, he hit .372 at Braves Field and .401 on the road.)

On May 25, a special day to benefit the St. Louis playgrounds, brought an overflow crowd of 25,000, including Judge Kenesaw Mountain Landis to Sportsman's Park. The Pirates topped the Cards, 7–3, but Hornsby was a perfect 3-for-3 with his tenth homer. He homered again the next day as the Cards rebounded to win, 6–2, and lined two more home runs in a 4–3 triumph over the Bucs two days later, propelling him past St. Louis Browns slugger Ken Williams and into the major league lead.

At the beginning of June, the *Sporting News* said of Hornsby: "He's had to work with a green hand alongside at short; Jack Fournier is no Sisler on first, and Milton Stock isn't covering the ground that Heinie Groh does at third. The team would be in a sad way without Hornsby. He's not the most showy or the noisiest player in the game, but his quiet thoroughness can't be equaled anywhere." The newspaper added, "Rogers is about two-thirds of the Cardinal infield when it comes to defense and everybody knows what he is on offense."[12]

This comment flies in the face of the belief that Hornsby was a poor fielder, especially at going back for pop flies. (Lefty Gomez quipped, "He never hit any so how would he know how to catch them?"[13]) The rap on his fielding may have been a result of his bitter unpopularity with his peers as well as his long fade after the operation on his heel in 1929 that limited his productivity.

Hornsby maintained that his fielding would have kept him in the major leagues even if he was an average hitter. His fielding statistics for 1922 back that up. He led all NL second basemen with 398 putouts, 81 double plays, and a .967 fielding percentage. He was second in assists with 473.

On June 12, in Philadelphia, the Cards swatted ten hits in a row during the sixth inning of a 14–7 thrashing of the Phils. Hornsby enjoyed another perfect afternoon with four of the Cardinals' 23 hits, including a three-run homer. He hit .522 at Baker Bowl in 1922. What might he have hit had he been a Phillie?

On June 15, Hornsby's tenth-inning RBI double beat Brooklyn, 4–3. He added two singles and homer number 15 the following day, but the Cards lost in Flatbush, 12–2. On June 22, he was hitting .397. His closest competitor in the league was Pittsburgh's Carson Bigbee at .363. On June 29, his first-inning homer in an 8–5 win in Pittsburgh was being compared with the longest balls ever hit at Forbes Field. On July 1, he boomed two doubles, a triple, and a home run in a doubleheader split with the Pirates.

On the Fourth of July, the Cards split a doubleheader with the Reds in St. Louis. The Reds won the morning game, 11–9. Hornsby was ejected from the contest for disputing a call at first base. The newspapermen thought he had beaten out an infield bouncer in the fourth inning, but umpire Charles Pfirman didn't see it that way. Hornsby angrily pointed a finger at Pfirman, poking him in the nose with it. That was his ticket to the clubhouse. Such occurrences were rare for Hornsby. As long as his base hits kept coming, he paid little attention to umpires.

The ejection seemed to spark the team. The Redbirds went on a rampage, winning 17 of their next 20 games, including 10 by one run. They won the afternoon game, 6–5, as Hornsby returned to slam his 19th homer. He hit his 20th homer the following day as the Cards routed the Reds, 11–4. Brooklyn was the next unfortunate visitor to Sportsman's Park. A 20-hit attack, including two by Hornsby, crushed Uncle Robbie's ballclub, 14–2, in the opener. On July 7, Hornsby knocked out three hits and won the game, 6–5, with a ninth-inning home run off Dazzy Vance. He had four hits and two stolen bases on July 8 as the Cards beat Brooklyn again, 10–7. The Cards then won their sixth straight, 6–5, as Hornsby doubled, tripled, and threw a Robins runner out at the plate to save the game. On July 10, his three-run homer in the seventh inning was the difference in a 4–1 win, which allowed St. Louis to complete its sweep of the Robins. In 1922, Hornsby was a nightmare for Brooklyn pitchers at Sportsman's Park, hitting .533 with a 1.022 slugging percentage.

Even Hornsby's foul balls were doing damage. The *Sporting News* reported that a professional singer named Eleanor McLaughlin filed suit against him for $15,000. She claimed that the shock of being struck by a foul ball from his bat on July 10 ruined her voice.[14]

Hornsby tied Gaavy Cravath's post–1900 single-season NL homer record on July 14 with his 24th blast. It ignited a seven-run rally in the seventh inning as the Redbirds beat the Phils, 9–5. The Cards had cut New York's lead to 2½ games, and the Giants were due in town for a four-game series. A record total of 75,000 fans jammed the ballpark for the four-game series with the Cards winning three. In the final game, Hornsby doubled twice and singled to spark a 9–8 victory. He hit .409 against the Giants in 1922 —.395 in St. Louis and .422 at the Polo Grounds — with eight home runs.

Hornsby always hit well against the Giants. He once hit a line drive that caromed off the chest of New York pitcher Art Nehf. Almost a week later the name A.G. Spalding was still stenciled on Neft's skin like a tattoo.[15] During a series in 1924, Hornsby made 13 hits in 14 at-bats against the Giants, prompting National League president John Heydler, who was in attendance, to proclaim him "the greatest batsman of all-time."[16]

The Boston Braves followed the Giants into baseball-crazy St. Louis. Hornsby won the first game, 7–6, with a dramatic ninth-inning, three-run homer. A crowd of 25,000 fans ran out on the field and mobbed him. He was carried off the diamond on their shoulders, and then thousands waited for him at the clubhouse door and gave him another ovation as he left the park.

Twenty-four hours later he was back, slugging a two-run homer off Rube Marquard as the Cards beat the Braves in 10 innings, 5–4. Although Hornsby was a right-handed batter, he seemed to hit right-handed pitchers better than left-handed pitchers. Twenty-one of his first 26 homers in 1922 came against right-handers.

The next day the Cards exploded for six runs in the seventh inning, highlighted by first baseman Jack Fournier's grand slam, to beat the Braves, 6–1. With McHenry gone, Fournier was the only other power threat in the St. Louis lineup other than Hornsby. Fournier hit .295 with 10 homers in 128 games in 1922 but he was a slow-footed, inept fielder. The Cards replaced him with rookie "Sunny Jim" Bottomley in August. Bottomley hit .325 in 37 games in 1922 to begin his trek to the Baseball Hall of Fame.

On July 22, the Cards took over first place by exploding for six runs in the eighth inning in a 9–8 win over the Braves. Hornsby contributed a single and two doubles. Hundreds of straw hats sailed onto the field at the game's conclusion. The other St. Louis team, the Browns, routed the A's with 20 hits in a 10–1 win that day to tighten their grip on first place in the AL. The dream of an all–St. Louis World Series was a possibility.

Listen to what Clyde Sukeforth, a catcher for ten years for Cincinnati and Brooklyn, told author Donald Honig:

> Hornsby was in his heyday when I broke in. The greatest hitter of all time, I'd say, or if not, then damn close to it. How did you pitch to him? You pitched and you prayed, was how. There was no way you could fool him. Just look at those averages. When Hornsby stepped into the cage to take batting practice before a game, everything on the field stopped. Everybody turned to watch him swing. And that included the old-timers, the tough old pros. Now that's an impressive tribute, I'd say. And he wasn't what you'd call a popular ballplayer either. Hornsby was a brutally frank man who always spoke his mind. But when he had a bat in his hand, he had nothing but admirers.[17]

On July 23, the Cards left cozy Sportsman's Park and boarded a train for New York for a big five-game series. The Giants scored 42 runs to win four of the contests. Hornsby was "held" to eight hits in 22 at-bats in the series, including three doubles and a home run. The four-bagger tied him with Ned Williamson for the all-time NL single-season home run record. Williamson had hit 27 homers while playing for the Chicago Colts in 1884.

July proved to be Hornsby's best month for power. He slammed 16 doubles, three triples, and 10 home runs, and drove in 42 runs in 35 games. Ballplayers commonly became worn down by the sizzling summer heat in St. Louis. Not Hornsby. As a youngster in the Lone Star State his energy seemed inexhaustible. He carried that same endurance into the major leagues. In 1924, he hit .509 in August.

But Hornsby did have other things on his mind besides a pennant race in 1922. Midway through the season he met a pretty brunette named Jeannette Pennington Hine at a dog-racing track in Collinsville, Illinois. They were mutually attracted and chatted for a while. On many occasions after that he found her waiting at the Sportsman's Park pass gate after games. Both were married at the time. Although he was not known as the romantic type, Hornsby fell in love and began an affair. Jeannette Pennington Hine was a sharp contrast to his down-to-earth Texas wife, Sarah, who became suspicious and hired detectives to follow her husband. When her suspicions were confirmed, she took her son, Rogers Jr., and left to live with her widowed mother in Los Angeles. A divorce followed in June 1923. She received a $25,000 lump-sum settlement and custody of her son. Hornsby married Jeanette in February 1924.

Back on the field, St. Louis rallied to enjoy its last day in first place on August 10 by topping the Braves in Boston, 7–3. From then their fortunes slid downhill. Not so for Hornsby. On August 13, his homer in a 16–5 loss to the Cubs started his 33-game hitting streak.

The Giants entered St. Louis for the final time of the season on August 25 and swept the Cards three straight. St. Louis's pennant hopes were dead. Hornsby went 9-for-12 in the series with two triples and three homers. He ended August hitting .389.

The season was winding down, but Hornsby's bat was still white hot. In a five-game series against Cincinnati in early September, the St. Louis hitting machine went 10-for-24, including a double, two triples off Eppa Rixey, and an inside-the-park homer that rebounded off the facing of the right-field bleachers at Redland Park. His next stop was Philadelphia, where he rattled Baker Bowl for 12 hits in 19 at-bats, including four doubles and two homers. He had hit in 30 straight games.

Hornsby's hitting streak was stopped at 33 by Burleigh Grimes's moist delivery in the first game of a doubleheader in Brooklyn on September 20. In the second game of the day, Hornsby clouted homers in the first and ninth innings, sandwiched around a single, as the Cards won, 13–7.

In the technological jet age we live in today, computer charts are used by managers to give them numbers on how a hitter fares against a pitcher. Often managers make out their lineup cards accordingly. Hornsby never believed in that; he was convinced that there never was a pitcher he couldn't hit. He declared, "Most batters have the idea in the back of their heads that a certain pitcher is hard for them to hit. How foolish! They don't have to hit the pitchers. All they are called upon to do is to meet the ball. It's the same ball whether Alexander handles it or some unknown rookie. The eye can travel much faster than the ball and so can the bat. The batter can meet the ball no matter who throws it."[18]

The Cards last visit to the Polo Grounds on September 23 was memorable. Hornsby singled and hit his 40th homer in the opener, but the Giants won, 7–6. New York center fielder Casey Stengel had a big day, beating out three bunt singles and tagging a homer. Stengel hit .368 in 84 games while being platooned with Billy Cunningham. The Cards won the second game, 10–6, as Hornsby singled once and homered twice more. One of his homers was a bomb that kited deep into the top of the right-field stands while the other was a towering fly to left-center that Rogers beat out for an inside-the-parker with a terrific sprint between third base and home.

In game three, the walloping Texan singled twice and tripled but the Giants clinched the pennant with a 5–4 win in ten innings. In the last game Cardinal pitcher Jesse Haines, incensed at being taken out in the fifth inning, chucked the ball over the grandstand roof. The Giants won, 6–3.

Shortly before the Cardinals took the field in Chicago for their final game of the year, James M. Gould of the *St. Louis Dispatch* told Hornsby that he needed three hits to finish the season above .400. He got them. He had saved his best hitting for September, when he wore out opposing hurlers for a .438 average.

After hitting .424 in 1924, Hornsby almost duplicated his feat of combining 40 home runs with a .400 batting average in 1925. He hit .403 with 39 homers and a career-high .756 slugging percentage. Cardinal owner Sam Breadon grew disenchanted with Rickey's managing during the season and asked Hornsby to take over the dugout helm. Hornsby agreed, but only after Breadon helped him buy Rickey's 1,167 shares of stock in the franchise (approximately 12.5 percent). Rickey moved up to general manager. After a 13–25 start under Rickey, Hornsby turned the club around with a 64–51 record for the rest of the 1925 season.

As player-manager in 1926, Hornsby led the Cardinals to the world championship over Ruth's Yankees. Ironically, in the only world championship season of his career, Hornsby was not great with the bat. In a game against Cincinnati on May 6, Hornsby collided with Reds catcher Val Picinich at second base, displacing two vertebrae in his back. Although he was back in the lineup three days later, he played the rest of the season with pain. In 134 games he batted .317 with 11 homers and was the darling of St. Louis when the Cards bested the Yankees in the World Series in seven games.

After the season was over Hornsby declared that he was unhappy in his present position. He had not been paid a nickel more than his $33,000-a-year salary to take on the additional duty of managing. He asked Breadon for a three-year contract at $50,000 per season. Breadon instead traded him to McGraw's Giants for Frankie Frisch and pitcher Jimmy Ring.

Hornsby still owned part of the St. Louis franchise and NL president John Heydler wouldn't allow a player to play for one ballclub while holding stock in another. Hornsby held out for top dollar before selling his Cardinals stock for $100,000, plus another $12,000 to cover legal costs. Breadon paid $86,000 of it. The other seven clubs in the league paid $2,000 each, with the Giants picking up the extra $12,000.

In 1927 Hornsby played all 155 games for the Giants, hit .361, and drove in 125 runs. When McGraw became ill during the season, Hornsby took over temporarily as manager. He piloted the club during most of its sensational 45–12 stretch that brought the Giants to a 92–62 finish, just two games behind pennant-winning Pittsburgh. Yet Hornsby's blunt tongue got him in trouble with New York owner Charles Stoneham and was shipped to the Boston Braves.

Hornsby won his seventh and last batting title (.387) with the Braves. He also took over as player-manager again after 31 games. Hornsby would never enjoy success as a major league manager again. The Braves record under him was a woeful 39–83. The Braves could not afford to keep Hornsby and traded him to the Chicago Cubs for $200,000 and five players.

Playing with his fourth ballclub in four years, Hornsby enjoyed his last great season (.380, 39 homers, 149 RBIs and 156 runs), leading the Cubs to a pennant. But in November 1929, he had a dozen bone particles removed from his right heel with surgery. The operation was not a success. Hornsby tried to play in 1930 with a specially made shoe but limped noticeably and was benched by manager Joe McCarthy. He then fractured his left ankle while sliding into third base on Memorial Day, which left him a baseball cripple thereafter at age 34. He never played a full season again. The Cubs finished in second place, two games behind St. Louis. Before the season ended, Cubs owner William K. Wrigley Jr. replaced McCarthy with Hornsby as manager.

The Cubs floundered under Hornsby, and he was fired 97 games into his second year, in 1932. The official reason given was his addiction to gambling, but few of the Cub players liked him. Cub first baseman Charlie Grimm took over as manager and the team rallied to win the pennant. The Cub players did not vote Hornsby a single penny of their World Series money. After the unsuccessful heel operation in 1929, Hornsby managed to hit .313 in 719 at-bats while serving as a player-manager with the Cubs and then the Browns until 1937. He came back again to manage for another half-season with the Browns and a season-plus with the Reds in the 1950s. Wherever he went in the major leagues, Hornsby was harsh and unpopular, often expressing disdain for players who could not play the game as well as he had.

In his 1962 book, *My War with Baseball*, Hornsby declared:

> When I was a little boy in north Fort Worth, Texas, my mother started me in baseball by sewing me a uniform. Then she taught me not to drink or smoke, and above everything to always tell the truth. Unfortunately not everybody likes to hear the truth. I called a spade a spade, and sometimes I think this got me in more trouble than I would have gotten in if I had been a drinker. That's why I haven't got a high-paying job now. I didn't "yes" anybody. Truth hurts most people. It shortened my managing career in the major leagues. I'd rather have a modest job — or no job — and be truthful and satisfied, than be a frustrated, scared liar with a good managing job.[19]

During the 1920s Hornsby owned the NL while batting .382 in 5,451 at-bats. He led the NL in batting seven times, slugging nine times, on-base percentage eight times, runs five times, RBIs four times, home runs twice, hits four times, doubles four times, triples twice, walks three times and total bases seven times. Lifetime, in his shortened career, he had 2,930 hits (35 percent for extra bases), 301 home runs, and a .358 batting average (second only to Ty Cobb). As an offensive force, he was on the same level as Williams, Mays, Aaron, Cobb, Bonds — and even Ruth. A good argument still can be made that he was the best right-handed batter that ever lived and the greatest-hitting middle infielder who ever played. It is doubtful we will see his likes again

Chapter 5

The Sizzler and His Browns:
George Sisler in 1922

When baseball enthusiasts discuss the great first basemen of the old days, Lou Gehrig, Jimmy Foxx, and Hank Greenberg are mentioned. Yet there was a guy who played for the St. Louis Browns, George Sisler, who deserves to be included in the same company. Sisler could not match the Herculean power of Gehrig, Foxx, or Greenberg, but what he lacked in clout he made up for in other ways. Revisiting his 1922 season reveals how magnificent "the Picture Player's" talents were at the zenith of his career.

Ty Cobb called Sisler "the nearest thing to a perfect ballplayer."[1] In 1922 the left-handed-hitting Sisler ran off a 41-game hitting streak, peppered the diamond with 246 hits in 142 games, and paced the American League in runs scored (134), stolen bases (51), triples (18), assists (125) and batting average (.420). He also had 105 RBIs and whacked 42 doubles. He struck out only 14 times.

Unfortunately, the 1922 season was the last to showcase the real Sisler. After the season, sinusitis infected his optic nerves. For a while he had double vision. A sinus operation followed. Sisler missed the 1923 season, and his eyes never regained their former acuity. He came back in 1924 but was not the same ballplayer.

Sisler recalled his bout with sinusitis: "All season long (1923), I suffered. I felt sorry for the fans, for my teammates, for everyone except myself. I planned to get back into uniform for 1924. I just had to meet a ball with a good swing again, and then run. The doctors all said I'd never play again, but when you're fighting for something that actually keeps you alive — well, the human will is all you need."[2] Sisler managed to hit .320 in 4,112 at-bats from 1924 to 1930 and ended with a .340 lifetime mark. But the world never had a chance to witness the kind of career that could have been for "the Sizzler."

In 1922 Christy Mathewson wrote of George Sisler, "He is every bit as valuable as Ruth, some people think more valuable. But he has another temperament. When he makes a great hit or a great play and the crowd is ready to idolize him, he modestly touches his cap and fades out of sight." Sisler batted .420 in 1922 as his Browns finished just one game behind Ruth's Yankees for the pennant.

Branch Rickey, a shrewd judge of baseball talent and Sisler's first manager with the St. Louis Browns, said of his first baseman, "My, but he was lightning fast and graceful — effortless. His reflexes were unbelievable. His movements were so fast that you simply couldn't keep up with what he was doing. You knew what had happened only when you saw the ball streak through the air."[3]

Sisler's entrance into the major leagues sparked controversy. He signed a contract while he was underage with Akron of the old Ohio-Penn League in 1911. Although he played no games and received no money, his contract was sold to Columbus and then to the Pittsburgh Pirates while he attended the University of Michigan. Sisler graduated from Michigan with a degree in mechanical engineering. He was coached by Rickey in his sophomore year and starred as a .400 hitter while playing as a pitcher, first baseman and outfielder. He made Vanity Fair's All-America team three times and led the Wolverines to the mythical national championship in 1914. By 1915 he was the nation's top college player, and a flock of scouts followed him. They hoped Pirate owner Barney Dreyfuss would cede his rights to Sisler because the player had signed his contract while underage. Dreyfuss had no intention of doing so.

The Sisler family turned to Rickey, who possessed a law degree, for unofficial legal advice. Rickey traveled to Ohio to talk with Sisler's father and to make certain George had signed the contract without parental approval. Once he was sure of this, Rickey suggested Sisler's father inform the major leagues' National Commission and dare them to defy his paternal authority in a court of law. Sisler's dad did just that and said his son should be declared a free agent.

Rickey wrote the three-man National Commission, which was a predecessor of the commissioner's office, urging them not to enforce the "illegal contract." Rickey warned the commission that if it chose to enforce the "illegal contract," it would run the risk of offending families and high schools when gullible young ballplayers signed contracts without parental approval.

The AL and NL presidents voted along party lines but the third member of the commission, Reds president Gary Herrmann, broke ranks and voted for Sisler to become a free agent. Dreyfuss tried to sign Sisler anyway by offering $5,200. Rickey had an ulterior motive besides the welfare of Sisler. At the end of 1913 he had left Michigan and become manager of the St. Louis Browns. In June, Sisler telegraphed Dreyfuss: "Have decided to join the St. Louis American League team."[4] The Browns signed Sisler for $7,400.

Sisler entered the major leagues with the lowly Browns in 1915 as a pitcher, outfielder, and first baseman. That year he split eight decisions in 15 games on the mound and batted .285 while appearing in 37 games at first base and 29 games in the outfield. He even outpitched his idol, Walter Johnson, in one of his wins, a 2–1 decision. In 1916 he bested Johnson again, 1–0. Sisler could pitch. He had a 2.35 ERA in 111 career innings, but like Ruth, his hitting was too good to be restricted to a pitcher's schedule. He was switched to first base where he hit .337 from 1916 to 1919 while swiping 37 bases per season. In 1918 he served his country during World War I in the Chemical Warfare Division. He was on the verge of being sent overseas when the armistice ended the war.

Rickey eventually left the Browns but he and Sisler began a friendship that would last more than 50 years. Sisler was always respectful towards his former tutor, calling him "Mr. Rickey." Rickey, in turn, idolized Sisler, his manner, and his family life, and cited him as a model to other athletes.[5]

At age 37, Rickey, married and with four children, also volunteered for the Chemical Warfare Division. Unlike Sisler, he was sent to the front. His writings reveal his horror of seeing the dead, gassed and maimed, that passed through his sector, and he never forgot the screams of suffering young men.

Later in life he would sign the first African American ballplayer, Jackie Robinson, to a major league contract.

History shows that the years just before 1920 were among the toughest of the century for hitters; approximately 28 percent of Sisler's career at-bats took place then. Hitting increased dramatically in the 1920s. Not only were trick pitches like the spitball and shineball outlawed, but umpires were told to throw discolored balls out of play. This was a result of the fatal beaning of Ray Chapman. Shiny white balls are easier to see and hit. Historians are not in agreement whether the baseballs used during the 1920s were livelier than those used before. Circumstantial evidence suggests they were. Sisler's hitting exploded in 1920. He rapped 257 hits, the record until Ichiro Suzuki slapped his way to 262 hits, including 225 singles, in 2004. Suzuki had the benefit of a 162-game season and did not surpass Sisler's record in 154 games. Sisler played every inning of every game in 1920 and batted .407. He finished the season at a blistering pace, hitting .442 in August and .448 in September. At Sportsman's Park he hit .473, the second-highest home park average ever. (Joe Jackson hit .483 in Cleveland in 1912.) Ruth led the majors in home runs, but Sisler's combination of doubles (49), triples (18), and homers (19) helped him top the Babe in total bases (399 to 388). The Yankees purchased Ruth from the Red Sox for $100,000 after 1919. After 1920, they offered $200,000 for Sisler.

In 1921 Sisler "slumped" to .371 with 216 hits in 138 games, but in 1922 he and his Browns tore the cover off the ball while battling the Yankees down to the wire for the pennant. In 1922 St. Louis topped the Yanks in runs, hits, doubles, triples, homers, stolen bases, batting average (.313 to .287), and pitching ERA (3.38 to 3.39). The Yanks were without Ruth and Meusel for the first six weeks of the season due to suspensions by Commissioner Landis for participating in an illegal barnstorming tour. Major league rules at the time forbade barnstorming tours by participants in the World Series, believing that such events would cheapen the World Series. The Yanks kept pace with the Browns until their two sluggers returned. The Pinstripers' secret to success was their airtight defense that committed 44 fewer errors than the Browns defenders.

The Browns opened the season before 20,000 fans at Comiskey Park in Chicago. Their ace, Urban Shocker, bested Chicago's ace, Red Faber, 3–2. Sisler's first-inning double keyed a two-run rally. The next day Sisler socked an apparent two-out bases-loaded single against the Chisox, but teammate Frank Ellerbe missed second base to wipe out a hit and two RBIs for George. St. Louis won anyway, 4–2, and completed a sweep two days later, 14–0, with Sisler contributing four of the Browns' 21 hits.

On April 19 in Cleveland, the Browns ripped 20 hits and stole eight bases in routing the Indians, 15–1. Elam Vangilder tossed a three-hitter and also cracked three hits, including a homer. Vangilder compiled a 19–13 record with a 3.42 ERA in 245 innings as the Browns' number-two starter. He also batted .344. Sisler's work for the day included two singles, a double, a triple, five runs scored, and three stolen bases, including one of home.

Back in St. Louis on April 22, Sisler singled three times in front of three homers by left fielder Ken Williams as the Browns topped Chicago, 10–7. Williams grew up in Oregon. His mother was a logging-camp cook who later operated an all-night restaurant that served the train crews at Grants Pass junction.[6] Williams enjoyed his best year in 1922 when he led the AL in homers (39) and RBIs (155) while batting .337 in the clean-up spot behind Sisler. He also stole 37 bases, making him baseball's original 30–30 man. But in July 1924, he fractured an ankle while sliding and missed 40 games. In 1925, headed for his best season ever with 25 homers and 105 RBIs in 102 games, he suffered a near-fatal beaning and missed the final 52 games. Although he came back to play several more seasons, he had become noticeably ball-shy and was never the same batter again.[7]

The following day Williams went 3-for-3 with another home run, and the Browns' lead-off hitter, Jack Tobin, beat the White Sox, 4–3, with a tenth-inning drive into the right-field bleachers. A left-handed, 5'8", 142-pound right fielder, Tobin possessed surprising power for a little guy. He was also adept at making perfect drag bunts. In 1922 he whacked 207 hits including 13 homers, scored 122 runs, and batted .331.

Detroit followed the White Sox into the Mound City. The Browns won the opener, 6–2. Sisler singled and doubled and Williams banged another homer. The Browns' centerfielder, William "Baby Doll" Jacobson, added a three-run homer. Jacobson joined Williams and Tobin as the third member of the Browns' outfield. He was the league's biggest man at 6'3" and 215 pounds but used a light bat to smack base hits rather than try for homers. In 1922 he batted .317 with nine home runs and 102 RBIs.

On April 25 the Browns defeated the Tigers, 5–3. Sisler legged out a first-inning triple, followed by Williams' sixth homer in four days. On April 28 Williams homered again in a 3–2 win over Cleveland. He then knocked his eighth and ninth homers in nine days during a 6–5 victory over the Indians on April 29.

On April 30, a sunny Sunday afternoon attracted 27,000 fans to Sportsman's Park, which then had a seating capacity of 19,000. The Browns won their third straight from Cleveland in a 29-hit battle, 11–9. The game featured a triple play by the Indians, and was ultimately decided when Duster Mails balked in the tie-breaking run in the eighth inning. Sisler slapped two more base hits and swiped two bases.

The Browns completed their four-game sweep of the Tribe on May Day, 13–2, as Sisler singled twice and tripled. The victory kept St. Louis in the league lead at 12–5. New York was one game behind. Sisler's three singles on May 4 pushed his average up to .442, but Detroit bested the Browns, 6–5, on Harry Heilmann's three-run homer in the ninth inning. Williams hammered his tenth homer and was right behind Sisler at .397. His head start in the race for the home run crown proved too much for Ruth to overcome.

Sisler's value to the Browns transcended his hitting and baserunning stats. He was commonly regarded as the best fielding first baseman of his era. His 1,535 assists are third on the all-time list. But stats don't always tell the whole story. Sisler's fielding plays sometimes bordered on the impossible. In a game against Boston in 1916, the Red Sox had runners on first and third with no outs. The next batter lifted a routine fly to Burt Shotton in left field. Conceding the run, Shotton threw to Sisler to get the runner returning to first. After making the putout there, Sisler whirled and fired a perfect strike to catcher Hank Severeid for a triple play. Early in 1922 against Washington, Sisler anticipated a squeeze bunt by Roger Peckinpaugh. Racing in with the pitch, he fielded the ball about 15 feet up the line, brush-tagged Peckinpaugh, and then threw out Joe Judge at the plate. Two outs on a squeeze-bunt grounder are not the norm, but that was George.

In a three-game series in Philadelphia in May, Sisler knocked out 11 hits in 15 at-bats, including a double and three homers, but the A's captured two of the contests. The Browns were in the midst of a mini-slump that left them a half-game behind the Yanks. The lead in the pennant race would flip-flop back and forth between the two teams all summer.

The Browns made their first visit to the Polo Grounds on May 20. This was the day the suspensions to Ruth and Meusel ended. A crowd of 40,000 fans showed up to see the return of the two sluggers. Ruth arrived at the ballpark in a limousine and was given a boisterous cheer by thousands of fans standing around the entrance gates. Just prior to game time he was presented with an award by the National Vaudeville Association. The Babe had made more than $50,000 in the past year in vaudeville. But Ruth was rusty, and he failed to get the ball out of the infield in four trips to the plate. The Browns scored seven runs after two were out in the ninth inning to win, 8–2. Sisler smacked three singles, but Jacobson's grand slam was the big blow.

New York rebounded to win the next game in ten innings, 6–5. Ruth knocked out a double in five at-bats but boos started down from the seats in his direction. On the following day Ruth blasted a home run off Vangilder in the eighth inning and the boos turned to cheers. Tobin's throwing error helped the Yanks tie the game with two runs in the ninth, and New York won in 13 innings, 4–3. St. Louis won the final game of the series, 11–3. Ruth managed a double and a homer in 16 at-bats in the series. Sisler had six singles, a double, and a homer in 19 at-bats and swiped four bases. He left New York hitting .439. Cobb and Bing Miller were also over .400 at .402 each.

On Memorial Day the Browns split two with the Tigers in St. Louis, losing the morning game, 6–5, before rebounding to win the afternoon tilt in 16 innings, 2–1. Sisler slashed five singles and a triple. As June opened, George beat the Chisox with an RBI single in the twelfth inning, 4–3. He put together his seventh four-hit game of the season the next day as the Browns trounced the Pale Hose, 12–4. He enjoyed yet another four-hit day on June 9 as St. Louis humbled the Red Sox, 8–1. He finished the season with 13 four-hit games. His closest rival in the batting race, Cobb, had a record four five-hit games and batted .401 in 1922.

Most people remember Cobb as being an egotistical wildcat driven to win at all costs. Sisler, conversely, was an easygoing man. Ray Gillespie of the *St. Louis Star* recalled:

> Everybody on the ball club sort of looked up to him. Like little boy blue, could do no wrong. "Sis," that was the nickname, that was how they referred to him. I think they regarded him with reverence, kindness. ... He was so good, exceptional that year. Everybody knew how hard he was trying, all the heroics and things. ... Likable? Yes. Very much so. He was a shy person, wasn't a pushy type. Very shy. Generally spoke when he was spoken to. Had very little to say. Bashful. Actually bashful. That's the kind of person he was.[8]

A visit to Sisler's home would find his shelves filled with books of a technical nature as well as a collection of classics. He was an exceptional billiards player, a good golfer, a scientific boxer, and a skilled bridge player. A conversation with him would reveal he was well informed on all current events.

The Yankees arrived in St. Louis on June 10 with their bats waving wildly, routing Shocker and the Browns, 14–5. Ruth's three hits included his sixth homer. The next day 30,000 fans somehow squeezed into Sportsman's Park. The *Sporting News* reported the crowd would have been twice that figure if there had been room. The Yanks sent the crowd home disappointed while winning, 8–4, behind Hoyt.

The Browns regrouped to win the third game, 7–1, as rookie Hubert Pruett tossed a six-hitter, fanning Ruth three times. Pruett struck out Ruth nine of the first 12 times he faced him. The youngster explained to sportswriters, "No trick to it, just bend one in on him and he'll miss it by a mile."[9] St. Louis also won the fourth game, 13–4, as Sisler singled twice and tripled twice.

On June 14 Sisler belted a grand slam to help beat the Senators, 7–6. He was not regarded as a power hitter, but with the batting surge of the 1920s his line drives found gaps for extra-base hits. He used his speed to turn singles into doubles and doubles into triples. He stood just under six feet, packing a streamlined 170 pounds into his frame. Admitting that he patterned his hitting style after Cobb, Sisler choked his 42-ounce bat and preferred the place-hitting science rather than trying to slug. In the three years from 1920 to 1922, before his eyes were damaged, Sisler smacked 719 hits in 1,799 at-bats for a .400 batting average.

The Yanks went into a tailspin in mid–June and lost eight straight. Cobb's Tigers won 22 of 26 before Heilmann was forced out of action with a back injury. By June 25 the Browns led the league at 40–28, with the Yanks 1½ games back and the Tigers four games out. Sisler was on top in the batting race at .429.

And the hits kept coming as George went 6-for-9 in a doubleheader in Boston on July 7 with two doubles and a triple. The *Sporting News* reported he played for two weeks in July with a "dislocated thumb" that bothered his gripping of the bat. Nevertheless, he was on a pace to record 275 hits.[10]

Cobb made his run at Sisler in the batting race in July and early August. On July 20 Sisler's lead over Cobb shrank to four points — .413 to .409. The Yanks invaded St. Louis in early July and took three of four games to jump back on top. Bad news followed when Sisler was spiked below the knee while sliding into first base on July 29, causing him to miss six games. In his first at-bat back, he lined into a triple play against the A's, but he followed that up with a single and triple as the Browns beat the Mackmen, 4–1. By August 10 Cobb had overtaken Sisler, .410 to .409.

Ruth was also starting to warm up as he beat the White Sox with a dramatic three-run homer in the ninth inning at the Polo Grounds on August 20. The Babe batted .315 with 35 homers in 406 at-bats. Down the stretch he saved three games with strong throws. The Yanks were strengthened by a one-sided trade that brought Joe Bush, Sam Jones, and Everett Scott from the Red Sox. Bush enjoyed a career season in winning 26 games against only seven defeats. Jones compiled a 13–13 record in 28 starts and 17 relief appearances and lead the AL in saves. Together they offset an off year by Mays, who slumped to 12–14 with a 3.60 ERA and ended the season in Miller Huggins' doghouse. Scott was the best gloveman in baseball. He led AL shortstops in fielding from 1916 to 1923 and played in 1,307 consecutive games.

The Yanks picked up center fielder Lawton "Whitey" Witt just after Opening Day from Philadelphia for cash. Witt batted .297 in the leadoff spot, led the league with 89 walks, and scored 98 runs. A trade that really allowed the Yanks to win the pennant was the acquisition of Joe Dugan and Elmer Smith from Boston on July 23 for four second-line players and $50,000. Dugan filled a gaping hole at third base. Frank Baker had seen his best days. The trade brought an uproar from fans, who called the Yankees "the Checkbook Champions."

Sisler regained the batting lead from Cobb (.416 to .401) by spraying 10 hits in 15 at-bats as the Browns swept three straight from the Red Sox in Fenway, from August 22 to August 24. The Browns entered the Polo Grounds for a four-game series on August 25. The Yanks won three of the contests to forge in front by 1½ games. Shocker won the opener, 3–1, but lost the fourth game, 2–1, in 11 innings to the Yanks' Bob Shawkey. Shawkey was the Yankees' top workhorse in 1922, hurling 300 innings with a 20–12 record and a 2.91 ERA. He was called "Sailor Bob" because he spent 1918 as a petty officer aboard the battleship *Arkansas*. Shocker was the Browns' iron man. He hurled 348 innings with a 24–17 record and a 2.97 ERA.

Shocker arrived in the major leagues as a catcher, but he showed such speed and accuracy in his throws that he was switched to pitcher. His delivery was aided by a permanent crook in his ring finger, an injury he suffered as a catcher. He maintained that the crooked finger improved his grip on the ball and his effectiveness as a pitcher. In 13 years he won 187 games. When he died at age 38 in 1928, his death was attributed to an overstrained "athlete's heart."

As August closed and September opened, Sisler's hits were coming in bunches. On August 30 he whacked two singles and a triple and stole a base as the Browns won in Cleveland, 11–3. The next day he singled once and doubled twice but the Indians came from behind with five runs in the ninth to win, 7–6. On September 1 in Detroit, Shocker tamed the Tigers, 4–1, and Sisler singled twice more. He added two singles, including a key base hit in the Browns' game-winning rally in the eighth inning, as St. Louis won again in Detroit, 5–4, on September 2. Sisler had hit safely in 31 straight games and was challenging Cobb's record of 40 consecutive games. Detroit won the final game of the series thanks to a remarkable play by left fielder Bobby Veach. In the ninth inning Veach ranged far to the foul line to make a bare-handed catch of a drive by Eddie Foster with two outs and the bases loaded. The Tigers won in 11 innings, 4–3.

On Labor Day in St. Louis, the Browns blitzed the Indians, 10–3 and 12–1. Sisler made seven hits in nine at-bats, including three doubles and a triple, stole another base, and scored seven times. The *Sporting News* described the chaotic scene at Sportsman's Park: "Thousands of fans, unable to get in the park in the ordinary way, because of a shortage of entrance gates, broke down the fences, uprooted turnstiles and went in like a raging flood. One estimate is that 5,000 milling bugs overcame the slim force of ticket sellers and takers and forced their ways into the stands and onto the field."[11] The city was baseball mad!

The Browns retook first place the succeeding day with a 10–9 conquest of Cleveland. Williams clubbed a grand slam and Sisler socked two singles and pilfered three bases. "The Sizzler's" hitting streak was up to 35 games.

That night thousands packed the biggest theater in St. Louis, where the Browns were given gold watches and asked to make speeches. The crowd would not let Sisler leave the building until he had addressed the audience.

Sisler was at the peak of his career. In the August 30 issue of *Outlook*, Christy Mathewson said, "Now there is Sisler of the St. Louis team — he is every bit as valuable as Ruth, some people think more valuable. But he has another temperament. When he makes a great hit or a great play and the crowd is ready to idolize him, he modestly touches his cap and fades out of sight."[12]

The *Sporting News* quoted a writer in the Yankees' hometown as saying this about the Browns' superstar: "If there is anything he cannot do in the national pastime I would like to see it. Whether it is hitting the ball, playing first base, sliding into a bag or beating out a throw, it makes no difference. He can do one just as well as the other. I rate him the greatest player we ever had in the baseball sport."[13]

Sisler raised his hitting streak to 38 games with two singles and a triple as the Browns slaughtered Cobb's Tigers, 16–0, on September 9. Vangilder tossed the shutout and joined in the hitting spree with two doubles and a triple. Williams pumped his 37th homer; Jacobson tripled three times and singled.

On September 11 the Browns topped the Tigers, 5–4. Sisler tied the score at 4–4 with a two-out ninth-inning RBI triple and then scored the winning run on a Marty McManus single. The game proved to be disastrous to the Browns' pennant chances. In the seventh inning Cobb grounded to short and Wally Gerber made a wide throw. Sisler stretched so far to catch the ball that he fell forward on his right shoulder. Nothing was made of the play at the time, and Sisler helped win the game with his triple in the ninth inning. But the next day Sisler failed to appear for the game until the second inning. His shoulder had caused such pain during the night that he could not sleep and he consulted medical specialists in the morning.

The team physician, Dr. Robert Hyland, explained the injury to the St. Louis press: "Sisler is suffering from a severe and extremely painful strain of the deltoid muscle of the right shoulder. Movement of the arm caused him so much misery that I immobilized the arm and shoulder in tape and have ordered him to keep it so for a week."[14]

Hyland added, "I feel that Sisler will be very fortunate to completely recover before the close of the season, though he doubtless will try to play. For one week it is certain he ought not to attempt anything on the ball field, but I guess he will try to get into the Yankee series despite my advice."[15]

Sisler missed four games but was in the lineup when the Yankees arrived in town for the showdown series. St. Louis fans waited in line for hours to buy tickets for the opener. Sisler tied Cobb's record of 40 consecutive games with a hit by smashing a double off second baseman Aaron Ward's shins in the fourth inning. He came to bat against Shawkey again in the sixth frame with the bases loaded, one out, and his team trailing, 2–1. He socked what appeared to be a sure single to the right side of the infield. A base hit would have scored two runs and put the Browns ahead. But Aaron Ward flung himself with a desperate lunge toward his bare-hand side and made a great stop. He then flipped the ball to shortstop Scott, who made the force play at second, and then fired to first for a sensational double play. Sisler probably would have beaten the relay to first, but with his arm dangling almost lifeless at his side he could not pump it to help him run.

In the ninth inning someone in the crowd hurled a pop bottle that struck Yankee center fielder Witt in the head. The bottle knocked Witt cold, and he was carried off the field bleeding. Shawkey ended up besting Shocker, 2–1.

Pruett was chosen by Browns manager Lee Fohl to oppose Hoyt in the second game. Ruth broke a 0–0 tie in the top of the sixth with his only career homer off Pruett, giving the Yanks a 1–0 lead. In the bottom of the sixth, however, Foster walked and Sisler promptly singled to break Cobb's record. Williams lined a single over Pipp's head into right field, scoring Foster. McManus fanned, but Williams got into scoring position by stealing second. Catcher Hank Severeid, a .321 hitter on the year, socked a base hit into center, scoring both Sisler and Williams for a 3–1 Browns lead. In the eighth Sisler drew a walk and Williams pulverized his 38th homer. Another overflow crowd of 30,000 fans were on hand that day. They exploded into cheers when the Browns won game two, 5–1.

In the rubber game St. Louis sent Frank Davis to the mound against Bush. Again a crowd of 30,000 jammed Sportsman's Park. The day before police were told by the umpires to stop St. Louis fans in the center-field bleachers from waving white handkerchiefs every time the Yankees came to bat. The handkerchief-waving was a ploy to distract Yankee hitters. On this day the center-field fans thought up a new trick. They wore white shirts, locked arms, and swayed back and forth to provide a moving background for Yankee batters. In the seventh inning Williams and McManus drilled ground-rule doubles into the overflow crowd, which was standing in the outfield in roped-off areas. The two doubles helped give the Browns a 2–0 lead.

But the Yanks were far from finished. They got one run back in the eighth when Dugan doubled and scored on a throwing error by McManus. In the top of the ninth, Witt came to the plate with one out and the bases loaded against Shocker, who was pitching in relief. Witt's head was swathed in bandages after he had been hit by the bottle, and doctors told him he had suffered a brain concussion, advising him not to play again in the series. Witt replied that there was no way he wasn't going to play. He had already socked two singles on the day. This time he singled sharply to the center lawn, driving in the tying and go-ahead runs. The ballpark was silent as a tomb. Bush retired the Browns in order in the bottom of the ninth, including Sisler on a ground ball to second base, and the Yanks left town in first place. Bush had broken Sisler's streak at 41 games, during which he had hit .460.

In remembering the race, Sisler remarked that the "Pop Bottle Incident" seemed to take some heart out of the Browns players.[16] The *Sporting News* said of Sisler's attempt to play in the series, "George Sisler, suffering from a crippled shoulder that had kept him out of the Boston series, made good his word and got back in the battles against the Yankees, but it was Sisler in name only. His right arm hung almost lifeless at his side and he could neither field nor hit up to form."[17]

In the Browns' next game, a 4–3 loss to Washington, Sisler pinch-hit and struck out against Walter Johnson. He missed the following two games before returning to rap a single in the Browns' 11–5 win over the A's on September 22. The A's then beat the Browns, 6–5, pushing St. Louis 4½ games back. To tie for the pennant the Browns would have to win their last four games while the Yankees lost their final five.

It almost happened. St. Louis beat Philly, 7–4, on September 24 while Cleveland's George Uhle blanked the Yanks, 3–0. Sisler smacked three singles, stole two bases, and forced two errors with daring baserunning. The Browns were idle on September 28 but Boston beat New York, 3–1. On September 29, the Browns topped Chicago, 3–2, as Shocker bested Faber and Tobin banged two homers. Boston beat New York again, 1–0, as former Yankee Jack Quinn outdueled Shawkey. The Browns were now two games out with two to play. AL president Ban Johnson had declared that in the event of a tie, the pennant race between St. Louis and New York would be decided by a best-of-three-game series at a neutral ballpark.

The Browns outscored Chicago, 11–7, on September 30 as Sisler singled, doubled, and drilled a homer into the right-field bleachers. In Boston, Red Sox manager Hugh Duffy planned to pitch Herb Pennock against the Yanks. Pennock had beaten New York three times. Before the game, though, Boston owner Harry Frazee came into the clubhouse and ordered Duffy to start Alex Ferguson, who had been clobbered in his last two outings against the Yanks. Ferguson gave up three first-inning runs before being relieved by Pennock. Pennock pitched shutout ball for the last eight innings. The damage had been done, however, as Hoyt with relief help from Bush pitched New York to the pennant, 3–1.

St. Louis won its final game, 2–1, and the Yankees lost, 6–1, making the New York margin of victory a single game. Many St. Louis fans looked forward to the 1923 season with optimism, but Sisler's eye problems ruined what should have been an interesting next few years in Brownieville.

Without Sisler in the lineup the Browns' attendance dropped 40 percent in 1923. George sat in the stands with sunglasses all summer surveying the action. When Sisler returned to play in 1924, he took on the additional responsibility of managing the Browns. He was still a slick-fielding .300 hitter but only a shadow of the ballplayer the AL saw from 1920 to 1922.

Sisler was hired by Branch Rickey, who was president of the Brooklyn Dodgers in the 1940s, as a batting coach. There he helped teach Jackie Robinson the knack of hitting to the opposite field; Jackie won the National League batting crown in 1949 with a .342 average. Ironically, it was George's son, Dick Sisler, who beat Brooklyn with a tenth-inning home run on the last day of the 1950 season to allow the Phils to nose out the Dodgers for the pennant. Dick Sisler couldn't hit like his father, but he was a solid player who batted .276 in eight seasons at first base. Another son of George's, Dave Sisler, pitched seven seasons in the majors, posting a 38–44 record in 247 games. Fans of today's home run happy baseball tend to trivialize the value of Sisler's play in the 1920s. Tell them to call the next time someone bats .420 while leading the league in stolen bases and fielding his position better than anyone in the game. It would be interesting to know how much money that player receives in his next contract.

Chapter 6

How to Drive in 191 Runs: Hack Wilson in 1930

Lewis Robert "Hack" Wilson was the most unlikely looking slugger who ever laced up spikes. Wilson stood 5'6", weighed 190 pounds, wore a size five-and-a-half shoe and a size eighteen collar. His physique inspired humorous nicknames, including "the Hardest Hitting Hydrant of All Time." Pitching to Hack, however, was no laughing matter. With his stature he possessed a small strike zone. Anything pitchers dared throw in there he swung at with a murderous cut. In 1930 he pounded 208 hits, 35 doubles, six triples, and 56 home runs, batted .356, scored 146 runs, and drove in an astounding 191 runs for the Chicago Cubs. His 191 RBIs represent a major league record that may never be broken.

Like Babe Ruth, Wilson experienced an unhappy childhood. He was born in Ellwood City, Pennsylvania, an illegitimate son of a sixteen-year-old factory girl and a heavy-drinking mill worker. His mother, Jennie Kaughn, died of a burst appendix when Hack was seven years old. He lived in a boarding house with his father, Robert Wilson.

Later Hack moved to Chester, Pennsylvania, and he quit school at age sixteen in the sixth grade. He became a devil at the Edystone Print Works while working twelve hours a day. He remembered, "I worked at the print shop for two years, during which time I carried a million pounds of lead and was getting to be a big, husky kid."[1]

Hack was a strong kid but the butt of jokes because of his dwarfish appearance. He recalled, "When I was a kid, they never let me forget I was ugly. They'd ask me what tree I lived in. They'd tell me not to step on my tail or they'd say, 'Hey, freakie, come over here.' I made my mind up early that I would get even with those blankety-blanks."[2]

When Hack wasn't working he was playing stickball. From Chester, Hack and his father moved to another boarding house in Edystone. There Hack found a job at the Baldwin Locomotive Works. He swung a sledgehammer driving red-hot rivets into metal. Like the fabled steel-driving man of the ballad "John Henry," Wilson built up huge muscles.

When Wilson wasn't driving steel, he played ball as a catcher. He signed to play pro baseball for Martinsburg of the Blue Ridge League. In his first minor league game, he caught a spike while sliding and wrenched his right leg. The injury was diagnosed as a compound fracture below the calf; he was advised not to play baseball again.

He spent a month in a hospital and was introduced to a friend of one of the nurses, Virginia Riddleburger. At 34 years old, Virginia was 12 years older than Hack. She had been married and abandoned before. Virginia gave Hack the stableness he needed, and within eight weeks of the injury he was back in the lineup. He returned strongly batting .356 as his girlfriend, Virginia, cheered him on from the stands. The next season he switched to the outfield and batted .366 with 30 homers in 322 at-bats.

In 1923 he was sold to Portsmouth in the Virginia League for $500. He crushed the ball, batting .388 with 19 homers and 101 RBIs in 448 at-bats. He also married his biggest fan, Virginia. The owner of the Portsmouth Truckers, Frank Lawrence, contacted John McGraw about his star player. McGraw attended a Truckers game in which Hack ripped three hits and he was intrigued by the hard-hitting dwarf-like phenom. He gave Lawrence $11,000 plus two players for Wilson and a pitcher. In 1924 Hack looked promising while hitting .295 for the pennant-winning Giants in 383 at-bats.

In 1925 Hack fell into a slump. He was hitting .239 in 180 at-bats when McGraw farmed him to Toledo. Wilson blamed his bad showing on the fact that he was worried about Virginia, who was pregnant. Hack also exhibited a weakness of not being able to hit a major league curveball. He saw a steady diet of hooks and flailed away in futility. McGraw told him to become a more disciplined hitter and he promised he would bring Wilson up next spring.

Wilson was nicknamed "Hack" while with the Giants because he resembled a popular wrestler, George Hackenschmidt. Wilson never wore a Giants uniform again. He hit well at Toledo (.343, 42 RBIs in 55 games), but the New York front office made a clerical error, leaving him exposed to the annual draft of minor league players. The Cubs acquired him for $5,000. At least that is McGraw's version of how the Giants lost Wilson. Some believe McGraw soured on Wilson and that there was no clerical mistake. They said McGraw made up the story so he wouldn't look foolish after Hack became a star.[3]

Hack was a sensation for manager Joe McCarthy's Cubs, leading the league in homers from 1926 to 1928 with 21, 30, and 31 while driving in 109, 129, and 120 runs. He also hit for average at .321, .318, and .313. At first glance fans might think the Cubs would hide their odd-shaped slugger in the

Hack Wilson stood 5'6", weighed 190 pounds, wore a size five-and-a-half shoe, and a size eighteen collar. His stubby shape inspired many humorous nicknames, including "The Hardest Hitting Hydrant of All Time." Pitching to Hack, however, was no laughing matter. In 1930 he drove in 191 runs, a record that may never be broken.

field, yet they put him in center field. One scout that saw Wilson play in the minors commented, "The report is he has bad legs. It's not true or he could not cover the ground as he does." In 1927 Hack led all NL center fielders with 400 putouts.

Chicago fans fell in love with their pudgy home run artist. Wilson visited many of the Windy City's speakeasies and was reputed to be a high-ball hitter on and off the field. He spent money as fast as he made it, picking up the tab for his pals during a night on the town. His wife, Virginia, became less of a steadying influence on him despite the birth of his son. As his stardom grew so did Hack's carousing. There seemed to be a kind of strike-back-at-the-world motivation to his behavior.

Bill Veeck, the son of Cubs president William Veeck, was a teenager when Hack was in his heyday. Veeck recalled:

> Hack's only trouble was that he was overgenerous. He gave everything away he had. His money, the shirt off his back — little things like that. Chicago was a toddling town in those days. Hack's drinking buddies, a rollicking crew of about two dozen Chicagoans, would wait for him after the game and they'd toddle over to the joints on the North Side and the West Side. Hack picked up every check.... The players' favorite joint was the Hole in the Wall over in Cicero, a speakeasy which could easily be defined as the fallout shelter of the Prohibition era; it was the gangster hangout and that made it the safest place in town.[4]

Poet Carl Sandburg labeled Chicago "the stormy, husky, brawling City of Big Shoulders." In 1929 the Cubs took it by storm. The North Siders drew a then-record 1,485,166 fans to Wrigley Field while winning the pennant. No team surpassed that attendance until 1946. Wilson was a big cog in the Cubs offense, batting .345 with 39 homers, 135 runs scored, and 159 RBIs.

He had plenty of help. Rogers Hornsby batted .380 with 229 hits, 39 homers, 156 runs and 149 RBIs. Kiki Cuyler hit .360 with 111 runs and 102 RBIs while patrolling right field and stealing 43 bases. Left fielder Riggs Stephenson hit .362 with 110 RBIs. Pitchers Pat Malone, Charlie Root, and Guy Bush combined for 59 wins. The Cubs romped to the pennant with a 98–54 record.

The 1929 World Series against the Philadelphia A's proved to be a fiasco. In Game 4 of the Series, the Cubs led the A's, 8–0, going into the seventh inning before the roof caved in. Connie Mack's A's exploded for ten runs and won, 10–8. The rally was made possible by two fly balls that Wilson lost in the sun. The first fly fell for a single. The second fly off the bat of "Mule" Haas rolled to the center-field wall for a disastrous three-run homer.

Wilson was mortified at the game's conclusion. Writing in the *Sporting News,* Sam Murphy reported Hack stormed into the clubhouse after the loss angry and silent. McCarthy tried to console him but it did no good. Wilson shoved him aside without a word. "There was fire in his eyes and who knows what was in his heart that minute.... He seemed dazed as he stepped outside," wrote Murphy. Wilson then met his four-year-old son, Bobby. Murphy continued "Hack picked up that child, kissed him, hugged him. His sturdy frame shook with emotion. He wept."[5]

The loss was the turning point of the Series as the A's won in five games. On the train back to Chicago, the Cubs were awakened by a pounding sound. Looking out of their berths they saw Wilson banging the floor with his fists and cursing uncontrollably. Wilson was the leading hitter in the Series at .471 and made several brilliant catches. But he was branded as the goat because of the two balls he lost in the sun. The terrible experience left him determined to redeem himself in 1930.

In those days bench-jockeying was considered part of the game and often became vicious. Wilson's stubby shape gave the bench jockeys plenty of ammunition. Among other insults, they called him "Caliban," after William Shakespeare's deformed savage slave in *Tempest*.

The Cubs started 1930 on April 15 in St. Louis by beating the Cardinals, 9–8. Wilson drove in his first run of the year with a sacrifice fly and also doubled. The double became news because it was his first career hit ever on an Opening Day. Hack declared, "I ought to celebrate that now, but I'll wait until after the Cubs get into the World Series."[6] Wilson began his epochal season slow by getting two hits in 14 at-bats as the Cubs split a four-game series in St. Louis.

On April 21 in Cincinnati, Hack launched a 425-foot three-run homer as the Cubs drubbed the Reds, 9–1. The clout was satisfying for Hack because the Reds fans had booed him vociferously since his fights with Cincinnati pitchers Ray Kolp and Pete Donahue in 1929. The Reds also had insulted him with some nasty bench-jockeying. Hack could hit like 30 mules with each hand. The Reds were shocked by the vicious power of his punches.

In Chicago's home opener before 42,000 fans, Wilson hammered another three-run homer. This one came off the Cardinals' "Wild Bill" Hallahan. All it did, however, was spoil Hallahan's shutout, as St. Louis won, 8–3. Despite the two homers, Hack was barely hitting .200. The real bad news for the Cubs was the failure of the heel surgery to their other big star, Hornsby. Rogers was using a specially made shoe but still limped. Many felt "the Mighty Rajah" was playing on nerve alone. Hornsby was benched by McCarthy, who hoped the injury would heal with rest.

On April 25 in Chicago, Wilson's hard-drinking buddy, Pat Malone, hurled 12 innings of a 6–5 win over the Reds. Hack contributed a single, double, homer, and two RBIs. Malone would be the Cubs' top winner with a 20–9 record. On the last day of April, Wilson sent his third homer of the spring soaring 25 feet over the left-field wall at Wrigley as Malone beat the Pirates, 5–2. But the Cubs ended April with an 8–8 record, and fans wondered whether they could contend for the flag without a healthy Hornsby.

The Cubs answered that question in early May by winning their first seven games. On May 4, Hack went 3-for-3 with a double and two RBIs as the Cubs bested the Phils, 8–7, before 40,000 at Wrigley. On May 6, the Brooklyn Robins arrived in town with a seven-game win streak. The Robins' top hitter was Babe Herman, who assaulted pitchers terribly batting .393 with 241 hits, including 35 homers.

Herman got his team on the board with a first-inning homer. In the bottom of the first Wilson answered with a two-run shot off Robins ace Dazzy Vance. Vance rivaled the A's Lefty Grove as the game's fastest pitcher. In 1930 Dazzy led the league with a 2.61 ERA and won 17 games. This is remarkable because 1930 was considered the year of the hitter. Historians agree a juiced ball with sunken stitches was used that season. The sunken stitches made it difficult for pitchers to get a grip on the ball in order to throw breaking pitches. The entire NL batted .303 and the league's ERA was 4.97. This caused many to belittle Wilson's RBI total, which for a long time kept him out of Cooperstown. Eventually Baseball Hall of Fame voters realized how amazing Hack's record was, and he was enshrined in 1979. His homer off Vance helped the Cubs win, 3–1, and was good news for Wilson in another way. He had been an easy strikeout victim for Vance, a so-called cousin. Dazzy once struck him out six times in succession. But in 1930 Hack would hit Vance and be a cousin for no one.

The Cubs won the next two games from Brooklyn and then catapulted into first place with a 6–5 win over the Giants on May 9. Wilson went 7-for-12 in the three wins with a homer, two doubles, and seven RBIs. On May 10 he slammed a first-inning, two-run homer against the Giants, bringing 37,000 at Wrigley to their feet. But the Giants rallied to win, 9–4, as their first-baseman, Bill Terry, smacked two singles, a double, and a homer. Terry knocked out an NL-record 254 hits in 1930 and batted .401. Terry's teammates, Fred Lindstrom and Mel Ott, weren't bad either. They hit .379 and .349, respectively. The Giants batted .319, the highest average for any team during the century.

The Giants retook first place by winning the next two contests, 9–7 and 14–12. In the latter game they led 14–1 after five innings. The Cubs fought back, tying a then–major league record with four homers in the seventh inning (one by Wilson) but ran out of outs.

Through mid–May, Wilson was hitting .359 with 27 RBIs in 27 games, tying him with the Phils' Chuck Klein for the league lead in RBIs. On May 18 the Cubs split two in St. Louis, winning 9–6 and losing 8–2 before 32,000. Wilson hammered two homers. The Cards would join the Cubs, Robins, and

Giants as contenders for the pennant and win the flag. They were a streaky team with a well-balanced attack. Their entire lineup boasted of .300 hitters, including Jim Bottomley, Frankie Frisch, and "Chick" Hafey. They hit .314 and scored an NL-record 1,004 runs.

The May 22 issue of the *Sporting News* featured a picture of Wilson with the headline "HACKING AT BAMBINO'S CROWN." The story reported that the "wide-shouldered swatsmith" was the first batter to reach 11 homers and added, "Hack's circuit smashing proclivities have done much to keep the Chicago Cubs in the pennant race while Rogers Hornsby limps about on that now famous overgrown heel of his and since Riggs Stephenson has been out of action because of an injury."[7] By May 26, however, the Cubs had fallen back into fourth place at 19–19. The Cards won 15 of 16 games and were now on top at 23–13.

On May 27, Cub pitcher Hal Carlson arrived at the ballpark scheduled to take the mound. The game was rained out. At 4:00 A.M. the next day he died of a hemorrhage of the stomach, leaving a wife and four-year-old daughter behind. Carlson was a member of the 308th Machine Gun Corps during World War I and was hospitalized by a gas attack. He developed tuberculosis in 1928. The gas attack was blamed for his death.

The Cubs won that day over the Reds, 6–5, as Hack whacked a two-run triple in the first inning followed by a bounce homer by Cuyler. Prior to 1931 balls that bounced into the stands in fair territory were considered home runs rather than ground-rule doubles in the NL. On May 29 the Cubs canceled their game. Before their doubleheader on Memorial Day, the team gathered around McCarthy and vowed to win for the spirit of Hal Carlson. Charlie Root shut out the Cardinals in the morning game, 2–0. The Cubs won the afternoon tilt, 9–8, as Wilson smacked his 14th homer and Cuyler singled twice, doubled, and swiped two bases.

The Cubs' sweep knocked the Cards out of first place. But in the morning game Hornsby tried to stop his slide into third base and fractured his left ankle. He was expected to be out of action three months. He tried to come back late in the season but wasn't mended. Rogers was a non-factor in the Cubs' offense in 1930, hitting .308 with two homers in 104 at-bats.

After Carlson's death the Cubs won nine straight while scoring runs like crazy. On June 1 they clobbered the Pirates, 16–4, as Hack singled, doubled, bashed homers number 15 and 16, and drove in five runs. Two days later "Footsie" Blair socked four of the Bruins' 17 hits in a 15–2 win in Boston. The next day Chicago buried the Braves with 20 hits, 18–10. Hack contributed a single, double, and RBI number 51. Cuyler and Stephenson were the big guns with five hits each. Cuyler singled three times, doubled, and homered. Stephenson singled three times and doubled twice.

Cuyler hit .355 with 228 hits, including 50 doubles, 17 triples, and 13 homers. He scored 155 runs and added 134 RBIs with 37 stolen bases. While batting in the third spot, Cuyler drew 72 walks and scored 53 times on Hack's RBIs. Although he appeared chunky at 5'10" and 180 pounds, Cuyler could run like the wind, recording as many as 26 triples in a season and winning four stolen base crowns.

Stephenson was bothered by a combination of injuries in 1930. When he was in the lineup he added a big bat. In 109 games he batted .367. In 14 seasons he hit .336. Cubs leadoff hitter Woody English enjoyed a career season by batting .335 and scoring 152 runs. He drew 100 walks and scored 47 times as Hack's RBIs.

The biggest addition to the Cubs' lineup in 1930 was catcher Gabby Hartnett. Hartnett had missed almost the entire 1929 season with an arm injury but returned in top form in 1930, hitting .339 with 37 homers and 122 RBIs. A Cub batting order with a healthy Hornsby and a healthy Hartnett would have been something to behold. The 1930 Cubs outscored their 1929 team 998 to 982, and are the second-highest scoring juggernaut in NL history.

The Cubs finished their sweep of the Braves, 10–7, on June 5 as Wilson and Hartnett homered. They opened up in Brooklyn the next day with a 13–0 pounding of Vance. The Robins ended Chicago's nine-game win streak the following afternoon, 12–9, despite Wilson's 18th homer. The Robins also won the rubber game, 8–0, as Dolf Luque fired a two-hitter. On June 9 Brooklyn was in first place at 30–17, with the Cubs in second at 28–22.

On June 14 the Cubs topped the Giants before 35,000 at the Polo Grounds, 8–5. Hack got the Cubs started with a two-run single in the first inning, giving him 56 RBIs in 52 games. The Giants won game two before 45,000, 7–4, powered by Shanty Hogan's three-run, seventh-inning homer. The Cubs won the final game, 8–5, on Charlie Grimm's two-out, ninth-inning grand slam off Carl Hubbell. The Cubs left New York trailing the Robins by 3½ games. The Giants were in third place, six games back. The Cards hit the skids, winning just three of 18 games, and checked in with a 26–28 record, 9½ games back. It looked like Brooklyn's year.

Hack kept hacking away. On June 23 he smacked two singles, a double, a triple, and homer number 22, and chased home five runs as the Cubs slaughtered the Phils, 21–8. Brooklyn murdered the Pirates that day, 19–6, with 28 hits. Herman banged two homers. The Robins ripped 12 straight hits in the game.

The Robins arrived in Chicago for a four-game series on June 26. The stands were packed. The Robins won game one, 7–1, behind Vance. The Cubs took game two, 7–5, on Cuyler's two-run homer in the tenth inning. In game three Chicago's Malone outpitched Babe Phelps, 4–2. On June 29, the 66th birthday of Robins manager Wilbert Robinson, the Cubs knocked Brooklyn out of first place, 5–1.

Close to 50,000 fans attended games two and four of the series at Wrigley. The press reported that every available space in the stands was occupied; many fans had to be turned away. The stock market had crashed in October 1929, but the extent of the catastrophe had yet to be felt. Some unemployed found baseball a good way to pass the time until better days arrived. Major league baseball drew a then-record 10,132,262 fans in 1930, the most it would attract until 1945. The Cubs almost equaled their record attendance of 1929, drawing 1,463,624 customers.

Chewing gum millionaire and Cub owner William Wrigley Jr. took pride in the upkeep of his ballpark. The park glittered with freshly painted signs, and efforts were made to keep the place spotless. This led to record attendance figures, but some of the customers were not your everyday Joe Fan. Al Capone, who ran the most infamous bootlegging-operation in the United States, was a big Cubs fan. His rival in the bootlegging business, Bugs Moran, was also a Cubs booster. The Cubs put on a pre-game exhibition, complete with fungo hitting and a razzmatazz infield drill. The gangsters liked to arrive at the ballpark early to see it. Cub firstbaseman Charlie Grimm recalled, "They used to come out and watch us practice. They'd sit right behind our bench, and there was never a peep out of them."[8]

Hack was the most popular player on the Cubs. He drew attention with his mannerisms. No matter how clean his uniform was at the start, it would be a mess at game's end. Every time Hack arrived at the plate, he grabbed some dirt and rubbed it into his uniform. He perspired profusely, soaking his uniform with sweat. He talked to himself constantly while batting and swung his arms in all directions. A favorite gesture to his bench jockeys was to put his thumb to his nose. He liked to argue with umpires after being called out on strikes. He often broke the handle of his bat by slamming it down on the plate after one of his league-leading 84 whiffs.

On July 3, Wilson was hitting .347 with 23 homers and 73 RBIs in 71 games. He was having a gigantic season, but so were others. The Phils' Chuck Klein was batting .399 with 19 homers and 77 RBIs. In the AL, Gehrig was at .383 with 86 RBIs and Ruth was hitting .375 with 81 RBIs and a major league-leading 31 home runs. In the first game of a double header against the White Sox on July 2, Ruth hit his 31st blast, putting him 21 days ahead of his 1927 pace. He predicted he would hit 75 homers.

In the second game of the day, however, Ruth got his hand caught in the wiring of the right-field stands at Yankee Stadium in an attempt to rob Chicago's Carl Reynolds of a homer. He tore the entire nail off the ring finger of his left hand and departed in extreme pain. The injury bothered him during the second half of the season. He belted 49 homers, good enough to lead the AL, but disappointing considering his blazing start.

It was Wilson's second half of the season that would make him the king of sluggers. In the final 83 games (two games were ties), Hack drove in 118 runs. At this time rumors circulated that Hornsby was after McCarthy's job. Before he broke his ankle on Memorial Day, Hornsby wanted to play more often, and he was bitter at McCarthy for keeping him on the bench. Late in the season when his ankle was healing, Hornsby felt McCarthy kept him out of the lineup too much. There were reports of a feud on the team between pro–McCarthy and pro–Hornsby factions and rumors that a fistfight between two Cub teammates had occurred because of the conflict.

On Wednesday, July 16, the Cubs entered Brooklyn for a big five-game series against what looked like the team to beat. Over 30,000 fans showed up at Ebbets Field for a mid-week doubleheader and 15,000 were turned away. The Cubs won the opener, 6–4, as Wilson doubled, scored twice, and knocked in a pair of runs. In the eighth inning Brooklyn's Del Bissonette collided with Hartnett at the plate while trying for an inside-the-park homer. Bissonette was tagged out as well as knocked out. In the dressing room after the game, Bissonette was unaware he had even hit the ball.

Brooklyn took the second game of the day, 5–3, as Luque outpitched Root. The Cubs won the third game of the series, 6–3, in 13 innings. The next day Wilson singled, doubled, and banged homer number 25 off Jumbo Elliott as the Cubs triumphed again, 6–2. They won the fifth game too, 5–4, as Wilson drilled a two-run homer on a sixth-inning offering from Vance. Hack led the league in walks in 1930 with 105. As the season wore on, pitchers realized that giving the slugging runt a free pass was the best way of dealing with him. The Cubs' winning ways in Flatbush left them in second place, four percentage points behind Uncle Robbie's Robins.

On to the Polo Grounds, where Wilson hit homer number 27 off Fred Fitzsimmons to give the Cubs a 5–3 lead in the first of four games, but the Giants came back to rout Bush, 13–5. On July 21 Wilson slugged two homers and Malone mowed down McGraw's batsmen, 6–0. The two teams split a doubleheader on July 22. The Cubs peppered Pete Donahue with 13 singles (three by Wilson) to win the opener, 5–4, before the Giants prevailed, 7–1, in the finale. The Cubs' success in Flatbush and Manhattan was encouraging.

In the Baker Bowl on July 24, the Cubs rolled up a 13–3 lead after two innings and held on to beat the Phils, 19–15. Two days later Wilson sent homers number 30, 31, and 32 orbiting into the seats and drove home five runs as the Cubs smacked 21 hits to complete a three-game sweep of the "Phutile" Phillies, 16–2. The 1930 Phils set a major league record by slashing

1,783 hits. They compiled a .315 batting average but finished last at 52–102. The reason was a pitching staff that was pounded for a 6.71 ERA.

Klein finished at .386 with 250 hits, 40 homers, and 170 RBIs, and Lefty O'Doul hit .383 with 22 homers and 122 runs scored. Baker Bowl was a bandbox. A 60-foot-high tin wall loomed over right field, 281 feet from home plate. Klein posted a record 44 assists in 1930 by playing the Ping-Pong shots off the tin wall and making strong throws. Curiously, Hack's best year with his bat was his worst defensively. He made 19 errors.

August was Wilson's most productive month. In 31 games he homered 13 times and drove in 54 runs. He was visiting plenty of speakeasies during this hot streak, causing his manager, McCarthy, to ask, "What am I supposed to do? Tell him to live a clean life and he'll hit better?"[9]

Bill Terry claimed he kept Wilson's drinking under control while Hack was with the Giants. In Chicago, McCarthy tried a different approach. Charlie Grimm recalled, "Joe McCarthy was a great psychologist. He loved the guy (Wilson). On the road Joe would frequently have him up to his room and talk things over. He kept him straight."[10] Wilson might not have been straight twenty-four hours a day, but he was functioning as a clutch batsman like no one had ever seen.

Grimm also told sportswriter Ed Wilks, "He made the money for us, and never mind the two fly balls he lost in the sun in the 1929 World Series. He was vicious with the bat. The word would go along in the dugout when we needed runs, 'Let somebody get on base and give Hack another at-bat.'"[11]

Wilson was especially dangerous in Chicago. He batted .381 at Wrigley compared to .324 on the road and drove in 115 of his 191 runs in Chi-Town. Thirty-three of his 56 homers also came there. The Cubs won 51 games and lost 26 at home. Their road record was 39–38. After Hornsby went down, Hack put the Cubs on his back and carried them as far they could go. He sent runners scurrying around the paths with miraculous regularity, swinging his bat just as productively as the sledgehammer he had driven steel with.

Wilson possessed small hands and was one of the first sluggers to use a thin-handled bat. Sometimes he shaved the handle. Woody English remembered, "He broke more bats after he struck out. He'd take the bat by the big end and hit the little end on home plate and it would fly. Did you ever see him? He was a wonderful guy, a colorful guy. He was a short heavyset guy. Had a red neck — not much neck at all. He could hit that ball, that long ball."[12]

Wilson continued his torrid pace in September with 10 homers and 34 RBIs. McCarthy recalled, "I never saw a guy win games the way he did that year. We never lost a game all year if he came up in the late innings with a chance to get a hit that would win it for us.... No tougher player ever lived than Hack Wilson."[13]

Wilson's slugging feats would carry the Cubs over the Robins and the Giants, but the Cardinals were just as hot as Wilson. St. Louis would win 36 of its final 46 games, including 21 of its final 25, to charge past the whole pack with a furious sprint.

Hack homered on July 29, August 2, August 3, and August 5 to bring his total to 36. On August 10, the Cubs trounced the Braves, 6–0 and 17–1, in a Sunday doubleheader before 45,000 at Wrigley. Wilson slammed homers number 37, 38, and 39 and brought home seven runs. In St. Louis the Cards beat the Robins twice, 8–2 and 4–0. The next day Chicago passed Brooklyn in the standings with a 4–2 win over the Braves. Wilson misjudged a fly ball by Wally Berger to give him an inside-the-park homer but also delivered two singles. In St. Louis, the Cards scored three runs in the bottom of the ninth to upend the Robins again, 7–6.

Brooklyn limped into Chicago for a four-game series on August 12, and the Cubs won three of them. A total of 140,000 paid plus 17,500 free ladies saw the weekday series. Hack hit his 40th homer in game two and contributed a big single in a game-winning, tenth-inning rally in the final contest. He drove in eight runs in the series. He was at .347 with 126 RBIs in 113 games.

On August 18, Hack singled three times and hit his 42nd homer to ignite a six-run rally in the eighth as the Cubs buried the Phillies, 17–3. He added four RBIs. Contrary to what has now become legend, Wilson did not spend all his free time in speakeasies. After that game he went to Chicago's Municipal Tuberculosis Hospital, where he cheered ailing children until 10:00 P.M.

The following afternoon Hack singled twice and tied Klein for the then-single-season NL home run record with blast number 43. Out in right field Klein saluted Wilson as the stumpy slugger trotted toward second base. The *Sporting News* called Klein's gesture a "splendid bit of sportsmanship."[14]

The Giants made their last serious bid for the pennant with a visit to Wrigley on August 21. The Boys of Broadway exploded for six runs in the first inning of the opener to beat the Cubs, 13–6. The Cubs won game two, 12–4, as Hartnett belted a grand slam. Wilson decided game three with a two-run single in the eighth inning, 4–2. Danny Taylor swiped home in the ninth inning of the final game as Bush and the Cubs bested Fitzsimmons, 2–1. Wrigley Field was jumping as a total of 178,000 fans came out for the series. The Cubs had beaten off challenges from the Robins and Giants and were in first place with a five-game lead. It surely looked like Chicago's year.

On August 26 Hack called his shot against the Pirates. Lloyd Waner lined a ball toward Wilson in center. Wilson fell while chasing the ball, and the sphere rolled to the wall for an inside-the-park homer. At the end of the inning, Wilson apologized to his pitcher, "Sheriff" Blake, who like Hack made his home in West Virginia.

Hack announced, "Sheriff, it seems like things always happen to you that never happened before. That belly-buster couldn't have occurred behind any other pitcher. But for your sake and for the pride of West Virginia, I'm going to get that home run back with a legitimate homer. And in this very inning."[15] Wilson, who had already socked a two-run single and driven in a run with a sacrifice fly, sent the ball into the seats as the Cubs rallied to win, 7–5. The circuit clout was Hack's 44th of the year, breaking Klein's record. Ruth made a point of looking up Wilson while Hack was in New York and told the chubby Cub, "Kid, you're the best!"[16]

Disaster struck the Cubs the succeeding afternoon. Charlie Root failed to record an out in the first inning before retiring with a muscle pull in his arm. He was not an effective pitcher for the rest of the season. Hack singled and doubled and drove in three runs, but the Bucs banged 20 hits in winning, 10–8. Pie Traynor socked five of Pittsburgh's hits and Gus Suhr's eighth-inning, two-run homer was the difference. On August 16 Grimm had suffered a four-inch spike wound in his left leg from the Phils' Lefty O'Doul. Stephenson was handicapped all season with a variety of injuries. Hornsby tried to come back for the stretch drive but still could not run well. The death of Carlson hurt the pitching staff. It seemed Hack was fighting an uphill battle.

The high-flying Cardinals came into Chicago on August 28 for a four-game set. They won the opener, 8–7 in a game that lasted 20 innings. Wilson pulled a muscle in his back due to a tremendous swing and miss and left the game. He missed his only contest of the season the next day but the Cubs won in 13 innings, 9–8. The Cubs used their entire pitching staff in the 33 innings. Years later McCarthy painfully recalled, "That was the end of the Cubs. The pitching staff was shot.... If we had lost (the two games) in nine, we would have won the championship."[17] Wilson was back in the third game with a two-run single and homers number 45 and 46 as the Cubs won, 16–4. The Cards won the getaway game, 8–3, as Hallahan fired a four-hitter and fanned 12. Hallahan walked Wilson intentionally four times. During the final month the Cubs could not keep up with the Redbirds.

On September 6 the Cubs scored four runs in the eighth inning and six in the ninth to overtake the Pirates, 19–14. Wilson drove in four runs with two singles and his 47th homer. The series with Pittsburgh was not a success for the Cubs, however. They scored 49 runs in five games but lost three of them.

The final turning point downward for the Cubs came next in Brooklyn. The Robins beat them three straight, 3–0, 6–0, and 2–1, as Phelps, Luque, and Vance silenced the Chicago bats. A Wilson homer off Vance was the Cubs' only run.

Hack tried to rally his team going 5-for-5, including two doubles, homer number 49, and six RBIs, in a 17–4 rout of the Phils on September 12. The

next day he socked two singles and a double and scored three times, but the
Phils won, 7–5, on O'Doul's two-run, pinch-hit homer in the eighth inning.
On September 15 the two teams split a doubleheader. O'Doul was poison
again for the Cubs, as his home run onto Broad Street in the ninth gave the
Phils the opener, 12–11. Hack went 3-for-8 on the day with his 50th homer.

McCarthy had received a telegram signed by 3,600 fans wishing the
Cubs good luck on their road trip. The eastern swing became a nightmare for
the Irishman, however, and the *Sporting News* reported, "The consensus seems
to be that square-jawed Joe is going to get the air not many days after the
season has officially closed."[18]

The Robins lost 19 of 27 games in August, but the unpredictable "Daffi-
ness Boys" reawakened to win 11 straight in early September. By September
16 they were back in the lead at 84–60. The Cards trailed by only a single
game, with the fading Cubs 1½ back.

On September 17 Wilson clubbed two skyscraping two-run homers into
the upper right-field stands at the Polo Grounds as the Cubs beat New York,
5–2. His four RBIs on the day gave him 177 as he passed Lou Gehrig's single-season major league mark of 175. But the Cubs were tamed by Hubbell,
7–0, and by Fitzsimmons, 6–2, in the other two games of the series. In the
process they lost more ground to the Cardinals.

In McCarthy's last game as Chicago's skipper, Wilson hammered a two-
run homer in the first inning and added an RBI single in the ninth frame.
The Cubs won in Boston, 6–2. The Cubs had played 21 of their last 22 games
on the road. Despite the victory, Wrigley announced, "We planned to offer
Hornsby a contract a few days after the season closes. We didn't want to
embarrass McCarthy. Now that all sorts of rumors are flying around, the matter will be taken up immediately." Wrigley added, "I have always wanted a
world's championship team and I am not sure that Joe McCarthy is the man
to give me that kind of team."[19]

McCarthy went on to win seven world championships with the Yankees
and retired as skipper of the Red Sox 62 games into the 1950 season with the
highest winning percentage of any manager in history. The Cubs have not
won a world's championship since 1908.

When McCarthy learned of Wrigley's intentions, he quit before being
fired. When William Veeck was quoted saying that McCarthy lost control of
the club, Joe was furious. He replied, "It must have taken Veeck a long time
to make that one up. The only players who ran around at night were Hack
Wilson and Pat Malone, and Hack's hitting and Pat's pitching won the pennant for us last year and kept us in the race all this year."[20]

The *Sporting News* said that some players on the Cubs team were "in
bad" with Hornsby for "not attending strictly to business" and that "rumors

of house cleaning were being dispensed freely."[21] The bible of baseball went on to say that Hack was unfriendly toward Hornsby and that Hornsby didn't count out trading Wilson.

The Cubs won their last four games of the year to finish in second place. On September 26, Chicago topped Cincinnati, 7–5, as Wilson's two-run homer in the seventh frame was the difference. The same day in St. Louis, the Cards clinched the flag with a 10–5 win over the Pirates. On September 27, Hack sent flying homers 55 and 56 and drove in four runs in a 13–8 thrashing of the Reds. He socked two singles, coaxed a bases-loaded walk, and drove in runs 190 and 191 in the Cubs' final regular-season game, a 13–11 win over Cincinnati.

Cincinnati catcher Clyde Sukeforth claimed that Hack actually hit 57 homers in 1930. Sukeforth told author Bill Honig the following during the 1970s:

> Hack, you know, holds the National League record for home runs in a season — 56, in 1930. Everybody knows that, right? Well, I'll tell you something that everybody doesn't know — he hit 57 that year, except that the record book doesn't show it. He hit one in Cincinnati one day, way up in the seats, hit it so hard that it bounced right back onto the field. The umpire had a bad angle on it and ruled that it had hit the screen and bounced back. I was sitting in the Cincinnati bullpen, and of course, we weren't going to say anything. But Hack really hit 57 that year.[22]

In 1931 the National League deadened the ball to stop the deluge of hitting. They put a thicker cover on it and raised the seams of the stitching to help the pitchers. Hack only hit .261 with 13 homers and 61 RBIs in 112 games before being suspended in September by the Cubs. The suspension came after a fight between Malone and a couple of sportswriters at a train platform in Cincinnati on September 5. Wilson had accompanied Malone on a night on the town after a disappointing loss. When they reached the platform the next morning to catch the train back to Chicago, the fight started. Wilson swore that he didn't participate, although he probably helped instigate the bout and looked on with apparent approval.

Hornsby wasn't much help to his slugger. Rogers berated Hack for his carousing, and Hack was fined $6,500 during the year. Hornsby also humiliated Hack by playing pitcher Bud Teachout in center one day, and gave Hack take signs on 2–0, 3–1, and 3–0 pitches. McCarthy had given Wilson the green light on such pitches.

Years later Hack told writer J. Roy Stockton, "Some people said I was a batting flop because I was carousing around too much. That was all wrong. I went out occasionally, but not as much as I did the year before, when I was hitting all those home runs. You have to do something for recreation, but I was in condition to play every day."[23]

The Cubs traded Wilson to St. Louis in December 1931, and the Cards dealt him to Brooklyn. There he enjoyed a revival, batting .297 with 23 homers and 123 RBIs, but it was his last hurrah. He was out of baseball by 1935. A costly divorce in 1938 also hurt him. Wilson remarried, shuffled from job to job, and ended up in Baltimore, where he died a pauper in 1948. He died from the complications of a head wound suffered due to a fall. He was 48 years old.

His body went unclaimed for three days. His first wife died in 1940. His second wife, Hazel, had become ill, and her family had taken her back to Martinsburg. When notified of Hack's death and asked about the disposition of his body, his son, Robert, sent a telegram with the reply, "Am not responsible."[24]

The president of the NL, Ford Frick, wired $350 to pay for a funeral in Baltimore, attended by about fifty people. Plans were made to bury Hack in Baltimore until word came from Martinsburg to cancel the burial. Hazel, who had been sent to a mental hospital in West Virginia by her family, gave approval for Hack's body to be sent back to Martinsburg for a more dignified burial.

Wilson's lodge brothers, fellow members of the Order of the Elks, drove his body back to Martinsburg, where it was laid out for viewing at a funeral home. About one thousand people came to see it. Two hundred people, including Hazel, then attended his funeral and burial. A season like Hack Wilson enjoyed in 1930 would have set him up for life today. The most he earned in a season was $33,000.

Hack's son had a successful career as a teacher, principal, and school superintendent. Although bitter at his father for his shortcomings as a parent, Robert told writer Bob Broeg that he chose to remember fondly the Hack Wilson who loved to hunt, fish, and attend sporting events.[25] Robert appeared at Hack's overdue induction into the Baseball Hall of Fame.

Back in 1931 at the baseball writers' convention, a member urged that they petition Commissioner Landis to get Wilson thrown out of baseball. The dean of the writers, Grantland Rice, probably described Hack best when he replied, "My boy, don't you recognize a genuine miracle when you see one?"[26]

Chapter 7

The Beast of the White Elephants: Jimmie Foxx in 1932

Shibe Park opened in 1909 and was home to Connie Mack's A's until the team moved to Kansas City in 1955. The heyday at Shibe occurred from 1929 to 1931, when Mack's A's captured three pennants while winning more than 100 games each year. Clad in their bright white uniforms with sharp blue trim and a stately letter A on the shirt, these A's are still considered one of the best ballclubs ever. The slugger on Mack's A's team was Jimmie Foxx, who could hit a ball as far as anyone. He was at his best in 1932 when he challenged Ruth for the then-single-season home run record by hammering 58-round trippers.

Foxx possessed more than power. He was a lifetime .325 hitter. In 1932 he batted .364 and led the AL in runs (151), RBIs (169), and homers. He missed the Triple Crown because Dale Alexander nosed him out of the batting title with a .367 average. Alexander had 454 plate appearances; today's rules require 502 plate appearances.

The reason Foxx did not break Ruth's home run record centered on the playing conditions, which had changed between 1927 and 1932. During that time screens were installed above the fences in Cleveland, Detroit, and St. Louis. Balls hit into the screens were no longer home runs, falling instead for doubles or triples. Foxx had 33 doubles and nine triples among his 213 hits. At Sportsman's Park in St. Louis, a 21 foot high-screen was erected on top of the 11 foot-high wall in right. In an interview with writer Fred Lieb in the *Sporting News,* Foxx said he hit six balls against that screen during the season that would have been homers in 1927.[1] It's also possible that Foxx might have hit the screens in Cleveland and Detroit.

Foxx had another factor working against him. After 1930 the bounce home run was abolished. Prior to then balls that bounced into the stands were considered home runs rather than ground-rule doubles. Foxx might have hit a few ground-rule doubles in 1932. He also had two homers wiped out by games called because of rain. "Double X" batted fifth in the A's order, with Mickey Cochrane third and Al Simmons fourth. If Foxx had batted third or fourth, he would have received more plate appearances.

Foxx grew up in Sudlersville, Maryland. He played pitcher, catcher, and any position his high school needed him. In his junior year, his last season of high school ball, he batted .552. Foxx was not just a muscleman; he was a star in track and soccer in high school. In 1924, at age sixteen, Foxx signed to play baseball for the Easton, Maryland, team in the Class D Eastern Shore League.

The manager of Easton was Frank Baker, the former star for the A's who was impressed with Foxx's natural ability. Foxx played any position that Baker asked him to play. Before the season was over Baker contacted Miller Huggins to tell him about this phenom. Huggins was not interested. Baker then contacted Mack, who sent a scout.

A's scout Mike Brennan reported that although Foxx was sixteen, he possessed the physique of a man of twenty-five. Foxx was six feet tall and weighed 175 pounds. Brennan said Foxx was "all muscle" and that he was not only the hardest hitter in the league but also its fastest runner. Foxx played catcher for most of the season. Brennan noted Foxx could fire the ball like a streak to second from a squatting position behind home plate.[2]

Mack signed Foxx for $2,000, one of the all-time bargains. Two years earlier he had purchased Robert "Lefty" Grove from Baltimore of the International League for $100,600 and spent $35,000 to get Al Simmons from the minor league Milwaukee Brewers. He bought the entire Portland franchise in the Pacific Coast League to acquire catcher Mickey Cochrane. These four players were the cornerstones of Mack's teams.

Mack sent Foxx to play for Providence of the International League in 1925. He played catcher, right field, and first base and hit .327. The A's already had a top catcher in Cochrane, who hit .331 in 134 games and handled the chores behind the plate better than anyone. It was obvious Mack had to find another position for Foxx.

In 1926 Foxx sat beside Mack while studying the game. He appeared in 15 contests and hit .313. The next year he played in 61 games, including 32 at first base, and hit .323. In 1928 Mack's inability to find a permanent spot for Foxx cost Philadelphia the pennant. The Yankees stormed out to a huge lead, winning 40 of their first 50 games. Fans thought that a repeat of 1927, when the Yankees won 110 games and captured the pennant by 19 games, was underway. But the A's won 25 of 33 games in July and stayed hot through August. They pulled even with the Yanks on September 7, and passed the Pinstripers with a victory the next day. On September 9, Mack's Athletics came into Yankee Stadium for a doubleheader. A record crowd of 85,264 saw the Yanks finally halt the momentum of the stampeding White Elephants, 3–0 and

In 1932 Jimmie Foxx blasted 58 homers to go along with a .364 batting average, 169 RBIs, and 151 runs scored. Probably the main reason he didn't break Ruth's then-single-season record of 60 homers was that high screens had been erected above the outfield walls in St. Louis, Detroit, and Cleveland since Ruth hit his 60 in 1927.

7–3. New York won the pennant by 2½ games. Foxx appeared in 60 games at third base, 19 at catcher, 30 at first base, and nine as a pinch-hitter and batted .328 with 13 homers in 400 at-bats.

In 1929 Mack tossed Foxx a first baseman's mitt and told him the position was his. For much of the season he was hitting around .400 and belting some of the longest homers ever seen. On July 29 his picture ran on the cover of *Time* magazine. He batted .354 with 33 homers and 117 RBIs as the A's won 104 games and dethroned the Yankees.

In 1930 Foxx pounded 37 homers and drove in 156 runs while batting .335. The A's won 102 games and easily took another pennant. They bested the Cardinals in the World Series for their second straight championship. The 1931 season began on a bad note for Foxx. In the second game of the season he fell while rounding second base and ripped a tendon. He was out until May 5. In June, Jimmy Dykes was injured and Foxx was pressed into action for 20 games at third base. On September 9, Washington's Heinie Manush spiked Foxx while crossing first base. Foxx was on crutches for a spell and missed ten days. His average dipped to .291. For the season he hit 30 homers with 120 RBIs. The A's played .777 ball through May, June, and July, and won 107 games overall. They outdistanced the Yankees by 13½ games. New York scored a still-record 1,067 runs to the A's 858 runs, but the A's pitching (3.47 ERA) far outclassed the Yankees (4.20 ERA). Philadelphia lost the World Series to the Cardinals in seven games.

Foxx was one of the premier sluggers but was severely underpaid. In 1930 he signed a three-year contract for $50,000, earning him a yearly salary of $16,666. At the same time Mack was paying Simmons and Cochrane a yearly salary of $30,000. When Foxx outslugged Ruth in 1932, his $16,666 salary was dwarfed by Ruth's $75,000 salary.

Foxx cut off the sleeves of his A's uniform to show his biceps. He said the freedom this provided his arms gave him extra power. Some of his home runs were traveling 500 feet, a distance previously reserved only for Ruth and Gehrig. His menacing appearance at the plate led to his nickname "the Beast."

Ruth, at age thirty-seven, possessed a huge torso. His home runs were rain-making bombs that seemed to take an eternity before returning to earth. Ruth generated a lot of his power from his upper body. Foxx possessed a sculptured body. Lefty Gomez once quipped, "He's so strong, he's got muscles in his hair."[3] Foxx's homers took off as low line drives that rose until they seemed to soar into orbit.

Foxx possessed quick and powerful wrists. He held his bat lower than most sluggers. He used a quick hitch to start his swing. Foxx said, "I'm not as large as Ruth, but I have the proper timing and thorough coordination of hands, wrists, shoulders, and eyes. My fingers and wrists are very strong and

I use a thinner handled bat than him, with more weight at the end. The lighter the bat, the faster you can swing it."[4] Actually, Foxx switched to a lighter model bat in 1932 with a thinner handle and bigger barrel.

When asked if he tried for homers, Foxx replied, "No. Once I did that I was licked. A proper bat, a good swing and meet the ball squarely was my method. If you have enough power and meet the ball right it's going to go out of the park anyway. There is no difference between a ball hit 400 feet and one hit 500 feet. They're both homers."[5]

When asked about his longest homer, Foxx recalled a shot he hit while touring Japan in 1934 with an All-American all-star team in Tokyo. Foxx related, "The distance to the left-field stands was 400 feet. Now there were an awful lot of rows between the base of the stands and the top. Well, I got hold of one. It was a high towering one that hit right on the top of the back wall behind all those fans and skipped right out of the park. How far did it go? It must have gone 600 feet, they told me."[6]

The A's had reason to be confident in 1932. The average age of the A's was twenty-eight. Outfielder Bing Miller and third baseman Jimmy Dykes were the oldest of the regulars at thirty-seven and thirty-five, respectively. Mack planned on making his team stronger by using young outfield prospects Ed Coleman and Doc Cramer instead of Miller. Coleman batted .342 in 30 games before breaking his left ankle and Cramer batted .336 in 92 games before breaking his collar bone. Both were lost for the remainder of the season. Miller wound up playing 95 games and batting .295. Mack also replaced light-hitting shortstop Joe Boley with Eric McNair, who hit .295 with 47 doubles, 18 homers and 95 RBIs.

Offensively, the Athletics were stronger than ever in 1932. They scored 981 times, second to New York's 1,002 runs. Unlike the National League the AL did not put a heavier cover on its ball after 1930. The AL did raise the stitches on the ball to help the pitchers' breaking pitches. In their three pennant-winning seasons of 1929, 1930, and 1931, the A's had scored 901, 951, and 858 runs, respectively. The problem in 1932 was Philadelphia's pitching. The 1932 Yankees outpitched the A's for the first time since 1927. Led by Lefty Gomez and his 24 victories, the Yanks league-leading ERA of 3.98 was considerably better than Philly's 4.45 ERA. Grove won 25 games and led the league in ERA at 2.84, but he was the only A's pitcher with an ERA under 3.84.

There is a myth that Mack's pennant-winning A's were unbeatable until Connie sold off his stars to make financial ends meet during the Depression. In fact, Mack didn't begin breaking up his ballclub until 1933. In 1932 the Yankees won 107 games and beat Mack's juggernaut at full strength by 13 games.

On April 12, Opening Day at Shibe, the Yankees outslugged the A's, 12–6. Ruth smashed two homers off George Earnshaw onto the roofs of the houses beyond the right-field barrier. Gehrig also homered and rattled a triple off the wall. Earnshaw was battered for ten runs in four innings. Foxx went 2-for-5 with a single and homer off Lefty Gomez. His homer was the longest belt of the day, rocketing over the center-field fence near the flagpole, some 468 feet from home plate.

After cold weather postponed two games, the series resumed on April 15 with Philly topping the Yanks, 9–8. Foxx hit another solo homer and Cochrane also knocked a round-tripper. Simmons and Mule Haas added three hits each. Dykes won the game with a sacrifice fly.

The Senators invaded Philly next and Grove stopped them with a six-hitter, 4–2. Foxx singled twice and swiped a base. The A's won the following day, 11–3, as Foxx singled twice and crushed a three-run homer off Firpo Marberry. Foxx then went 3-for-3 in game three of the series with a single, double, and homer, but the Senators prevailed, 15–7, as Heinie Manush drove in five runs.

On April 20 the A's traveled to New York for Opening Day at Yankee Stadium before 58,322. Gomez beat the Mackmen, 8–3, as Ruth, Bill Dickey, and Lyn Lary homered. The A's rebounded to win game two, 8–6. Foxx smacked a single and two triples and Cochrane walloped a ninth-inning grand slam. Foxx was hitting .500 through the first eight games. In game three the A's routed Yankee starter Gordon Rhodes for five runs in the top of the first inning but New York came back to rout Rube Walberg with six runs in the bottom of the first. Foxx delivered a two-run single in the first-inning rally. The Yanks rolled up a 16–5 win.

The loss sent the A's into a tailspin as they lost their next six games. The streak was broken on May 2 when Foxx's eleventh-inning homer beat the Red Sox at Fenway, 3–2. Washington was leading the league with a 13–4 record. The Yanks were in third place at 10–5 and the A's were in seventh place at 5–10. This bad start was fatal to Philly's pennant hopes.

On May 5, Foxx singled twice, tagged a homer, scored five runs, and drove in four as the A's routed Cleveland's Wes Ferrell, 15–8. On May 7, "the Beast" singled, tripled, and knocked out his seventh homer of the young season. The Indians, however, routed four Philly pitchers with 18 hits to win, 10–7.

On May 10, Grove shut out the Chisox, 9–0. Two days later Earnshaw beat St. Louis, 9–4. Foxx slashed six singles and a double in nine at-bats in the two wins. The two games were bad news for Connie Mack, however. A combined total of only 5,000 fans came out to Shibe to see them. The Depression was getting worse. In the winter of 1932-1933, the nation's unemployment rate would reach twenty-five percent. More than 5,000 banks had closed in the previous two-and-a-half years. The national income had dropped to less than one-half of what it was before Black Friday in October 1929.

Mack, who was owner as well as manager of the A's, was hit harder than most owners. In the mid-1920s Shibe underwent renovations. Mack had borrowed from banks. The debt was in excess of $800,000 and a great deal was outstanding in the 1930s.[7] The A's also possessed the highest payroll in baseball. Philadelphia's attendance figures declined steadily. In their championship season of 1929 they drew 839,176 and in 1930 and 1931 their attendance declined to 721,663 and 627,464, respectively. In both years the A's jumped out to big leads in the pennant races in the first half of the season. With the drama of a close race gone, fans stayed away. In 1932 attendance dropped to 405,500.

Mack's financial difficulties would cause him to sell off his stars in the next few seasons. Foxx was the last to go, in 1936. The A's financial woes affected Foxx's pocketbook. After Foxx put together one of the greatest offensive seasons for any batter in history, Mack had no choice but to cut the player's salary $366.

In mid–May the *Sporting News* reported:

> Never before so protracted a period has Foxx whaled the hosshide as he has this season. The explanation is that Jimmy is swinging this year more than ever, taking fewer good ones than used to be his wont. It was said and it was true, that Foxx tried to outguess the pitchers. Frequently they outguessed him, sending him back to the bench a strikeout victim, while he kept his bat aloof. But all of that has since been changed. Jimmy is taking his cuts. And is that hosshide going places.[8]

The A's rallied with a seven-game win streak starting on May 17. On that day Earnshaw spun a four-hitter at Detroit and Foxx singled and rode home on Dykes' double for the go-ahead run in a 2–0 win. On May 18 he hit a two-run homer as Grove tamed the Tigers, 8–2. On May 19 his first-inning grand slam was all Roy Mahaffey needed to beat the Red Sox, 4–2. He singled once and doubled twice on May 20 as Rube Walberg stymied Boston again, 6–1. On May 21 he bashed two homers and drove in six runs as the A's finished off Boston in a doubleheader, 18–6 and 6–3.

On May 21 the A's rode into Yankee Stadium and bested the Pinstripers, 4–2. Grove fired a six-hitter. Foxx, Simmons, and Cochrane homered. The win streak put the A's in third place at 18–14, 4½ games behind the now-first-place Yanks. Foxx was leading the AL in homers with 14; Ruth had 10. But the Yanks won the next two games, 6–5 and 3–1, respectively. In the third game Gomez threw a three-hitter, fanning 13. Foxx was switched to third base in the series.

He played third base again in Boston on May 26 and homered as Earnshaw won, 7–1. His eleven-game hitting streak was stopped on May 28, but on May 29 he played third and homered again in a doubleheader split in Fenway. He was quoted in the *Sporting News* as saying, "I am going after anything that's near the plate. I'm not letting anything go by that looks good."[9]

On Memorial Day the A's swept a doubleheader from the Senators at Shibe, 13–2 and 8–6. Simmons whacked four hits, including two homers in the morning game. Foxx singled and hit homer number 17 for three RBIs in the afternoon outing. Dykes enjoyed a big day with two homers, a single, a double, and eight RBIs. The A's could not make up any ground as the Yanks swept the Red Sox, 7–5 and 13–3.

Seven teams scored as many as 1,000 runs during a season in the twentieth century. The Yankees, from 1930 to 1932, did it three years in a row. The big boppers for the 1932 Yanks were still Ruth (.341, 41 homers, 137 RBIs) and Gehrig (.349, 34 homers, 151 RBIs). Tony Lazzeri and Ben Chapman drove in 113 and 107 runs, respectively. Catcher Bill Dickey hit .315, and leadoff batter Earle Combs hit .321 with 143 runs. What separated the 1932 team from the Yankee squads of 1930 and 1931 were improvements in defense and pitching.

Rookie shortstop Frankie Crosetti solidified New York's defense. Pitcher Lefty Gomez was known for his humor and was nicknamed "Goofy." But Gomez could do more than clown. In 1932, he hurled 265 innings and won 24 games including seven victories over the A's. Six-foot-two, 205-pound Red Ruffing rounded into top form (18–7 with a 3.09 ERA in 259 innings). Rookie Johnny Allen (17–4, 192 innings, 3.70 ERA) and George Pipgras (16–9, 219 innings, 4.19 ERA) completed the staff.

On the first day of June the Yankees arrived in Philly for a six-game series. The A's were in fourth place, six games behind New York. A good series might have turned the pennant race around. A crowd of 31,000 turned out for a doubleheader and the A's swept the Yanks, 8–7 and 7–6, to move within four games. In the first game Ruth's RBI single in the top of the sixteenth inning put the Yanks up, 7–6, but the A's Max Bishop slugged a game-winning, two-run homer in the bottom of the sixteenth. In the second game Foxx's two-run homer in the seventh inning off Pipgras landed on top of the left-field roof and put the A's up to stay.

But New York's Gomez won game three, 5–1, fanning ten. Game four had to be seen to be believed. The Yanks smashed seven homers and broke the record for total bases in a game with 50 as they hammered the A's, 20–13. Foxx tripled, homered, and scored three times, but Gehrig stole the show. In his first three times at bat, Gehrig blasted homers over the right-field wall off Earnshaw. Mack took the distraught Earnshaw out of the game and instructed him, "Sit here for a few minutes, son. I want you to see how Mahaffey does it. You've been pitching entirely wrong to Gehrig." Gehrig then sent a fastball from Mahaffey that disappeared over the left-field barrier. "I understand now," Earnshaw said. "Mahaffey made Lou change his direction. Can I shower now?"[10]

Gehrig had two more times at bat. In the eighth inning he grounded out. In the ninth he belted a shot off Eddie Rommel to the deepest part of center-field. Simmons, playing center in place of Cramer, raced to the far corner, leaped and robbed Gehrig of possibly a fifth home run. The ball was not going to clear the fence, but if it had hit the wall and bounced around Lou might have had an inside-the-park homer. Afterwards Gehrig said, "I think that last one was the hardest ball I hit."[11]

The series concluded with a doubleheader split between the two teams. Foxx, Bishop, Cochrane, and Simmons homered in the opener as the A's won, 10–7. The Yanks' Ben Chapman then doubled, tripled, and drove in four runs as New York captured the second game, 7–4. The A's would never get within four games of McCarthy's team again. On June 5 Foxx was hitting .401.

The Depression was hitting baseball hard. In 1929 ten million fans attended games. By 1932 fan attendance had shrunk to three-and-a-half million. The music of the times reflected the country's mood with songs like "Brother, Can You Spare a Dime."

After one game in Washington, where Foxx singled and slugged his twenty-first homer during an 11–7 win, the A's headed to Cleveland for a four-game series. Foxx managed just four hits as the two teams split the series. But while in Cleveland he did something more heroic than any deed he performed on a ball field. One night an apartment house near the hotel where the A's were staying erupted in fire followed by an explosion. The building was ablaze and people were screaming for help. Before the arrival of fire trucks, Foxx and Cochrane helped rescue three young girls and a man from the burning building.[12]

In the following four-game series in Detroit, "the Beast" slammed four homers, bringing his season total to 25, as the A's won three games. One of the homers was a ninth-inning, three-run shot off Tommy Bridges that clinched the victory. In Chicago on June 20, Foxx singled, doubled, stole a base, and blasted his 27th homer in an 18–11 Philly triumph. The homer was only the second ball ever to clear the high wall in left-center at Comiskey Park. The other was one Foxx hit the season before. Cramer went 6-for-6 with six singles to tie an AL record.

On June 25, Foxx tagged New York's Gomez for a tape-measure three-run homer in the fourth inning but Gomez won his eleventh straight game, 7–4. The homer was one of the longest in Yankee Stadium history. It sailed into the upper tier of the left-field grandstand. Had it been several feet more towards center, it would have left the stadium. Two "Xs" were later painted on the seat where the ball hit. That seat remained marked with the "Xs" until Yankee Stadium was renovated in 1974. The next day Ruffing pitched New York to a 6–2 win over the A's. Foxx wasn't giving up, however. He rallied the A's to a doubleheader sweep over the Red Sox in Philly on June 27 with five hits in seven at-bats. He was hitting over .380 and leading the league in homers and RBIs. The A's, however, were in third place at 39–30, 8½ games out.

On July 4, the A's were rained out. In New York the Senators beat the Yanks twice, 5–3 and 12–6, breaking Gomez's eleven-game win streak. Washington's Carl Reynolds had a jarring collision with Yanks catcher Bill Dickey at home plate. After the play Dickey delivered a haymaker punch to Reynolds' face. Reynolds was out of action for six weeks with a broken jaw and Dickey was suspended for thirty days. In his first game back, on August 4, he singled three times and hit a grand slam as the Yanks routed Chicago, 15–3.

Dickey was becoming a rival to Cochrane, hitting .315 in 108 games with 15 homers and 85 RBIs in 1932. Cochrane hit .293 with 23 homers, 118 runs, and 112 RBIs. During the 1929–1931 years, Cochrane hit a combined .346. He was a graduate of Boston University where he starred on the football field as a quarterback. He was an unusually speedy baserunner for a catcher and occasionally batted lead off. His lifetime batting average of .320 is tops among catchers.

Cochrane was an avid admirer of Connie Mack. He told Boston writer George C. Carens in 1934, "I don't know about other systems, but I do know that Connie Mack handles a team as individuals. He talks to each man calmly and peacefully. And he can 'lay it in' when he thinks it necessary. He's just as likely to hop on you when you're going good. Thinks you can take it better, maybe. He hates a loafer. Tries to make a man know what it means to do his best. Thinks a player can eat and sleep better when he makes baseball a game of play, of fun. He figures slumps come when a man loafs or sulks."[13] Mack managed until age 87. He won 3,731 games and lost 3,948. He stood 6'1" and weighed 150 pounds. He managed in street clothes, wearing a collared shirt, suit, tie, and hat as he moved his outfielders with a wave of his scorecard.

On July 8, the A's pulled back within 6½ games of New York by sweeping a doubleheader from the White Sox, 6–4 and 11–2. Foxx hit his 30th homer in the opener and Simmons banged a three-run homer in the second game. The next day the two teams split. Ted Lyons beat Grove in the first game, 7–0. The loss broke Grove's eleven-game win streak. In 1931 Grove won 16 straight while racking up 31 victories against just four losses. When he lost his bid for 17 straight by a 1–0 score, he ripped his shirt and three lockers to pieces.

On July 10 the A's won an 18-inning marathon game in Cleveland, 18–17. Foxx had six hits, including homers number 31, 32, and 33 plus a double. He scored four times, including the winning run in the eighteenth inning, and drove home eight runs. His two-run single in the ninth inning had put the A's up, 15–14, but the Indians tied the score in the bottom of the inning. Cleveland's Johnny Burnett broke a record with nine hits. The Tribe whacked 33 hits and the A's whacked 25 for a total of 58. The game was played on a Sunday. Blue laws prohibited baseball on Sundays in Philadelphia. Since the game was just a one-day stopover in Cleveland before the two teams traveled to Philly, Mack brought along two pitchers. Lew Krause was hit hard and Eddie Rommel came in relief in the second inning. Rommel received the win despite giving up 29 hits, 14 runs, and eight walks.

The win moved the A's to within six games of the top again, but their pennant hopes took a nose-dive the following afternoon when the Indians beat them twice back in Philly, 9–8 and 12–7. Foxx went 4-for-9 in the doubleheader with his 34th homer, a belt over the left-field roof off Mel Harder. From here onward the A's steadily fell farther and farther behind.

Foxx was having a great season, but not many Americans remembered 1932 as a good year. The Democratic nominee for president, Franklin D. Roosevelt, who had given his "Forgotten Man" speech back in April, tried to rally hope in the country with his campaign. He would win the election over Herbert Hoover by a landslide in November and declare in his inaugural address, "The only thing we have to fear is fear itself."

After losing two more to the Indians, the A's finally won on July 14 against Detroit, 9–2. The Mackmen exploded for seven runs in the seventh inning, highlighted by Foxx's three-run homer off Tommy Bridges that cleared the left-field roof. In game two of the series the Tigers topped the A's in 11 innings, 11–10, trumping three homers and six RBIs by Simmons. Despite a slow start that had Philadelphia fans booing him early in the season, Simmons wound up at .322 with 35 homers and 151 RBIs. Born Aloysius Harry Simmons in Milwaukee, he finished his career with 539 doubles, 149 triples, 307 homers, 2,927 hits, and a .334 batting average. In 1925 he challenged the single-season hits record by banging 253 safeties while batting .384. Fiercely proud of his Polish heritage, Simmons was said to work himself into a maniacal rage before facing a pitcher. A right-handed hitter, Simmons had a habit of striding with a step toward third base while batting. This was known as a flaw called "stepping in the bucket" but Mack never messed with Al's style.

In game three of the series Grove gained his 13th win, 14–3, despite giving up two homers to the Tigers' Charlie Gehringer. Foxx slammed a three-run homer in the eighth inning, again clearing the left-field roof. In game four Foxx tagged two more homers, this time off a young Whitlow Wyatt, as the A's eked out a 4–3 win. One of the homers again flew over Shibe's left-field roof. The *Philadelphia Inquirer* declared that Foxx now had a "copyright" on roof-clearing homers at Shibe.[14]

Foxx was challenging Ruth's mark of 60 homers and the press began calling him the "new King of Swat." Foxx was not the carouser that Ruth had been in his early days. In fact, Foxx seemed embarrassed by the attention he was receiving. He was described as a modest, genial, and happily married gentleman. One writer said that if one didn't know better, he might mistake Foxx for the team's water boy. He played bridge, read western stories, and enjoyed golf, bowling, and hunting. He dressed meticulously and visited a manicurist.

On July 19 at Shibe, the A's toppled the Browns, 9–8 and 16–6. Foxx went 4-for-7 with three doubles, five runs scored, an inside-the-park homer, and three RBIs. The inside-the-parker rebounded off the top of the center-field wall as Jimmie easily crossed the plate. It was his 39th homer, putting him 32 days ahead of Ruth's 1927 pace. During the five-game series against the Browns, Cramer was on fire, rapping 17 hits in 24 at-bats. On July 25, however, Cramer broke his collar bone on a diving try for a fly ball.

On July 23 in Washington, Foxx launched another huge belt. This one settled into the center-field bleachers at Griffith Stadium, which were 422 feet from home plate. Mack was quoted in the *Philadelphia Inquirer's* July 24 edition, "As soon as I saw Foxx take his stance at the plate I felt sure he was going to be a great hitter. The remarkable point of Foxx's homers this year has been their 'carry.' He hits them as if they were shot out of a gun and the majority of them steam out of the park."[15]

On July 27 the A's kept their hold on second place by tagging the Tigers in Detroit, 13–8 and 4–0. Foxx clouted homer number 41 and veteran Bing Miller slashed six hits and pushed home five runs. On the last day of the month, what was declared a major league-record crowd of 89,284 turned out for the opening game at Cleveland's new Municipal Stadium. Grove outdueled Mel Harder, 1–0. Foxx ended July with 41 homers.

As August opened Foxx slowed down and went into his only slump of the season. From August 1 to August 19 he hit only two homers. His wife, Helen, was confined to a hospital bed at St. Joseph's Hospital in Philadelphia. Although not gravely ill, her condition was enough to worry Jimmie. Perhaps a bigger reason for his slump was an injury he suffered while doing chores around the house. He was standing on a ladder trying to put in a curtain fixture when he started to fall. In attempting to stop his fall he sprained his left wrist. The injury did not keep Jimmie out of the lineup but it did affect his batting.

Foxx's 42nd homer on August 5 in St. Louis was another big-time clout flying into the center-field bleachers at Sportsman's Park, a good 445 feet from home plate. But Grove lost the game in relief, 9–8, despite knocking out a homer of his own. Foxx's next homer on August 14 went over the center-field wall in the third inning of a 6–1 win at Fenway Park, traveling at least 460 feet. In the first inning of the game he had just missed a four-bagger with a triple off the top of the right-field wall.

By August 20 Jimmie's wrist couldn't have been bothering him too much. On that day he launched a 500-foot home run off Ted Lyons at Shibe. It disappeared over the center-field wall and carried well past a neighboring factory building. "The Beast" then connected for homers on August 24, 25, 26, and 30, and ended August with 48. Ruth's record was within striking distance.

On September 2, Foxx went 4-for-6 with his 49th homer as the A's split a doubleheader with the Red Sox, winning the second game, 15–0. McNair clouted three homers and Simmons hit two three-run blasts, giving him 31 circuit clouts on the year. The succeeding afternoon against Boston, Foxx hit solo home runs in the first and ninth innings. The second round-tripper tied the score at 3–3, whereupon McNair followed with his fourth homer in two days for the winner.

On Labor Day, 70,772 at Yankee Stadium saw the McCarthymen beat Philly twice, 8–6 and 6–3. This increased the Yankee lead to 12½ games. Gomez bested the A's for the seventh time in eight tries in the opener and Johnny Allen ran his record to 16–2 with his tenth straight win in the second game.

The Athletics were able to handle any team except New York. They beat Detroit, 5–4, on September 11, with Foxx's seventh-inning homer the deciding blow. On September 14, they exploded for eight runs in the ninth inning to overtake the Browns, 13–6. Foxx had just two singles, but Simmons ripped five hits, including two doubles, and Cochrane doubled twice and homered.

The bats of Foxx and Simmons kept smoking. The A's bested the Chisox twice, 4–3 and 7–4, on September 18. Foxx went 5-for-9 with five RBIs and another homer off Lyons. Simmons laced six singles and a double. The A's finally beat New York on September 21, 8–4. Foxx slammed a three-run dinger off Ruffing, his 54th blast of the campaign, and Simmons and McNair also went deep. The Yanks topped the A's in 14 of 22 meetings in 1932 and won the final game between the two teams the following day, 8–7, in eleven innings. Foxx clobbered a grand slam off Gomez in the third inning and added a solo shot in the seventh but it wasn't enough.

On September 24, Foxx clubbed another grand slam. This one came off Washington's Bill McAfee during a ten-inning, 8–7 loss. With only one game left to play in the season, "the Beast" had 57 homers. In the final game Washington's Alvin Crowder stifled the A's, 3–1, for his 26th win of the year and 15th in a row. Foxx went 3-for-3 with homer number 58. Foxx gave Ruth's record a valiant challenge but the cards seemed stacked against him.

Of Foxx's 58 homers, 31 came at Shibe Park and 27 on the road. He hit 45 home runs off right-handers and 13 against left-handers. His 438 total bases and .749 slugging percentage led the league. After 1932, Mack sold Simmons, Dykes, and Mule Haas to the White Sox for $100,000. Foxx responded to his cut in salary in 1933 by winning the Triple Crown. He hit .356 with 48 homers and 163 RBIs. The A's finished in third place at 79–72, well behind pennant-winning Washington. Mack sold Grove, Walberg, and Bishop to

Boston for $125,000. He also sold Cochrane to Detroit for $100,000 and George Earnshaw to the Chisox for $25,000.

Foxx continued pounding the ball hard, but after a last-place finish in 1935, Mack sold him to Boston along with pitcher Johnny Marcum for $250,000. The trade helped Foxx as Boston owner Tom Yawkey gave him a $7,000 raise, to $25,000. Foxx had some big years in Boston. In 1938 he batted .349 with 50 homers and 175 RBIs. He missed another Triple Crown because Detroit's Hank Greenberg clocked 58 homers.

In 1940, Foxx's last big year, he suggested to Boston manager Joe Cronin that he could do some catching if Cronin wanted to get Lou Finney's bat in the lineup at first base. The Red Sox were in contention for the pennant. Foxx thought the move might help his team win. Foxx caught 42 games and played first base in 95 games, batting .297 with 36 homers and 119 RBIs. The Red Sox finished in fourth place, eight games behind champion Detroit. In 1941 Foxx hit .300 with 19 homers and 105 RBIs. He slumped in 1942 and Boston waived him to the Cubs, where he hit .205 in 205 at-bats. He was washed up at an early age.

Foxx retired for a year and came back as a player-coach with the Cubs in 1944. He had been declared 4-F, probably because of a chronic sinus condition that affected his eyesight. He managed one hit in 20 at-bats for Chicago before being sent to the Cubs minor league Portsmouth club.

In 1945 Foxx tried to come back again, this time with the Phillies. He batted .268 with seven homers in 224 at-bats. He also pitched 22 innings for the Phils, sporting a 1.59 ERA, but said his arm was "dead tired" after going five-and-two-thirds innings in his only start. With the return of many major leaguers from the war, Foxx was no longer needed.

Foxx's last good year in the majors was 1941. He was only 34 when he lost his ability. He was the youngest player at the time to reach 500 home runs and finished with 534. What caused the decline of Foxx is not clear. Some believe the 1940 season, when he volunteered to catch, took a lot out of his legs. But the chronic sinus problem that affected his eyesight was probably the main reason. The accompanying pain that went along with the condition contributed to his increasing use of alcohol.

Foxx lost more than $40,000 in a failed golf course venture during World War II. He began a pattern of moving from job to job. In 1952 he managed the Fort Wayne Daisies of the All-American Girls Professional Baseball League that was portrayed in the movie *A League of Their Own*. He also managed the University of Miami baseball team and was batting coach for the minor league Miami Marlins and Minneapolis Millers.

Foxx retired before a pension plan was set up for major league baseball players. He struggled financially to make ends meet for the rest of his life.

Foxx's health failed him as he aged. A fall down a flight of stairs in 1960 resulted in partial paralysis and he suffered two heart attacks. He died at age 59, choking to death on a piece of meat. The big seasons that Foxx enjoyed would have made him a multi-millionaire today. Instead, life was a struggle for Foxx after his career ended. His 1932 season and his glory years with the A's, however, will remain a legend as long as baseball is played.

Chapter 8

Mr. Dean at His Dizziest:
Dizzy Dean in 1934

Few pitchers have captured the imagination of the baseball world like "Dizzy" Dean did when he led the St. Louis Cardinals to the world championship in 1934. The self-proclaimed "Great One" won 30 decisions against just seven defeats while appearing in 50 games and hurling 312 innings for the notorious Gas House Gang. He also led the National League with 195 strikeouts and was second only to the New York Giants' Carl Hubbell with a 2.65 ERA. His brother, Paul "Daffy" Dean, won 19 games against 11 losses while working 233 innings with a 3.44 ERA. In addition, Dizzy and Daffy each won two games as the Cards bested the Detroit Tigers in a hard-fought World Series.

In spring training of 1934 Dizzy astounded the sportswriters with a prediction. He announced, "Me 'n' Paul are gonna have a family contest. If I win more games than he does, I'll lead the league. And if Paul wins more games than me, I'll run second. I don't see how anybody can beat us Redbirds now with two Deans on the ballclub. We'll be sure to win 45 games between us and if we have six more pitchers who can win about 50 other games, that will put us in the World Series. It oughta be a breeze from here on."[1]

The writers saw Dizzy as a brash young farm boy just shooting off his mouth. Yet when 1934 was finished, the Cardinals had won 95 games, just as Diz predicted, and captured the NL pennant. And the Dean brothers had pitched the Redbirds to not 45, but 49 victories, plus two each in the World Series. Diz, with his rubber arm, exploding fastball, and boasting predictions became the most talked-about attraction in the 1930s. The 23-year-old, 6'2" right-hander was all legs and arms. His fastball was smoke.

Diz was born in 1910 in Lucas, Arkansas, one of three sons of Albert Dean. His mother died when Diz was seven years old. There has been much debate about how far Diz advanced in school. After he became a star, Diz claimed to have never gotten past the second, third, or fourth grade, depending on which version of his life story he was telling. By 1951 Paul Dean, tired of the exaggeration of Diz's supposed ignorance, refuted all this. In an interview with the *Sporting News,* Paul said that Diz actually reached the seventh grade and was an average student in reading and writing.[2]

The debate over how far Diz got in school obscures the fact that Diz worked picking cotton as early as age 12 for 50 cents a day. He went to school when he could, but because the Deans were poor nomad laborers and moved frequently, his schooling was interrupted often.

At age 16, Diz ran away from home. He lied about his age and enlisted in the army. He earned his nickname of "Dizzy" because he drove his sergeant, James Brought, crazy. Diz's off-duty time was consumed with playing baseball. Brought recognized Diz's ability as a pitcher and made a project out of helping him control his fastball. Diz developed into a sensational pitcher for Brought's army team.

There have been different stories told about how Diz got out of the army before his hitch was up. The true story is that the San Antonio Public Service

Dizzy Dean, shown here with Negro League legend Satchel Paige, won 30 games for St. Louis in 1934 plus two more in the World Series. His brother, Daffy Dean, won 19 games during the regular season plus two in the World Series. Legend has it that Satchel once beat Dizzy in a 13-inning exhibition game, 1–0, at Hollywood Park.

Company bought Diz out of the army for $150 in 1929.[3] The company gave him a job so he could pitch for its semi-pro team. This came after a game in which the San Antonio team beat Diz and Brought's army team, 2–1, in eleven innings.

While pitching semi-pro ball in San Antonio, the dizzy one was discovered and signed by a part-time scout for the Class AAA Houston Buffaloes, Don Curtis, for $100 a month. The Buffaloes were a farm team of the St. Louis Cardinals. When he reported to the Buffaloes in the spring of 1930, it was decided that Diz wasn't ready for Class AAA ball. He was sent to the St. Joseph, Missouri, team of the Class C Western Association. He won 17 games by mid–August and was promoted to Houston, where he won eight of ten decisions. The Cardinals called him up late in 1930 and he pitched a three-hitter, beating the Pirates, 3–1.

The Cardinals were planning on bringing Diz up in 1931, but he infuriated the veterans on the team with his braggadocio. He began sleeping through practice sessions. Furthermore, Diz started signing for everything he bought, expecting management to pay for it. This caused club president Branch Rickey to inform local merchants that Diz needed to pay cash. He put Diz on a dollar-a-day allowance. A couple of weeks after the regular season began, Diz was back in Houston.

In Houston, Diz rang up a 26–10 record with 303 strikeouts in 304 innings and a 1.57 ERA. He was brought up by St. Louis to stay in 1932. The fans in St. Louis loved Diz. He went 18–15 with the Cards in 1932, leading the NL in strikeouts (191), shutouts (four) and innings pitched (286) while posting a 3.30 ERA. In 1933 he went 20–18 with a 3.04 ERA in 293 innings and led the league again with 199 strikeouts. On July 30 he set a then-major league record by striking out 17 batters against the Cubs. In typical Dean fashion he told reporters, "If I'd'a knowed I was near a record, I'd'a struck out 20 o' them bums, easy."[4]

By 1934 Diz was still suspicious and somewhat antagonistic towards those who had enjoyed the benefit of a higher education, but his hick-like fashions of a few years earlier were gone. He was happily married and his wife, Patricia, protected him by watching his finances closely. Diz had met Patricia while he was in Houston in 1931. Pat was a good-looking woman. Legend says that he met her in a clothing store and married her after a one-day courtship. This is not true, but it was a quick courtship. He did not arrive in Houston that year until May 2. He announced their engagement on June 1, and two weeks later they were married. Until "Dizzy" died in 1974, her sensibility balanced her husband's unpredictable behavior.

On Opening Day, 1934, at Sportsman's Park, Diz pitched the Cards to a 7–1 win over Pittsburgh. Outfielder Joe "Ducky" Medwick drove in three runs with a homer and two singles and third baseman John "Pepper" Martin doubled twice. The Giants' Carl Hubbell, Dean's chief rival as the best pitcher in the league, threw a four-hitter at the Phils in New York, winning, 4–1, before 40,000. Hubbell, a left-handed screwball pitcher, would produce 21 wins against 12 losses, toss 313 innings, and lead the majors with a 2.30 ERA.

The player-manager of the world champion Giants, Bill Terry, made a remark back in February that he would regret. While being surrounded by a bunch of sportswriters, Terry was asked about the upcoming season. Roscoe McGowan of the *New York Times* asked, "How about Brooklyn, Bill?" Terry answered, "Brooklyn? Is Brooklyn still in the league?"[5] The writers laughed. Near the end of the season, Terry's Giants hosted the Dodgers in two games that would decide New York's fate in the pennant race. The Dodgers would remember Terry's little witty remark. It would come back to haunt him.

Paul Dean got his first start in the season's second game. He yielded a first-inning, two-run homer to the Bucs' Pie Traynor and a home run to Gus Suhr in the second inning. He left the game trailing, 4–0, after just two innings. The Cards got him off the hook by tying the game at 6–6 before Cookie Lavagetto decided it for Pittsburgh with a homer in the eighth inning. Cards player-manager Frankie Frisch told Paul afterward, "You've got the speed, but it won't matter how hard you throw. If it's down the middle, these fellows are going to hit it."[6] Paul was a 20-year-old, 6'0" 175-pound right-hand fastball pitcher. During the second half of the season he would be dubbed "Daffy" by the writers, but he was actually shy and serious.

On April 22, the Cubs knocked Diz out of the box during a 15–2 romp. The Cubs were still angry at Diz for ridiculing them after he struck out 17 in his triumph the previous July. On April 28, the Cubs drove Diz from the mound again with four runs in the third inning on the way to a 7–1 win. Two days later Diz was hit hard yet again, this time by the Reds. He gave up nine hits and five runs before being lifted in the seventh inning, but the Cards' bats bailed him out with a 10–6 win. As April closed the Cubs were on top at 10–2, with the Giants right behind at 8–3. The Cards were struggling at 4–7.

The Cards then got hot as a pistol, winning 12 of 13 games. Diz earned his first of seven saves on the year on May 2. He rescued starter Tex Carleton after the first two Reds batters had singled in the ninth inning and preserved a 4–1 win. The next day Paul earned his first win after pitching five innings in relief, although he was hit hard by the Phils. Medwick's grand slam powered the Cards to an 8–7 win.

Medwick batted .319 with 40 doubles, 18 triples, 18 homers, and 106 RBIs in 1934. He was nicknamed "Ducky" because of his waddling walk. On May 15 he cut in front of Carleton during batting practice and slugged Carleton when Tex objected. He was the Cards' clean-up hitter and the least-liked member of the team. In 17 seasons, Ducky ripped 2,471 hits and batted .324.

On May 5, Diz was back in form, striking out seven while stopping the Phils, 7–1. On May 9, the Giants arrived in St. Louis and Diz shut them out, 4–0, fanning seven batters. Two days later Paul outdueled Hubbell in ten innings, 3–2. the *Sporting News* reported; "The youngster from Columbus, who has shown but little in previous assignments, matched Carl Hubbell, ace of the world's champions, all the way and looked every inch a big league hurler."[7] Diz told the writers, "Them Giants don't have a pig's chance in winter of beatin' me 'n' Paul."[8]

Diz beat Brooklyn, 12–7, on May 13 despite five errors committed by his infielders. On May 17 in Boston, Paul beat the Braves, 5–3, socking a single and a double and scoring twice in the process. The Cards invaded the Polo Grounds on May 20 and Diz beat Hubbell, 9–5. Medwick and Cards first baseman James "Ripper" Collins homered. Collins had a career season in 1934 while batting .333 with 35 homers and 128 RBIs. He was a former coal miner who liked singing cowboy songs. He dabbled as a part-time journalist, contributing short stories to newspapers and enjoyed nightclubs.[9] His 35 homers tied him with the Giants' Mel Ott for the NL crown in 1934.

On May 22 Paul beat the Giants again, 7–4, for his fourth win and third complete game in a row. Medwick's bases-loaded triple in the ninth inning off Dolf Luque decided the issue. In Philadelphia on May 27, Diz beat the Phils, 5–2, winning his own game with a mammoth homer through a strong wind at Baker Bowl in the tenth inning. The next day the Cards' Bill Hallahan blanked the Phils, 10–0, as St. Louis took over undisputed possession of first place with a 22–13 record. The standings were tight as a drum with Pittsburgh, New York, and Chicago all within 1½ games. This was the day that bank robbers Bonnie and Clyde were shot in Louisiana. A total of 167 bullets were fired into their car as they raced along, trying to escape an ambush by the Texas Rangers.

On Memorial Day the Cards beat the Reds in a doubleheader, 9–6 and 9–2. Paul and Diz combined to win the first game, with Diz going the final 1⅔ innings. Catcher Bill DeLancey led the Redbird offense with two singles, a triple, a home run, and four RBIs. Carleton, who won 16 games against 11 losses in 241 innings, went the route in the second game, backed by five hits from Medwick, the guy who had slugged him in the batting cage two weeks earlier. DeLancey was a country boy like Diz. He hailed from North Carolina and hit .316 with 13 homers in 253 at-bats while platooning at catcher with Virgil Davis. He was usually the catcher when the Deans pitched.

On the last day of May the Cards beat the Reds again, 3–2, in ten innings. Paul pitched the tenth inning in relief to get credit for one of his two saves on the year. After the game Diz told Frisch that neither he nor Paul would pitch another game for the Cards unless Paul received a $2,000 raise.

Diz had been pestering Frisch day and night about getting Paul more money. When the Cards arrived in Pittsburgh the next day, Diz was scheduled to take the mound. Diz informed Frisch that he had a sore arm and couldn't pitch. Frisch told Diz to get out of his uniform if he didn't want to pitch, and added that Paul could do the same if he had a sore arm too.[10] Paul remained in uniform, but Diz changed into civilian clothes and watched the game from the grandstand at Forbes Field. The Pirates scored three times in the ninth to upend the Cards, 4–3.

Diz told the press, "Frisch promised me in New York he would see to it that Paul got some more money, but last night he tells me he ain't goin' to do nothin' a the sort. I'm satisfied with my contract — even if I ain't gettin' half a what I'm worth (Diz's salary was $7,500) — but it ain't right to expect my brother to pitch the way he can pitch for what he's makin.'"[11] Paul's record was 5–0 and Diz's was 6–2. What happened next is not known. Owner Sam Breadon probably told Paul that he would be well compensated sometime during the year if he kept pitching well. At any rate Diz returned to action the next day and beat the Bucs, 13–4, backed by a triple, two home runs, and seven RBIs from Collins.

On June 5, Paul outpitched the Cubs' Lon Warneke, 4–3, as Collins' two-run homer put the Cards ahead to stay. The next day the Cubs knocked Diz out with five runs in five innings. Paul came in later in the game and pitched three shutout innings, but the North Siders scored six times in the thirteenth inning to win, 12–6. The Cards thought they had the game won when Medwick appeared to slide in safe on a close play at the plate in the twelfth. But to the surprise of the 4,700 fans present, he was called out by umpire Charles Rigler. Frisch stormed out of the dugout and bumped Rigler, who in turn swung his mask at Frisch. Both were subsequently fined $100 by NL president John Heydler. The loss knocked the Cards out of first place.

June would not be a good month for St. Louis. The Cards struggled, winning 13 games and losing 14. The Deans accounted for 11 of the 13 St. Louis wins. On June 10, Diz went all the way while beating Pittsburgh, 3–2. He said of the Pirates afterward, "They really aren't tough, if you know how to pitch. ... Why, those palookas are lucky whenever they get a run off me and Paul."[12] Two days later Paul scattered 13 hits to beat Boston, 7–3, backed by a single, triple, and home run from Martin. On June 14, Diz pitched three innings in relief of a 12–9 win over the Braves, highlighted by shortstop Leo Durocher's inside-the-park grand slam.

Martin came from Oklahoma, and played third base with his chest as well as his glove. He hit .289 in the lead-off spot and paced the league with 23 stolen bases, specializing in head-first slides. Rickey enjoyed spreading a ridiculous story of how Martin was discovered by scout Charlie Barrett. The story goes that Barrett was driving 60 miles per hour on the plains of Oklahoma and suddenly looked up to see a jackrabbit run by his car while being pursued by Martin. "Anyone who can run that fast can play baseball," Barrett was supposed to have said before stopping his automobile to sign Martin.

On June 17, Paul shut out the Phils, 6–0, in the first game of a doubleheader and Diz hurled three innings to win the second game in relief, 7–5. On June 21, Diz won his tenth of the year by stifling the Dodgers, 9–2. The next day Paul fanned ten batters and beat Brooklyn again, 7–2, for his ninth win. Frisch whacked five hits and Collins pumped his 16th homer. The day after that Diz pitched three innings of scoreless relief, handing the Dodgers another defeat, 5–4.

The league-leading Giants arrived in St. Louis for a four-game series on June 24. The strength of the Giants lay in their four top hitters — Bill Terry, Mel Ott, Travis Jackson, and Jo-Jo Moore — plus a pitching staff that led the majors with a 3.19 ERA. They were the defending world champs, having defeated the Washington Senators in the 1933 World Series in five games. The Broadwayites won the first two games by 9–7 and 10–7 scores, respectively. Paul went the distance despite giving up 15 hits to win game three, 13–7. Diz won game four, 8–7, on DeLancey's ninth-inning homer. As the month closed, Diz was sporting a 12–3 record while Paul's record was 10–2. They appeared in 18 of the Cards' 27 games in June. The Cards' record was 38–27. It was becoming increasingly clear that St. Louis would be nowhere without the Deans.

On June 29, Gary Schumacher of the *New York Evening Journal* wrote, "The Deans are all the St. Louis fans talk about. When anybody else starts on the mound, the fans chant in unison, 'We want Dean.'"[13]

As July opened Diz pitched 17 innings of an 18-inning, 8–6 win in Cincinnati. Diz and Paul were not complaining about their work load despite enduring one of the hottest summers of the century. Since May the Midwest had been going through a wicked heat wave that would last the entire summer and kill more than 1,000 people. Missouri was facing a terrible farm crisis as no rain had been in sight for weeks. In St. Louis the temperature was 100 degrees or hotter for thirty days.[14] In addition to the sweltering heat, there were terrible dust storms that ruined farms. Children would die of dust pneumonia, and families would sleep with their faces covered by wet towels. An entire region would be turned into a worthless Dust Bowl. With the dust, the drought, and the Depression, hundreds of thousands of refugees took to the road to escape their situation.

Diz was thrown out of a game along with Frisch on July 2 for disputing the alleged failure of umpire Bill Klem to call an infield fly with the bases loaded. Paul and the Cards lost the game, 7–4, to the second-place Cubs.

The Cubs trailed the Giants by two games, with the Cards perched four games back. The Deans had Independence Day off while the Cards and Cubs swapped 4–2 decisions in a doubleheader before 21,500 in St. Louis. In New York the Giants celebrated the nation's birthday by routing the Braves twice, 9–1 and 15–0, before 43,000. Freddie Fitzsimmons and Hubbell pitched strong games while the Giants ripped 29 hits, including two home runs each by Mel Ott and Lefty O'Doul. The next day the Giants poured it on the Braves, 13–7, with 15 hits, including a pinch-hit grand slam by Jo-Jo Moore. The Giants looked like the class of the league.

On July 8, Diz mowed down the Reds in the first game of a doubleheader with ten strikeouts in a 6–1 win over Paul Derringer. Paul Dean was knocked out with six runs in the third inning of the second game as the Reds rebounded to win, 8–4. The Reds rode the younger Dean hard with some tough bench-jockeying, prompting him to walk off the mound and challenge the entire Cincinnati dugout. He was intercepted by Collins at first base, but soon brother Diz was buzzing around in front of the Cincinnati bench, challenging the Reds to come out and fight.

The All-Star game was held before 48,363 fans at the Polo Grounds, and Hubbell outpolled Diz in the fans vote, 86,000 to 62,000. Hubbell started the contest, hurled three scoreless innings, and became the talk of baseball when he fanned Ruth, Gehrig, Foxx, Simmons, and Joe Cronin in succession. But the AL triumphed, 9–7, teeing off on Warneke and Van Lingle Mungo for eight runs. Diz appeared in the seventh and allowed one run and five hits in three innings.

The Cards began the second half of the season with bad luck on July 12 when Paul sprained his ankle sliding into third base in Philadelphia. He was carried from the field. Diz took the mound and pitched 3⅔ innings of shutout ball, fanning eight and picking up his 15th win, 8–5. In Brooklyn on July 15, Diz blew away the Dodgers, 2–0, with a four-hitter and drilled a homer.

It was during this visit to Brooklyn that three sportswriters were sent on the same day to do a feature story on Diz. Tommy Holmes of the *Brooklyn Eagle*, Bill McCullough of the *Brooklyn Times-Union*, and Roscoe McGowen of the *New York Times* all took turns sitting with Diz in the clubhouse.

Diz was asked by each of the writers where and when he was born. He later described his answers. "Tommy comes first and I told him I was born in Lucas, Arkansas, January 16, 1911. Then McCullough comes along and I wasn't going to have his boss bawl him out for gettin' the same story, so I told him I was born at Bond, Mississippi. That's where my wife comes from, and I pick February 22. McGowen wanted the same story but I give him a break and told him Holdenville, Oklahoma, August 22. They do their stories and their bosses are all happy with em' see, because they all got their scoops."[15]

On July 19 in Boston, Diz beat the Braves, 4–2, producing the go-ahead run with an RBI fly ball in the sixth. The Cards came into New York for a four-game series on July 23, trailing the Giants by four games. Diz went all the way in the opener, winning for the fourth time of the season against the world champs, 6–5. Collins went 5-for-5 with his 21st homer. In Chicago gangster John Dillinger was finally shot down by FBI agents on his way out of a movie theater.

Roy Parmelee shut out the Cards on four singles the following day, 5–0, to even the series. In game three, Paul made his first start since spraining his ankle and lasted seven innings, limiting the Giants to six hits and two runs. Diz relieved and retired the last six batters in order as the Cards won, 7–2. New York's Fitzsimmons won the final game, 6–3, and Terry's team retained their four-game advantage.

The Cards opened August in Chicago as Paul blanked the Cubs on five hits, 4–0. In Boston, the Giants pounded the Braves for 30 hits in sweeping a doubleheader, 11–2 and 10–3. Hal Schumacher coasted on the mound for his 16th victory and banged his fifth homer of the year in the second game. He finished 1934 with a 23–10 record and 3.18 ERA in 297 innings. Ott had two homers, three doubles, a single, and seven RBIs. He ended 1934 at .326 with a league-leading 35 homers and 135 RBIs.

On August 3, Diz scattered 11 hits in beating the Pirates, 9–3. He also doubled, tripled, scored twice, and drove in two runs. The next day he bailed out Carleton after Pittsburgh had scored twice in the ninth inning, and nailed down a 6–4 win. On August 7 in Cincinnati, Diz whitewashed the Reds on six hits, 2–0, for his 20th win. Twenty-four hours later he relieved Paul in the tenth inning and pitched three shutout innings to gain win number 21. Medwick's bases-loaded triple was the big blow in a six-run Cards rally in the twelfth. The Redbirds won, 10–4.

Back home in St. Louis, the Cards routed Chicago's Warneke with nine runs in the third inning in a 21-hit, 17–3 win. The Cards' great double-play combination of Frisch and Durocher socked four singles each. At age 35, Frisch was in the midst of the 16th season of a Hall of Fame career. As a manager he was a tough-minded leader in the tradition of his former skipper, John McGraw. As a second baseman, he batted third in the lineup and hit .305. He was known as a money player.

Durocher was the team captain and the best fielding shortstop in baseball. He was also its sharpest dresser and a frequenter of the most expensive nightclubs. He lived beyond his means yet somehow managed to survive. He batted eighth in the Cardinals lineup and hit .260. He was reputed to be the most dangerous .260 hitter in either league. His hits seemed to come at times when they hurt the opposition the most. He drove in 70 runs.

A crowd of 36,073 fans were at Sportsman's Park for a Sunday double-header against the Cubs on August 12. Both Deans were scheduled to pitch, but the Cubs clubbed Paul in the opener, 7–2, as Babe Herman and Billy Herman homered. They then racked up Diz in the second game, 6–4, as Kiki Cuyler ripped two singles, a double, and a triple. This was the first time that both Deans had lost on the same day, and the defeats pushed the Cards 7½ games behind the Giants.

After the game, the St. Louis players were told to hurry to the train depot for a trip to Detroit. The Cardinals were scheduled to play the Tigers in an exhibition game. Diz and Paul decided to disobey orders. There were 40,000 fans at Navin Field in Detroit, many of them young boys waiting to see the amazing Dean brothers. They were disappointed when the Deans did not show.

In the Cards' clubhouse the next morning, Frisch came out of a meeting with Breadon and Rickey and told Diz he was fined $100. He told Paul that he was fined $50. Diz claimed that he didn't make the trip because his arm was sore, and Paul said that his ankle hadn't healed completely. Frisch said the fines would stick. When Diz and Paul refused to go out on the field, Frisch told them to take off their uniforms. Diz took off his uniform and ripped it to shreds. The two brothers threatened to go fishing in Florida for the rest of the year.

The Deans sat behind the Philadelphia dugout wise-cracking and signing autographs. They later moved to the press box before leaving in the fourth inning. The Cards won, 6–1, as old-timers Dazzy Vance and Jesse Haines combined pitching efforts. Diz told the press, "The Cards don't need us none now. Anybody can beat them Phillies, but the Giants are comin' in here next week and we figure Rickey will be beggin' us to let them give us our money back. It takes ol' Diz 'n' Paul to stop them Giants and he knows it."[16]

The Cardinal management showed no signs of caving in. Rickey called Diz's bluff by offering to pay for a one-way train ticket to Florida. The public turned against the Deans. Baseball was struggling through the Depression, fighting for its survival. Only 256,171 fans came out to see the Cards in 1933 and just 325,056 showed in 1934. More than 17 million people were on relief. The Deans were viewed as spoiled brats who should be happy they had a job.

Diz and Paul decided to end their revolt and pay the fines. The Cards reinstated Paul immediately but decided to punish Diz by suspending him for ten days without pay. On August 17, Paul pitched seven innings of shutout relief as the Cards beat the Phils for the fourth straight time, 12–2. On August 19, however, he relieved and gave up the winning run in the ninth inning of a 10–9 loss against Boston in the first game of a doubleheader. The Cards won the second game of the day, 3–1, behind Bill Walker for their sixth triumph in seven games without Diz.

Dizzy had been ready to apologize and rejoin the team immediately. When he was hit with the suspension, he decided to plead his case to Commissioner Landis. He drove to Chicago to ask the baseball czar for a hearing. Landis set the hearing for the morning of August 20 at the Park Plaza Hotel in St. Louis.

With Breadon, Rickey, Frisch, and Durocher present, Landis listened to both parties and sided with the Cards management. Diz was ordered to make a public apology to his team and wire an apology to the Tigers. Breadon said he would reduce the suspension to seven days if everyone else agreed, which they did. Diz took his medicine, saying, "I weren't meant to be no lawyer, anyway"[17] and blanked the Giants with a five-hitter four days later, 5–0. On August 28, Paul shut out the Dodgers, 2–0, for his 14th win. On the last day of August, Diz beat the Cubs, 3–1, for his first conquest of the Bruins since the 17-strikeout game. He had failed in seven previous starts. The win left the Cards and Cubs tied for second place, 5½ games behind New York.

If the Cards had any chance of catching the Giants, they seemed to blow it in a doubleheader loss on Labor Day in Pittsburgh. In the opener Paul was shelled for eight runs in the third inning as the Bucs won, 12–2. Diz relieved Walker in the ninth inning of the second game with the Cards leading, 5–3. He proceeded to get tagged for three runs as the Bucs rallied to win again, 6–5. Meanwhile, the Giants beat the Phils with dramatic ninth-inning rallies twice in Philadelphia, 3–2 and 6–5. Hank Leiber's RBI double decided the first game as Hubbell won his 19th. Jo-Jo Moore's two-run homer won the second game, and the Giants' lead stood at seven games.

Frisch remembered his players arriving at the clubhouse at Ebbets Field with their heads hanging on September 5. He delivered a scalding pep talk, and later told writer Sid Keener, "I burned them like they'd never been burned before. 'Are you fellows going to quit now?' I shouted. 'This race is just getting hot. It's not over yet and don't give up. We're going to fight to the finish, and, I'm telling you, we won't be beaten"[18]

Diz then fired a three-hitter at the Dodgers, defeating them, 2–1, for his 24th win. Collins tied the game with a homer in the eighth inning and DeLancey won it with a ninth-inning blast. On September 9, the Cards swept a twin-bill from the Phils, 6–1 and 7–3. Paul won the first game with a ten-strikeout four-hitter. At the Polo Grounds, Pittsburgh's Larry French beat Fitzsimmons, 1–0, on Gus Suhr's ninth-inning homer. Diz beat the Phils, 4–1, the next day with a five-hitter while whiffing seven. In New York, the Pirates scored five runs in the ninth inning to upend the Giants, 9–7. The Giants made three crucial errors. Hubbell tried to rescue Schumacher in the ninth but failed. The momentum was shifting.

The Cards entered the Polo Grounds on September 13 trailing by 5½ games. In the opener Paul pitched a gem, beating Fitzsimmons, 1–0, in 12 innings. Schumacher evened the series by beating Walker in game two, 4–1. On September 16, a then–NL record crowd of 62,573 showed up as both Deans took on the Giants in a doubleheader. Diz went six innings in the opener, yielding three runs before retiring for a pinch-hitter. The Cards rallied for four runs in the seventh frame to win, 5–3. Paul then outpitched Hubbell for a 3–1 win in 11 innings. Collins' homer in the seventh inning tied the game and Martin's homer in the eleventh decided it. The Giants' lead was down to 3½ games.

The Cards were idle the next two days while New York won two of three against the Reds. Their only loss came when Cincy's Bennie Frey beat Fitzsimmons in 10 innings, 2–0, on a Chick Hafey homer. The Giants had not scored for Fitzsimmons in 31 innings. On September 20, the Cards won twice in Boston, 4–1 and 1–0, on stellar pitching efforts by Carleton and Walker. In New York, Hubbell stopped the Reds, 4–3, winning his own game with an RBI single in the ninth inning.

On September 21, 18,000 fans turned out at Ebbets Field to see the Dean brothers face the Dodgers in a doubleheader. Diz won the first game easy, 13–0, and didn't allow a hit until Buzz Boyle beat out a slow infield roller in the eighth inning. Paul won the second game with a no-hit masterpiece, 3–0. Legend has it that Diz exclaimed afterward, "If I'd'a knowed Paul was goin' to pitch a no-hitter, I'd'a throwed one, too." But if he did say this it didn't appear in any major newspapers.[19]

Diz did tell Roy Stockton of the *St. Louis Post-Dispatch*, "I didn't know that I had a no-hitter. I was way out front and I was just coasting along. Boy if I had known that I was so near to a no-hitter I'd have given those Dodgers so much smoke and fancy curves that they wouldn't have even seen the ball."[20]

The Giants' lead dwindled to 2½ games the following day as Schumacher walked in the winning run in the eleventh inning to hand the Braves a 3–2 win in Boston. The Cards split two in Cincinnati on September 23, while the Giants split two in Boston. The Giants were idle the following day, and the Redbirds' Walker befuddled the Cubs in Chicago, 3–1, on the strength of Martin's two-run homer. The Giants' lead was just two games.

Durocher recalled in his autobiography a clubhouse meeting that Frisch called to discuss the final games. Diz told his manager, "I'll pitch today, and if I get in trouble Paul will relieve me. And he'll pitch tomorrow, and if he gets in trouble I'll relieve him. And I'll pitch the next day and Paul will pitch the day after that and I'll pitch the last one. Don't worry, we'll win five straight."[21]

On September 25, Diz outpitched Pittsburgh's Larry French, 3–2, surviving a two-run homer by Arky Vaughan in the ninth inning. In New York, Philly's Curt Davis threw a four-hit shutout at the Giants. The lead was down to a single game. The next afternoon Pittsburgh's veteran Waite Hoyt outdueled Paul, 3–0, yielding just two hits as Vaughan connected for another two-run homer. In Manhattan, Giants catcher Gus Mancuso slugged two homers and drove in four runs but allowed the winning run to score on a passed ball in the ninth inning as the Phils won, 5–4.

On September 27, the Giants were idle and the Cards took advantage of three errors by Cincinnati to score five runs in the first inning and beat Derringer, 8–5. The Giants were idle again on September 28, and Diz shut out the Reds, 2–0, on two days' rest in a sprinkle of rain in St. Louis. The Cards and Giants were now in a flat-footed tie with two games remaining.

The full-page headline in Saturday's *Brooklyn Eagle* shouted: "DODGERS SET TO SHOW THEY ARE IN LEAGUE." Brooklyn beat the Giants in the last two games, 5–1 and 8–5, to knock New York out of the pennant race. St. Louis won twice. Paul beat Cincinnati, 6–1, on two days' rest, scattering 11 hits. Diz, pitching on one day's rest, then blanked the Reds, 9–0. A crowd of 37,402 saw him win his 30th game, supported by homers from DeLancey and Collins. The Cards had won 19 of their last 24 games; 11 of the wins were recorded by the Deans.

In the Cardinal clubhouse, Martin and Medwick were singing "I Want a Girl Just Like the Girl That Married Dear Old Dad."[22] Frisch was being interviewed on NBC radio. Dean seemed uncharacteristically quiet. In the past five days he had hurled 27 innings, yielding two runs. Three days later he opened the World Series in Detroit on two days' rest.

The 1934 Detroit Tigers were loaded with talent. Player-manager Mickey Cochrane hit .320 and caught 129 games. The Tigers hit .300 and led the majors with 958 runs. They were led by Charley Gehringer (.356, 127 RBIs, 134 runs), "Goose" Goslin (.305, 100 RBIs, 106 runs) and Hank Greenberg (.339, 139 RBIs, 118 runs, 26 homers, 63 doubles). Detroit won 101 games.

Cochrane decided not to throw his ace, "Schoolboy" Rowe, against Diz in the opener. A crowd of 42,502 saw Diz win, 8–3, besting surprise starter Alvin Crowder. Medwick was the batting hero with four hits, including a home run. Game 2 belonged to Schoolboy Rowe as the Tigers beat the Cards in 12 innings, 3–2, on Goslin's RBI single. Rowe was awesome, retiring 26 of the last 27 batters. Back in St. Louis in Game 3 the Tigers had Paul Dean on the ropes in several innings. But Paul escaped from the predicaments like Harry Houdini to best Tommy Bridges, 4–1. Martin jump-started the Redbird offense by doubling, tripling, and scoring twice.

The Tiger bats woke up in Game 4 tagging five Cardinal pitchers for 13 hits in a 10–4 win. Greenberg singled twice, doubled twice, and drove in three runs. Frisch put Diz in the game as a pinch-runner in the fourth inning. Diz was hit in the right temple by a throw while trying to break up a double play. The crowd of 37,492 at Sportsman's Park held its breath in silence as Diz stumbled for several steps and collapsed unconscious. After several minutes he regained consciousness and was carried from the field. Dean's first utterance when he came to was, "They didn't get Pepper at first, did they?"[23]

Diz was scheduled to pitch the next day, but many believed he might not be able to. Tests revealed, however, that no serious damage had been done. Legend says that headlines in the papers read, "X-RAYS OF DEAN'S HEAD REVEAL NOTHING." A crowd of 38,536 saw Bridges outpitch Diz, though, as the Tigers won, 3–1, to go up 3–2 in the Series.

Thousands arrived at the train station in Detroit to greet the Tigers. With Rowe scheduled to pitch Game 6 44,551 Tiger rooters filled Navin Field. Paul Dean opposed Rowe. With the score tied at 1–1 in the fifth, Durocher singled through the box. Paul dropped a good sacrifice bunt, and Martin lined a single to left. Goslin's throw to the plate went wild as Durocher scored. Martin flew all the way to third base and then scored on Jack Rothrock's ground-ball out. The Cards led, 3–1.

The Tigers narrowed the gap to 3–2 in the sixth, helped by a bobble by Paul on a soft tapper off the bat of Gehringer. With runners on first and second and nobody out, Goslin dropped a bunt. DeLancey fired a bullet to Martin at third, forcing Cochrane. The Tigers insisted Cochrane was safe. Photos taken of the play support the Tigers' contention.[24] It was the turning point of the Series. Greenberg singled in Gehringer to tie the game at 3–3, but Paul escaped further damage.

Durocher laced a double off Rowe in the seventh. Paul then singled to right, chasing Durocher home. Paul stayed tough in the pinches by retiring Greenberg on a pop-up with two runners on base in the eighth. The Cards lived to played another day with a 4–3 victory.

The question now was who Frisch would start on the mound for Game 7 against Eldon Auker. Diz had only one day's rest. Hallahan pitched eight strong innings in Game 2 and was the winner of two games in the 1931 World Series. He was well rested.

Before the game Frisch asked Diz, "How do you feel?"

Diz replied, "You wouldn't think of pitching anybody else with the greatest pitcher in the world sitting here?"

Frisch said, "Great. As far as I'm concerned, that's all I have to hear. Pay attention. We'll go over the hitters."

As Frisch carefully discussed each hitter, Diz seemed impatient. Finally, he stood up and told Frisch, "What the hell you going over the hitters for? They're not going to get any runs off of me." He then began pulling the musical instruments of Pepper Martin's Mudcat Band out of a trunk. He handed the instruments to his teammates and soon they were singing "She'll Be Coming, 'Round the Mountain."

Frisch began cussing out Diz and announced, "Hallahan is the pitcher!"[25]

Durocher recalled begging Diz to go over and apologize to Frisch. Diz couldn't believe Frisch would not pitch him. Durocher wrote in the names of the starters on the lineup card per Frisch's instructions before bringing it to home plate. He desperately wanted Diz to pitch. In his autobiography he described the moments just prior to game time: "When we were ready to go out, I said to Frank, 'He's going to pitch, isn't he?' Frank said, 'That dirty sonafa —.' I said, 'He'll be great, Frank. Isn't he great? He's ready today, you can see how ready he is, can't you, Frank?' And when Frank didn't say anything, I whipped the card out, wrote J. Dean in the pitcher's spot and shoved it back in my pocket."[26]

Diz fired a six-hit shutout. He did not walk a batter and struck out Greenberg three times. With one out in the third inning, Diz blooped a single to right and then shocked Goslin by stretching it into a double. Martin beat out a tapper to Greenberg with Diz racing into third. Martin stole second on the first pitch and the rattled Auker walked Rothrock to load the bases. Frisch ran the count to 2-and-2, fouled off four pitches, and rammed a three-run double over first base. That was the ballgame.

Cochrane brought in Rowe, Chief Hogsett, and Bridges as the Cards scored seven times. Diz came up again in the inning with the bases loaded, topped the ball down the third-base line, and beat it out. After the big inning Diz was in his glory while chuckling with everybody. Frisch tried to tell him that it was still early in the game. Diz replied to Frisch's instructions to sit down and rest by answering, "It's all over. I told you at the meeting, one was all I needed. They're not going to get any."[27]

In the sixth inning Medwick tripled and slid hard into Detroit third baseman Marv Owen. As Owen tripped and accidentally came down on Medwick's leg, Ducky kicked at him. Owen and Medwick had words and were separated. Both dugouts emptied. This was a Series of country hardball, with more than the usual bench-jockeying, jarring collisions, and flying spikes. The Cardinals earned their nickname of the "Gas House Gang" in the Series. Joe Williams of the *World-Telegram* described the Redbirds as a "bunch of boys from the *gas house* district who had crossed the railroad tracks for a game of ball with the nice kids."[28]

When Medwick took his position, the frustrated Tiger fans vented their disappointment by showering him with garbage. Commissioner Landis demanded that Frisch remove Medwick from the contest so the game could continue. The Cards won the lopsided affair, 11–0.

After pitching three complete games in the last five days of the regular season, Diz had pitched another three complete games in seven days during the World Series. In 26 innings he compiled a 1.73 ERA in the World Series with 17 strikeouts. Paul had pitched 18 innings with 11 strikeouts, a 1.00 ERA, and the other two St. Louis victories.

Diz went 28–12 in 1935 and 24–13 in 1936. In 1937 he was at 12–7 when he was chosen to start the All-Star game. In the third inning of the contest Earl Averill slashed a line drive that broke the big toe in Dean's left foot. Diz tried to pitch again before the toe healed. He felt something pop in his arm and his legendary fastball was gone forever. He was traded to the Cubs in 1938 and pitched part-time for three more seasons before retiring in 1941. In the five years, from 1932 to 1936, Diz averaged 24 wins, 306⅔ innings and 194 strikeouts per season with a 3.04 ERA while pitching in an era friendly to hitters. Paul went 19–12 in 1935 and then hurt his arm in 1936, never enjoying pitching success again.

After leaving the Cubs, Diz announced the St. Louis Browns games on radio. He was a natural with his quick wit, country charm, and knowledge of the game. He butchered the English language in his descriptions of the action. Many of his remarks ("The baserunner slud into third base" and "The players returned to their respectable bases") temporarily drew the ire of English teachers throughout the country. But in the end he was well respected by the majority of his listeners.

Diz later signed to announce television's *CBS Game of the Week*, where he became a popular voice for more than a decade. Hollywood produced a movie of his life entitled *Pride of St. Louis*. He and Pat managed their money well and made solid investments. When he retired from broadcasting, the former son of a cotton-picker was a millionaire.

Chapter 9

Larrupin' Lou and McCarthy's Bombers: Lou Gehrig in 1936

Henry Louis Gehrig was the greatest run producer ever. In 17 seasons with the Yankees, the left-handed first baseman drove in 1,995 runs in 2,164 games, an average of .9219 RBIs per contest. No major leaguer ever had a better RBI per-game percentage. The 6'1", 205-pound "Iron Horse" was at his best with men on base. Hits ricocheted off his bat like cannon shots while runners circled the basepaths as if on a pinball machine treadmill. He crashed a record 23 grand slams. Over a span of 13 consecutive seasons he averaged 147 RBIs per campaign. This is amazing because Lou batted behind two of history's greatest base-cleaners in Babe Ruth and Joe DiMaggio.

Gehrig scored 1,888 times, an average of .8725 runs per contest. No post–1900 player has had a higher per-game ratio. For 13 straight seasons "Laruppin' Lou" scored more than 100 runs. Lou could run well for a big man. In 1926 he led the AL in triples with 20 and added 18 triples in 1927. He stole home 15 times in his career.

For many seasons Lou played in the shadow of Ruth. The extent of his run production was lost in the public eye due to the flamboyance of the Bambino. Tirelessly, Lou plugged away in 2,130 consecutive games while maintaining his unmatched production. Yet no matter what Lou did, Ruth was the idol of millions and the guy that put people in the stands. At one point, Ruth drew a salary of $80,000. Lou's highest salary was $39,500.

Gehrig summed up his feelings of playing second fiddle to Babe: "I'm not a headline guy, and we might as well face it. I'm just a guy who's in there every day, the fellow who follows the Babe in the batting order. When Babe's turn at bat is over, whether he strikes out or belts a home run, the fans are still talking about him when I come up. If I stood on my head at the plate, nobody'd pay any attention."[1]

Joe DiMaggio once wrote, "Gehrig was the type of ball player to command respect, even if you weren't his teammate. To see his broad back and muscular arms as he spread himself at the plate was to give the impression of power as no other ball player I ever saw gave it." Gehrig still holds the career record for most RBIs per game, and for a span of 13 straight seasons he averaged 147 RBIs.

In 1936 Gehrig emerged from Ruth's shadow. With the Babe retired, Lou took over as leader of the Yankees. He tied a career high with 49 homers to top the AL and also led the league in runs (167), walks (130), on-base percentage (.478), and slugging percentage (.696). He batted .354, drove home 152 runs, and amassed 403 total bases to power the Yankees to their first pennant since 1932.

Everything went right for Lou in 1936. He belted his first All-Star game home run at Braves Field. In October he drilled two key home runs in the World Series as the Yanks beat the Giants, four games to two. His home run off Carl Hubbell was the deciding blow in sending "the Meal Ticket" down to his first defeat in 18 games. The homer was noted as the turning point of the Series.

In 1936 Lou got some overdue recognition. His picture appeared on the cover of *Time* magazine. Offers came for him to endorse products. For the second time in his career, he was voted MVP, and he was recognized by most fans as simply the best player in baseball. In June 1936, the *Sporting News* said of Gehrig, "He never looked better in his life, and he is 33."[2] Lou appeared to have many productive years left in pinstripes. His physique was so impressive that in the offseason after 1936 he was sought by Hollywood to succeed Johnny Weissmuller in Tarzan movies. He posed in promotion photos wearing leopard skin before producers decided Gehrig's legs were too muscular.

Three years after reaching his crescendo, the seemingly indestructible "Iron Horse" took himself out of the Yankee lineup. He had started the 1939 season's first eight games, but managed only four singles in 28 at-bats. He felt as weak as a kitten. He checked into the Mayo Clinic in Minnesota in June 1939, where it was learned he was suffering from amyotrophic lateral sclerosis. The affliction is known nowadays as "Lou Gehrig's Disease" and results in an incurable physical deterioration before death. Many times ALS strikes people who appear to be the strongest and healthiest. Lou was just 35 years old.

On July 4, 1939, Gehrig stood before a microphone and told 62,000 people at Yankee Stadium, "Fans, for the past two weeks you have been reading about a bad break I got. Yet today I consider myself the luckiest man on the face of the earth. I have been in ball parks for 17 years and I have never received anything but kindness and encouragement from you fans." Lou talked for several minutes, thanking his parents for pointing him in the right direction. He thanked his wife, Eleanor, saying she "has been a tower of strength and shown more courage than you dreamed existed," and ended by saying, "I might have had a bad break, but I have an awful lot to live for."[3] The rafters of Yankee Stadium shook from a thunderous ovation as the great man walked off the diamond.

Less than two years after making his farewell speech, Gehrig died in June 1941. A movie of his life story entitled *Pride of the Yankees* became a box-office success in 1942. Gary Cooper was nominated for an Academy Award for his portrayal of Gehrig. During World War II, when Cooper toured military posts near combat zones, the GIs never failed to call on him to recite Gehrig's speech. As Cooper re-enacted that emotional moment, the usually raucous GIs listened in respectful silence.[4]

Gehrig was born in New York City in 1903, the son of German immigrant parents. His mother, Christina, had four children but only Lou lived past infancy. His father was an art-metal mechanic who suffered health problems and was out of work for long periods. For much of Lou's youth, it was up to his mother, a tall woman who weighed 200 pounds, to put food on the table. She said of Lou, "He's the only big egg I have in my basket. He's the only one of four who lived, so I want him to be the best."[5] While his mother worked full-time at a Columbia University fraternity scrubbing, cooking, and cleaning, Lou pounded the pavement running errands to bring home nickels and dimes. Later he was noticed for his football and baseball skills at Commerce High.

Momma Gehrig saw sports as a means of getting Lou a scholarship to college. She said baseball was a "game for bummers." Lou received a football scholarship to Columbia, where he played fullback and tackle and studied engineering. While there, Lou waited on tables and performed other menial tasks at a fraternity to help finance his education. He also played minor league baseball at Hartford under the assumed name of Lou Lewis. He needed the extra money as his mother began having health problems. He was assured by Giants scout Art Devlin that playing for Hartford wouldn't affect his eligibility for college athletics.

When college officials discovered who the Lou Lewis in box scores for Hartford was, Gehrig was barred from participating in sports at Columbia. Columbia baseball coach Andy Coakley, however, persuaded officials that the youngster had made an innocent mistake. Lou got a second chance, and he starred as a pitcher and first baseman. He won six games pitching, struck out 17 batters against Williams College, and batted .444. Fifteen of his 28 hits went for extra bases, including seven homers. His slugging percentage was .937.

Yankee scout Paul Krichell asked Coakley about his team. Coakley said he had a pitcher worthy of Krichell's attention. Kritchell attended a game against Rutgers and Gehrig crushed two tremendous homers. Kritchell reported to Yankee general manager Ed Barrow, "I think I've just seen another Babe Ruth."[6] Barrow was skeptical and told Kritchell to take another look. The next game Kritchell saw, Lou belt a home run out of Columbia's South Field, with the ball bounding down the pavement of 116th Street, 450 feet away. That homer was the second longest hit in the history of South Field. The longest was one Lou hit three weeks later against Wesleyan. It bounced up the steps of the university's journalism school.[7]

Lou was signed with the Yankees for a $1,500 bonus and a first-year salary of $2,000. He quit college because money was desperately needed. His mother had a bout with pneumonia and his father needed a serious operation. Years later he said he had no choice.

After 13 games with the Yankees in 1923, Lou was sent to the minors at Hartford. There he fell into a slump, hitting .062. His manager, Paddy O'Connor, had been told by Barrow to put him on first base and leave him there, but O'Connor was running out of patience. He called Kritchell to complain.

For Lou, in the beginning of his baseball career it was always work, work, work to improve himself so he could send money home to take care of medical expenses. He spent almost nothing on himself. His roommate at Hartford, Harry Hesse, remembered, "I realized the guy didn't have a dime. ... After his father got over that operation, Lou sent them on the first vacation they ever had. To do it, he had to strip himself down to nothing. He didn't have money for clothes. He looked like a tramp. When he was in that first slump, I've never seen anyone suffer so much. He took everything to heart. He was a guy who needed friends, but didn't know how to go about getting them."[8]

Kritchell was sent to talk to Lou. There he found a homesick young man under a ton of emotional strain. Lou was convinced that he would never hit again. Kritchell recognized that his prospect's fear of failure was paralyzing him. He advised him to relax and to try to hit the ball through the middle. The talk worked wonders. Lou began to hit and soon his home runs started flying out of the Eastern League parks. He improved his average to .304 and finished with 24 homers. In 1924 Lou tore up minor league pitching, batting .383 with 37 homers at Hartford. He was promoted to New York in 1925.

On June 1, 1925, Lou's streak of 2,130 consecutive games started when he pinch-hit for Pee Wee Wanninger. The next day Wally Pipp was beaned in the temple in batting practice and sent to the hospital. He remained hospitalized for two weeks while Gehrig took over at first base. Pipp never got his job back, and was traded to Cincinnati. Lou batted .295 with 20 homers in 437 at-bats.

With Lou joining Ruth in the Yankee lineup in 1926, the Pinstripers battled to the top of the AL for the first time since 1923. They won pennants in 1926, 1927, and 1928 and world titles in 1927 and 1928. In 1927 Gehrig and Ruth were neck-and-neck in a battle for the home run crown. Ruth pulled away in the final month and hit 60. Lou tailed off in September and finished with 47. On September 7, Gehrig was batting .389 with 45 home runs and 161 RBIs. In the last 22 games, he hit .275 with two homers and 14 RBIs. Sportswriter Fred Lieb said Gehrig slumped because he was worried sick about his mother, who was suffering from an inflammation of the thyroid gland that required surgery. Lou said, "I'm so worried about Mom, that I can't see straight."[9] Gehrig did break Babe's then–single-season RBI record with 175.

When Miller Huggins died in 1929, Gehrig lost a real friend. From the start Huggins made a special project of working baseball savvy into Gehrig. Huggins once said of Gehrig, "Only Lou's willingness and lack of conceit will make him into a complete ball player. That and those muscles are all he has."[10]

Gehrig said of Huggins, "I guess I'll miss him more than anyone else. Next to my mother and father, he was the best friend a boy could have. When I first came up he told me I was the rawest, most awkward rookie he'd ever seen or come across in baseball. He taught me everything I know."[11]

In 1930 Gehrig was putting together his best season when bad luck struck. He finished the year batting .379 with 41 homers and 174 RBIs. One wonders what he could have done had he not played the final three weeks with a broken finger. After the last game Lou had his finger repaired with surgery. He also was suffering from bone chips in his elbow that required surgery.

In 1931, Joe McCarthy was hired as manager of the Yankees. Lou reset his own AL record with 184 RBIs. The A's superior pitching kept New York out of the World Series for a third consecutive year. Gehrig had found another friend in McCarthy, however. McCarthy recognized Lou was a chronic worrier and praised Gehrig openly to build up his confidence.

For 14 seasons Lou never missed a game. He seemed as afraid to lose his job as the greenest rookie just up from the bushes. As Jack Sher wrote, "He played with fractured hands, doubled over with lumbago, woozy from being hit in the head by wild pitches. He stayed in games grinning crazily, like a macabre dancer in a grueling marathon."[12] Sports scribe Dan Daniel said, "All his career, Gehrig feared his ability to hit a ball would leave him overnight."[13]

Lou married Eleanor Twitchell in 1933. It was a good match. In a way she was the opposite of Lou. An attractive, vivacious woman from Chicago, Eleanor was very outgoing and mixed easily with people. On the day their engagement was announced, Eleanor was in the stands when Lou hit a home run. He waved to her as he crossed home plate and remembered the day as the happiest of his life. A date was set for September 30, but Lou couldn't face the attention of a formal wedding. He talked her into a quiet ceremony among a small group of friends. Eleanor recalled, "Less than an hour after we were married, Lou was on his way to the Stadium to play baseball."[14]

The marriage took place despite the objections of Lou's mother, to whom he was deeply devoted. The pair enjoyed the short time they had together before Lou's illness. They took a trip around the world. Even when Lou was dying, Eleanor invited theater stars, singers, comedians, and sports stars to buffet suppers to keep her husband's mind off his illness. She recalled, "The house was like a circus but they were all welcome. I wanted to keep Lou entertained. All the activity kept me from thinking too."[15]

After Lou's death, Eleanor reflected, "No matter what his achievements, he was dogged by a sense of failure and a need, constantly, to prove himself. Success brought Lou no sense of attainment, no relaxation. It was like something ephemeral to be clutched with both hands. He was afraid if he loosened his grip for a moment, everything he had struggled for would slip away from him."[16]

At the end of the 1938 season, when the disease first began to affect him, he struggled noticeably game after game. His strength slipped away. His wife pleaded, "Please give yourself a rest, Lou. Your record is safe. You need a rest."[17] Lou kept playing, determined to work himself out of his slump while not knowing how doomed a man he was.

In 1936, McCarthy's Yankee team was just as powerful as any club Ruth played on. That includes the 1927 Murderer's Row outfit. They hit .300 and hammered a then-record 182 home runs. They also scored 1,065 runs, just two behind the record 1,067 scored by the 1931 Yanks. They won 102 games and captured the pennant by the largest margin in history, 19½ games. They led the league in pitching and set a record for total bases (2,703) that lasted until 1997.

Gehrig led the way but he had help. Rookie sensation Joe DiMaggio hit .323 with 29 homers, 125 RBIs and 132 runs. Also driving in more than 100 runs were second baseman Tony Lazzeri (109), outfielder George Selkirk (107), and catcher Bill Dickey (107). Shortstop Frankie Crosetti batted .288 with 90 walks and scored 137 times. Third baseman Red Rolfe hit .319, scored 116 runs, and tied DiMaggio for the league lead with 15 triples. Jake Powell and Myril Hoag split duty in center field and hit a combined .304. The pitching staff included Red Ruffing (20–12), Monte Pearson (19–7), Bump Hadley (14–4), Lefty Gomez (13–7), Johnny Broaca (12–7), and relievers Pat Malone (12–4) and Johnny Murphy (9–3).

President Franklin D. Roosevelt threw out the first ball on Opening Day in Washington as 31,000 saw the Senators' Bobo Newsom outduel the Yanks' Lefty Gomez, 1–0. The Yanks were also shut out in their home opener, 6–0, by Boston's Lefty Grove. A shivering crowd of 22,256 saw Grove fire a two-hitter. Gehrig posted both hits, one of them a smash off Jimmie Foxx's shins.

New York was not the favorite to win the pennant in 1936. McCarthy had won one pennant in five years since taking the Yankee helm. He was called "Second Place Joe" and sportswriters believed his job was in jeopardy. Ruth wanted to manage the Yankees. The Yankees offered Babe a position as manager of their top minor league team in Newark, but Ruth had no intentions of starting in the minors.

Gehrig ripped three singles and Selkirk singled, doubled, and tripled in a 10–2 win over the Senators on April 24. The Yankee offense began to show signs of its potential. Two days later the Red Sox scored six runs in the first inning at Fenway, but New York came back with seven runs in the second to triumph, 12–9. Gehrig tripled, homered, and drove in three runs. Crosetti slapped five hits and netted three RBIs. Dickey singled twice, doubled twice, and chased home four runs.

On April 28, Gehrig belted his third homer of the spring as Red Ruffing blanked Cleveland with a four-hitter, 2–0. The homer was one of 14 Lou hit off Indians pitching in 1936. The next day Washington's Jake Powell ran into Detroit slugger Hank Greenberg at first base, breaking Greenberg's wrist and sidelining him for the season. On the last day of April, Detroit player-manager Mickey Cochrane suffered a broken finger. He missed nearly the whole season. The dual blow proved to be too much for the world champion Detroiters to overcome and paved the way for a New York romp. Powell would be traded to the Yanks on June 14 for Ben Chapman.

On May 3, Joe DiMaggio made his long-awaited debut before 25,490 fans at Yankee Stadium. He started the season late because of a foot injury.

The Yanks pummeled the Browns, 14–5, as Joe D singled twice and tripled while playing left field. McCarthy would not station him in center field until past midseason. Gehrig singled four times, scored five runs, and knocked in two. The Yanks were in second place at 12–6, just a half-game behind Boston.

DiMaggio also had three hits in his second game, as the Yanks tagged the Browns, 8–3. Gehrig was even better, whacking four hits, including two doubles. On May 7, Lou was hitting .402 with 26 runs and 16 RBIs in 21 games. Dickey, who homered twice during a 6–5 win over Detroit that day, was at .357. The Yankee catcher finished the season at .362, the highest ever for an AL catcher until Joe Mauer batted .365 in 2009.

In mid–May DiMaggio wowed fans while batting in the number-three spot. On May 14, he went 4-for-5 with three doubles in St. Louis. The next afternoon he went 4-for-5 again with two doubles in Chicago. On May 19, he was hit in the ribs by a throw from Cleveland second baseman Bill Knickerbocker while trying to break up a double play. Lazzeri, who was very protective of his new Italian American teammate, rushed out to fight Knickerbocker. The two were separated before any solid blows were landed. The Yanks won, 10–4, as Gehrig hit his sixth homer and scored three times. On May 21, DiMaggio was hitting .411.

The Yankees really began to flex their muscles on May 23 in a doubleheader in Philadelphia. They routed the A's, 12–6 and 15–1, socking a total of 30 hits. Gehrig singled twice and tripled in the opener. Selkirk went 4-for-4 with two doubles in the second game. Lazzeri pumped three of his 14 homers on the year in the double romp.

The next afternoon the Yankees combined 19 hits with 16 walks to humble Mack's White Elephants, 25–2. Lazzeri hit three homers, including two grand slams, added a triple, and set a single-game AL record with 11 RBIs. Even Crosetti homered twice. DiMaggio homered once and singled twice. Dickey legged out two triples and Gehrig singled twice and scored three times. The 1936 Yankees were being hailed as the new Murderer's Row. They led the league with a 25–12 record, 1½ games ahead of Boston.

The Yanks arrived in Boston for a three-game series on May 26. "Yawkey's Millionaires," as the Red Sox were called in the *Sporting News,* won the opener, 5–4, as Wes Ferrell pitched a complete game and Jimmie Foxx launched his 12th homer. In the fourth inning, Boston's Eric McNair crashed into Dickey at home plate with the force of a freight train. Dickey was rushed to St. Elizabeth Hospital. For a while it was thought his spleen had been punctured. Tests showed that his left kidney was damaged. He missed a month. At the time, Dickey had driven in 50 runs in 39 games. The Red Sox were now a half-game out of first place.

The Yankees responded to the Red Sox challenge. Rolfe doubled, tripled, and plated Crosetti with a single in the eleventh inning for a 9–8 New York win in the second game of the series. The Yanks won the rubber game. DiMaggio was the star with two singles, a triple, three runs scored, and three RBIs. The Yanks came back from a 4–1 deficit to prevail, 10–6.

On Memorial Day, McCarthy's team swept a doubleheader from the Senators, 7–1 and 6–1, before 71,750 fans at Yankee Stadium. Gehrig went 3-for-6 with his seventh homer. DiMaggio laced three doubles and Selkirk tripled and homered. On the final day of the month, New York topped Boston again, 5–4, in 12 innings before 41,781 in the Bronx to open up a 4½-game lead. Gehrig homered and doubled. DiMaggio singled three times and won the game with an RBI triple in the twelfth inning. Joe D was in the midst of an 18-game hitting streak. On June 4 he was hitting .379. Gehrig was batting .360 with eight homers, 56 runs, and 32 RBIs in 46 games. Lou would respond to the competition of DiMaggio just as he had with Ruth.

DiMaggio once wrote, "Gehrig was the type of ball player to command respect, even if you weren't his teammate. To see his broad back and muscular arms as he spread himself at the plate was to give the impression of power as no other ball player I ever saw gave it."[18] On June 5, Lou played in his 1,700th consecutive game and sparked a 4–3 Yankee win over Cleveland with an inside-the-park homer. The next day he homered off the Tribe's Mel Harder in a 4–2 loss. He managed two singles in seven at-bats in the final game of the Indians series as the Yanks won in 16 innings on Selkirk's home run, 5–4. Ruffing pitched 16 innings to get the win and also singled, doubled, and homered.

On June 8, the combination of Gehrig and DiMaggio buried St. Louis, 12–3. Lou swatted a single, double, and homer for three RBIs and "the Jolter" singled, tripled, and homered for five RBIs. On June 11, Gehrig clouted his 12th homer, scored twice, and knocked in two runs as New York beat Detroit in ten innings, 10–9. Rolfe had quite an afternoon with three doubles and a triple, chasing home the winning run with his tenth-inning double. On June 16, Lou hit homers number 13 and 14 in an 8–4 loss in Cleveland. The next day the Yanks came back to clobber the Indians twice, 15–4 and 12–2, smacking 38 hits. Lou went 6-for-11, including two triples, a homer, five runs scored, and five RBIs. In the final game of the series in Cleveland, Lou went 4-for-4 with a single, two doubles, and a homer off ex-teammate Johnny Allen as the Yanks won again, 6–5.

Gehrig celebrated his 33rd birthday in Detroit on June 19 by socking three doubles off Eldon Auker as New York triumphed, 5–2. Lou was robbed of a fourth double when first baseman Jack Burns made an acrobatic stop of his hot smash down the right-field line. In Chicago on June 24, the Yanks routed the Chisox with 25 hits, 18–11. Lou went 4-for-5 with two doubles and scored four times. DiMaggio smashed two homers in New York's ten-run fifth inning and added two doubles before the slaughter was over. Dickey, now back in the lineup, joined in with three singles, a homer, and four RBIs.

Gehrig was by no means the only big sports star from New York City. James J. Braddock, nicknamed "the Cinderella Man," was heavyweight boxing champ of the world after having stunned Max Baer in a 15-round unanimous decision in 1935. Braddock's story was a heart-warming one as he was hit hard by the Depression and forced to seek work on the docks before being given a second chance in boxing.

On June 27, Gehrig, Dickey, and Rolfe connected for homers off Chicago's Ted Lyons as the Yanks pounded out a 7–6 victory. The next day the new Murderer's Row belted six homers in a 10–6 triumph in St. Louis. Selkirk flew around the bases with a three-run inside-the-park homer. Crosetti nailed two home runs and Gehrig, DiMaggio, and Ruffing also went deep. Gehrig was now leading the league in batting average (.402), hits (102), and runs (81). His 56 RBIs put him in third place behind Foxx (66) and Dickey (63). Dickey was hitting .373. DiMaggio had slipped to .350. As a newcomer, Joe D may have taken some attention away from Gehrig's 1936 season. New York writers had written about Lou for years, and the new Italian kid from San Francisco played with a distinctive flair. But even Joe D was not Babe Ruth.

On the last day of June, 54,046 fans at Yankee Stadium saw their heroes beat up on Boston in a doubleheader, 10–5 and 6–2, to open up a 9½-game lead. Gehrig singled twice and homered twice, scored four times, and drove in four runs. His 20 homers on the year put him in second place behind Foxx. McCarthy gave Lou the ultimate compliment during June. He told sportswriters Lou was "the greatest ballplayer of all time."[19]

In the All-Star game at Braves Field, Lou hammered a 430-foot homer off Curt Davis. The National League won the game, however, 4–3. DiMaggio was the goat. He played a second-inning sinking liner by Gabby Hartnett into an RBI triple by missing a shoestring catch. In the fifth, Joe bobbled a single by Billy Herman, allowing Herman to reach second base. Herman then scored the deciding run on Joe Medwick's single.

While on the road, Gehrig was a movie fan. The silver screen was his main diversion. He even tried his hand at acting in 1937, appearing in a western called *Rawhide*. His acting was panned by critics. He was a well-read man and opera fan. He liked poetry and comic strips. He liked being around kids. He did not feel at home in sophisticated circles and was not a conversationalist. Sportswriters found his personality boring. Some say the grin he often wore was a shield against situations he found uncomfortable. Gehrig never realized how much his steady play was admired by fans. He told author Jack Sher in his last interview that he received 30,000 letters from fans after he quit. It took him and his wife eight months to answer them.[20]

Lou began the second half of the season with a two-run, first-inning home run against Cleveland, but the potent Tribe offense rebounded to win, 11–4. Cleveland first baseman Hal Trosky homered twice and tripled. The 6'2", 207-pound left-handed-hitting Trosky would have a career season (.343, 216 hits, 124 runs, 42 homers, and 162 RBIs). The fifth-place Indians paced the AL with a .304 team batting average and tied the Tigers for second place with 921 runs, but their pitching was tagged for a 4.83 ERA.

The Tribe's pitching ineptitude was demonstrated the next day. The Yanks got revenge with a 20-hit, 18–0 laugher over manager Steve O'Neill's ballclub. Lou connected for a two-run homer off Lloyd Brown in the first inning and hit another two-run homer off Willis Hudlin in the third inning. The two blasts put Gehrig in the league lead in home runs with 23.

While wielding his 36-ounce bat, "Larrupin' Lou" was a picture of concentration in his open stance. In terms of physical safety for opposing pitchers, Lou was feared more than Ruth. Ruth batted third in the Yankee order and wore number three. Gehrig batted fourth and wore number four. Lou's number four was referred to as "the hard number" by rival pitchers. There was fear that one of his shots that resembled a two-iron might one day decapitate a pitcher.

Gehrig hit 493 homers in his career. Unlike most sluggers, he was tough to strike out. He fanned only 46 times in 1936. For an extremely hard swinger, Lou was an excellent contact hitter. His total of 205 hits in 1936 was one of eight seasons that he ripped 200 or more safeties. Only Pete Rose, Ty Cobb, and Ichiro Suzuki had more 200-hit seasons and they did not slug .632.

The Yanks invaded Chicago on July 25 to take on the red-hot White Sox. The Pale Hose had won 17 of their last 21 games to move into second place. Two of their stars, shortstop Luke Appling and left fielder Rip Radcliff, were tied for the league lead in batting at .378. Appling, who once fouled off 17 pitches before banging a triple, eventually led the league at .388. Gehrig had dropped to third place at .371.

More than 50,000 fans showed up for the doubleheader against the New Yorkers. The Yanks won the first game easily, 12–3, as Gehrig crushed a three-run homer off Pat "Sugar" Cain in the second inning and added an RBI single. The second game was a riotous spectacle. Gehrig hit homer number 30 off Bill Deitrich in the sixth inning to give New York a lead. In the eighth stanza, Chicago's Radcliff rapped a bouncer to Gehrig, who tossed the ball to pitcher Pat Malone covering first. Umpire Charles Johnson called Radcliff out and then turned, failing to see that the ball had been knocked out of Malone's glove in a collision with the Chicago outfielder. When Johnson saw the ball lying on the ground, he conferred with third-base umpire Bill Summers.

Summers ruled that the ball was knocked out of Malone's glove after the putout had been completed. Beer cans and pop bottles were tossed from the stands by irate Chicago fans. The situation was ugly.

In the ninth inning Chicago's Zeke Bonura slammed a dramatic two-out, two-run homer to tie the game at 8–8. A bottle was tossed from the stands that struck Summers, who collapsed prior to being revived and was assisted to the clubhouse. Commissioner Landis announced over the amplifying system a reward of $5,000 would be paid for any information leading to the arrest of the assailant. In the eleventh inning, Gehrig reached second base on a wild throw by second baseman Jack Hayes. Lou moved to third when pitcher Russell Evans fumbled Selkirk's bunt, and scored the eventual winning run on Lazzeri's slow tapper to Appling. The White Sox challenge had been met.

On July 28 in Detroit, Gehrig had another field day. He singled once, doubled twice, homered, scored five runs, and knocked in five as the Yanks routed the crippled Bengals, 16–6. In the sixth inning a frightening play occurred. Yankee center fielder Myril Hoag collided with DiMaggio while chasing a drive to the gap. Both outfielders were knocked unconscious while Goose Goslin circled the bases for a homer. DiMaggio recovered to stay in the game but Hoag was taken out. The next day the Yanks routed the Tigers by another football score, 13–3. This time Gehrig singled twice, homered, and drove in three runs. Hoag was back in center field and managed a single in five at-bats. After the game he was rushed to Harper Hospital for emergency surgery. Doctors said he had suffered a concussion in his collision with DiMaggio the day before. Hoag missed the rest of the season.

On July 31 in Cleveland, DiMaggio played his first game in center field during an 11–7 win over the Indians at League Park. Gehrig, who was back on top in the batting race at .381, singled, hit homer number 33, scored twice, and knocked in three runs. The Yanks were in first place by 8½ games over now-second-place Cleveland with Dickey (.346), DiMaggio (.344), Selkirk (.320), Hoag (.301) and Rolfe (.300) hitting well.

Gehrig's parents were born in Germany but there is no record of them ever showing support for the Nazis. Gehrig played in exhibition games against black teams on barnstorming trips and recognized how good they were. The owners of major league baseball defended their segregation practices by saying that the blacks were inferior players. It was clear to see how black teams exposed this falsehood. Gehrig was one of the few white ballplayers to go on record at that time for the integration of baseball. He stated, "There is no room in baseball for discrimination. It is our national pastime and a game for all."[21]

On August 2, the Marx Brothers entertained 65,342 fans at Municipal Stadium while Cleveland took batting practice. The ensuing game lasted 16 innings prior to being called because of darkness and ending in a 4–4 tie.

Gehrig went 3-for-6 with a double and two RBIs. In the thirteenth inning he left the game after straining his back with a ferocious swing and miss. The Yanks had an off-day on August 3 and Lou got a chance to rest before taking the field for his 1,754th consecutive game in Boston on August 4.

Back in New York on August 9, a throng of 50,685 fans saw the Yanks sweep the A's in a doubleheader, 7–6 and 3–0. Gehrig hit homer number 34 in the opener, and his bases-loaded triple in game two off Gordon Rhodes provided Pearson with all the runs he needed.

In Philadelphia on August 16, Gehrig singled, doubled, and launched a grand slam as New York won again easily, 16–2. The two teams split a doubleheader the following afternoon. Gehrig banged two home runs and knocked in four runs as New York took the first game at Shibe, 10–2. He doubled and tripled in defeat as the A's captured the second game, 2–1. During the doubleheader, Philly fans gave Lou an outburst of applause when he was seen offering A's rookie Chubby Dean some pointers on technique at playing first base. When Lou arrived in the majors, he seemed to make one bad play a game at first base. Then it became one bad play a week. Eventually it became one bad play a month as Lou evolved into one of the league's better glovemen. Connie Mack had handed Dean a note to give Gehrig, asking him if he could help out the rookie. Lou happily obliged.

The *Sporting News* quoted Gehrig in August, "In the past, I played ball without thinking, without wondering why things happen and why expected results did not become facts. Now, I am giving the pitchers a mental tussle and I personally feel that I was never as good as I am today. Perhaps, it's what you call the peak."[22]

On August 22, Gehrig's homer in the seventh inning off Boston's Lefty Grove put the Yanks up, 2–1. Jimmie Foxx tied the contest with one of his 41 circuit clouts of the season in the ninth inning, but New York emerged victorious after 13 innings, 3–2. Gehrig's single in the thirteenth chased Rolfe to third base from where he scored on Dickey's one-base jab. There were 63,969 fans at Yankee Stadium to see the two teams in a doubleheader the following day. Six hundred of them, including a brass band, came from Hartford to pay tribute to Lou. Gehrig slammed homer number 40 as the Yanks took the first game from Boston, 5–3. Manager Joe Cronin's Beantown boys, who fell all the way to sixth place in the second half of the season, won the second contest, 6–3.

The *Sporting News* said Lou was playing most of August with a painful chipped bone in his middle finger. It went on to say, "But instead of slowing down Locomotive Lou, the injury has found him going better than ever. The Yankee star has his heart set on establishing a number of records this season."[23] Among the records mentioned was Al Simmons' mark of 11 straight seasons of 100 or more RBIs. Lou tied Simmons' record in 1936 and broke it in 1937. Sixteen times during Lou's career he suffered chipped bones in his hands.

The Yankees increased their league lead to 12½ games on August 28 by manhandling the Tigers in a doubleheader, 14–5 and 19–4. The second game was mercifully called for darkness in the seventh inning. Lou went 4-for-7 on the day with two homers and five RBIs.

In the next 13 games, however, Gehrig went into his only slump of the year, managing five hits in 39 at-bats. The *Sporting News* explained, "Lou has suffered from rheumatic symptoms in his back and has not been himself at all. He has not been taking his natural cut at the ball."[24] Chipped bones in his fingers could not slow Lou down, but apparently back problems could.

On September 9, Lou seemed back in form as he creamed a grand slam during a 12–9 win in Cleveland. The victory clinched the pennant for the Yanks as they now held an 18-game lead over second-place Chicago. In Detroit on September 11, Lou walked and hit a three-run homer during a nine-run New York rally in the eighth inning. The Yanks toppled the Tigers, 14–4. The Yankees broke the then–major league single-season team record for home runs in St. Louis during a doubleheader sweep of the Browns. The new Murderer's Row crashed eight home runs, winning 10–7 and 12–1. DiMaggio belted three of the homers and Gehrig hammered two.

Back in the stadium on September 19, New York City Mayor La Guardia presented Gehrig with a scroll celebrating Lou's 1,800th consecutive game. The scroll was filled with prose admiring Lou for his mental and physical attributes. Lou singled and doubled and Dickey finished off the Senators with a ninth-inning homer in the 6–5 win. On September 24, Lou hit his 49th homer of the campaign in a 4–3 loss to Philadelphia.

The 1936 Yankees' margin of victory in the pennant race was 19½ games, breaking the 1927 Yankees' record of 19 games. Some sportswriters said the Pinstripers' easy win caused them to play sluggish down the stretch and might adversely affect their chances in the World Series. Gehrig laughed off the sluggishness talk, saying, "Put the dough on the line, give a ball club the great financial and glory incentive such as you get in the Series, and there is no sluggishness. There is a new edge immediately. In fact I would rather go into the Series from an easy race like ours than from a tough, nerve-racking affair such as the Giants have been through."[25]

The Giants' Carl Hubbell started the opening game of the World Series against the Yankees' Ruffing. Hubbell posted a 26–6 record with a 2.31 ERA while winning his last 16 decisions. His screwball was the most devastating pitch in baseball. His control of the pitch was incredible. On July 2, 1933, he pitched 18 innings against the Cardinals without walking a man while striking out 12. He won 23 games that year with ten shutouts and a 1.66 ERA.

In the 1933 World Series against Washington, he hurled 20 innings without allowing an earned run. He made it 17 victories in a row for 1936 with a 6–1 taming of the potent Yankee lineup at the Polo Grounds.

The Yanks teed off on the Giants' Hal Schumacher in Game 2 though, scoring 18 runs in an 18–4 romp. Gehrig drove in three runs with two singles A crowd of 64,842 was on hand at Yankee Stadium for Game 3 to witness a pitching duel between the Giants' Fred Fitzsimmons and the Yanks' Bump Hadley. Gehrig swatted a big homer in the second inning and Crosetti's RBI single in the eighth was the decider in a 2–1 Yankee win.

Game 4 saw Hubbell take the mound before a then–World Series record crowd of 66,669 at Yankee Stadium. Gehrig came up in the third inning and worked the count to 3-and-2. Player-manager Bill Terry walked over and told Hubbell to be cautious and not give Lou anything good to hit. Hubbell's next pitch was a curve, high and inside. Lou would have walked if he had it taken, but instead he swung, picking the ball off his right ear and driving it like a rope into the right-field stands. The two-run belt put the Yanks up, 4–0, and was the only homer hit off Hubbell all year with a man on base. Hubbell allowed seven homers in 304 innings during the regular season. Lou would later double off Hubbell and score again as the Yanks prevailed in the pivotal game behind the pitching of Pearson, 5–2.

The Giants survived elimination by winning Game 5, 5–4, in ten innings. The Yanks clinched the Series with a rout in Game 6, 13–5. After the Series, Lou declared, "He was all pitcher, that Hubbell. If he had stopped us that day, with that incredible pitch of his, he would have been very tough in a seventh game. I've had thrills galore. But I don't think any of them top that one."[26]

For the Series, Lou batted .292 and tied Lazzeri for the lead in RBIs with seven. Lou had always been a great World Series player. Somehow the Babe seemed to overshadow him. In the 1928 Series, Lou batted .545 with four homers, but Ruth batted .625 with three homers, including one remarkable blast off a quick pitch by Cardinal pitcher Willie Sherdel. In the 1932 Series, Lou batted .529 with three homers in the four-game sweep of the Cubs. Ruth batted .333 with two homers. He also became the talk of the nation with his theatrical "called shot" in Game 3. In 41 World Series games, Ruth batted .326 with 15 homers, 37 runs, and 33 RBIs. In 34 World Series contests, Gehrig batted .361 with 10 homers, 30 runs, and 35 RBIs.

Gehrig enjoyed his last super season in 1937, batting .351 with 200 hits, 37 homers, 138 runs, and 159 RBIs as the Yanks ran away with the pennant. DiMaggio enjoyed an even better year (.346, 46 homers, 151 runs, and 167 RBIs). "Joltin' Joe's" seemingly effortless virtuosity captivated the imagination of sportswriters. He was the talk of baseball and hailed as "the next Babe

Ruth." Once again, Lou was pushed into the background. After only his second season in the majors, Joe D demanded $40,000 for 1938, more than Gehrig had ever made in a season. The new Yankee superstar declared, "I know what I'm worth." He held out until April 25 before signing for $25,000.

Lou didn't know it at the time, but in 1938 he was battling the beginnings of a disease that would take his life three years later. He was in the line up every day, batting .295 with 29 homers and 114 RBIs as the Yanks took their third world championship in succession. Eight games into the 1939 season, the Yankee captain asked McCarthy to take him out of the lineup. When the extent of Lou's failing health was revealed, "the Iron Horse" retired with his unforgettable speech. Lou was a picture of courage. He declared himself "the luckiest man on the face of the earth," and spent the last two years of his life helping kids as a parole officer.

Lou could have enjoyed more good years in a Yankee uniform had fate not dealt him such a cruel blow. Lou's baseball experience could be characterized by what happened on June 3, 1932. That was the day Lou hit a record four homers and was robbed of a fifth on a super catch by Al Simmons in Philadelphia. The next day, however, the top headlines in the sports pages across America were filled with a different story, the news that John McGraw had retired after 30 years as manager of the Giants. On the day of his top performance, Lou received second billing.

Chapter 10

The Motor City's Big RBI Man: Hank Greenberg in 1937

Lou Gehrig had a worthy challenger in the RBI business of the 1930s. He was Detroit's Henry Benjamin (Hank) Greenberg. The original "Hammerin' Hank" drove home 183 runs during the summer of 1937. Nobody has driven in more since then. Greenberg's 1937 total is just one behind Gehrig's AL record of 184. In his career, Greenberg knocked in .9153 runs per game. Only Gehrig's .9219 RBI-per-game percentage tops Hank's. The towering 6'4", 215-pound right-handed slugger of the Motor City led the Tigers to pennants in 1934, 1935, 1940 and again in 1945 after spending 4 years in the Army Air Force during World War II. The Greenberg-led Bengals were a potent rival for Joe McCarthy's Yankee teams of the 1930s and early 1940s.

Baseball fans remember Greenberg mostly for his 1938 season when he hit 58 home runs to challenge Babe Ruth's mark of 60, but Greenberg considered 1937 as his best season. In his autobiography, *Hank Greenberg: The Story of My Life*, Greenberg states, "Nineteen thirty-seven was, personally, my best year. I say this because ballplayers appreciate that runs batted in are all that's important to a ball team. It isn't how many doubles you get or how many home runs you hit. Those are important, but the bottom line is who drives in the runs."[1]

Greenberg was the first great Jewish baseball player and felt added pressure and a special responsibility to perform well for that reason. He took a lot of abuse from some opposing players and fans. Longtime teammate Birdie Tebbetts remembered, "There was nobody in the history of the game who took more abuse than Greenberg, unless it was Jackie Robinson. ... I was there with Hank when it was happening and I heard it. However, Hank was not only equal to it, he was superior to most of the people who were yelling at him."[2]

Tebbetts added, "Nobody else could have ever withstood the foul invectives that were directed toward Greenberg, and he had to eat them. Or else he would be out of every game he played."[3]

Hank recalled: "Some of the things they yelled were pretty nasty but I could always handle it pretty well. That's because everybody got it. Italians were wops, Germans were krauts, and the Polish players were dumb polacks. Me, I was a kike or a sheeny or a mockey. I was big so I made a good target. The only thing that bothered me was there were a lot of Italians, Germans, and Poles, but I was the only Jewish player who was making a name for himself and so they reserved a little extra for me."[4]

Hank was born on January 1, 1911, in Greenwich Village of New York City. His parents immigrated to America from Romania. When Hank was six years old, the family moved to the Bronx. Hank loved baseball and spent countless hours playing or practicing the game across the street from his house at Crotona Park. As was the case with the other legendary RBI man from New York City, Lou Gehrig, Hank's parents were not too keen on baseball. They saw the hours that Hank was spending on baseball as wasted time. They thought he should spend more of his efforts studying his school work. Hank's two brothers and his lone sister all graduated from college and went into educated professional work, but Hank stubbornly made up his mind to stick to baseball. He passed his courses in school but admitted that athletics occupied 85 percent of his time.

When a friend tried to get Hank a tryout with his favorite team, the New York Giants, he was refused. The Giants said they had scouted Hank and were convinced he would never make it as a major leaguer. Still, Hank followed his dream and played semi-pro ball for the Bay Parkways in the summer of 1929. Soon he was playing in the Blackstone Valley League in Massachusetts for more money. Yankee scout Paul Kritchell, the same scout who had signed Gehrig, was impressed with Hank's bat. He invited him to Yankee Stadium to see the final Bronx Bombers game of the season. While there, Hank got a good look at Yanks' first baseman Gehrig and said to himself, "No way I'm going to sign with this team, not with him playing first base."[5] Hank signed with Detroit for $9,000. He was accepted to New York University on a basketball scholarship, but he talked his father into letting him quit NYU in his freshman year. He joined Detroit's training camp in the spring of 1930. He explained to his father he could always go back to college, but right now he had to play baseball.

Hank was sent to Class A Hartford but was in over his head. At one point he struck out 13 straight times and in his own words was "awkward as a giraffe" around first base.[6] He was sent to Class C Raleigh, where he settled in, hitting .314. He slugged his way up in the minors, from Raleigh in 1930 to Class AA Beaumont in 1932, where he was MVP of the Texas League. In 1933, Greenberg showed he was ready for the big show by hitting .301 with 87 RBIs in 449 at-bats with Detroit. In 1934 he blossomed into a full-fledged star. He led the Tigers to the pennant, batting .339 with 26 homers, 63 doubles, and 139 RBIs.

Charlie Gehringer once said of Hank Greenberg: "Hank loved to drive those runs in. ... Everybody likes to drive in runs, but with Hank it was a passion. I think he got just as big a kick out of driving in a run with a single as he did with a home run." In 1937 Hank drove in 183 runs. No one has driven in that many since then.

During the heat of the 1934 pennant race, Hank faced a tough dilemma of whether he should play on the Jewish New Year's holiday of Rosh Hashanah. His family was an Orthodox family. He did not want to offend his faith by playing in the game, but he did not want to let down his teammates by refusing to play.

Teammate Charlie Gehringer recalled:

> We're in a real tight pennant race with the Yankees in September and we're about to play the Red Sox, who were tough. We needed every win and Hank Greenberg wanted to play, but it was an important Jewish holiday, Rosh Hashanah, and he was going to have to sit out and pray that day. The press made a big deal out of it and really put a lot of pressure on him to play. I remember he consulted Detroit's top rabbi, who decided Greenberg could play because it says in the Old Testament (the Talmud, actually) that the boys should be playing that day. But now the entire city is watching him, all the local Jews are watching him and the Tigers are counting on him.[7]

Gehringer continued: "So Hank plays and it's a drizzly overcast day; I remember I had trouble seeing the ball. Hank hits two home runs off Dusty Rhodes and we won, 2–1, with his homer winning it in the tenth. I thought that was really something, and I said to him after the game, 'You should see how I hit on Christmas.' He laughed. I just really think that was an enormous amount of pressure to put on a man and he came through."[8]

The Jewish holiday of Yom Kippur was eight days later. Yom Kippur is the day of atonement, the most sacred holiday of the year for Jews. The Tigers' lead in the standings was more secure but the pennant was not decided. This time Hank decided not to play and attended a synagogue, where he was greeted with a spontaneous ovation.[9]

Greenberg was even better in 1935. He led the Tigers to the pennant again while batting .328 and leading the AL with 36 homers and 170 RBIs. In 1936, however, he suffered a broken wrist after 12 games when Washington's Jake Powell ran into him as Hank was reaching down the line for an errant throw. Hank missed the rest of the 1936 season.

In 1937 the Tigers insisted Greenberg sign a $1-a-year contract. They said he had to demonstrate in spring training that he was physically sound enough to play before they would offer him the same contract he had in 1936. Greenberg left no doubt during exhibition games that he could still play at a high level and was offered a new $25,000-a-year contract before Opening Day.

The 1937 season began for the Tigers in Detroit as 38,200 saw them edge Cleveland, 4–3. Greenberg did not manage a hit against Mel Harder but teammate Gee Walker hit for the cycle in reverse order. Walker began the season by hitting safely in his first 27 games and wound up batting .335. He could be a bungler on the base paths, however, and was traded to the White Sox in 1938.

Greenberg began his assault on the RBI record in Chicago's home opener with a single, double, homer, and three ribbies as the Tigers won, 10–3. On April 28, the Detroiters peppered the Browns with 15 hits as Hank notched two RBIs in an 11–5 rout. On May 2, the Tigers nipped Chicago, 6–5. Walker went 3-for-3 with a game-deciding homer in the seventh. On May 3, Hank pulverized a grand slam over the scoreboard at Navin Field off Pat Cain as Detroit toppled the White Sox again, 12–9. The Tigers reached first place on May 6 with a 12–6 win over the Yankees. Greenberg doubled, tripled, and homered for four RBIs. He was hitting .340 with 16 RBIs in 11 games. He finished 1937 with 49 doubles, 14 triples, 40 homers, 137 runs, and a .337 batting average along with his 183 RBIs.

In Philadelphia on May 20, Hank's first-inning, two-run triple at Shibe keyed a 3–2 win. The next day he belted a two-run homer off Lefty Grove as the Tigers topped Boston in 11 innings, 4–2. On May 22, the *Sporting News* reported that Hank "was credited with hitting the longest home run ever seen in Boston, when he poled a 500-foot wallop over the center field wall in the third inning."[10]

Disaster struck the Tigers on May 25, however, when their catcher and manager, Mickey Cochrane, was beaned by a pitch from "Bump" Hadley in the fifth inning at Yankee Stadium. Cochrane's skull was fractured in three places and for a while he lay between life and death at St. Elizabeth Hospital. Cochrane was hitting .306 with 27 runs scored in 27 games while batting second in the Tigers order. He never played another game. Walker moved up to the number-two slot for the remainder of the year.

Greenberg helped knock Hadley out of the game with an RBI single in the ninth inning that day, but Johnny Murphy came to the rescue as the Pinstripers prevailed, 4–3. Coach Del Baker took over managerial duties while letters streamed in to Cochrane from well-wishers all over the country. The next day the dazed Tigers seemingly went through the motions, losing to Lefty Gomez, 7–0.

Greenberg had high praise for Cochrane, who had become the Tigers' player-manager in 1934. Hank said in his autobiography, "We needed somebody to take charge and show us how to win and that's what Mickey did. We didn't always drive a runner in with hits; there was a strategy of winning ball games with sacrifice flies and ground balls. Cochrane was the one who taught us how to do it. He was an inspirational leader."[11]

Greenberg was obsessed with getting his teammates across home plate. Gehringer, who batted third in the Tiger order and led the league in 1937 with a .371 average, recalled, "Hank loved to drive those runs in. If there was a man on first, he'd always say to me, 'Get him over to third, just get him over to third.' Everybody likes to drive in runs, but with Hank it was a passion. I think he got just as big a kick out of driving in a run with a single as he did with a home run."[12]

The Tigers finally beat the Yankees, 5–4, in 13 innings on May 27. Greenberg homered but retired with a charley horse in the fifth inning. He was back the next day in Detroit with a single, double, homer, and three RBIs as the Tigers swept two from the Browns, 6–5 and 7–3. Hank singled and tripled with two RBIs in a 13–9 loss to the Browns on May 29 and then went 5-for-5 with two homers, a double, and five RBIs in an 18–3 slaughter of St. Louis on May 30.

On June 3, Hank tagged a 400-foot single as well as a triple and homer but the Bengals lost to Washington, 5–4. The 400-foot single came about because Walker held at first base, thinking Ben Chapman would catch Greenberg's drive that rebounded off the center-field wall. But Hank kept hammering. He blasted a two-run homer off Lefty Gomez to help beat the Yanks, 4–3, on June 7. He singled, doubled, and homered on June 8 as Eldon Auker blanked the A's with a one-hitter, 6–0. By June 10 Hank's average was up to .379 with a league-leading 57 RBIs in 46 games. Gehrig led the league at .380. Chicago's Zeke Bonura was second in RBIs with 52.

The Tigers made a move that enhanced Greenberg's chances at the RBI record by bringing up slugger Rudy York from Toledo and batting him just behind Hank, in the number-five slot. York played 41 games at third base and 54 games at catcher and hit 35 home runs in just 375 at-bats. On June 20, "Wrecking Rudy," as the sportswriters called him, homered in both games of a doubleheader as Detroit swept Philly, 6–3 and 8–1, to get within a game of the first place Yanks.

Detroit's initial replacement for Cochrane at catcher, Ray Hayworth, suffered a fracture between the wrist and elbow when he was hit by a fastball from Bobo Newsom. With Hayworth out of action, Birdie Tebbetts received much of the catching chores. While sound defensively, Tebbetts batted only .191 in 162 at-bats. The injury woes didn't end there. Third baseman Marv Owen had his hand fractured by a pitch from the A's Harry Kelley. When Owen came back, York was converted to catcher. He was a defensive liability there despite tutelage from Cochrane.

The Tigers scored an impressive 935 runs in 1937. The Yanks were even more powerful on offense by scoring 979 runs. New York's pitchers (3.65 team ERA) far outclassed Detroit's hurlers (4.87 ERA). The Tigers pitching corps missed Cochrane's expert handling. In addition, Lynwood "Schoolboy" Rowe, a winner of 19 games in 1936, came down with a sore arm and managed just one victory against four defeats. Baker tried to stay upbeat, telling the press, "If we can hang in there until Owen, Hayworth and Rowe get back, we'll give the Yankees or any other club a battle. In its crippled condition, the team has done as well, or better than anybody had a right to expect."[13] From this portion of the season onward the Yanks would leave the Tigers in the dust, winning the pennant by 13 games.

The Yankee runaway didn't stop Hank from driving in his runs. In examining the box scores of the 1937 season, it seems that Greenberg managed to drive in a run almost every game. Sometimes the RBIs came in bunches, like his first-inning grand slam off Jack Wilson in Fenway Park on June 23, but more often Greenberg's assault on the RBI record came in his consistency of plating a run a game.

Every productive cleanup hitter needs a good leadoff man and the Tigers had an excellent one in Pete Fox. Fox hit .331 and joined Greenberg, Gehringer, and Walker as the fourth batter on the team to rack up 200 hits in 1937.

On the last day before the All-Star break, Hank cracked a single, double, and his 18th homer and drove in five more runs as the Tigers swept two from Chicago, 8–4 and 7–4. He was still leading in RBIs with 74 in 67 games. He was picked for the All-Star game but sat on the bench throughout the contest. Manager Joe McCarthy played almost all his Yankees the entire game. The experience angered Greenberg. In 1935 he had more than 100 RBIs by the All-Star break yet was not even picked. Sure, Gehrig and Foxx were in the same league, but Greenberg rightfully believed he had been slighted. When he was picked for the All-Star game in 1938, he refused to join the team.

York got the Tigers off strong in the second half of the season by tagging a three-run, first-inning homer on July 9 in a 10–8 triumph over Cleveland. Hank doubled, scored twice, and plated a pair of runs. The Tigers and Indians combined for 25 extra-base hits and eight homers in splitting a doubleheader the next day. Detroit won the first game, 12–11, as Greenberg and rookie Chet Laabs homered during a five-run Tiger seventh. Cleveland's Hal Trosky belted two of his three homers on the day in an 8–7 Indian win in the second game. On July 11, a Tiger rookie with the illustrious name of Cletus Elwood "Boots" Poffenberger outpitched Cleveland's young wunderkind, Bob Feller, 3–2. Feller allowed just two hits, one of them a third-inning RBI single by Greenberg, but got into trouble with walks. Feller walked the bases loaded in the sixth. He then fanned Greenberg but followed up by allowing a run to score on a wild pitch. He walked two more in the ninth when the Tigers scored the winner. Shortstop Lyn Lary fell while trying to scoop York's slow roller, allowing Gehringer to cross home with the clincher. Poffenberger celebrated by getting married the next day.

The Yanks came into Detroit next and mauled the Tigers, 10–2 and 13–6, to run their winning streak to ten games. The Tigers won the final game, 14–7, but the Yanks had opened up a seven-game lead. Greenberg smacked a single, triple, and homer in nine at-bats in the important series, good for three RBIs. Yankee outfielder Jake Powell was booed loudly by Tiger fans. A local newspaper suggested that his bone-rattling collision with Greenberg early in 1936 was nothing short of a deliberate act to injure the Tiger superstar.

Greenberg went 3-for-5 with his 21st homer and four RBIs on July 19 as the Tigers completed a three-game sweep of Washington, 8–4. The following day Hank's two-out single in the tenth inning drove home the winning run in a 10–9 conquest of Boston. Hank finished the day with three singles in six at-bats. York's three-run homer in the ninth had tied the game. On July 22, Hank ignited a 17–4 rout of Boston by tagging Bobo Newsom for a two-run, first-inning homer. Newsom boasted before the game that he liked to fool Greenberg with his pitches more than any batter in the league. After he was knocked out in the second inning, the Tiger players razzed Bobo and threw towels out of the dugout in his direction.

On July 25, Greenberg sent another blast disappearing over the fence, tripled, singled, scored three times, and drove in two to help propel Detroit over the A's, 12–9. The Tigers arrived for a three-game set in New York on July 27 trailing the Yanks by six games. Red Rolfe's eleventh-inning, walk-off homer won the opener for the Yanks, 6–5. Detroit routed Lefty Gomez, 8–1, in game two, but Bill Dickey's walk-off homer in the ninth inning settled the rubber game, 7–6. Hank went 5-for-11 in the series with three doubles, a triple, and three RBIs.

York was a terror in August. He broke Ruth's September 1927 record with 18 homers in a single month and added 48 RBIs. York was half–Native American and was named MVP of the Texas League in 1935 and MVP of the American Association in 1936. But as a first baseman, he was trapped behind Greenberg. As a catcher he was a defensive liability. In 1940 Greenberg agreed to switch to the outfield so York could play first base. The move resulted in a Tiger pennant.

Cochrane was back in uniform in early August in Philadelphia. He completely exonerated Hadley from any notion the beaning had been intentional. He had missed most of 1936, too, due to a nervous collapse. He spent most of that summer recuperating on a ranch in Wyoming. Rumors were circulating now the Red Sox were interested in hiring him as skipper. Detroit ended the gossip by signing Mickey to a two-year contract for 1938 and 1939. In September 1937, however, he took a European vacation and visited Naples, Rome, Berlin, Paris, and London for some relaxation. The Tigers replaced him with Baker after a poor 47–50 start in 1938.

York may have been breaking records in August but Greenberg was no slouch either. His three-run homer on the fifth day of the month helped Auker beat the A's, 5–3. His first-inning, three-run homer on August 13 off Oral Hildebrand powered Detroit to a 7–6 win over the Browns. The next day the Tigers scored a record 36 runs and socked 40 hits in slaughtering the Browns, 16–1 and 20–7. Greenberg went 4-for-10 in the afternoon massacre, scoring six times and picking up two more ribbies. Gehringer went 7-for-8 with two homers and six RBIs. St. Louis reserve infielder Gerald Liscombe finished both games on the mound.

The Tigers' booming bats were keeping the turnstiles clicking in the Motor City. The 1937 Tiger team drew a then-team record 1,072,276 fans to Navin Field. In the franchise's history, only the 1934 Tiger team outscored the 1937 ballclub. Economic times were slowly getting better. Americans tried to dance their way out of the Depression to the solid sounds and wild syncopation of swing bands across the nation. Songs like Billie Holiday's "Swing It Brother Swing," Duke Ellington's "Take the A Train," Count Basie's "One O'Clock Jump," Artie Shaw's "Begin the Beguine," Woody Herman's "Woodchopper's Ball," and Benny Goodman's all-time house rocker, "Sing, Sing, Sing," would fill the airwaves of America's favorite toy, the radio, during the next few years. Americans tapping feet seemed to make them forget their troubles.

Greenberg possessed a keen mind, which never stopped working overtime in his drive for improvement. He experimented with a huge first baseman's mitt, which writers said resembled a lobster trap, and wound up using it. Bud Shaver of the *Detroit Times* wrote in 1934 that Greenberg was "the most energetic researcher in baseball ... (and is) tireless in his quest for perfection, wants to know all the answers and isn't backward about asking. He argues continually with anybody at any time, probing calmly into other people's minds for information, knowledge, and ideas. He has a mind of his own, too, a good one, which he exercises as religiously as he does his muscles." Later in the story Shaver declared, "Baseball is no two-hour job for Greenberg. He works at it 24 hours a day, because when he dreams he dreams about the day when he will be a great ballplayer."[14]

On August 20 in St. Louis, the Browns' Jim Walkup was charged with "an awarded ball" for taking too much time while pitching to Greenberg in the fifth inning. The *Sporting News* said that Walkup "did everything but take a nap" out on the mound.[15] The "awarded ball" was ball four. In the seventh the Browns decided to pitch to Hank, and Greenberg clouted a three-run homer. Gehringer went through a streak of 12 games when he hit .500, and on August 26 he led the league at .387. Greenberg tagged yet another three-run homer that day as Detroit bested Boston, 6–5. On the previous afternoon he had banged three doubles for two RBIs as the striped cats humbled the A's, 10–4. York went 3-for-5 with his 26th homer. When Rudy struck out, the Detroit fans gave him a rousing spontaneous ovation.

Hank was a self-made ballplayer if ever there was one. At Crotona Park he used to cajole his pals into hitting him grounders in pepper games by the hour. When the sun was going down, he would ask the boys hanging around the park to stay late and pitch to him or shag fly balls from his booming bat. One of those friends remembered, "I guess we sort of humored him. Nobody thought he was going to make it. But we were willing to help him out; he was always a nice kid. What impressed us more than anything else was the belief he had in himself. Lord, was he ever determined!"[16]

The *Sporting News* headlines read "TIGER SLUGGERS PUT ON THREE-RING S.3" at the end of August.[17] On August 30, Greenberg's two-run, first-inning homer (number 30) combined with York's 28th blast and Gehringer's tie-breaking RBI single to pace Detroit to a 5–4 win over the Yanks. The following afternoon York drove in seven runs with two singles and two homers and Greenberg chipped in with two singles and two RBIs as Detroit tore apart the Senators, 12–3. Then on September 2, Greenberg tripled once and homered twice, defeating the Senators with a tenth-inning round-tripper, 9–8.

Greenberg always considered himself a guess hitter. He kept a book on the pitchers and believed it was a big advantage if he knew what pitch was coming.

Del Baker attempted to help Greenberg by stealing signs. A sidebar in the *Sporting News* relates one instance late in 1937 when Baker signaled to his slugger that a particular rookie pitcher was going to throw a fastball three straight times. Greenberg swung and missed on three straight curves. He told Baker afterward, "Never mind about telling me what this guy is going to throw hereafter, Del. Why, that rookie doesn't know himself what he's going to throw."[18]

Baker had better luck stealing signs in 1940 when he managed the Tigers to a pennant. He posted guys in the upper deck at Detroit who were equipped with a telescopic lens during a crucial Tiger homestand in the stretch. From September 4 to September 19, Greenberg went 27-for-59 for a .458 average with 13 homers, five doubles, two triples, and only seven singles, scoring 30 runs and driving in 33. Detroit won the pennant by one game over Cleveland.

The Bengals kept right on swatting the ball hard as they swept the Browns, 10–9 and 5–2, on Labor Day, with Greenberg contributing three singles, a triple, homer number 33, and four RBIs. On September 8, Hank sent homers 34 and 35 soaring into the seats in a 10–5 win over Cleveland. On September 10, Hank singled, doubled, and rang up three more RBIs as the Tigers knocked out Feller. But the Tribe came back to overtake the Tigers, 6–5, in a game shortened to six innings by rain. The next day the Tigers solidified their hold on second place by sweeping a twin-bill from Chicago, 9–5 and 4–2. Hank went 2-for-9 with a triple and two RBIs.

On September 15, Greenberg chose not to play. Instead, he observed the Jewish holiday of Yom Kippur. Had he played and knocked in a single run, he would have wound up tying Gehrig's RBI record. He doubled and hit the first homer ever to land in the center-field bleachers at Yankee Stadium for three RBIs in an 8–1 win on September 19. The *Sporting News* commented: "The Tigers throw no fear in the Yankees now only because of the wide gap separating them."[19]

After he became established in the major leagues, Hank continued to work at baseball like a driven man with practice, practice and more practice. One day at Shibe Park in Philadelphia, the groundskeeper interrupted a session of Hank's extra batting practice by informing him he had to leave. As Hank and his teammates, who were pitching and shagging flies for him, started to leave, an elderly gentleman called Hank over to the stands. The man was the vice president of the A's, John Shibe. Shibe told Hank, "I very much admire what you are doing, young man. You tell the groundskeeper to assist you in every way possible. Tell him that those are John Shibe's instructions. And if he doesn't like it, send him right up here to see me."[20]

Hank was now closing in on the record. He knocked in five runs with two homers in a 12–7 loss to Boston on September 21. The next day, York's three-run homer off Newsom and Hank's 170th RBI highlighted a 6–4 Tiger win in Fenway. Gehringer's batting average was at .380. While leaving New York on the Italian ocean liner *Conte di Savoiato* to begin his European tour on September 11, Cochrane shouted to the writers "Vote for Charlie Gehringer for that Most Valuable Player."[21] The scribes would heed Cochrane's advice, but Greenberg was probably the more fitting choice.

Gehringer was signed off the University of Michigan campus on the advice of Bobby Veach in 1924. In 19 seasons, he batted .320, knocking out as many as 60 doubles, 19 triples, and 20 homers in a season. He topped 200 hits seven times, scored more than 100 runs 12 times (including 133 in 1937), and drove in more than 100 runs seven times. He covered second base with a seemingly effortless manner and led the position in fielding nine times. His silence and consistency were legendary. He was nicknamed "the Mechanical Man." Former teammate Doc Cramer explained, "You wind him up on Opening Day and forget him." Cochrane once said of Gehringer, "Charlie says 'hello' on Opening Day, 'good-bye' on closing day, and in between hits .350."[22]

On September 28, Greenberg forced in the winning run with a bases-loaded walk off Whitlow Wyatt to beat the Indians, 2–1. He drove in six runs with two homers and a double on October 1 as the Tigers routed St. Louis, 14–4. This gave him 181 RBIs with two games to play.

On October 2 against Cleveland, Greenberg came to bat with the bases loaded against Mel Harder. The entire Indians outfield was shifted around to the left. He hit a checked-swing looper down the right-field line that landed foul by a whisker. If it had landed fair, three runners would have scored, giving him 184 RBIs. He did manage to bring in one run with a fly ball.

Going into the last game of the year, Hank had 182 RBIs. In this game the Tigers were going up against a red-hot pitcher in Cleveland's Johnny Allen. Allen was going for a record 16th consecutive win. He had compiled a 15–0 record in 19 starts and four relief appearances. Greenberg slapped an RBI single in the first inning for RBI number 183, which was all Detroit hurler Jake Wade needed. He pitched a one-hitter as the Tigers won, 1–0. Unfortunately, Hank did not get RBI number 184; it was the biggest disappointment of his baseball career.

After challenging Gehrig's RBI mark in 1937, Greenberg flirted with Ruth's home run mark in 1938, finishing with 58. Some fans believed pitchers down the stretch walked Greenberg on purpose so he wouldn't break the Babe's mark. Greenberg commented on this: "Some people still have it fixed in their minds that the reason I didn't break Ruth's record was because I was Jewish, that the ballplayers did everything they could to stop me. That's pure baloney. The fact is quite the opposite. So far as I could tell, the players were mostly rooting for me, aside from the pitchers."[23]

According to the box scores from September 1 to the end of the Tigers' season on October 2, 1938, Hank was walked 27 times in 32 games. He was walked 13 times in the last 19 games.

Greenberg added: "Naturally I was disappointed in not getting the record after having come so close. But as a matter of fact, my 58 home runs didn't afford me any thrill. I never compared myself to the Babe, and I wasn't that kind of a home-run hitter. I averaged around 35, so this was just a freak season for me. My goal in baseball was always RBIs, to break Gehrig's record of 184 RBIs. I would have loved to do that. I didn't accomplish it, but I came awfully close."[24]

In 1940 Greenberg agreed to switch to the outfield for a $10,000 bonus in order to make room for York's bat at first base. Hank hit 41 homers, drove in 150 runs, played left field adequately, and led the Tigers to the pennant. He was named MVP for the second time. Yankee great Joe DiMaggio said of Greenberg's switch, "He didn't have to yield his position at first base. When he made the change, he asked me about charging base hits in the outfield. I told him that you can't come in too fast, but you have to try to float in. ... Hank learned to play the outfield well. He was one of the most determined men I've ever known."[25]

On May 7, 1941, Greenberg was the first baseball star drafted into the army. He hit two home runs against the Yankees in his last game before leaving to serve Uncle Sam. He was thirty years old. In August 1941, Congress passed a law stating that men over twenty-eight years of age were not to be drafted. Hank was released from the army on December 5, 1941. He hoped to get ready for the 1942 baseball season, but the Japanese bombed Pearl Harbor on December 7. On December 9, Hank told the press, "I'm going back in. We are in trouble and there is only one thing to do — return to service. I have not been called back. I am going back of my own accord. ... Baseball is out the window as far as I'm concerned. I don't know if I'll ever return to baseball."[26]

Hank served as a captain in the Army Air Corps in India, Burma, and China, spending 11 months in war zones. He took part in the first land-based bombing of Japan. In the summer of 1945, almost 4½ years after he had entered the service, Hank returned to the Tigers to play 78 games and bat .311. While in the service Greenberg played only one baseball game. Yet when he returned, he homered in his first game back before 55,000 fans in Detroit. He then clinched the pennant for the Tigers with a grand slam off Nelson Potter on the final day of the season in St. Louis. In 1946 Hank led the AL with 44 homers and 127 RBIs while batting .277, but his fielding skills back at first base had eroded. The Tigers waived him out of the league to Pittsburgh.

Hank was ready to retire but Pittsburgh owner John Galbreath talked him into playing one more season for more than $100,000. He hit 25 homers in that last season, helping the Pirates set a team attendance record and teaching their young slugger, Ralph Kiner, to be more selective at the plate. Kiner's home run total jumped from 23 to 51.

Greenberg's career included just nine full seasons. In those years, particularly his biggest RBI season in 1937, baseball fans got to see how truly great a ballplayer he was. The tragedy is that the baseball world didn't get to see enough of Hank Greenberg. Add five prime years back to Greenberg's career that he lost and he could very well have reached 500 home runs and, more impressively, amassed 2,000 RBIs.

Chapter 11

Boston's Kid Bats .406:
Ted Williams in 1941

Baseball's last .400 hitter might have been the best hitter ever. In 1941 Boston Red Sox slugger Ted Williams batted .406. More than sixty years have passed since then and no one has duplicated Ted's feat. Hitters such as Rod Carew, George Brett, Tony Gwynn, and Todd Helton have flirted with .400 averages but fell short in the stretch.

In 1941 Williams whacked 185 hits, 33 doubles, three triples, and a league-leading 37 homers in 456 at-bats. He also walked 147 times, giving him a .553 on-base percentage, the highest on-base percentage until Barry Bonds walked 198 times with a .582 on-base percentage in 2002. Bonds then drew 232 walks with a .609 on base percentage in 2004.

Williams also led in slugging percentage in 1941 (.735) and struck out only 27 times. He led the AL with 135 runs and finished third to the Joe DiMaggio and Charlie Keller in RBIs with 120. DiMaggio hit .357 with 125 RBIs and set a record by hitting in 56 consecutive games. During the summer of 1941, America's last summer before its entry into World War II, Williams and DiMaggio took turns grabbing the headlines in the sports pages. Their names have been forever linked in baseball lore since, and countless comparisons have been made between them. Under today's rules Williams would have been credited with a .411 batting average in 1941. In 1941 a fly ball that drove in a runner from third base counted as a time at-bat and not as a sacrifice fly. Williams was charged with a time at-bat for six such fly balls in 1941.

Ted's career batting average of .344 is sixth all-time and the highest since Hornsby retired in 1937 at .358. Williams holds the highest career on-base percentage at .483. Ruth is second at .474. Williams' career .634 slugging percentage is second only to Ruth's .690. Probably the best measure of a player's offensive value is total average. This is derived by dividing a player's bases made (total bases + stolen bases + walks + times hit by pitches — number

Ted Williams batted .406 in 1941. Baseball's last .400 hitter wrote in his autobiography, "I wanted to be the greatest hitter who ever lived.... Eddie Collins used to say I lived for my next turn at bat, and that's the way it was. If there was ever a man born to be a hitter it was me. As a kid, I wished it on every falling star."

of times caught stealing) by his outs made (at-bats — hits + times caught stealing + times grounded into double play). Williams owns the second-highest all-time total average at 1.320. Ruth is first at 1.399.

Ruth's figure was inflated because the stat for times grounded into double plays was not recorded for individual players until 1935. Ruth went to the plate 1.075 as many times as Williams. Williams grounded into 197 double plays. If one uses speculation and multiplies the 197 by 1.075, it comes out to 212 double plays that Ruth may have grounded into (giving him a 1.35 total average). That total seems high since the number of double plays made in Ruth's era was significantly lower than the number of twin killings in Williams' era. Ruth was a slow runner for the latter part of his career. Yet even if we give him 250 double plays, his total average is still higher than Williams at 1.341. Bonds had a total average of 1.249 with a .607 slugging percentage and .444 on-base percentage.

Williams recorded these stats despite losing more time to military service than any player in history. He missed all of the 1943, 1944, and 1945 seasons when he served as a Marines fighter pilot in World War II. He missed all but 43 games to the Korean War in 1952 and 1953 for the same reason. He missed 727 games during his peak years. Consider the number of games he missed plus the difficulty of hitting major league pitching at so high a level after returning from such long periods of absence and the magnitude of Williams' statistical greatness becomes staggering.

In the first page of Williams' autobiography, Ted says, "I wanted to be the greatest hitter who ever lived. A man has to have goals — for a day, for a lifetime — and that was mine, to have people say, 'There goes Ted Williams, the greatest hitter who ever lived.' Certainly nobody ever worked harder at it. It was the center of my heart, hitting a baseball. Eddie Collins used to say I lived for my next turn at bat, and that's the way it was. If there was ever a man born to be a hitter it was me. As a kid, I wished it on every falling star."[1] Many fans still believe Ted was the best hitter ever. Even with the stats accumulated by sluggers during the steroids era, Williams' record compares favorably.

The only knock on Ted was that he walked too much. Ty Cobb criticized Williams for this. Many writers went as far as to say that Ted was "begging walks" and too concerned with his batting average. Williams defended himself against this charge. He contended that he might only be a .250 batter if he tried to hit pitches out of the strike zone. And that if a pitcher, having walked Ted, had to throw strikes to the guy behind him, that guy possibly became a .300 hitter. Ted believed he was more help to his team by not going after pitches off the plate.

Like most great hitters of the old days, Williams grew up in humble surroundings. His mother was gone all day and most of the night while working the streets for the Salvation Army during the bleakest Depression years. They called her "Salvation May." His father owned a photography shop in San Diego and wouldn't get home from work until late at night. Ted remembered, "Many nights my brother, Danny, and I would be out on the front porch past ten o'clock waiting for one of them to come home. I was maybe eight at the time, and Danny was six. I know the neighbors must have thought it was terrible for us, but kids don't think in those terms. ... You don't think of yourself being 'deprived' as a kid unless someone tells you are."[2]

Ted found his outlet in hitting a baseball. He spent hour upon hour at the North End playground. The playground had lights and Ted would stay there until nine o'clock. He hit against the backstop playing a two-man game called "Big League" by the hour. He also recalled batting 100 times in some sandlot games.

After high school Ted played two seasons for the San Diego Padres of the Pacific Coast League. The Boston Red Sox saw his talent and acquired him for $35,000 plus two players in 1937. Bosox general manager Eddie Collins first noticed Ted's ability the year before and signed him to a two-year contract for $7,500 plus a $1,000 bonus that his parents insisted on. The Red Sox sent Ted to Minneapolis of the American Association, where he batted .366 with 43 homers and 143 RBIs.

By the time he reached the Red Sox in 1939, Ted's 6'4" frame had filled out to 175 pounds and he was hitting balls more than 400 feet. Williams gave the Fenway faithful an inkling of things to come in 1939. He batted .327 with 31 homers and led the league in RBIs with 145. Batting in front of Jimmie Foxx helped. Foxx enjoyed his last big season, batting .360 and leading the league in homers (35) and slugging percentage (.694). Ted, at age twenty, also began to be known for his boyish cockiness. In one game in Detroit he blasted a homer off Bob Harris that landed on top of the right-field pavilion at Briggs Stadium. As he crossed the plate he told Tiger catcher Birdie Tebbetts, "I hope that guy is still pitching the next time I come up. I'll knock it clear over the roof." That is exactly what Ted did the next time up.[3]

Sometimes he practiced his swing while standing in the outfield. He did not fare well playing right field, the sun field, at Fenway. The next season he would be shifted to left, where he eventually became an underrated flychaser. There were times he sulked after tapping a ground ball and did not run hard to first base. If he had a bad day at the plate, it might effect his fielding. The Boston writers, led by Dave Egan, magnified his mistakes. In 1939 Ted's father and mother separated. He decided not to go home during the winter. He sent money to his mother, but home was not a happy place.

In 1940 Ted's relationship with the writers worsened. The first time Williams did something to displease sports reporter Harold Kaese, Kaese wrote, "Well, what do you expect from a guy who won't even go see his mother in the off season."[4] It was comments like this that turned Williams against the writers. He explained, "Before this, I was willing to believe a writer was my friend until he proved otherwise. Now my guard's up all the time, always watching for critical stuff. If I saw something, I'd read it twenty times, and I'd burn without knowing how to fight it. How could I fight it?"[5]

In 1940 Ted batted .344 but his power numbers fell to 23 homers and 113 RBIs. Only seven of his homers came at Fenway. After being booed upon striking out and following it up with an error, Williams vowed never to tip his cap again. He never did tip it again during his playing days, even after homering in his final at-bat in 1960.

Ted's way of dealing with the bad press was to tell the writers off. This increased his problem. It cost him votes in the MVP balloting. He did he not win MVP after batting .406 in 1941. He also did not win it after capturing the Triple Crown in 1942 and 1947. In 1947 he lost MVP honors to Joe DiMaggio by one point.

The 1941 season, however, was probably Ted's most enjoyable. His most zealous critics could find little fault with him that summer. It was the hitting perfectionist's perfect season. The so-called kid with the swelled head proved to the world how remarkable a talent he was. He proved he was the equal of anyone playing baseball and won many fans over to him. From then until the end of his career, the potshots the press took at him could not deny his true greatness.

The 1941 season didn't start in a promising way for Williams. He was a no-show on opening day of spring training. He phoned Eddie Collins the next day and explained he had been busy hunting wolves in Minnesota and lost track of time. He promised to hop in his car and drive straight down. In the second exhibition game Ted caught his spikes while sliding and chipped a bone in his right ankle. He ended spring training relegated to pinch-hitting duties.

On April 15, an Opening Day crowd of 15,000 at Fenway saw the Red Sox rally for three runs in the ninth to top Washington, 7–6. Ted delivered a pinch-hit single in the rally. A bases-loaded walk to player-manager Joe Cronin forced in the winning run. Ted's teammate Bobby Doerr believed that Williams' ankle injury might have helped Ted hit .406. Doerr explained, "I remember him going into the trainer's room every day to get his ankle taped up. In batting practice you could see him kind of favoring it. I kind of wondered then, and I kind of got to thinking as the season went on, that it was sensitive enough to make him stay back for as long as possible to keep the pressure off his front foot."[6]

Williams agrees that he was able to hold back longer in 1941. However, Ted said, "But I never thought it was because of my ankle. I never thought that. From 1941 on, I was getting stronger and stronger and stronger. I was late to mature, and I think I was strongest between the ages of twenty-two and thirty-two. As a result, I was able to hold back and hold back, getting quicker and stronger than at any time."[7]

On April 20, Boston won its fifth straight, 14–8, in Washington. Red Sox center fielder Dom DiMaggio slashed a single and three doubles and stole two bases. His brother Joe belted a grand slam and drove in six runs as the Yanks humbled the A's, 19–5. The Red Sox winning streak ended the next day with a 6–5 loss to the Senators. Williams tried to play left field at Griffith Stadium during a 12–5 loss to Washington on April 22. He whacked a single and a double but aggravated the injury. In the next four games he appeared once, pinch-hitting unsuccessfully in a 6–3 loss in New York. Ted never was a good cold-weather hitter. Fenway almost always had chilling winds during the first couple of weeks of the season. Not being in the lineup every day then probably helped Ted bat .406.

Ted was back in left field on April 29 in Detroit. He bashed a long double and a 440-foot home run off Johnny Gorsica, but Gorsica outpitched Lefty Grove to win, 5–3. Ted always considered Detroit as his favorite park to hit in with its short right field. In 585 career at-bats there, he homered 55 times with 151 runs scored and 162 RBIs despite going against classy hurlers like Hal Newhouser, Dizzy Trout, Frank Lary, and Jim Bunning.

On May 7 in Chicago, Williams walloped a 500-foot two-run homer into the upper right-field stands at Comiskey Park off Johnny Rigney. Rigney liked to challenge hitters with high fastballs. The book on Ted was that he murdered the high fastball.[8] Ted came to bat against Rigney again in the eleventh inning with the score tied at 3–3. Rigney tried to surprise Williams with a slow curve. Ted drove it over the roof of the second tier in the deepest part of right-center and sent it bouncing into a parking lot 600 feet from home. Only Ruth and Gehrig had cleared that roof before.

Williams now had 17 hits in 42 at-bats for a .404 average. Washington shortstop Cecil Travis was leading the league at .459. Travis finished second to Ted in the batting race at .359 and topped the league in hits with 218. But he suffered frozen feet during the Battle of the Bulge and was never the same player after World War II. Travis batted .327 in 4,191 at-bats before the war. He hit .241 after he returned from combat.

The Yankees arrived in Boston on May 11 and the Red Sox routed New York, 13–5, before 34,500. Ted singled twice and doubled in six at-bats while Joe DiMaggio singled three times in five at-bats. Joe was off to a slow start, barely batting .300, when he began his 56-game hitting streak on May 15 with a single against Chicago's Ed Smith. Ted singled once in three at-bats that day during a 6–4 loss to the first-place Indians. In the ninth he came to the plate with two runners on against Bob Feller. Williams smashed a laser line shot toward first base that was speared by Hal Trosky. Trosky then doubled up Lou Finney with a toss to second base to end the game.

Ted's single that day started a 23-game hitting streak of his own. In those 23 games, Ted batted .487 (43-for-88) while DiMaggio batted .368 (32-for-87). On May 21, Ted went 4-for-5 with a double off the Browns' Bob Harris in an 8–6 Red Sox win. Williams was always a terror against the Browns. In 1941 he hit .426 with nine homers and 26 RBIs in 61 at-bats against them. From 1939 to 1953, he feasted on Brownie pitching, batting .393 with 60 homers and 223 RBIs in 754 at-bats.

The Red Sox played three games at Yankee Stadium, from May 23 to May 25. The first game was called because of darkness with the score tied, 9–9. The Yanks won the second game, 7–6, as DiMaggio's two-run single in the seventh inning was the deciding blow. Boston took the final game, 10–3, as Williams singled three times and doubled to bring his average to .404.

During a four-game series against the A's from May 27 to May 29, Ted ripped eight hits in 15 at-bats, including a double and two homers, to bring his average up to .421. On Memorial Day in Boston, the Yanks and Red Sox divided a doubleheader. New York won the opener, 4–3, and Boston took the second game, 13–0. Ted was 3-for-5 on the day with a double and scored four times. DiMaggio had two singles in five at-bats but experienced the worst day of his career on defense, making four errors. Ted ended May at .429. He had hit .436 for the month.

The *Sporting News* opined,

> Unless all people who know anything are 100 percent wrong, Williams is due to firmly establish himself this year as one of the truly great left-handed batsmen. There isn't anything particularly new about this estimate of his ability, either. In 1939, his first complete season in the major leagues, Williams did things with a bat and ball that made all wonder where his limits were. He hit homers in many parks that went so far as to be almost unbelievable. He didn't hit them off young or unskilled pitchers altogether either. [9]

As June opened an announcement was made that all servicemen would be admitted free for the remainder of the season at major league ballparks. Ted began June in Detroit with four hits in nine at-bats, including his eighth homer of the year, as the Red Sox swept a doubleheader, 7–6 and 6–5. Lou Gehrig died on June 2 and flags were flown at half-staff in major league parks on the day of his funeral. Cleveland led the league on June 2 at 30–19. Chicago was 1½ games out. The Yanks were three games back. Boston was four out with a 22–19 record. Bob Feller had won 11 of the Indians games, including three shutouts.

The Red Sox teed off on Cleveland pitching on June 5, socking 16 hits in a 14–1 win. Williams singled twice, homered, drove in three runs, and scored four times. The next day his average reached its high-water mark for the season at .438 as he doubled and clouted a two-run homer off Rigney in a 6–3 win in Chicago.

Around this time Carl Felker characterized Williams in the *Sporting News*:

> Ted Williams rolled up a newspaper, gritted his teeth, faced the mirror in a hotel room in St. Louis and took a cut at an imaginary ball. "Hitting is the biggest thing in my life," he exclaimed. "I love it. And the thing I like next best is to hunt ducks in Minnesota." But right now, duck hunting doesn't occupy any part of Ted's thoughts. He is concentrating on the job of trying to top the .400 mark in hitting for the 1941 season. And he believes he has a good chance to reach his goal — perhaps even to smash the all-time figure at .438 set away back in 1894 by Hugh Duffy, now a coach with the Red Sox. "If you don't have confidence in yourself, who will?," asks the Boston kid.[10]

Felker continued: "Every chance he gets, Williams practices hitting. 'I've always done that,' he declared. 'It's my pet theory — practice your swing all the time, from morning to night. Strengthen those muscles you're going to use. I go out to the ball park in the morning for batting drill. Even when I'm in the outfield, I take my imaginary cuts at the ball. I'm always taking swings in my room. It all helps.'"[11]

Felker also wrote of the young sensation:

> His love of cowboy pictures is just one of many evidences that Ted Williams, 22 years old, still is in his boyhood, as far as his emotions are concerned....He has an unconcealed boyish delight in his own batting success, a youngster's high enthusiasm over being a part of baseball's Big Show, a quick hearty laugh and equal quickness to speak his mind, without a moment's reflection to choose his words, as is the case with older players. He has a boy's pleasure in praise and a quick, youthful resentment of criticism, a trait that possibly led to his famous feud with sports writers during his first two seasons in the majors.[12]

Williams' 23-game hitting streak was stopped in Chicago on June 8 by Ted Lyons. Lyons walked him three times, including once with the bases loaded. The Red Sox won, 5–3, in ten innings behind Grove. The Red Sox were pitching the 41-year-old Grove once a week and Lefty was doing well. He had compiled a 20-game win streak in Fenway.

On June 12 in St. Louis, Ted's two-run homer off knuckleballer Johnny Niggeling was the difference in a 3–2 win. Back in Boston on June 15, Ted whacked four hits in six at-bats, including another double and homer, as the Yawkeyites swept the White Sox in a Sunday doubleheader before 34,000, 8–6 and 6–4.

On Bunker Hill Day in Boston, the Red Sox took the opener of a doubleheader from Detroit, 14–6, but dropped the second game, 8–5. Ted drilled a two-run homer and doubled in five at-bats. In New York, the Yanks completed a three-game sweep of Cleveland. "Joltin' Joe" ran his streak to 29 consecutive games, tying the Yankee club record shared by Earle Combs and Roger Peckinpaugh.

On June 23 Cleveland still led the league at 40–25 when they entered Boston for a three-game set. The Yanks were two games back and Boston was within striking distance at 33–26, four games back. The Red Sox won the opener, routing Mel Harder and his successors with 18 hits, 13–2. The next day Williams cracked a two-run homer in the fourth inning to tie the score at 2–2 and Boston went on to win, 7–2. The loss knocked the Indians out of first place as New York took over the top by besting St. Louis, 7–5. "Joltin' Joe" homered in the fourth inning, bringing his streak to 37 games. In the final game, Cleveland rebounded to win, 11–8. Feller, showing strains of overwork, was hit hard but recorded his 16th win. Williams went 5-for-10 in the series, scoring six runs and knocking in three. He was now at .412 with 53 RBIs and 63 runs. DiMaggio was at .349 with 62 runs and 57 RBIs.

The Red Sox invaded Yankee Stadium for a doubleheader on July 1, trailing the Bronx Bombers by five games. It was Boston's last real chance to get into the pennant race. But 52,832 saw the Yanks win, 7–2 and 9–2. After Joe DiMaggio broke Sisler's record of 41 consecutive games, Willie Keeler's 1896 record of 44 games was resurrected. Joe stroked three singles in the doubleheader sweep to tie Keeler's mark. He broke it the next day with a three-run homer that flew over Ted's head and sailed into the left-field seats. The Yanks won again, 8–4, to open an eight-game lead over third-place Boston. Lefty Gomez quipped that Joe broke Keeler's mark by using Wee Willie's formula, "Hitting them where they ain't."[13]

Ted managed three singles in nine at-bats in the series without an RBI. He said afterward, "I know it sounds corny, but I really wish I could hit like that guy Joe DiMaggio. I'm honest, Joe's big and strong and he can club that ball without any effort. These hot days I wear myself out laying into it, and I lose seven or eight pounds out there. When it's hot I lose my snap or something."[14]

On July 3 in Philadelphia, Grove won his 299th career game, 5–2, backed by a two-run homer from Williams. On the last day before the All-Star break, Ted went 4-for-8 with two doubles as the Bosox topped the Senators twice, 6–2 and 4–3, at Fenway. In New York, 60,948 fans showed up at Yankee Stadium as Gehrig's monument in center field was dedicated. The Yanks beat the A's twice, 8–4 and 3–1. DiMaggio smacked six hits, including a double and a triple. Before each game started at Yankee Stadium, Joe would go to Stevens Brothers refreshment booth and drink cups of black coffee. His streak had reached 48 games and was the talk of baseball. The life-and-death drama of the streak had fans asking each day, "Did he get one?" Ted was getting second billing during Joe's streak, but he was drawing attention with his .405 average at the break.

The All-Star game was considered as big an event as the World Series in those days. Both leagues played for keeps and for bragging rights. Going into the last of the ninth at Detroit, the AL trailed, 5–3. A few minutes later the bases were loaded with one out and Joe DiMaggio at the plate. Joe rapped what appeared to be a game-ending double play ball to shortstop Eddie Miller, but second baseman Billy Herman's relay to first pulled Frank McCormick off the bag. One run scored, and Williams walked to the plate to face the Cubs' Claude Passeau with two on and two out.

Ted fouled off the first pitch, took two balls, and then lifted a fly ball toward the foul line in right. He described his historic homer in his autobiography:

> I had pulled it to right field, no doubt about that, but I was afraid I hadn't got enough of the bat on the ball. But gee, it just kept going, up, up, way up into the right-field stands in Detroit.... Halfway down to first, seeing that ball going out, I stopped running and started leaping and jumping and clapping my hands, and I was so happy I laughed out loud. I've never been so happy, and I've never seen so many happy guys. They carried me off the field, DiMaggio and Bob Feller, who had pitched early in the game and was already in street clothes. [15]

The Red Sox stayed in Detroit for a four-game series after the All-Star game. On July 12, Ted received a base on balls and then took a big lead off first base. The Tigers pitched out and Birdie Tebbetts fired down to Rudy York, trying to pick Williams off. Ted slid back to first hard, and when he did his foot hit the corner of the bag and twisted. It was the same foot he had injured in the spring. He limped around a few more innings before retiring to the clubhouse. The ankle swelled. He had received three walks in the game before fouling out in his last at-bat. On the previous day he had been collared in four at-bats by Bobo Newsom, as Bobo denied Grove his 300th win, 2–0. Ted's average had dipped to .397 and the dream of a .400 season seemed in jeopardy.

Meanwhile, Joe DiMaggio ran his streak to 56 games before being stopped on July 17 before 67,468 in a night game in Cleveland. From the time he broke Keeler's record until the end of the streak, he was on fire, whacking 24 hits in 44 at-bats. He now led the league in RBIs with 76 and home runs with 20. During one span in the streak, the Yankees won 30 of 35 games to run away into a solid lead. On July 21 they led Cleveland by seven games and Boston by 14. Joe's average was up to .375, and he told reporters that he hadn't given up on catching Ted for the batting title. During the streak he had hit .408. During the same period, Ted hit .412.

Ted spent 12 games on the bench. He pinch-hit four times — he walked once, hit an RBI fly ball, popped out, and cranked a three-run homer. He returned to left field in Fenway on July 22 and tagged Chicago's Rigney again for a gigantic homer into the right-center bleachers in the second inning. Stan Spence replaced him in the field later, but Ted was back for nine innings the next day, socking a single and double. In his first 12 games back from the injury, Ted ripped 19 hits in 35 at-bats to bring his average back up to .412.

On July 25, 1941, the Nazis were stalled 230 miles from Moscow and Lefty Grove won his 300th game, beating Cleveland, 10–6. In the fifth inning Ted belted a two-run homer to tie the game at 4–4, but he quickly gave both runs back by misplaying a ball in the outfield. In the seventh inning he walked and third baseman Jim Tabor followed with a home run to knot the score again at 6–6. Ted fouled out weakly in the eighth with two runners on and angrily flung his bat in the air, but Foxx followed by slamming the ball off the center-field wall for a triple. Foxx's blast scored two runs, and Jimmie chugged home when the throw skipped past third.

Ted does not remember the game with any pleasure, however, because he was nowhere to be seen in the post-game picture of Grove celebrating. Williams was hurt by the accusation that he was so mad at not having come through with the winning hit for Grove that he was sulking in the trainer's room while pictures were being taken. He explained, "I drove in two and let in three that day, and that's why I was so mad at myself. And I'm mad now that I'm not in the picture with my arm around Lefty Grove. That's a picture I really wish I had."[16]

Grove was quoted after his 300th victory, boasting, "I'm on my way to 500 now!"[17] In his next game he gave up four runs to Detroit before retiring a batter. He never won another game.

After DiMaggio's streak was stopped in Cleveland, he ran off another 16-game streak to hit safely in 72 of 73 games. He went almost two months without striking out. Yet Ted was pulling away again in the batting race. His three singles on July 26 denied Feller his 20th win. His two-run homer on July 29 was the key blow in a 3–2 win over St. Louis. He smashed a grand slam against the Browns the next day. He ended July at .409 to "Joltin' Joe's" .377. On August 1 he went fishing on an off-day and caught a 374-pound tuna.

In two doubleheaders in St. Louis, on August 19 and August 20, Ted went 8-for-14 with five homers, seven runs, and eight RBIs. DiMaggio cooled off and dipped to .356. Joe then sprained his ankle on August 19. He missed three weeks. DiMaggio's injury gave Ted a good chance at the Triple Crown — if the pitchers did not walk him too much. He was in the midst of a 21-game road trip, when he was walked 32 times in 96 plate appearances. He had 26 hits. He hit .406 on the trip with a .623 on-base percentage. On August 30 he celebrated his twenty-third birthday with a single and home run during a 12–3 win over the A's.

The *Sporting News* reported:

> The orders the pitchers get now when Ted comes to bat, particularly with men on base is to walk him. They start walking him as early as the first inning. If he isn't walked intentionally with the catcher moving off to one side, they might as well put on the act, because they pitch so wide to Ted it would be silly for him to swing on any of the pitches.... It is the exception when Ted is pitched a ball not down near his left knee or so far on the outside as to be almost a wild pitch. Therefore his chances of hitting are kept away down. Ted has one of the best eyes for pitches of any batter in baseball. [18]

While in the U.S. Marines, Ted's eyesight would be tested at 20/10, and he set the gunnery record at Jacksonville.

On Labor Day in Boston, Ted smashed three tremendous home runs in a doubleheader sweep of the Senators. This gave him 34 homers on the season, passing New York's Charlie Keller for the league lead. He was also walked four more times. One of the homers came off Bill Zuber, the pitcher who came close to ending Ted's career with a beaning at Minneapolis in 1938. The writers said it was the longest homer Ted had hit at Fenway all season. [19]

The Yanks clinched the pennant with a 6–3 win at Fenway on September 4. Atley Donald, a pitcher noted for his control, walked Ted four straight times, before Williams singled in his final time at-bat. They were the only walks Donald gave up. The same frustrating experience happened to Ted three weeks earlier at Yankee Stadium. After a first-inning RBI single, he was walked four straight times to an accompaniment of boos from New York fans.

On September 7 at Yankee Stadium, Ted laced a single and a pair of doubles off Lefty Gomez in an 8–5 loss. His first time up he banged a drive high off the foul pole. The ball ricocheted into the stands in foul territory for a double. Under the rules at the time, if a ball hit off the inside of the foul pole and landed in the stands foul, it was a double. Under today's rules, any ball hitting the foul pole is a homer.

Yankee Stadium was the only park in which Ted did not hit a home run that summer. In the fifth inning, however, he crushed a 450-foot double off the top of the center-field wall, missing a round-tripper by inches. The next inning Gomez walked him on four pitches with the bases loaded, giving Ted his only RBI of the day.

Many fans believed Williams would have been even more of a terror if he had played for the Yanks. Yankee Stadium had a short right-field porch, ideal for a left-handed pull hitter like Williams. Ted said, however, he always considered Yankee Stadium a tough park to hit in because off its background of white shirts in the bleachers and afternoon shadows. In 1941 he knocked out 16 hits in 33 at-bats for a .489 average there, the best mark of his career at the stadium. Lifetime in 475 at-bats there, he hit .309 with 30 homers.

Williams believed the best thing he had going for him was playing in Fenway. Yawkey had blotted out the signs. There was a green background everywhere to help batters see the ball. The shadows were not bad, and there was that close left-field wall. In 1941 Williams had 104 hits in 243 at-bats at Fenway for a .428 average. He also homered 19 times and drove in 62 runs with a .574 on-base percentage and .765 slugging percentage. He hit .380 on the road. For his career he batted .361 in Fenway and .328 on the road.

Ted believed the Green Monster was a big help to him even though he didn't hit to left often. He said the close wall gave him the luxury of waiting longer on a pitch. He always knew that balls he sliced to left or balls hit late could still clang off that wall or go out. By being able to wait longer, Ted believed he got fooled less often by pitches and was able to protect the plate better with two strikes.

On September 15, Ted belted his 35th homer of the season, a three-run shot off Chicago's Johnny Rigney in a 6–1 triumph at Fenway. His three RBIs tied him with Joe DiMaggio at 116. Keller was leading the league at 122, but he twisted his ankle on September 7 and was lost for the season. It was possible both Ted and Joe could pass him in RBIs.

When the Yanks came into Fenway on September 20, Joe and Ted were still tied in RBIs at 116. Ted had two-thirds of the Triple Crown locked up and was battling Joe for the RBI crown. The Yanks won the first game, 8–1. Joe singled, doubled, and drove in two runs to take the lead again at 118. The next day Boston clinched second place by winning, 4–1. Ted launched a two-run homer off Ernie Bonham, tying Joe for the RBI lead again.

Ted now was hitting .406 with six games left to play. He was quoted as saying: "Lots of times I could belt the ball into the stands if I wanted to take a chance, but I have to think about my average this season. Next year, everybody will be talking about my 1941 mark. Then I'll be swinging from my heels and giving the home run record a whirl. I'll go after em' all, one at a time. I'll beat Gehrig's mark for runs batted in, Hornsby's and Cobb's batting records and Ruth in homers. I'm the boy to do it, too."[20]

The *Sporting News* remarked:

> From the rock-bound coast of Maine to the sun-kissed shores of California, the real fans are rooting almost to a man for Ted to continue above the .400 mark.... Williams has a grip on the fans of the country that is remarkable. He is only a

youngster, having become 23 on August 30. It may be that his great ability as a batter for one so young has appealed to the fans. There is a boyishness about Ted that gets everybody. A string bean in build, with a frame so shy of the usual sinew and muscle which great hitters of other days have had, he does not appear to have the power to do what he does and yet he does it. [21]

On September 23 and 24, the Red Sox played three games in Washington and Ted managed two singles in ten at-bats. His average dropped to .402. Meanwhile in New York, DiMaggio smashed two home runs and drove in three runs to take the RBI lead for keeps. On September 27, Ted got just one hit in four at-bats, a double to deep center, against A's knuckleballer Roger Wolff during a 5–1 Red Sox win. His average dipped to .39955 with a season-ending doubleheader scheduled the next day at Shibe.

Ted described the evening before the doubleheader in his book:

> The night before the game Cronin offered to take me out of the lineup to preserve the .400 (.39955 rounds off to .400). I told Cronin I didn't want that. If I couldn't hit .400 all the way I didn't deserve it. It sure as hell meant something to me then, and Johnny Orlando, the clubhouse boy, always a guy who was there when I needed him, must have walked ten miles with me the night before, talking it over and just walking around. Johnny really didn't like to walk as much as I did, so I'd wait outside while he ducked into a bar for a quick one to keep his strength up. The way he tells it, he made two stops for scotch and I made two stops for ice cream walking the streets of Philadelphia. [22]

On the last day of the season the weather turned cold at Shibe. A crowd of 10,000 showed up. Ted recalled, "As I came to bat for the first time that day, the Philadelphia catcher, Frankie Hayes, said: 'Ted, Mr. Mack told us if we let up on you he'll run us out of baseball. I wish you all the luck in the world, but we're not giving you a damn thing. [23]

Williams started the first game with a line single between first and second off Dick Fowler. The next time up he homered 440 feet over the right-center-field fence. Then he hit two singles off a left-hander he had never seen, Porter Vaughn. He finished the game at 4-for-5 as the Red Sox won, 12–11. In the second game he hit a ground single to right and then doubled off a loud-speaker horn in right center. Mack had to have the horn replaced in the winter. For the day he wound up with six hits in eight at-bats to finish at .406. He added to his story, "I don't remember celebrating that night, but I probably went out and had a chocolate milk shake."[24]

This wasn't the last time Ted rose to the occasion. On Opening Day in 1946, in this first game back after three years in the military, Ted blasted a 400-foot homer in Washington. In 1952, in his last game before leaving for Korea, Ted broke a 3–3 tie with Detroit by creaming a homer off Dizzy Trout. Ted flew 39 combat missions over Korea. When hit by small-arms fire during one mission, he crash landed his damaged jet and escaped from the flaming wreckage fortunate to be alive. In his first Fenway appearance back from the cockpit near the end of the 1953 season, he homered off Mike Garcia and went on to bat an incredible .407 in 37 games.

In 1957, at age 39, Ted topped the league with a .388 batting average and slammed 38 homers. He batted .453 during the second half of 1957. Off the field, his concern for charitable causes in Boston and his efforts on behalf of the Jimmy Fund were numerous, often unpublicized, and made genuinely from his heart. Today he is remembered most for hitting .406 in 1941, but Ted Williams' entire career — both on and off the field — was nothing short of colossal.

Chapter 12

Rapid Robert's Triumphant Return: Bob Feller in 1946

In 1946 Bob Feller returned triumphant from 3½ years of service in the U.S. Navy during World War II to put together a season that few have matched. Feller's performance in 1946 is a bit overlooked today. He appeared in 48 games, completed 36 of 42 starts, threw 371 innings with a 2.18 ERA, hurled 10 shutouts, struck out 348 batters, and won 26 games for a Cleveland team that only scored 537 runs.

When the season ended Feller's 348 strikeouts was thought to be the all-time single-season record. Huge crowds turned out to see "Rapid Robert" mow batsmen down in his quest to break Rube Waddell's supposed record of 343 in 1904. After the season ended, research by historians discovered that Waddell struck out 349 batters in 1904. The point is moot now. Sandy Koufax (382 in 1965) and Nolan Ryan (383 in 1973) have broken the record.

Feller took pride in his number of innings pitched. His 36 complete games in 1946 haven't been equaled since. His total of 371 innings in 1946 has been exceeded twice, both by left-handers (Wilbur Wood's 376.2 innings in 1972 and Mickey Lolich's 376 innings in 1971). Neither pitched as effectively as Feller. Feller then threw an estimated 80 more innings in a barn-storming series of games that he organized, mostly against the Satchel Paige All-Stars. Paige's team featured many of the best African American ballplayers. All total Feller pitched more than 450 innings against top-flight talent in 1946.

Bob Feller grew up on his family's farm in Van Meter, Iowa. He was nurtured along as a pitcher by his father, Bill. When Bob was 12 years old, he and his father built a ballpark right on the farm next to the corn, cows, and chickens and formed their own team. Feller wrote of the ballpark, "We charged 25 cents to get in — 35 cents for a doubleheader — and Dad formed a team and scheduled games for every Sunday all summer long. On most Sundays, two or three hundred people came to watch our team of players in their teens and their 20s and one 13-year-old play baseball against good teams from Des Moines and other cities."[1]

Before leaving for the war, Feller was the best pitcher in the game. He signed a contract for $40,000 for 1940, making him one of the game's highest-paid players. He built a $25,000 brick house for his parents on the farm back in Van Meter with indoor plumbing, electricity, and air conditioning. His father had been diagnosed with inoperable brain cancer. Bob knew he owed his success as a ballplayer to his dad, and wrote in his 2001 book, *Bob Feller's Little Black Book of Baseball Wisdom*, "There wasn't anything my father wouldn't do for me."[2]

In 1940 Feller tossed the only Opening Day no-hitter in history when he blanked the Chicago White Sox, 1–0, at Comiskey Park. He compiled a 27–11 record with 261 strikeouts and a 2.62 ERA in 320 innings. In 1941 his success continued as he hurled 343 innings, won 25 games against 13 losses, and fanned 260 batters with a 3.15 ERA.

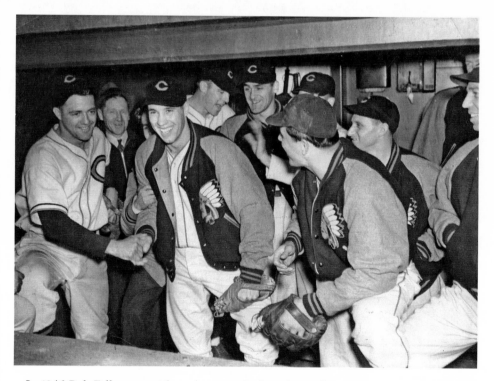

In 1946 Bob Feller returned on the mound triumphant after 3½ years of service in the U.S. Navy during World War II. He completed 36 of 42 starts, compiled a 2.18 ERA in 371 innings, struck out 348 batters, hurled a no-hitter plus two one-hitters, and won 26 games for a Cleveland team that scored only 537 runs.

Feller enlisted in the navy two days after the bombing of Pearl Harbor. He left an income, including endorsements of $50,000 a year, for a navy salary of $80 a month. He did not have to join up; he was not eligible for the draft because he was the sole support of his family. His father, Bill, was ill and would die in 1943.

Feller was put in charge of a 24-man crew manning a .40 millimeter Bofors anti-aircraft mount on the USS Alabama battleship. From March to August 1943, the ship was utilized to escort convoys to Britain in the North Atlantic. Then the USS Alabama sailed through the Panama Canal to the Pacific war. It was used to escort carriers and soften up the Japanese defenses by providing shore bombardment. A number of times the USS Alabama came under attack from Japanese planes. It was Feller's vital task to determine where the AA guns would aim during these heated fights. The USS Alabama fought in the Battle of the Philippine Sea, where the Japanese launched approximately 430 planes and lost all but 35. Three Japanese carriers were sunk. Feller called the battle "the most exciting 13 hours of my life."[3]

And Feller did not feel special about his service time. In an interview with author John Sickels on October 18, 2002, for Sickel's definitive biography of the legendary pitcher entitled *Bob Feller: Ace of the Greatest Generation*, Feller declared, "I'm no hero. Get this straight. The heroes didn't come back. Only the survivors did."[4]

Feller was discharged in August 1945. He started nine games at the end of the 1945 season, finishing with a 5–3 record in 72 innings. In spring training of 1946, Feller did not pitch well. His velocity seemed to be less than overpowering. In an exhibition series against the Giants, he was raked for 20 hits in 16 innings. Skeptics said Feller had left his fastball in the navy.

The 1946 Indians were not a good offensive team. They batted .245 with 79 homers and scored 537 runs to finish in sixth place with a 68–86 record. Player-manager Lou Boudreau, the Cleveland shortstop, was the best everyday guy in the lineup, batting .293 with a team-high 62 RBIs. Pat Seery hit 26 homers but also whiffed 101 times and batted .225. George Case was the fastest runner in the majors, swiping an AL-leading 28 bases, but he batted .225. Hank Edwards led the Clevelanders, batting .301 in 458 at-bats, but Kenny Keltner had an off-year at .241.

On Opening Day 1946, the Indians visited Comiskey Park. Feller temporarily silenced the skeptics by hanging nine zeroes up on the scoreboard to outpitch Bill Dietrich, 1–0. Feller didn't allow a hit until Taft Wright lined a two-out single to right in the fifth inning. Feller issued his only walk of the day to Bob Kennedy in the ninth. Kennedy was bunted to second. Jake Jones then blooped what looked like a game-tying single to center field. Bob Lemon, who started the 1946 season as a center fielder before being switched to pitcher, raced in and made a sensational diving catch. Lemon then tossed the ball to Boudreau at second to double up Kennedy and end the game. Feller allowed just three hits and fanned ten.

In his next start Feller lost by a 3–2 score in 10 innings to Detroit. Tigers moundsmen Stubby Overmire and Virgil Trucks combined to beat Feller. Overmire tied the game with a perfect squeeze bunt in the seventh. In the tenth Feller walked Eddie Lake, who scored the winner on Eddie Mayo's double. Again Feller fanned ten. Feller also lost on April 26 to Chicago, 4–2. A wind-blown pop eluded second baseman Ray Mack for a gift double to start a four-run Chicago rally in the fifth inning.

The rumors began again that "Rapid Robert's" fastball wasn't as rapid as before the war. Feller wrote in 1947 in his first autobiography, *Strikeout Story*, that one particular newspaper article espousing this theory "maddened me as nothing ever written about me had before."[5] On April 30, Bob took the mound at Yankee Stadium before 37,000 fans determined to kill these rumors.

The big right-hander succeeded. He fired 133 pitches in no-hitting the Bronx Bombers, 1–0. After the first batter for the Yankees, Phil Rizzuto, was retired on a soft bouncer to third, "Snuffy" Stirnweiss socked a hard grounder through the box past Feller. The *Sporting News* described shortstop Lou Boudreau's sparkling play: "Flashing across second base, cutting in front of the startled Mack, came Boudreau almost literally from nowhere to scoop up the ball and tumble head over heels, but not until he had fired a perfect throw to Les Fleming at first base. If Feller had done anything less than pitch a no-hit game that play would have been the headline of the day."[6]

Feller walked Tommy Henrich but got DiMaggio on a come-backer to the mound to end the first frame. Charlie Keller walked to lead off the Yankee second but was thrown out trying to steal. Feller then fanned Nick Etten and Joe Gordon. Bill Dickey walked to begin the Yankee third but Feller whiffed pitcher Bill Bevens, Rizzuto, and Stirnweiss. In the fourth Feller struck out Keller and Etten. In the fifth he struck out Dickey and Bevens. There were no Feller strikeouts in the sixth but he retired the side in order. The *Sporting News* reported, "There was an electric hum of expectancy in the arena."[7]

In the seventh Fleming momentarily lost Keller's pop fly to short right in the sun but made a last-second lunge to snare the ball. Etten fanned for the third time and Gordon bounced to Ken Keltner at third base. The *Sporting News* recorded, "Now there was no doubt of the crowd's allegiance. Unreservedly, the roaring stands swung behind the Cleveland fire thrower."[8]

In the eighth Dickey tapped a routine grounder to Boudreau. Bevens, who was also pitching a shutout, fanned for the third time. Rizzuto hit a foul pop-up in back of third but Keltner dropped the ball. The *Sporting News* described Boudreau's second sparkling play: "Rizzuto then grounded hard to

Keltner's left and Ken made a frantic lunge for the ball. He couldn't reach it but Boudreau could. Almost on the grass and well to the right of his usual position, the manager launched a mighty throw and little Phil was out by a half a step."[9]

In the top of the ninth Cleveland catcher Frankie Hayes broke the scoreless tie with a homer. The *Sporting News* picked up the action in the bottom of the inning:

> The tension of the ninth defies description. Stirnweiss bunted straight at Fleming and Les fumbled the ball for an error. Henrich sacrificed, Keltner to Fleming. DiMaggio worked the count to three and two, then grounded easily to Boudreau, Stirnweiss reaching third. Stirnweiss danced exasperatedly off third as Keller took his place in the batter's box. The park was a madhouse. Feller's first pitch was a fast ball, a called strike. So was his second and Keller took a full swing but missed. The next offering also was fast, but high, for ball one. Then Feller threw the slider which he had used so effectively against the Yankees right-handed hitters. Keller bounced it gently toward Mack. For one suffocating fraction of a second, the big keystoner slipped and fell on his hands. But he recovered in plenty of time to make the play and pandemonium broke around the big farm boy from Iowa.[10]

Before the game Feller was asked about the skeptics who were saying he had lost something off his fastball. "I guess I'll have to show a few of those guys," he told the *Sporting News*. The bible of baseball remarked, "And to make the demonstration all the more convincing he picked the Yankees, with their notorious Murderer's Row, as the guinea pigs to prove to doubting Thomases that the Feller of 1946 is just as good as the sturdy young Iowa lad who marched off to war after Pearl Harbor. ... He was a great Feller before the war, a great Feller in the war. And he's a great Feller with the war over."[11]

Four days after the no-hitter, Feller struck out nine Red Sox in six innings but gave up 10 hits, including a homer by Ted Williams, and five runs before exiting in defeat. The Red Sox got off to the fastest start in history, winning 41 of their first 50 games, and coasted to the pennant by 12 games over Detroit. Feller was not one to sulk after a bad outing. On May 7 following a day game in Washington, he entertained wounded soldiers at Walter Reed Hospital for nearly three hours. In 2002 he told John Sickels, "After coming out of war, you realize that sports are insignificant. Sports are only a game. A lot of people don't understand that. It's only a damn game."[12]

On May 8, Feller halted a seven-game Cleveland losing streak by striking out 11 and beating the A's, 5–2. Five days later he fanned 12 and beat the Browns, 4–3, in 10 innings. George Case's bases-loaded single won it for the Tribe in the tenth. Feller ran his record to 5–3 on May 17 by shutting out the Senators, 3–0. He struck out 14, giving him 85 whiffs in 71 innings. The

Sporting News declared, "The speed king's more optimistic admirers started hoping he would become the first Major League pitcher to register 300 whiffs since Walter Johnson cracked that stratospheric total in 1912."[13]

On May 21, Feller beat the Yankees again, 5–2. He extended his hitless streak against the Bronx Bombers to 13⅔ innings before Dickey singled in the fifth. Hayes provided the big blow with a three-run double off Bevens in the first inning. Five days later Feller went the full nine but gave up 15 hits to the Browns, losing, 8–2. But the "Van Meter Meteor" rebounded on May 30 to shut out the Chisox, 3–0. Again Hayes banged the key hit, belting a two-run homer in the second inning. The White Sox protested the four-bagger, saying a fan had interfered with Ralph Hodgin's attempt to catch the ball.

Feller won his eighth game on June 4 while registering 14 more strikeouts in beating Washington, 10–3, before 37,000 at Griffith Stadium. On June 8 in front of 50,000 at Yankee Stadium, Feller bested the New Yorkers yet again with a five-hitter, 2–1. Seery's two-run homer in the second inning held up. On June 12 before 33,534 fans, the largest crowd of the year at Fenway Park, Feller broke the Croninmen's 12-game win streak, 7–2. He struck out ten, giving him 136 punchouts in 124 innings.

Feller's record stood at 10–4, but there were two pitchers in the league challenging him in wins. On June 15, Detroit's "Prince Hal" Newhouser won his eleventh game, 3–1, over the Senators. Newhouser posted a 26–9 record with 275 strikeouts and a 1.94 ERA in 293 innings in 1946. In 1944 Newhouser won 29 games, and he won 25 more in 1945. He was named AL MVP for both seasons. He was classified as 4-F because of a congenital heart ailment, but he could pitch. The other pitcher challenging Feller was Boston's David "Boo" Ferriss. Ferriss won his first 10 decisions in 1946 before losing to Chicago, 7–6, on June 15. He would finish at 25–6 with a 3.25 ERA in 274 innings. Bothered by asthma and a sore arm, he never won more than 12 games in a season again.

Feller tied Newhouser for the league lead by tossing a 2–1 win in 11 innings with nine strikeouts against the A's on June 16. Both hurlers went for their 12th win five days later; only Newhouser succeeded. Feller lost to Boston's Tex Hughson, 1–0. The Red Sox tallied the lone run in the second inning when Bobby Doerr tripled and scored on a foul pop out in back of first base. Newhouser won his 12th by stopping the Yankees, 6–2. The Detroit ace had a two-hit shutout until DiMaggio smashed a two-run homer in the ninth.

On June 25, Feller fanned 13 more in besting the Yankees, 8–3, despite three singles and a homer by DiMaggio. In the eighth inning Feller experienced an unusual feeling in his right shoulder. The Yanks had two runs in and the bases loaded with one out. Feller went to the dugout to investigate and discovered the shoulder seam of his sweatshirt had let go. He changed shirts and proceeded to strike out Ken Silvestri and pinch-hitter Bill Dickey to get out of the jam. Afterward he said, "I knew I had lost my stuff but I didn't know why. My control was haywire and my shoulder felt all tied in knots. Was I relieved when I discovered what the trouble was."[14]

Newhouser passed Feller again the next day by winning a laugher over Boston, 16–2. He fanned 11 and hit his first major league homer. But Feller tied him on June 29 by shutting out the White Sox, 2–0, with nine whiffs. Young Gene Woodling broke up a scoreless tie with a two-run triple in the eighth.

Feller is best known for his fastball, but to many his curve was just as devastating. He threw three different types of curves and was not afraid to throw them on 2–0 and 3–1 counts. Hank Greenberg recalled, "Feller had a fantastic curve ball that was almost unhittable if you were a right-handed batter."[15] Feller wrote in his 1990 autobiography:

> I always had confidence in my curve because I had been throwing it since I was eight. I've never agreed with those who say kids shouldn't throw curves until their teens. I taught it to myself in throwing the ball back to Dad in our homemade batting cage. I threw it from then on, but I wasn't hurting my arm because I was throwing 12 months a year. That's the difference. How many kids throw year-round? But for those who do, curve balls are harmless — because the muscles in the kid's arm are strong and in condition and can therefore take the strain of a curve ball.[16]

The duel between Feller and Newhouser continued all summer. On July 3, Feller blanked the Browns, 6–0, with 10 strikeouts for his 14th win, but Newhouser won his 15th the same day, 2–1, over Chicago in 10 innings. "Prince Hal" only allowed one hit through the first nine innings and won his own game with an RBI double in the tenth. On July 7, Feller won his 15th, 3–2, over the Chisox with six strikeouts, giving him 190 whiffs in 180 innings at the All-Star break. Newhouser won his 16th with a 3–0 shutout of the Browns to keep the lead.

The American League trounced the National League in the All-Star game, 12–0, at Fenway Park. Feller, Newhouser, and the Browns' Jack Kramer each pitched three scoreless innings, limiting the NL stars to three singles. The star of the day was Ted Williams with two homers, two singles, and a walk.

Near the end of June the Cleveland team was sold to a syndicate headed by Bill Veeck. Veeck was a master wheeler-dealer and promotional genius. He was the son of former Chicago Cubs president William Veeck, Sr., and grew up around Wrigley Field assisting groundskeepers and selling soda in the stands. He fought as a member of the U.S. Marines against the Japanese near the end of the war, suffering wounds that required several operations and eventual amputation of his right foot in November 1946. Veeck recognized that Feller was the biggest box-office attraction on the

Indians and encouraged him to shoot for Waddell's strikeout record. Feller agreed to start on short rest and appear in relief in order to break Waddell's mark. Cleveland became known as "Strikeout City" as big crowds showed up to root Feller on.

Veeck roamed the stands talking with "average Joe" fans. He treated spectators to tremendous fireworks displays that lit up the summer skies across Lake Erie after night games. He hired baseball clown Max Patkin to entertain fans while coaching first base. Patkin was double-jointed and his hilarious, dancing, contortionist pantomime routines drew the ire of baseball purists, but had fans and even umpires roaring with laughter. Veeck also hired a former minor league shortstop named Jackie Price, who was a phenomenal pre-game entertainer. Price would hang upside down from the batting cage and swat pitched balls on a line to all fields. His best stunt, however, involved a jeep. He would shoot a baseball out of a pneumatic tube and drive a jeep across the outfield after it. Then he would somehow catch the ball backhanded while still controlling the moving jeep. Cleveland's attendance near the end of June was just 289,000, but after Veeck took over, it skyrocketed. By season's end the Indians had drawn a team-record 1,052,289 fans.

Pitching for the third time in five days, Feller was rocked by the Yankees, 9–1, on July 11 as Aaron Robinson homered twice, including a grand slam. But Robert bounced back five days later to beat the Red Sox, 6–3, backed by two Keltner homers. The Bosox socked nine hits, including four by Johnny Pesky, but Feller pitched out of trouble a number of times. On July 20, Feller won his 17th by a 10–2 score over Washington. Again Keltner was the hitting star with a homer, double, and two singles. On July 24, Feller blanked the A's, 1–0, with a three-hitter for his seventh shutout. Four days later he blanked the Senators, 2–0, with a four-hitter. He struck out ten and outdueled Bobo Newsom before 40,712 in Cleveland.

On the last day of July, Robert threw a one-hitter at the Red Sox, winning, 4–1. It was the seventh one-hitter of his career, tying Addie Joss for the record. The Croninmen scored their lone run in the first inning without a hit. Wally Moses walked and advanced to third on two ground-ball outs. Rudy York walked and then purposely got caught in a rundown between first and second. Moses took off from third and scored before York was tagged out. Doerr's second-inning single was the only hit off "Rapid Robert." Feller helped his own cause with a two-run triple. He struck out York three times and got his first whiff of Ted Williams of the season among his nine strikeouts. The win was his 20th of the year, tying Newhouser for the lead. About this time rumors appeared in the papers that Feller was about to be traded to the Yankees. Robert scoffed at the idea he could win as many as 40 games with a better hitting team, saying, "I don't want to go to New York and pitch for the Yankees. I'm perfectly satisfied where I am. ... I'll take my chances with Cleveland if nobody minds."[17]

On August 4, 74,000 fans turned out at Municipal Stadium to see Feller take on the Bronx Bombers. He had to leave the game after 6⅓ innings with the score tied at 0–0 because of a pulled back muscle. The Yanks won, 2–0, on Etten's two-run single off Lemon in the ninth inning. Things weren't much better for Newhouser that day. The Red Sox drove him from the box in a 9–4 win. Doerr homered twice and doubled for seven RBIs. Hal had been receiving treatment at Henry Ford Hospital for a nerve injury in his pitching arm. His record was now 20–4, with three of his losses to Boston.

On August 8, Feller broke Joss's record with his eighth career one-hitter, whitewashing the Chisox, 5–0. Ironically, his former catcher, Frankie Hayes, who had been traded to Chicago in June, socked the only hit off Feller. Hayes's single was a blooper to center that barely dropped in. Boudreau admitted responsibility for the gift single, saying, "I called for the ball too soon. It was my fault and not Seery's that he didn't get to the ball."[18] Hayes was hitting on borrowed time as Case had just missed catching a pop foul to right lifted by Hayes just before the single.

In between starts Feller made periodic appearances in relief and racked up strikeouts in his effort to break Waddell's record. Boudreau told the *Sporting News*, "Bob is by all odds the hardest worker in baseball. The records show that he pitches more than anyone else but that's only half the story. Even on the days he isn't pitching he is running and doing calisthenics, almost literally by the hour. I've never known an athlete who trained as conscientiously, and the results speak for themselves."[19]

In an interview with the *Sporting News*, Feller said he ate two good meals a day and revealed his diet. "At breakfast I start with a large orange juice, follow with Wheaties, then with eggs and some meats, ham or sausages, whole wheat toast and milk. ... For my late meal I prefer a shrimp cocktail, a thick soup, meat, salad and potatoes and milk."[20]

On August 13, Feller took the mound before 65,000 at Municipal Stadium and lost a 1–0 battle to Virgil Trucks and the Tigers. He had a no-hitter until the seventh inning. He gave up a walk, two singles, and a run in the eighth before leaving the game for a pinch-hitter. On August 15, Newhouser was back in form, blanking the Chisox, 3–0, on a three-hitter to tie Feller in wins with 21.

In his next start Feller's effort was sabotaged by three Cleveland errors in the eighth inning, helping the White Sox to four runs and a 4–1 win. On August 20 his effort was sabotaged again by errors in a 5–4 loss in Washington. This time the Tribe committed four miscues, including two by the usually reliable Boudreau. For a week before the game, Washington owner Clark

Griffith had been advertising a test to measure the speed of Feller's fastball. He planned to have Feller fire a few of his smokeballs before game time while a U.S. Army device called a "lumiline chronograph" tested their speed. The device was used to measure the velocity of artillery shells. It was said to be accurate to one ten-thousandth of a second.[21] But no one bothered to ask Feller's permission to participate in the exhibition.

Feller was miffed by Griffith's assumption that Bob would participate since the test took place just before a game that the Cleveland ace was scheduled to start. Feller voiced his displeasure to Griffith but agreed to take part for $700. He fired five pitches into the device. His fifth pitch shattered one of the wooden supports of the device and ended the test. His fastest pitch was measured at 98.6 miles per hour when it reached the plate. Modern-day radar guns measure the speed of a pitch when it leaves a pitcher's hand. This is usually three to four miles per hour faster than when the pitch crosses the plate. This means that Feller actually threw the ball 101 or 102 mph. Despite Feller's protestations, most observers believe he did throw faster before the war. It's possible he might have thrown 103 or 104 mph.

Feller was back on track on August 24 as he blanked the A's, 5–0, for his tenth shutout and 22nd win of the year. "Boo" Ferriss, however, passed him the next day, winning his 23rd by beating the Indians, 2–1. Doerr clouted two homers for Ferriss. Newhouser won his 22nd the same day, beating the Yankees, 7–2, with 10 strikeouts, including Keller three times. Hal also singled and homered for five RBIs.

A crowd of 71,551 showed up at Yankee Stadium for a Wednesday night game on August 28 to see Feller pitch. He was bested, however, by Ernie Bonham, 4–0. On the first day of September, Feller was beaten by Chicago's Joe Haynes, 4–1. Two days later he rescued Lemon by hurling 1⅔ innings in relief to earn a save in a 5–3 win over the Browns. Before the game George Case was challenged in the 100-yard dash by the great Jesse Owens. Case ran the 100 in 10 flat but Owens ran it in 9.9 seconds to win. On September 5, Feller suffered the worst drubbing of his career, giving up eight runs in four innings of a 10–0 loss to the Tigers.

It was apparent that the number of innings Feller was logging was affecting his performances. He said that in the last half of 1946, his first objective was to win games and his second was to strike out as many batters as possible. Most pitchers will tell you, however, that trying for strikeouts interferes with a hurler's effort to win a game. Sandy Koufax said some of the best games he pitched were games in which his strikeout total was low. Trying to strike out every batter runs up pitch counts and tires even the best pitchers. With all the publicity Feller's strikeout chase was getting, he was under a lot of pressure. That along with his relief appearances hurt his ability to win more games in 1946.

After the three straight losses, Feller won his 23rd by defeating the Browns, 3–2, on September 8. He registered eight more strikeouts giving him 301. Feller tied for the league lead again with his 24th win, stopping the front-running Red Sox, 4–1, on September 12. The victory delayed Boston's clinching of the pennant. He scattered eight hits, including a punch double to left by Williams against the shift. On September 15, Ferriss forged ahead again with win number 25, taming the White Sox, 4–1. Feller lost a 3–0 decision on the same day to the A's. Three days later Newhouser won his 25th while throwing a three-hitter and striking out 11 in a 2–1, ten-inning win over Philadelphia. The next day Feller made it a three-way tie with his 25th win, besting Ray Scarborough and the Senators, 5–1. Cleveland trailed 1–0 in the game prior to tallying five times in the eighth inning. On September 21, Ferriss lost his bid to win number 26. He left the game against Washington in the eighth, trailing, 5–4. The Red Sox rallied to tie the game and won in 11 innings, 7–5, for their 100th triumph of the year.

Bill Veeck touted the match-up between Feller and Newhouser on September 22 as "the Pitching Duel of the Century." A crowd of 38,103 turned out at Municipal Stadium. Newhouser was at his best, allowing no walks and just two singles in besting Feller, 3–0. He threw 97 pitches and struck out nine while winning his 26th. Feller threw 144 pitches, allowing eight hits and four walks while fanning seven.

On September 25, Feller failed in his bid for win 26 by a 4–1 score to Chicago. He struck out 10, giving him 337 whiffs, and allowed just four hits in defeat. Waddell's record was now tantalizingly within reach. Boudreau used Feller in relief for five innings in a 9–8 win over Detroit on September 27. Feller fanned six Tigers to tie Waddell's supposed record of 343. He fanned Johnny Outlaw in the ninth for victim number 343. Later in the inning he almost made Greenberg his record-smashing 344th victim, but catcher Jim Hegan barely missed holding a potential foul-tip third strike.

On September 28, Ferriss went for his 26th win and left the game after five innings with a 3–0 lead over Washington. The Red Sox were saving his arm for the World Series. But the Senators rallied to win, 4–3. On the last day of the regular season, Feller and Newhouser squared off in Cleveland. If Feller won, he would tie Newhouser for the league lead in wins with 26. And if Feller struck out just one batter, he would break Waddell's supposed record of 343. A crowd of 47,876 filled up most of Municipal Stadium. The Indians scored three times off Newhouser in the fourth inning. Feller won the game, 4–1, but did not strike out a batter until fanning Newhouser in the fifth. He later claimed that the Tigers were choking their bats and just trying to make contact in order to deny him the record. He pitched out of his only real jam by whiffing Dick Wakefield and Greenberg with two runners on base. He fanned Greenberg again in the eighth frame. He finished with five strikeouts to give him 348 on the year.

It is interesting that Feller finished with 348. Waddell's record was thought to be 343. As early as July, however, the *Sporting News* reported that Ernest Lanigan, the director of the Baseball Hall of Fame, said further research showed that Waddell struck out 347. Nowhere during the season does the number 349 appear in the *Sporting News*. If Feller had known the real record was 349, he could have picked up two more strikeouts by making an additional one or two relief appearances. Afterward Feller said, "That's my high water mark. I don't think I could do it again and I wouldn't want to if I could."[22]

Feller had several good seasons after 1946. In 1947 he won 20 games and led the league in strikeouts. In 1948 he helped pitch Cleveland to the pennant, winning 19 times and again leading in strikeouts. After dipping in wins to 15 in 1949 and 16 in 1950, Feller led the league for the sixth time in 1951 with a 22–8 record. In 1954 the Indians won a then–AL record 111 games and dethroned the Yankees for the pennant. Feller was used as a spot starter and posted a 13–3 record with a 3.09 ERA. Feller retired after 1956 with a 266–162 lifetime record and a 3.25 ERA. After 1946 he added the third no-hitter of his career and his ninth one-hitter. He holds the record along with Nolan Ryan of pitching 12 complete games in which he allowed one hit or less. The interesting thing to consider about Feller is what his final stats might have looked like had he not lost almost four prime years to the war. He could have easily won 300 games and perhaps as many as 340.

Chapter 13

The Pride of the Redbirds:
Stan Musial in 1948

No player in history has dominated a season offensively as thoroughly as Stan Musial did when he topped the National League in nine categories in 1948. "Stan The Man" paced the NL in hits (230), doubles (46), triples (18), runs (135), RBIs (131), batting average (.376), total bases (429), on-base percentage (.450) and slugging percentage (.702). He tagged 39 homers, one behind the 40 homers of co-leaders Ralph Kiner and Johnny Mize. His 429 total bases far surpassed the second-place total of Johnny Mize's 316, and are only 21 behind the all-time NL record of Rogers Hornsby. Stan was truly "the Man" in the summer of '48.

During the 1940s and 1950s, Musial was the NL's rival to Ted Williams. While Ted led the AL in batting seven times and slugging nine times, Stan was atop the NL in batting seven times and slugging six times. The most impressive stat in Stan's career is his total bases mark of 6,134, second all-time to Henry Aaron's 6,856 bases. Stan is also fourth in hits (3,630), third in doubles (725), tied for nineteenth in triples (177, the most since Paul Waner retired in 1945), sixth in RBIs (1,951) and ninth in runs (1,949). Although not a classic home-run hitter, he walloped 475 four-baggers and retired after 22 years in 1963 with a batting average of .331. Only Tony Gwynn has retired with a higher batting average since that time.

Stan rang up this collection of stats with one of the oddest-looking batting stances. He dug in his left foot on the back line of the batter's box. His right foot was placed twelve inches in front of his left. He took three left-handed practice swings and followed up with a hula-dance wiggle to help relax. He stooped over into a crouch and stirred his bat like a weapon in a low, slow-moving arc away from his body. As the pitcher let loose with his fling, "the Man" would cock his bat into a steady position, dip his right knee, and twist his body away from the pitcher so that he was concentrating at his adversary's delivery out of the corner of his keen eyes. He would then uncoil with his explosive swing.

Musial was born in 1920 in Donora, Pennsylvania, just twenty-eight miles south of Pittsburgh in the industrialized Monongahela Valley. Smokestacks from a zinc plant lined the river banks there and filled the air with a heavy sulfur smell. In October 1948, its fumes hovered over the town in a deadly poisonous smog for four days, killing twenty-one people. His father, Lukasz, was one of its eventual victims, dying just before Christmas that year.

Lukasz was born in Warsaw, Poland. He came to America on his own. He worked in the shipping department of Donora's wire mill. He handled 100-pound bundles of wire, stacking them into freight cars. Stan's mother, Mary Lancos, was of Czech descent. She went to work sorting nails in the same wire mill at age 14. It was there she met Lukasz, and they were married before she was 18.

Lukasz brought home only $11 every two weeks from his back-breaking labor and the couple paid $4 a month in rent. Despite this, they raised six children. In his 1964 autobiography, Stan recalled:

> We didn't have much except kindness. A family of eight — squeezed into a small five-room house. There were times, Mom recalls, when Ed (his lone brother) and I had to be sent to school in canvas-top sneakers because she couldn't afford shoes. But there never was a time when I didn't have a baseball. My mother made many for me out of a little bit of this and that, sewn together. I don't know whether it is significant, but, searching my memory these many years later, I can't recall any toy before I received my first ball. [1]

Musial wasn't only a great hitter; he was the complete package, a hustling ballplayer who came up through the tough St. Louis Cardinals farm system. But for all his accomplishments, Musial has become an overlooked man among baseball's post–World War II greats, and his astonishing 1948 season is seldom mentioned among the great individual campaigns.

Like Babe Ruth, Musial started his pro career as a pitcher, with Williamson of the Mountain States League. In 1938 and 1939 his record was a combined 15–8 with an ERA around 4.50. In 1940 the Cardinals sent him to their Daytona Beach team in the Florida State League. The team was managed by former White Sox pitching star Dickie Kerr. Under Kerr's tutelage, Stan posted an 18–5 record with a 2.62 ERA. Kerr also used Musial in the outfield, and Stan hit .311 with 70 RBIs in 405 at-bats. In August of 1940 he injured the shoulder of his pitching arm while attempting to make a diving catch. He was never an effective pitcher again.

In 1941 the Cardinals sent him to their Class C Springfield team as an outfielder. Stan pounded the ball for a .379 average with 26 homers and 94 RBIs in 87 games. He was promoted to the Cards' top minor league team,

Rochester, in July. In 54 games with Rochester, Stan hit .326. When their season ended, Stan received a wire telling him to report to the St. Louis Cardinals. The Cards were in the midst of a fierce pennant race with Brooklyn. Musial rapped 20 hits in 12 games and batted .426, but Durocher's Dodgers edged the Redbirds by 2½ games.

In 1942, Stan proved his impressive late-season stint with the Cards in 1941 was no fluke. He batted .315 in 135 games as manager Billy Southworth's Cards won 43 of their final 51 games to post 106 victories and overtake the Dodgers by two lengths. Brooklyn had led the Cards by ten games on August 5 but couldn't keep up with the lightning finish of the St. Louis Swifties, as New York sports cartoonist Willard Mullin called them. The Cards then rolled over the Yankees in the World Series in five games.

Musial became a superstar in 1943, leading the NL in hits (220), doubles (52), triples (20), batting average (.357), and slugging (.562) as the Cards won 105 games and another pennant. Stan was named MVP. In 1944 the Cards won 105 games for their third straight pennant and then topped the crosstown Browns in the World Series in six games. Stan led the NL in hits (197), runs (112), doubles (51), triples (14), and slugging (.549). His .347 batting average was second only to Brooklyn's Dixie Walker's .357.

Musial spent 1945 in the navy. He was assigned to ship repair duty at Pearl Harbor. He returned to the mainland with a bang in 1946 to lead the Cards to their fourth pennant and third world championship in five years. He paced the NL in hits (228), runs (124), doubles (50), triples (20), batting (.365), and slugging (.587). He earned his second MVP award. The Cards beat Brooklyn in a special playoff and then topped the Red Sox in the World Series in seven games. Stan was on top of the world. Little did he know that it would be his last World Series.

The 1947 season was a struggle. When the season began, Stan became mired in the worst slump of his career. In May, Stan complained of a "sick stomach" and was diagnosed with acute appendicitis while in New York. The attending physician recommended surgery. After conferring long-distance with team physician Dr. Robert Hyland, Cardinal manager Eddie Dyer decided to have Musial flown to St. Louis. There Hyland examined Stan and told him he had infected tonsils as well as appendicitis. But Hyland suggested that it might be possible to put off surgery until the end of the season by freezing the diseased parts. Stan said in his book, "The famed surgeon knew when not to operate, too. I was all for that."[2]

The appendix was frozen. Five days later Stan returned to the lineup. He went to bat 22 times without a hit before beating out a bunt. On May 19 he was hitting .140. By June 13, Stan's average had risen to .205. During the last 104 games of the season, "the Man" made a remarkable turnabout and

In 1948 Stan Musial led the NL in hits (230), doubles (46), triples (18), runs (135), RBIs (131), batting average (.376), total bases (429), on-base percentage (.450), and slugging percentage (.702). His 39 homers were just one behind co-leaders Ralph Kiner and Johnny Mize. His career total bases mark (6,134) is second only to that of Hank Aaron.

finished the season hitting .312 with 183 hits, 30 doubles, 13 triples, 19 homers, 95 RBIs, and 113 runs in 149 games. At season's end he underwent surgery to remove his appendix and his tonsils.

In spring training manager Eddie Dyer moved Stan back to the outfield for the first time since 1946 to make room for prospect Nippy Jones at first base. Stan had been switched to first base in 1946 for the final 114 games and spent all of 1947 at the infield position. In his career he played 1,016 games at first base and 1,896 games in the outfield, the first ballplayer to occupy more than one position for more than 1,000 games.

Stan recalled, "From the moment I picked up a bat in 1948, healthy and strong after off-season surgery, I knew this would be it, my big year.[3]... I was 27 now, at my athletic peak and healthier than I had been for as long as those low-grade infections had been gnawing at my system. Stronger, too, when I picked up a bat and swung it. The bat felt so light that instead of gripping it about an inch up the handle, as I had in the past, I went down to the knob."[4]

On Opening Day in St. Louis, the Cards' Murray Dickson scattered 10 hits in blanking Cincinnati, 4–0. In the third inning Hank Sauer and Johnny Wyrostek missed communications and let a fly ball by Stan fall for an RBI double, his only hit on the day. Two days later Stan stung a single, double, and triple against Cincinnati, but the Reds won in the ninth inning, 4–3, when catcher Del Wilber juggled Stan's perfect throw to the plate.

On April 24, Stan slashed an RBI triple in Chicago for his 1,000th career hit. St. Louis Post-Dispatch sportswriter Bob Broeg teased Stan afterwards, "Look, Banj (short for Banjo, a common term used to describe a weak hitter), if you're going to talk about hits, what about trying for 3,000."[5]

Stan had not considered getting 3,000 hits but told Broeg, "That's a long way off. Too many things could happen. Keep reminding me. This is a team game and I play to win, but a fella has to have little extra incentives. They keep him going when he's tired. They keep him from getting careless when the club is way ahead or far behind. It'll help my concentration."[6] For a span of fifteen seasons Stan whacked 2,947 hits and slugged .595.

On April 30 in Cincinnati, Stan knocked out the first of four five-hit games he enjoyed in 1948. He ripped an RBI single in the first inning. He cranked a two-run homer in the fifth frame. He lit a seven-run St. Louis rally in the seventh with a double and then capped it with a two-run single. In the ninth inning he doubled again, bringing his average at end of April up to .400. The Cards won, 13–7.

Brooklyn arrived in town on May 4, and home runs by Musial and Enos Slaughter helped top the defending-champion Dodgers, 5–4. Stan ended the game with a tumbling catch with two runners on base.

Musial was always trouble against the Dodgers. In fact, he received his nickname of "the Man" from Dodger fans during a three-game series at Ebbets Field in 1946. Stan ripped eight hits in 12 at-bats in that series. In the final game, Bob Broeg heard Brooklyn fans chanting something every time Stan came to the plate but couldn't decipher the words. At dinner that evening he asked traveling secretary Leo Ward if he knew what the Flatbush fans were saying. Ward told Broeg, "Every time Stan came up they chanted, 'Here comes the man!' [7] Broeg informed his St. Louis readers of the chant in his column the next day. One of the most famous nicknames in history was born.

At Ebbets Field in 1948, Stan smashed 25 hits in 48 at-bats for a .521 batting average. The 25 hits consisted of 10 singles, 10 doubles, a triple, and four home runs. He slugged 1.021 in Brooklyn. In his book, Stan said, "If I could have hit all season at Ebbets Field or the Polo Grounds or, for that matter, if I could have played the 1948 season on the road, I might have hit .400 and ripped the record book apart."[8] In 1948 Stan hit .415 on the road and .334 at Sportsman's Park.

The Cards arrived at Ebbets Field for the first time in 1948 on May 18. Musial singled and doubled off Ralph Branca as St. Louis took the opener, 4–3. The next night before 32,883 fans, the largest crowd at Ebbets Field thus far that season, the Cards tagged five Brooklyn pitchers for 18 hits in a 13–5 laugher. The Dodgers couldn't get Musial out in any of his six trips to the plate. "The Man" singled three times, doubled, tripled, and walked, scoring five runs and knocking in two. The Cards routed four Dodger twirlers for 14 more hits in the final game, winning, 13–4. "The Man" singled once, doubled twice, and hammered a seventh-inning homer off Hugh Casey. In the series he went 11-for-15.

During the series Durocher's pitchers sent Slaughter to the dirt to avoid a head-high pitch, drilled Cardinal third-baseman Whitey Kurowski in the back, and beaned catcher Del Rice, forcing him out of action. Such incidents were commonplace during Brooklyn-St. Louis battles throughout the 1940s.

Stan did his share of ducking too. In his book, *Nice Guys Finish Last*, Durocher recalled a game in 1948 when his star, Jackie Robinson, was sent sprawling to the dirt by a Cardinal pitch. Leo's pitcher retaliated by knocking down Musial with two pitches in succession. The second pitch hit Stan's bat as he was unloading, and he was thrown out while flat on his back. According to Leo, Stan stopped him on the field a couple of innings later and said, "Hey, Leo, I haven't got the ball out there. I didn't throw at your man." Leo recalled answering, "Stan, old boy, you better tell that man in there to let my man alone. As far as I know, I've got 25 players too. And Robinson is one of my best. You're the best player I know on the Cardinals. For every time my man gets one, it looks like you're gonna get two." Durocher ended the story, "We never had any more trouble with the Cardinals as far as Mr. Robinson was concerned."⁹

In 1948, however, St. Louis had to be worried about the Boston Braves as well as the Dodgers. Billy Southworth had moved from St. Louis to manage the Braves and he had them playing good ball. On May 21, Boston's Warren Spahn beat Harry Brecheen and the Cards, 3–1, despite a Musial homer. The next night the Cards turned the tables and sent Boston's other ace pitcher, Johnny Sain, to the showers on the way to a 6–4 win. St. Louis was in first place by 2½ games. Spahn, Sain, and the Braves would not go away, however. They would win their first pennant since 1914 despite Musial's gargantuan year.

In New York before a Wednesday night crowd of 44,128 at the Polo Grounds on May 26, Stan slugged his eighth and ninth homers of the season, but the Giants exploded for eight runs in the eighth inning to triumph, 10–7. The Cards were in the midst of a spell in which they lost eight of nine games before beating Brooklyn, 4–1, on June 3. Stan bashed a two-run homer in the first inning off Preacher Roe that day and Brecheen made it stand up by hurling a four-hitter.

On June 6, the Cards retook first place by sweeping the Phils in a doubleheader, 11–1 and 2–0. Musial's roommate, second baseman Red Schoendienst, banged four doubles and a home run in the sweep. The day before he had knocked out three doubles and a single in a 9–6 win against Brooklyn. A sure-handed man with the reflexes that made him a master at turning the double play, Red would be honored with a plaque at Cooperstown. In 1948 injuries kept him out of all but 96 games, a devastating blow to the Cards' pennant ambitions.

In three successive games, from June 15 to June 18, Musial was on fire, lacing 10 hits in 11 at-bats, including two doubles, a triple, and a homer. The Cards beat the Phils twice at Shibe Park, 2–1 and 4–1, and then won a 30-hit battle over the Giants at the Polo Grounds, 12–8.

On June 22 at Braves Field, "the Man" tied what was then the NL record by recording his third five-hit game of the season in a 5–2 win over Boston. All five hits were singles, including a bunt in the third inning. Before he went up to the plate in the ninth inning with the bases loaded, manager Eddie Dyer jokingly hollered out to him, "Hey boy, I'm afraid I'm going to have to send up a hitter for you."¹⁰ Stan did a double-take. The Cardinal bench laughed. Stan then socked Clyde Shoun's first pitch to center to drive in two runs and win the ballgame.

Three days later Stan tore apart the Dodgers at Ebbets Field again with two singles, a double, and his 16th homer. The Cards beat Joe Hatten, 6–3. He was hitting .408. The next night Brooklyn hurler Preacher Roe interrupted a St. Louis clubhouse meeting to tell the Cards he had figured out how to get

Musial out. The left-hander from Arkansas revealed his formula. "Walk 'im on foah pitches an pick 'im off first," he drawled, ducking out the door amidst chuckles.[11] The Dodgers managed to get Musial out three times that night, but in the seventh inning he homered off Paul Minner as the Cards beat Durocher again, 6–4.

By July 1, Musial had rapped out 101 hits in 252 at-bats for a .401 average. The relatively new phenomenon of night games was not hurting Stan. He was hitting .462 at night and also .437 against left-handers.

On the Fourth of July, the Cards split a doubleheader in Cincinnati. Musial banged out five singles and a double to raise his average to .405. The next day he smacked four singles as the Cards swept a doubleheader from the Cubs in a steady rain back in St. Louis, 6–3 and 5–2. The day after that he singled twice and homered but the Cubs prevailed, 12–10.

The 6'1", 175-pound Musial was flexing his muscles as never before. On July 9, he slammed his 20th homer off the Reds Herm Wehmeier in the fourth inning. That was a new career high for Musial, and for the next ten years he would become one the league's premier home run hitters, averaging 31 per season.

But the Cards were losing almost as often as they were winning. St. Louis went into the All-Star break six games behind the Braves. Musial was called into the front office before the break and given a $5,000 raise, to $36,000. Yet it seemed as if even Stan's best would not be good enough to help the Cards catch Southworth's Braves.

Boston fans coined the phrase "Spahn and Sain ... and pray for rain" in tribute to its two top pitchers, Warren Spahn and Johnny Sain. Sain hurled 315 innings with a 24–15 record and 2.60 ERA. Spahn, who won 15 and lost 12 with a 3.71 ERA in 257 innings, actually had one of the worst years of his career. He went on to win 363 games (fifth all-time and the most since World War II) with a 3.09 ERA in 21 seasons. This is remarkable because Spahn didn't begin his major league career until age 25, in 1946. He had pitched 15 innings in 1942 but spent the rest of the next few years in the army, earning a medal at Remagen Bridge. Spahn wasn't a mystery for Musial in 1948, however. Stan had his best success against Spahnie, going 11-for-22. In 107 career games against Spahn, Stan batted higher than .320. Spahn said of Musial, "If I could roll the ball up there, I think that's the way I might have pitched him."[12]

The Cardinals were racked by injuries to Schoendienst, Whitey Kurowski and center fielder Terry Moore. Kurowski played 65 games at third base and Moore patrolled center field for 71 games. Musial played all three outfield positions as well as some first base. The bright spots for the Cardinals besides Musial were the performances of Slaughter (.321, 90 RBIs) and Brecheen (20–7, 2.24 ERA, seven shutouts in 233 innings).

Slaughter went through an 0-for-34 funk early in the season, causing writers to speculate he was washed up. When asked about Slaughter's slump, Eddie Dyer replied, "I won't bench him because I want to win the pennant. The Cardinals can't win with Slaughter out. The day he's through, he'll know it and so will I. That will be the day he'll have to walk. He's not hitting now, and he didn't hit in spring training. I don't like it, but I'm not irked nearly as much as he is."[13]

Dyer had been Slaughter's manager back in the minors at Columbus in 1936. During a game that season, Slaughter trotted in from his position in right field at the end of an inning and then slowed to a walk upon reaching the infield. Dyer had given him a tongue lashing earlier for striking out on a pitch over his head. Dyer met Slaughter on the dugout steps and asked sarcastically, "What's the matter, son? Are you too tired to run all the way? If so, then I'll get you some help."[14]

Slaughter described his reaction to Dyer's words in his autobiography, "That changed my life right there. From that moment on, Enos Slaughter never loafed on a baseball field. I can't say I was in any better a mood when it was time for me to go back to right field, but I hightailed it out there as fast as I could. From then on, I ran full speed to my position once my foot hit the top step of the dugout, and I ran just as fast until I reached the dugout coming back. Those words Dyer said to me that night never left me."[15] Slaughter, hitting .220 at the time, rebounded to bat .325. In his 19 years in the majors, Slaughter batted .300 with 2,383 hits.

Musial led NL All-Star vote-getters, amassing 1,532,502 votes. At the break his average was .403. Stan delighted the hometown All-Star game crowd of 34,009 at Sportsman's Park with a first-inning, two-run homer into the right-center-field pavilion, but the AL won the contest, 5–2. Before retiring in 1963, Stan held All-Star records for most games played (22), hits (20), total bases (40), and homers (6).

On July 17 Musial resumed his assault on NL pitchers with a grand slam, but the Phils outscored the Cards, 11–10, as Granny Hamner drove in seven runs with a single and a pair of doubles. The next day a crowd of 32,761 showed up at Sportsman's Park to see the Cards and Dodgers divide a doubleheader. Both teams were in second place, eight games behind Boston.

The Dodgers were in the midst of a revival. On July 21 they swept a pair from the Cubs at Wrigley Field, 9–3 and 7–1, giving them 16 wins in their last 19 games and their seventh win in eight tries for new manager Burt Shotton. Durocher was fired by the Dodgers after a disappointing start, only to be hired by the crosstown Giants. "Leo the Lip," long despised by the fans at the Polo Grounds, replaced their idol, Mel Ott.

Shotton piloted Brooklyn to the 1947 pennant while Durocher was under a year's suspension imposed by commissioner Happy Chandler. Shotton was a calm, bespectacled elderly gentleman who managed in street clothes, the opposite of the fiery Durocher. He was the same guy who, while working for the Cardinals at Columbus back in 1941, first recommended that Musial be switched to the outfield. He came back from his front porch in Florida in 1948 to guide the Dodgers from last place, 10 games off the pace, back into the pennant chase. In 1949 he won another pennant in Brooklyn. After losing the flag to Philadelphia on the last day of the season in 1950, he was fired by owner Walter O'Malley.

Durocher's Giants followed Shotton's Dodgers into St. Louis. The Cards took two of three. In the final game Musial capped a six-run Redbird outburst in the seventh inning with a two-run homer that gave the Dyermen a 6–5 lead. Mize tied the game with a solo shot in the eighth before the Cards won on Nippy Jones' RBI single in the thirteenth inning, 7–6. Jones hit .254 with 10 homers and 81 RBIs in 1948.

Southworth's Braves arrived next and the Cardinals slowed them down by winning three of four to get back to within five games of the top. Musial went 7-for-16 in the series with a double and a triple.

The Cards, encouraged by their recent showing against the Braves, climbed aboard a train headed east to Brooklyn for a three-game series. Musial was his usual destructive self there with six hits in 12 at-bats, including four doubles. But the red-hot Dodgers won all three contests to drop the Cards to fourth place.

The Dyermen were greeted next in Boston by a crowd of 37,071 at Braves Field on July 30. Musial ignited a five-run rally in the eighth inning with a double as Brecheen bested Sain in the opener of three, 6–2. Stan tripled, homered, and scored three times the next day against Spahn. But Sibby Sisti tripled with the bases full to climax a four-run rally in the ninth inning and give the Braves a dramatic 7–6 victory before 31,841 fans. A record 1,455,439 fans came to Braves Field in 1948. The Cards rekindled their pennant hopes by winning the rubber game, 9–6. After striking out and grounding into two double plays, Stan doubled and scored in the eighth inning and punched an RBI single in the ninth.

The next stop was back in New York at the Polo Grounds. The Giants had won seven straight and moved past the Dodgers into second place. The Cards were not impressed. In the opener they pulverized the Giants' hurlers with 20 hits in winning a laugher, 21–5. Musial doubled, homered, and scored three times. The loss was the first home setback for the Giants under Durocher, but it set a tone for Cardinal-Giant games for the remainder of the season. Two days later the series resumed with the Cards sweeping a doubleheader, 7–2 and 3–0. Musial slammed a two-run homer off Sheldon Jones in the first game and Brecheen outpitched Larry Jansen with a two-hitter in the nightcap. The Cards were within four of Boston.

Under Ott the Giants had floundered with a 27–38 start. Under Durocher they would improve, winning 51 games against 38 losses. Yet behind Ott, the Giants had won six of 10 against St. Louis in 1948. After Durocher took over, the Cards won 11 of 12. Interestingly enough, the Cards had won eight of 11 from Durocher's Dodgers at the start of the season but could only win two of 11 from Shotton's Dodgers afterward. Musial explained the results in his autobiography, "Leo liked to play the game rough, liked to make it a game of intimidation. His tactics turned us from tabbies into tigers."[16] Stan was the most ferocious St. Louis tiger against the Giants in 1948 by tagging their moundsmen for 11 homers. In 1954 Stan belted five home runs and socked a single in a doubleheader against Durocher's eventual world-champion Giants at Sportsman's Park.

On August 9 in Cincinnati, Slaughter whacked two singles, a double, and a triple for five RBIs as Brecheen won, 6–2. Enos was in a 17-game hitting streak and on a 20-for-36 tear. Two days later Musial belted a solo home run off Cincinnati's Johnny Vander Meer in the first inning and then capped a six-run rally in the second inning with a three-run double in a 9–4 win.

Pittsburgh's Forbes Field, meanwhile, was a chamber of horrors for the Cards in 1948. The Pirates came up with four runs in the ninth inning to upend the Cards, 5–4 on August 13. Musial singled, doubled twice, and tripled in defeat. He came to bat for a fifth time, trying to tie Ty Cobb's record of four five-hit games in a season. He slashed the ball hard but right back at pitcher Bob Chesnes, who made a fine play. Brecheen finally beat the Bucs, 6–3, the following day. Musial ignited a five-run explosion in the fourth inning with another double.

The Cards pulled to within 2½ games of the Braves on August 16 with a 9–7 triumph over the Cubs. Musial singled twice, doubled, homered, and made an acrobatic catch while playing center field. In Boston 151,519 fans came out for a five-game series between the Braves and Dodgers. The Dodgers won three of the five to get to within two games of the top.

Musial used his defense to beat the Pirates back in St. Louis on August 20. In the first inning he made a sixty-yard sprint and circus catch of a blooper off the bat of Ralph Kiner with a man on base. In the second inning he made a somersaulting grab of a drive by Danny Murtaugh then jumped to his feet and doubled Ed Stevens off first base with a perfect throw. The Cards won, 7–4, and climbed to within a single game of first place the following day with a 9–2 drubbing of the Bucs. Musial singled twice, doubled, knocked in a run, and scored two. The win was the Cards' 17th in 23 games.

That same day the Braves invaded Brooklyn for a doubleheader. The Dodgers temporarily took over first place by a half-game, knocking out Sain with five runs in the first inning of an 8–7 win in the lidlifter. Spahn, however, pitched the Braves back into first place in the second game, 2–1. The next day the Dodgers stole eight bases, including Jackie Robinson's fourth theft of home of the year, but the Braves prevailed, 4–3. Boston captured the final game, 3–2, in 14 innings. Beantown had reason to be excited as the Red Sox were in the hunt for the AL pennant.

Southworth's ballclub arrived in St. Louis on August 24 with a 2½ game lead. Musial slugged a two-run homer off Sain in the first inning and made another patented diving catch of Phil Masi's liner to center in the sixth, but the Braves wore out Cardinal pitchers, winning, 9–3. The next night St. Louis slid 4½ games back as Spahn applied a coat of whitewash, 2–0.

But the Redbirds weren't ready to fold. Musial rallied them to a double-header sweep of the Giants on August 26, deciding the second game with a two-run ninth-inning homer in the 7–5 victory. Two days later the Cards swept another twinbill from the Giants, 5–4 and 7–6. In the first game Stan came to the plate with the bases loaded in the ninth inning of a 4–4 tie. He whacked a bullet to Mize at first base, who stepped on the bag for a rally-killing double play. Yet Stan came back to win the contest in the thirteenth inning with his 33rd homer of the year. The two sweeps put the Cards within 1½ games of first place because the Braves cooled off in Chicago, dropping three of four.

The beginning of the end started for St. Louis on August 29 as the Dodgers came to town and took over first place by sweeping a doubleheader. Musial singled, doubled and homered in the opener but the Bums kayoed Brecheen with four runs in the first inning on the way to a 12–7 win before 33,826 fans. Jackie Robinson slugged a two-run homer in the first inning and hit for the cycle. In the second game Musial tripled in two runs in the ninth inning to tie the score at 4–4, but Brooklyn received pinch-hits from Pete Reiser and Arky Vaughn in the tenth to win, 6–4.

Shotton's Dodgers increased their lead to 1½ games over Boston 24 hours later with another doubleheader sweep of the Cards. Musial played the doubleheader with a wrenched knee. The injury occurred when he slipped on the runway to the dugout prior to the first game while besieged by autograph seekers. He went hitless in six at-bats, dropping his average to .377. The Dodgers came up with four runs in the ninth inning in the first game, benefiting again from pinch-hits by Reiser and Vaughn to win, 6–5. They coasted to a 6–1 triumph in the second game behind Hatten's five-hitter.

Just when Shotton's magic seemed to be working wonders, the Dodgers went into a tailspin by dropping four of five in Chicago and then losing three of four to the Giants at Ebbets Field. Durocher knocked his old team out of first place with a doubleheader sweep on September 3. The fate of the Dodgers and Cards was then sealed on September 6. Pittsburgh swept two from the Cards in the Smoky City, 2–1 and 4–1, while the Braves took two from the

Bums in Beantown, 2–1 and 4–0. The next day Stan lined into a first-inning triple play in still another loss at Forbes Field. Boston now enjoyed a four-game bulge over the new second-place team, Pittsburgh. Time was running out. The Braves never were seriously challenged again.

Musial enjoyed a big September while leading the Cards to a second-place finish. On September 9 he was 4-for-4 with a double and a triple, knocking in two runs and scoring on a double steal. Brecheen blanked the Reds, 4–0. The next day Stan beat the Reds again, 6–5, with an RBI single in the ninth inning, representing his 200th hit of the year.

In the Cards' last visit to Brooklyn, Stan didn't manage a hit in four at-bats yet highlighted a 4–2 win by taking three hits away from Dodger batsmen with his glove work. In the third inning he tumbled to the turf while robbing Jackie Robinson of a double. In the sixth he sprinted over to the exit gate in left-center and flung his glove up to make a desperation grab of Pee Wee Reese's drive, stuffing a probable leadoff triple by Reese in his mitt. Then with two on and two out in the ninth, Brooklyn's Tommy Brown looped a short fly to center for an apparent two-run, game-tying hit. But "the Man" raced in, dove hard, and snatched the ball off the blades of the grass to preserve the victory.

Stan always took pride in his fielding. He told Bob Broeg in his autobiography, "Over the years, I'm proud to say, I had some of my best days defensively when I wasn't hitting. I never said much, but I thought my share about players who would let their chins drag when not hitting so that their fielding was affected, too. If I couldn't beat 'em with my bat, I certainly hoped to try with my glove."[17]

Stan had jammed his left hand making the circus catches but was in the lineup the next day. Dodger Carl Erskine struck Musial on the right hand with a pitch early in the game, but Stan tied the score at 2–2 with his 36th homer in the eighth off "Oisk." Erskine once explained how he pitched to Musial: "I just throw him my best stuff, then run over to back up third base." The Dodgers won the battle that day, however, on Reiser's pinch-hit RBI single in the ninth, 3–2. Musial left Brooklyn with injuries to both hands.

Braves Field was considered a tough ballpark for a batter. The wind blew in strongly off the Charles River. The occasional times when the wind did blow out, it favored left-handed batters. On those rare days the flag at the right-field foul pole would wave toward the small right-field bleachers, which were nicknamed the "jury box." September 22 was such a day at the ballyard that was constructed in 1914 along Commonwealth Avenue.

At the batting cage before the game, Broeg pointed to the flag and said to Musial, "A great day for the hitters, Banj."[18] Musial decided to rip off the tape that had been protecting his injured wrists and attempt to play without any bandaging. In the first inning he dumped a single to left off Spahn, punching the ball to the opposite field to lessen the strain on his wrists. In the third, Stan went to left again off Spahn, this time driving the ball over Mike McCormick's head for a double. In the fourth inning, new Braves pitcher Charley Barrett tried to puzzle Musial with a 2–0 changeup. Stan saw it coming and said to himself, "To hell with the wrists!" He pulled the ball into the jury box for a two-run homer. In the seventh inning, Stan grounded a single between third and short off Clyde Shoun for his fourth hit of the game.

Stan was aware that he needed one more hit to tie Cobb's record of four five-hit games. Braves hurler Al Lyons wasn't cooperating. In the eighth inning Lyons missed with two pitches. It looked as if Musial was going to walk in his last plate appearance. Lyons' third offering to Stan was a bit outside, but Musial hooked it between first and second for a "seeing-eye" single. In protecting his sore wrists, Stan had taken the minimum five swings during the game to get his five safeties. In an earlier five-hit day that season, "the Man" had knocked out all five hits with two-strike counts.

As October opened, Musial went 3-for-3 in a 6–4 win over the Cubs, breaking his previous personal-best total of 228 hits. The next day, Stan broke Rogers Hornsby's seasonal team record of 102 extra-base hits by ripping his 46th double. The Cards clinched second place by drubbing the Cubs, 9–0. St. Louis finished the campaign with an 85–69 record, one game ahead of Brooklyn and 6½ games behind Boston.

Musial led the NL in every hitting category in 1948 except home runs. Red Schoendienst remembered, however, that Stan hit a ball at Shibe Park one day that struck the PA system above the fence and bounded back on the field. Umpire Frank Dascoli called it a double, but Red was sure it should have been ruled a home run.[19] With that homer Stan would have tied Kiner and Mize for the crown and literally led the league in everything.

In 1949 the Cardinals battled Brooklyn in another torrid pennant chase to the last day of the season before losing by a single game. It was the last pennant race St. Louis would be in for another seven years. That did not stop Stan from turning in great performances. He led the NL in batting in 1950 (.346), 1951 (.355), 1952 (.336), and again in 1957 (.351) at age 36. He was named the *Sporting News* Player of the Decade in 1956 and appeared on the cover of *Newsweek* magazine in 1957.

Along the way Musial played in 896 consecutive games to establish the NL record, which was broken by the Cubs' Billy Williams in 1969. In 1958 he became the Cardinals' first $100,000 ballplayer. In 1962 at age 41, Stan challenged for his eighth batting crown, finishing at .330 in 505 plate appearances. He also tied a record by hitting four home runs in succession that year, including three in one game against Casey Stengel's Mets.

"Stan the Man" was thrown out of only one ballgame in his career and that came in the minor leagues. He did not berate writers or sound off in the newspapers. He didn't second-guess his many managers and never engaged in fisticuffs on the ball field.

Despite his calm demeanor, Musial was a man of quiet toughness and stoic endurance. He did not scare easy. In 1953 Cincinnati manager Rogers Hornsby ordered pitcher Clyde King to knock Musial down during a particular time at bat. King protested to his manager, "Rogers, over the years I've gotten Musial out, I guess as good as anybody, and there's no point in knocking him down." But Hornsby was adamant. King then recalled, "Sure enough, I knocked him down. The ball went right up here (under the chin) and the bat went one way and his body went another way. And he hit the next pitch on the roof in right field. Home run! He killed it!"[20] In 1968 a bronze statue of Musial was unveiled in front of the Cardinals' Busch Stadium. The inscription on the statue reads, "Here stands baseball's perfect warrior. Here stands baseball's perfect knight." That indeed was "Stan the Man."

Chapter 14

The Great DiMag:
Joe DiMaggio in 1948

Joe DiMaggio. The name rolled off the tongue of sportscasters like music. In 1941 when DiMaggio ran off his sensational 56-game hitting streak to the glee of millions of baseball fans all over America, a lively hit tune by Les Brown and His Band of Renown entitled "Joltin' Joe DiMaggio" filled the nation's airwaves. As Joe built his streak blow by blow and game by game, the song played on all summer.

DiMaggio played the game with such impeccable virtuosity that many fans saw him as the greatest all-around player ever. In his 13 seasons with the Yankees the Bronx Bombers won 10 pennants and nine world championships. No wonder the song says, "We want you on our side."

Tommy Henrich, who played alongside DiMaggio in the outfield for his entire career, wrote of Joe:

> I was his teammate longer than anyone else, so maybe I am in the best position to appreciate him. Joe was without a doubt the greatest player that I ever saw. I think he was the greatest baseball player of all time, with the possible exception of Babe Ruth who might rate higher because of his ability as a pitcher. I'm sure Joe would have broken the Babe's records for home runs if he had played in any park other than Yankee Stadium. A right-handed batter in a park built to order for lefties, Joe hit a ton of balls that died in "Death Valley," that deep, deep area in left center field. In any other park those shots would have fallen beyond the fence for home runs....If I had to pick one player from history to start a team with, Joe would be the man. [2]

DiMaggio was hurt by the ballpark he played in more than any player in baseball. Nevertheless, he left an indelible impression of his skills that has lasted for more than half a century. One could pick many seasons to showcase DiMaggio. In 1937 he slammed 46 homers (the most by any right-handed Yankee while the team played in the old dimensions of Yankee Stadium) and

Joe DiMaggio had many great seasons but his 1948 campaign seems to be the most of what DiMag was all about. Despite an assortment of painful injuries, Joe drove himself to the end of a torrid three-team pennant race. He was taped up so much he said, "I feel like a mummy." Incredibly, he missed only one game while batting .320 with 39 homers and 155 RBIs.

drove in 167 runs. In 1939 he batted over .400 into September before finishing at .381. In 1941, he posted his 56-game hitting streak and won the MVP award.

The 1948 season, however, seems to represent DiMaggio best. He underwent surgery on his heel and shoulder in the two previous seasons and the heel operation had not worked out well. Every time he ran he felt pain in his heel, similar to that of stepping on a nail. He played in constant pain throughout 1948 yet appeared in 153 games, whacked 190 hits, swatted 39 homers, drove in 155 runs, and batted .320. By late summer he was an exhausted physical specimen, yet he drove himself to the end in a torrid pennant race.

Joe was born in Martinez, California, in 1914, the son of a Sicilian fisherman named Giuseppe DiMaggio. Giuseppe and his wife soon moved to Fisherman's Wharf in San Francisco and raised nine children. Joe's two oldest brothers followed their father by working the boats. The third oldest, Vince, didn't. He ran

away to play baseball in the Lumber Leagues. He was underage, and when his
father refused to sign papers to let him play, Vince faked his age and left.

Vince soon was signed by the San Francisco Seals of the Pacific Coast
League. The Seals sent him to their farm team in Tucson. Vince played a few
months there and returned to show his father the $1,500 he had saved.
Giuseppe thought Vince had stolen the money. When he realized it was honest
money, he no longer frowned upon the time his fourth-oldest son, Joe, was
spending playing baseball. Vince played from 1937 to 1946 in the major
leagues, batted 3,849 times, and hit .249 with 125 homers.

In the spring and summer of 1932, Joe was a hitter who took his cuts
for the highest bidder while changing uniforms and playing for semi-pro
teams all over San Francisco. By summer 1932 Vince was up with the Seals,
and he got Joe on the team for the last three games.

In 1933 with the Seals, Joe slashed 254 hits, batted .340, popped 28
homers, and drove in 169 runs. He broke the PCL record by hitting in 61
consecutive games. Joe was the top prospect in the PCL until an accident
early in the 1934 season. During an evening on the town, Joe lost his footing
on the running board trying to get into a since-unidentified car. He fell near
Fourth and Market streets and tore the cartilage in his left knee.[3] In his autobiography, Joe's mythical version of injuring his knee while aboard a jitney
cab was concocted for some unknown reason. He tried to play afterward but
could no longer run. He spent two months trying to recuperate, hobbling in
and out of the lineup. Once thought to be worth $100,000, Joe was labeled
damaged goods. He had started the season picking up right where he left off
in 1933, but hit only .270 after the injury.

Most scouts lost interest in him. Yankee scout Bill Essick got the Yankees'
orthopedic specialist to examine Joe. Essick was told there was no reason why
a healthy 19-year-old couldn't heal up perfectly. The Yanks bought Joe from
the Seals for $25,000 and five players. The Seals, however, insisted Joe play
one more year with them, and the Yankees agreed. They were allowed to hold
onto their $25,000 until Joe's knee was proven sound.

In 1935 Joe destroyed PCL pitching, batting .398 with 270 hits, 34
homers, 154 RBIs, and 173 runs as the Seals captured the championship. Joe's
manager, "Lefty" O'Doul, worked with DiMaggio on pulling the ball down
the line. He knew what DiMaggio would be up against playing in Yankee
Stadium with its 457-foot power alley in left. Joe lost the batting crown to
Oscar Eckhardt, .3992 to .3987.

In 1936 Joe batted .323 with 206 hits, 132 runs, 125 RBIs, 44 doubles,
15 triples, and 29 homers for the world-champion Yankees. Italian Americans
filled the seats of Yankee Stadium, packing their hero sandwiches and wine
and waving red, white and green tricolor flags. Joe was putting a lot of fans

in the seats and he knew it. In 1937 he signed for $15,000 after a brief holdout and enjoyed his best statistical season by batting .346 and leading the AL in homers (46), runs, (151) total bases (418), and slugging (.673). He drove in 167 runs. By August 1 he had belted 31 homers in 89 games and was ahead of Ruth's 1927 pace. Later DiMaggio offered, "I could have hit 70 in a field which favored right-handers. In addition to the 46 homers I got that year, I hit 15 triples that could have been homers. It seemed that every long ball I got hold of that season was a 400-footer, even the outs."[4]

The Yanks won another world championship in 1937, but 1938 started with an ugly holdout by DiMaggio. He asked for $40,000. When Gehrig signed for $39,000, Joe was unfazed. He told the press, "It makes no difference to me Gehrig signed. I'm still dickering with Colonel Ruppert and I'm waiting for a satisfactory contract. I have returned my contract unsigned."[5]

The public turned against Joe for the first time. In 1938 eight million people were out of work. On April 20, Joe capitulated and signed for $25,000. He was booed for the first time in many ballparks. His image had deteriorated. The boos rang in his ears as he walked the floors of hotel rooms at night while chain-smoking, unable to sleep. But Joe took care of business. He batted .324 with 32 homers and 140 RBIs. The Yanks won their third straight world title.

Joe signed for $27,500 in 1939 and the boos turned to cheers. But on April 29 he ripped muscles in his right leg while slipping on the outfield grass. He writhed in agony before being assisted off the field. Gehrig had been stricken with ALS and was out of the lineup forever. Things didn't look good. But Joe rejoined the club in June and hit as never before. On September 8 his batting average had surged to .408. Then bad luck struck Joe again. His left eye became infected, swelling it nearly shut. It was his lead eye at the plate, and in the last three weeks of the season his average dipped to .381, good enough to win his first batting title but not at .400. Years later DiMaggio blamed Joe McCarthy for not letting him rest the eye for even one game, claiming that he could have hit .400 had his manager let him sit for awhile.

In 1940 Joe signed for $30,000 and won his second batting title at .352 with 31 homers and 133 RBIs, but the Yanks finished third, two games behind Detroit. In 1941 Joe played for $37,500 and recorded his famous 56-game streak. The day-to-day exploits of his streak were welcome relief from the war news that looked bleak. He finished at .357 with 30 homers and 125 RBIs. The Yanks won their fifth world title in six years.

With the attack on Pearl Harbor, baseball seemed unimportant to America. As a nation we were fighting for our survival. Joe held out in 1942 before signing for a $6,000 raise. His holdout brought more criticism. He heard the boos and catcalls again. The Yanks won another pennant but lost to the Cardinals in the World Series. Joe slumped to .305 with 21 homers. He had married actress Dorothy Arnold in 1939. Dorothy left behind a movie career and gave him a baby boy, but the marriage was not going well. He felt the sting of the public criticism of high-priced ballplayers being slow to respond to a national emergency. The marriage was close to divorce when Joe enlisted in the Army Air Force in February 1943.

He entertained troops by playing ball for the 7th Army Air Force team, batting .401 in 90 games. He was forced to quit playing because of ulcers. His marriage ended in divorce in 1944. Joe was reassigned to the physical training section of Special Services and received a medical discharge in September 1945.

New Yankee president Lee MacPhail signed DiMaggio for the same $43,500 salary Joe had earned prior to his departure. These were not the same old Yankees, however. McCarthy feuded with McPhail before resigning. The Yankees struggled through the season with three managers and finished 17 games behind the Red Sox. Joe batted .290 in 132 games with 25 homers and 95 RBIs. His career seemed on the downslide.

In January 1947, Joe underwent surgery to remove a three-inch bone spur in his left heel. The operation did not go as expected, and on March 11 a skin graft operation was performed over a 1½-inch open wound on the heel. He was not in the lineup on Opening Day. In late spring, the magic returned. Joe won four games with home runs and went on a three-week .493 tear. The inspired Yankees reeled off a 19-game win streak and ran away with the pennant. His popularity soared to new heights. Bothered by a strained neck muscle and problems with his left ankle, he was sidelined in August. He finished at .315 with 20 homers and 97 RBIs and was voted MVP for the third time. He homered twice and was robbed of a third by an incredible catch by Al Gionfriddo in a World Series win over Brooklyn.

At the end of the 1947 season, however, DiMaggio was a weary athlete. He still had pain in his heel after the surgery of the previous winter. Now he needed surgery to remove bone chips on his right elbow. During the last half of 1947, he was able to make only one hard throw a game. The other Yankee outfielders disguised the weakness by racing over to assist him whenever possible. Dr. George Bennett performed the surgery and declared, "The bone had been resting on a nerve and it must have given him terrific pain every time he threw."[6]

In January 1948, the Yanks signed DiMaggio for $70,000. Only Babe Ruth had received a bigger Yankee contract. MacPhail sold his share of the Yankees for $2 million after the 1947 World Series. DiMaggio's salary negotiations with new general manager George Weiss went smoothly. Joe said, "I found Mr. Weiss the most pleasant man I've ever dealt with."[7] When asked what kind of season he needed to justify his big raise, Joe answered, "I think help the Yankees win another pennant, of course, and 35 home runs and 150 runs batted in for me."[8]

The Yanks opened 1948 in Washington, where 31,728 fans saw President Harry Truman throw out the first ball. The Yanks exploded for seven runs in the first inning and coasted to a 12–4 win. Early Wynn took the pounding for the Senators until being relieved in the ninth. DiMaggio singled, doubled, and scored twice. Two days later he connected for a 450-foot homer to straightaway center at Griffith Stadium and made a tremendous throw to nail Mickey Vernon trying to stretch a double into a triple. Although the Yanks lost to the Senators, 6–3, Joe knew he could throw with his old confidence.

The Yankee home opener marked the 25th anniversary of Yankee Stadium. An ill and shrunken Babe Ruth suffering from throat cancer sat behind the Yankee dugout as Governor Thomas Dewey threw out the first ball. The Red Sox prevailed, 4–0. Mickey Harris fired a five-hitter before 44,619. Joe McCarthy was now managing in the Boston dugout. He would bring his new team to the brink of pennants in 1948 and 1949 before losing out on the last day of both seasons. The Yanks won the next two contests from the Red Sox. In the rubber game Joe swatted a first-inning, three-run homer and Joe Page snuffed out a ninth-inning rally by whiffing the last two batters of a 5–4 win before 68,021.

In Boston on April 29, DiMaggio singled, doubled and then drove in the winning run with a deep fly in the tenth inning as the Yanks topped Boston again, 5–4. The Bosox would start slow under McCarthy but come on like gangbusters in mid-summer.

Bill Veeck's Cleveland Indians came out of the gates winning their first six games. On Opening Day in Cleveland, Bob Feller tossed a two-hitter at the Browns before 73,163. On April 26, the Tribe beat Chicago, 12–11, in 14 innings as player-manager Lou Boudreau laced a single, two doubles, and two triples. The talented shortstop batted .355, scored 116 runs, and drove in 106 to lead the Indians to the pennant. While benefiting from Veeck's promotional genius, Cleveland would set a major league high for attendance as 2,260,627 fans clicked through the turnstiles at Municipal Stadium. The Indians gave away free nylons to women, flew orchids in from Hawaii, and opened a nursery underneath the stands so mothers could attend games.

On May 8, DiMaggio ripped a two-run triple off Hal Newhouser and the Yanks sent him to the showers in the seventh inning of a 9–1 rout. Joe doubled and homered on May 10 as the Yanks humbled the White Sox, 9–3, for their fifth win in six games. In Boston, the Indians completed a three-game sweep with a 12–7 pounding of the Red Sox. The sizzling Boudreau knocked in three runs and started a triple play on a line drive by Billy Goodman.

The Indians arrived in New York the next day and Yankee hurler Allie Reynolds cooled them off, outpitching Bob Lemon, 4–1. Prior to 1947 Yankee manager Bucky Harris told DiMaggio he was planning to trade second baseman Joe Gordon to Cleveland for a starting pitcher. DiMaggio told him not to make the deal unless he got Allie Reynolds. Reynolds was sporting a 5–0 record on the way to a 16–7 season. His one-quarter Creek Indian ancestry gave rise to his nickname of "Superchief." From 1947 to 1954, Superchief won 131 games against 60 losses and was a major reason why New York continued to accumulate pennants.

On May 20 in Chicago, Joe smacked a single, double, triple, and two home runs and drove in six runs as the Yanks won, 13–2. He was batting .311 with 25 RBIs in 24 games. The Yanks had a 15–9 record and were in third place, two games behind the Indians. Boudreau was hitting .439. Despite Boston's 11–14 start, Ted Williams was batting .372 with a league-leading 30 RBIs.

The Yanks came into Cleveland for a doubleheader on May 23 and 78,431 fans showed up. Bob Feller, the $85,000-a-year smoke ball artist, started the opener against New York. All DiMaggio did was homer three times and single to chase home all six runs in a 6–5 Yankee win. Two of the homers came off Feller, and the third against Bob Muncrief traveled 450 feet, over the center-field scoreboard.

Teammate Tommy Henrich once said of DiMaggio, "When we played Bob Feller you could see the veins sticking out of Joe's neck. He was determined that he was not going to look bad against the best."[9]

Boudreau was quoted, "Sometimes, I'd rather see an ordinary pitcher in there against DiMaggio instead of Feller. When it gets to be either Feller or DiMaggio, Joe gives it that little extra."[10]

On May 25 in Detroit, Henrich went 5-for-5 as the Yanks coasted, 16–5. Henrich was known as "Old Reliable" to Yankee fans because of his clutch hitting. He batted .308, led the league in runs (138) and triples (14), slugged 25 homers, and drove in 100 runs.

The surprise of the league was Connie Mack's A's. On May 30 his team split a doubleheader with the Yanks in Philly, winning the opener in 10 innings, 7–6, before losing a rain-shortened contest in five innings, 2–1. Mack began his pro career in 1886. He had seen it all, and declared, "DiMaggio is the greatest team player who ever lived."[11] After the second game was called, Mack was furious. The *Sporting News* reported that Mr. Mack "was so enraged by umpire Passarello's action that he seized the arbiter by the shoulders and shook him."[12]

Bobby Brown, a future surgeon and AL President, socked seven hits as New York swept a Memorial Day doubleheader from Washington, 10–0 and 5–4. At third base Brown batted .300 in 113 games. June 13 was Babe Ruth Day at Yankee Stadium. A morning-long rain held down the crowd to 49,641. The Babe made his final visit to the ballpark and spoke briefly, saying, "The only real game in the world, I think, is baseball."[13] The inspired Yanks took care of Cleveland, 5–3, as DiMaggio keyed rallies by tripling off Feller in the sixth and then tripling off knuckleballer Gene Bearden in the eighth.

On June 20 in St. Louis, DiMaggio slugged three homers and drove in six runs as the Yanks topped the Browns in a doubleheader, 4–2 and 6–2. In Cleveland, a then–major league record 82,781 fans saw the Tribe knock off the A's twice, 4–3 and 10–0, behind Feller and Lemon. The next day in Cleveland, the Yanks routed the front-running Indians, 13–2. DiMaggio touched off a rally in the fifth inning with a two-run blast off Bearden, his 15th homer of the season. Reynolds went the route for his eighth win and drove in four runs with three singles.

DiMaggio banged two singles and his 16th homer the next day off Sam Zoldak, but Cleveland evened the series with a 5–2 win. A Wednesday night crowd of 65,797 saw the Yanks win the third game on Henrich's grand slam in the eleventh inning, 5–1. In the fourth game, New York's Vic Raschi outpitched Feller, 4–0. DiMaggio crashed his 17th homer in the ninth inning to tie Cleveland's Ken Keltner for the league lead. New York was in second place with a 35–24 record, 1½ games behind Cleveland. The A's were two games back at 36–26. The Red Sox, at one time 12 games off the pace, had fought back to within six at 29–27.

Around this time Dan Daniel wrote in the *Sporting News*, "By looking at the pattern which DiMaggio and the Yankees have been following this season, it will be realized that, more then ever, Joe is New York and New York is Joe in the standing of the American League. More than ever, the Bombers go as DiMaggio goes, and those who follow the Yankees day after day will tell you so in no uncertain terms"[14]

Joe surged into the league lead in homers with a belt in Detroit off Newhouser on June 25, his seventh homer in five days. On June 29 in New York, he won $150 in a pre-game homer-hitting contest against Ted Williams. The Yanks cooled off Boston that Tuesday night before 70,941, 7–0. Yankee junkball artist Ed Lopat yielded just three singles.

The reason Boston was still alive in the race was the phenomenal hitting of Williams. On July 1, Ted was hitting .402 with a league-leading 70 RBIs. DiMaggio was at .300 with 67 RBIs. Ted outpolled Joe in the All-Star vote, 1,556,784 to 1,519,182. But Boston scribe Dave Egan still maintained Ted was hurting the team by "protecting his batting average."[15]

Washington manager Joe Kuhel accused DiMaggio of using an illegal "loaded" bat during a game on July 2. Umpire Ed Rommel checked the bat and found nothing wrong with it. DiMaggio delivered an RBI single in the third inning of the game as New York won in 12 innings, 2–1, behind the pitching of fireballer Tommy Byrne. On the Fourth of July, the Yanks topped the Senators again, 6–5. Phil Rizzuto tagged up and raced home from third just ahead of Bud Stewart's throw on a short fly by Yogi Berra to win the game. In Boston, the Red Sox scored 14 runs in the seventh inning on the way to a 19–5 rout of the A's.

The *Sporting News* reported in the beginning of July, "Joe DiMaggio is continuing in the Yankee lineup despite an annoying pain in his heel, diagnosed as bursitis. The heat treatment prescribed for the ailment has caused skin burns."[16] On July 9 in Washington, DiMaggio doubled, homered, and drove in four runs as Lopat's junk mesmerized Kuhel's Senators, 9–0. In Cleveland 41-year-old Negro League legend Leroy "Satchel" Paige made his major league debut, shutting out the Browns in the last two innings of a 5–3 win.

The news wasn't as good for the Red Sox. During a train ride from Boston to Philly, Ted Williams initiated a playful sparring match with out-fielder Sam Mele. An enthusiastic boxing fan, Ted often blew off steam by engaging in such playful boxing while imitating Joe Louis. Williams and Mele traded a few light jabs. One of Mele's jabs hit Williams under the ribs. The next game Ted went hitless in four trips to the plate and complained of pain. That night he could barely take a breath without it hurting. The sparring match had resulted in a damaged ligament for Ted. He missed 13 games.

DiMaggio was having his own problems. He developed a bone spur in his other heel, the right one, that required surgery at season's end. With both heels hurting and both knees swollen, DiMaggio was out of the Yankee lineup for one game just before the All-Star break. Incredibly, it was the only game he missed all season.

At the All-Star break Cleveland was atop the standings at 45–28. Mack's A's were a half-game back at 48–32. Before a July 15 doubleheader between the A's and the Indians, 20,000 fans had to be turned away from Shibe Park. Such was the extent of pennant fever in Philly.

Nobody expected the A's to remain in the hunt. New York was 2½ games back at 44–32 and Boston was 6½ back at 39–35. Williams led the league in batting at .388 and had driven in 72 runs. DiMaggio was at .302 and led in RBIs with 74. During the second half, Ted batted .349 to finish on top of the league at .369. He drove in 55 runs to finish with 127 RBIs. Joe batted .339 during the second half and drove in 81 runs to lead the league with 155.

One night in Toots Shor's after the 1946 season, the owners of the Yankees and Red Sox, Dan Topping and Tom Yawkey, decided during a drinking bout to swap DiMaggio and Williams straight up. DiMaggio could take aim at Fenway's inviting Green Monster; Williams would have Yankee Stadium's short porch in right to shoot for. Both hitters might slug 60 homers. In the morning Yawkey woke up, changed his mind, and phoned Topping to call off the deal.

With his body aching and tired, DiMaggio made a pinch-hitting appearance in the All-Star game and drove in a run with a long fly as the AL prevailed in St. Louis, 5–2. Yankee manager Bucky Harris expected Joe to be out of the lineup a few more games, but DiMaggio said he was ready to play again after his brief rest.

On July 21, the Indians invaded the Bronx for a doubleheader before 67,139 fans. DiMaggio singled, homered and brought in three runs as the Yanks took the opener, 7–3. The Indians came back to win the second game, 12–8, on Jim Hegan's eighth-inning grand slam despite two doubles and a homer by Henrich. In game three 68,258 fans came to boo Bob Feller. Feller had refused to show up for the All-Star Game and went hunting instead. Harris claimed Boudreau had encouraged Feller's defection so the Cleveland ace could pitch against Boston and New York the following week. In the fifth inning, DiMaggio came to bat against Feller with the bases loaded. The rafters shook at Yankee Stadium when "Joltin' Joe" launched a grand slam to left field. It was Joe's 21st homer of the year and his ninth off Cleveland pitching. The Yanks won, 6–5.

DiMaggio seemed to play baseball with an elitist regal bearing. When the Yankees took the field, Joe was always the last to surface from the dugout. Sportswriter Red Smith once told Joe how easy he made everything look. Joe replied, "People say that and I'm grateful. But let me tell you the truth. It isn't easy at all. It's hard as hell to do the things I do out there."[17]

The Yanks swept the White Sox in a doubleheader in New York on July 25, 5–3 and 7–3, as DiMaggio ripped three singles, a double, and two homers. Four times in the second game, in the second, fourth, fifth, and seventh innings, youngsters ran out to Joe in center field to ask for his autograph. That same day the Red Sox took over first place by beating Cleveland for the third straight game at Fenway, 3–0, on Joe Dobson's six-hitter. It was Boston's 12th win in a row and 15th victory in 16 games. Ted was back in the lineup and shortstop Vern Stephens was busting the ball like never before on the way to a 29 homers, and 137 RBIs for the season.

DiMaggio knocked in three more runs with two doubles off Bob Lemon and dashed home on a double steal as the Yanks beat Cleveland, 5–0, on August 7 behind Raschi. The next day the Indians beat New York twice, 8–6 and 2–1, before 73,484. Tribe slugger Eddie Robinson homered three times. It was Cleveland's fourth home crowd of more than 70,000 in a week. The Indians had regained first place.

The Yanks then dropped two straight to Boston at home by 9–6 and 5–2 scores despite the fact DiMaggio went 5-for-9 with a double and two RBIs. Joe's little brother, Red Sox center fielder Dom DiMaggio, made a super catch in each game to rob Henrich and Billy Johnson of extra bases. Dom batted leadoff for Boston and hit .285 with 101 walks and 127 runs scored. Joe was an excellent defensive center fielder but many insist Dom was superior. Boston fans devised a new chant to spur on Dom. It was sung to the tune of "Maryland My Maryland" whenever Joe or Dom appeared at the plate. It sounded like this: "He's better than his brother Joe. Dom-in-ic Di-Mag-gi-o!" Joe thought the chant was cute and was happy for Dom's popularity.

The first-place A's arrived in the Big Apple on August 13 sporting a 65–43 record. Was Mack having another brainstorm at age 86? Insiders said coach Al Simmons was running the team. Whoever was running the show in Philly, it was extremely successful through 108 games. The A's were led offensively by third baseman Hank Majeski (.310, 120 RBIs). First baseman Ferris Fain (.281, 113 walks) and shortstop Eddie Joost (.250, 119 walks) could get on base and outfielders Barney McCosky (.326) and Elmer Valo (.305) hit well. Dick Fowler was their top pitcher, winning 15 games. The A's had feasted on the three bottom teams in the league with a 36–14 record against them to date.

The Yanks won the first two games of the series, 8–5 and 14–3. DiMaggio singled twice, homered, and drove in four runs in the 14–3 laugher. He had 25 homers and 102 RBIs. His pre-season expectations of 35 homers and 150 RBIs seemed reachable.

On August 15, the largest Yankee home crowd of the season (72,468) came to the stadium to see a doubleheader against the A's. DiMaggio belted a two-run homer in the ninth inning of the lidlifter to tie the game at 2–2. Bedlam broke out in the stands. Bill "Bojangles" Robinson did a tap dance on top of the Yankee dugout amidst the celebration. The A's came back in the top of the tenth with three runs, however. In the bottom of the tenth, DiMaggio tripled in a run before Lou Brissie came on in relief to quell the rally. An infantryman in World War II, Brissie had his leg shattered by an exploding shell and the southpaw wore a brace on his leg whenever he pitched. He won 14 times against 10 losses with five saves in 39 games. The A's won the second game of the day, also by a 5–3 score.

Beginning on August 17, the Yanks got on a hot streak and won 20 of 23 games. Joe drove himself as never before. He was not only fighting for a pennant but he was also fighting to help manager Bucky Harris keep his job. Joe liked Bucky, and rumors were flying that Harris would be fired if the Yanks did not win the pennant.

DiMaggio confided to his friends that it felt as if an "icepick" was stabbing him in his right heel every time he ran. His knees were swollen and he was suffering from a charley horse. Off the field he had difficulty walking at times. He wore special street shoes with high arches to stop the stabbing in his heels. He took pain-killing medication and was smoking a pack of cigarettes a day. Before every game he came in early to have his thigh wrapped tightly with tape. Another cinch of tape was wrapped around his midriff to hold the tape up on his thigh. Said DiMaggio, "I feel like a mummy."[18]

On August 16, Babe Ruth died. The next evening his body lay inside the main entrance of Yankee Stadium for viewing. People passed his coffin until midnight and throughout the following day. Estimates of the people who came to pay their respects ran as high as 200,000. On August 19, 75,000, soaked by heavy rains, stood outside Babe's funeral at St. Patrick's Cathedral. Joe was the only active player invited to serve as an honorary pallbearer. Afterward he flew out of La Guardia Airport to Washington and joined the Yanks in the third inning. He led off the fourth by socking an Early Wynn pitch for a base hit to ignite a six-run uprising. The Yanks won, 8–1.

On August 23, the Yanks blitzed Chicago for their seventh win in a row, 11–1. Joe chased home four runs with a single and homer number 28. On August 28 in New York, Joe robbed Boudreau of a triple with a spectacular running backhanded catch to save a run in a 3–2 win over the Indians. The next day he fractured Detroit third baseman George Kell's jaw with a blistering grounder. On the last day of August, a sparkling relay from Joe to Snuffy Stirnweiss to Gus Niarhos nipped the potential tying run at the plate after St. Louis had scored five times in the ninth inning. The Yanks won, 10–9.

During a doubleheader sweep of the Senators on September 3, Joe drove in seven of the 11 Yankee runs with a single and a pair of three-run homers. The second homer was an inside-the-parker off Wynn that Joe somehow legged out in the nightcap. The succeeding day he singled twice, scored twice, and drove in two runs in a 9–7 win over Washington. The day after that he homered in the second inning to tie the game at 1–1 and then helped break a 3–3 tie with a fluke double in the sixth inning. Joe was ducking a high and tight pitch from the Senators Sid Hudson when the ball struck his bat and blooped safely into right field. Berra, who hit .305 with 98 RBIs in 1948, followed with a triple, and Rizzuto singled. The Yanks won, 5–3. During their 20-for-23 hot streak, the Pinstripers couldn't shake their rivals. Boston won 22 of 26 during the same span.

On the morning of September 8, the first-place Red Sox were at 82–48 with a 1½-game lead over the Yanks. Cleveland had slipped to 78–53, 4½ games back despite two sparkling shutouts by their 41-year-old rookie, Satchel Paige. Paige shut out the White Sox, 5–0, at Comiskey Park on August 13 before a night game crowd of more than 50,000 fans and then blanked them again, 1–0, before 78,832 a week later in Cleveland. In 21 games including seven starts, Paige won six of seven decisions with a 2.47 ERA for the Indians. They couldn't have won the flag without him. The AL's first African American ballplayer, outfielder Larry Doby, hit .301 in 439 at-bats for Cleveland in 1948.

Yawkey's Millionaires knocked the Yanks back to 3½ games out by beating them at Fenway, 10–6 and 9–4, on September 8 and 9. New York looked on the verge of dropping out of contention. But DiMaggio prevented a sweep and broke Boston's nine-game win streak with a 440-foot, tenth-inning grand slam off Earl Caldwell. During the three games in Boston, Joe smacked seven hits in 14 at-bats.

Joe belted his 300th career homer on September 16 in Detroit off Fred Hutchinson. In the second game of a doubleheader in St. Louis three days later, Joe launched two-run homers in the first and third innings before retiring in the fourth frame because of his ailing legs. The Yanks won, 9–6. He was back in the lineup the next day with two singles, his 39th homer of the season, and three more RBIs. The Yanks edged the Browns again, 8–7. Two of his homers in St. Louis went over the scoreboard behind the left-field bleachers at Sportsman's Park, which was 379 feet away.

On September 24 at the stadium against the Red Sox, Joe plated a run with a fly ball in the first inning and drove in another with a third-inning single. In the fifth he was passed intentionally. Billy Johnson responded by smashing Earl Caldwell's first pitch for a three-run homer. The Yanks won, 9–6, and were in first place for the first time since Opening Day. Actually there were three teams in first place. New York, Cleveland and Boston were in a tie. The A's finally folded down the stretch and finished 12½ games back. League officials met hurriedly to discuss what would happen in the event of a three-way tie. They decided on a playoff game on October 4 between Boston and Cleveland, with the survivor to meet the Yanks for all the marbles.

Boston and New York split the next two games while Cleveland won twice. The A's then handed the Yanks a disastrous 5–2 loss on September 28. In the first inning the A's Eddie Joost slammed a long fly to center. Joe, running with an obvious limp, could not get to it. A New York scribe wrote: "It was only a question of time when DiMaggio's inability to cover a reasonable amount of ground with only one good leg would catch up with the Yankees. A two-legged DiMaggio not only would have caught Joost's lofty shot in the first inning, he would have been under the ball waiting for it to come down."[19] Boston lost at home to Washington, 4–2. The Indians routed the White Sox, 11–0, before 60,405 on Mr. Average Fan — Joe Early Night. Cleveland led New York and Boston by two with four to play.

The Yanks regrouped to beat Philly, 4–2, on the strength of rookie Hank Bauer's three-run homer. In Cleveland, Feller, working on two days' rest, stopped Chicago, 5–2, for his 19th win. Joe Gordon's 32nd homer and Keltner's 30th round-tripper backed Feller. The 1948 Cleveland infield of Eddie Robinson, Gordon, Boudreau, and Keltner produced 432 RBIs. In Boston, Ellis Kinder beat the Senators, 5–1.

Cleveland was idle on September 30. New York topped the A's, 9–7, in a rain-swept contest at Shibe Park. In Boston, pessimism was taking over as 4,998 showed up to see the Red Sox stay alive by beating the Senators, 7–3.

New York and Boston were idle as October opened, but Detroit came from behind to overtake Cleveland with three runs in the ninth inning, 5–3. Jimmy Outlaw's two-run single severed a 3–3 tie. The Indians led by only a single game with two to play. The Yanks had to travel to Fenway for their last two games.

Boston eliminated the Yanks, 5–1, as Jack Kramer tossed a five-hitter for his 18th win. DiMaggio doubled and scored the only Yankee run. Cleveland stayed one game up on Boston by blanking the Tigers, 8–0. Bearden threw his second consecutive shutout.

The final day of the regular schedule saw Detroit's Newhouser shut down Cleveland, 7–1, for his 21st victory. In Fenway 31,304 regained hope and saw their Red Sox force a playoff by outscoring the Yanks, 10–5. Dom DiMaggio ripped two singles and a homer. Joe singled twice and doubled twice. When he singled in the ninth inning for his fourth straight hit, Harris sent Steve Souchock out to pinch-run. As Joe limped off the field, the Fenway faithful rose to give him one of the loudest ovations ever for an opposing player. Cleveland came into Fenway for a one-game sudden-death playoff and player-manager Boudreau capped an MVP season by tagging four hits, including two homers, as Bearden won his 20th, 8–3.

Harris was fired in October and Casey Stengel was the surprise choice as the new Yankee manager. When asked to comment about the change, Joe said, "You know me, boys. I'm just a ballplayer with only one ambition, and that is to give all I've got to help my ball club win. I've never played any other way."[20]

On November 11, DiMaggio underwent surgery to remove bone spurs from his right heel. The operation was deemed a success. In January 1949, DiMaggio asked for $100,000 to play the next season. He got it. But when spring training began, his heel wasn't right. He limped in pain despite wearing sponge-rubber inner soles. He was not in the Yankee lineup on Opening Day.

As the days wore on, sportswriters speculated that DiMaggio's days as a ballplayer were over. He spent hours as a recluse brooding in his elegant suite at the Hotel Elysée in Manhattan, unsure if he would ever play again. He missed the first 65 games of the season. Then one morning in June he awoke to discover the pain in his right heel had vanished as if by miracle. He played in the Mayor's Trophy game against the Giants and felt no pain. The Yanks were due in Boston the next night to start a big three-game series. Joe told Stengel he was ready to go.

Stengel's Yanks had held the fort and were in first place without Joe. Henrich hit a flock of game-winning home runs early in the year, and the Yanks were winning with pitching and defense. The Red Sox, however, had won 10 of their last 11 games and were just two games behind. This looked like the series when Boston would take over the lead.

But Joe destroyed them. In 11 official at-bats, he slugged four key home runs along with a single and drove in nine runs. The Yanks swept the shocked Yawkeyites by scores of 5–4, 9–7, and 6–3. Joe fielded flawlessly, making 13 putouts with plenty of range. Suddenly, he was the man of the moment again with his picture on the cover of *Life* magazine. Reports of his demise had been premature. Joe batted .346 with 14 homers and 67 RBIs in 76 games and led the Yanks to the pennant by one game over Boston. A World Series victory over Brooklyn followed.

In 1950 another tough pennant race challenged DiMaggio and the Yanks. Stengel juggled his lineup frantically to stay close, and on August 11 he decided to bench a slumping DiMaggio. Joe sat for six games in silence and the Yanks fell to four games back. When Stengel wrote his name in the clean-up spot again, DiMaggio came back with a vengeance. For the next six weeks he hit .376 with 11 home runs while driving in the big runs. The Yanks won the pennant and beat the Phillies in the World Series. DiMaggio finished at .301 with 32 homers, and 122 RBIs.

At age 36 in 1951, DiMaggio experienced difficulty getting around on a fastball. His heels and legs bothered him again, and he no longer covered center field with good range. He finished 1951 at .263 with 12 homers and 71 RBIs in 116 games. The Yanks won yet another World Series.

DiMaggio quit after the season ended. He stayed in the limelight by marrying actress Marilyn Monroe. The marriage ended in divorce, but Joe still held a torch for the blond bombshell until her death in 1961. DiMaggio was made a symbol of a seemingly simpler and more heroic America that existed decades ago. He made a fortune in the nostalgia craze, getting top dollar for his autograph. He aged gracefully with his full head of silver hair. He dressed meticulously in classy blue suits. Wherever he went people said, "You look great, Joe!" He was a type of cult figure. His performance in 1948 proved he was still the "Great DiMag." Many people remembered him that way forever.

Chapter 15

Jackie's MVP Season:
Jackie Robinson in 1949

Everybody who knows anything about the history of baseball knows that in 1947 Jackie Robinson broke the color barrier that had existed in major league baseball for more than a half-century. His number 42 has been retired in every major league ballpark in tribute to his accomplishments as a ballplayer and as a man. Babe Ruth changed the way the game was played, but Jackie Robinson changed who played the game. When he became a Brooklyn Dodger in 1947, there was staunch opposition to integration in major league baseball.

Some fans and players tried to throw Jackie off his game with hostile racial insults, but he fought back with determined play between the white lines. He helped Brooklyn to the 1947 pennant and won Rookie of the Year honors. In 151 games at first base, a new position for him, he batted .297 with 125 runs and 29 stolen bases. It wasn't only the stats that made Jackie's play remarkable. Far from being the stereotype of the African American who would choke when the going got tough, Jackie became one of the best clutch hitters in baseball. On the bases his huge dancing leads caused pitchers to lose concentration, resulting in Dodger rallies. He stole home 20 times in his career. No one has stolen home more often since then.

Jackie was a winning ballplayer. In his 10 seasons in Brooklyn, the Dodgers won the pennant six times. In 1950 they lost the pennant on the last day of the season, and in 1951 they lost in a special playoff. They came within two games of winning eight flags in 10 years. Although Brooklyn had other outstanding players, Jackie was the driving force. As coach Jack Pitler observed, "He's the indispensable man. When he hits we win. When he doesn't we just don't look the same."[1]

Jackie switched to second base in 1948 and led the NL in fielding three of the next four years. The season picked for this chapter, 1949, was Robinson's best. He won the batting title (.342) and whacked 203 hits, including 38

Despite racial taunts that came his way, Jackie Robinson fought back with determined play between the white lines. Giants manager Leo Durocher wrote, "Jackie and I were always needling each other. And the more I needled him the more he killed me. Every time I looked up, it seemed Jackie Robinson was getting the late-inning hit that either tied the game or beat us."

doubles, 12 triples, and 16 homers. He amassed 124 RBIs, scored 122 runs, stole 37 bases, owned a .432 on-base percentage, and led NL second basemen in double plays (119).

Jack Roosevelt Robinson's journey in life began in Georgia in 1919. He was the youngest of five children born to Jerry and Mallie Robinson. When he was one year old, his father ran away, leaving Mallie and her children to fend for themselves. At age 30, Mallie put her family aboard a train and traveled to Pasadena, California. She arrived with three dollars sewn into her petticoat. She soon found a job as a maid. She received some public assistance, but by 1924 she owned her own house. In 1939 she purchased the property next door and in 1946 bought a third adjoining lot.

Jack's third-oldest brother, Mack, became a one-man track team at Pasadena Junior College and finished second to Jesse Owens in the 200-meter dash in the 1936 Olympics. Jack followed Mack to P.J.C. before moving on to UCLA on an athletic scholarship. In 1939 "Jackrabbit Jack" was quarterback on an undefeated UCLA football team (including three ties), averaging 11.4 yards per carry. In 1940 the UCLA football team disappointed but Jack finished second in the Pacific Coast Conference in total offense and earned honorable mention All-America honors.

In basketball at UCLA, Jack led the P.C.C. in scoring twice. In baseball he didn't play well at UCLA, but in track he won the NCAA title in the broad jump. He would have competed in the 1940 Olympics if not for World War II. At one point in his life he was the best athlete in the nation.

Jackie was drafted into the army in 1942 and rose to lieutenant in the cavalry. He was then attached to a tank battalion at Fort Hood. He was tried in a court martial as a result of a dispute that started when he was ordered to the back of a bus. He refused to go. The court martial trial ended with a not guilty verdict. The defense contended the whole thing was "simply a situation in which a few individuals sought to vent their bigotry on a Negro they considered 'uppity' because he had the audacity to seek to exercise rights that belonged to him as an American and as a soldier."[2]

After leaving the army Jackie batted .345 for the Kansas City Monarchs of the Negro American League in 1945. He then received an offer he couldn't refuse. Brooklyn Dodger president Branch Rickey offered Jackie a contract to play for Brooklyn's top farm club in Montreal. Rickey promised Robinson that if he played well there, he would be promoted to the play for the Dodgers. Rickey warned Jackie of the racial taunts he would face. Robinson asked, "Are you looking for a Negro who is afraid to fight back?"[3]

Rickey exploded back, "I'm looking for a ballplayer with guts enough not to fight back."[4] Rickey explained that if Jackie fought back with his fists, it might send the integration of major league baseball back a decade. Jackie agreed to accept the challenge. He batted .349 for Montreal and then won Rookie of the Year honors in Brooklyn. Most fan mail was encouraging, but there was some hate mail, including threats to do harm to Jackie, his wife Rachel, and their infant son. By mid-season the battle was beginning to be won. Jackie's picture appeared on the cover of *Time* magazine. He had become one of the most admired people in the nation.

After 1948 a talk Jackie had with Rickey changed things. In his autobiography Robinson wrote, "Not being able to fight back is a form of severe punishment. I was relieved when Mr. Rickey finally called me into his office and said, 'Jackie, you're on your own now. You can be yourself now.'"[5]

Years later Rickey explained his decision:

> I realized the point would come when my almost filial relationship with Jackie would break with ill feeling if I did not issue an emancipation proclamation for him. I could see how the tensions had built up in two years and that this young man had come through with courage far beyond what I asked, yet...I knew also that while the wisest policy for Robinson during those first two years was to turn the other cheek and not fight back, there were many in baseball who would not understand his lack of action. They could be made to respect only the fighting back, the things that are the signs of courage to men who know courage only in its physical sense. So I told Robinson that he was on his own. Then I sat back happily, knowing that, with the restraints removed, Robinson was going to show the National League a thing or two.[6]

Robinson reported to the Dodgers in spring 1949 in top shape. On the first day of spring training he told sportswriters, "They'd better be rough on me this year because I'm sure going to be rough on them."[7]

Commissioner Happy Chandler called Robinson to his office after the statement. Jackie later wrote, "I couldn't help wondering if he would have called up Ty Cobb, Frankie Frisch, or Pepper Martin — all white and all given to sounding off — for the same thing. I told the commissioner exactly how I felt and that, while I had no intentions of creating problems, I was no longer going to turn my cheek to insults. Chandler completely understood my position, and that was the end of our interview."[8]

The season began at Ebbets Field before a record Opening Day crowd of 34,530. Jackie belted a homer off Larry Jansen in the fifth inning and singled twice as the Dodgers trounced the Giants, 10–3. In the Phillies home opener four days later, Jackie put on his running shoes, stole second, stole third, and then raced home on a wild throw. The Dodgers beat Robin Roberts, 8–6. Jackie swiped 37 bases, including home five times, in 1949.

On May 3, Brooklyn pitcher Ralph Branca won his fourth start in as many tries with a 3–0 whitewash of the Reds. Jackie supported Branca with a homer. Robinson followed with an RBI double in a 5–1 win the next day, and singled, doubled, and scored twice the day after that as the Bums swept Cincinnati, 7–5.

With a 9–7 record Brooklyn was tied for second place, a game behind Boston. Catcher Roy Campanella, the second black ballplayer to crack the Dodger lineup, was leading the league with a .442 batting average and 16 RBIs. Born in Philadelphia of a black mother and Italian father in 1921, Campy starred at age fifteen for a hometown semi-pro ballclub, the Bacharach Giants. His play was noticed there by the Baltimore Eilte Giants of the Negro National League. They signed him to play the very next season. Still in school, Campy caught for the Giants only on weekends. In 1938 he quit school and joined the Elite Giants full time at age 17.

In 1949 Campy would catch 127 games and bat .287 with 22 homers and 82 RBIs. He won the MVP of the NL in 1951, 1953, and 1955. In 1953 he hit .312 with 42 homers and 142 RBIs. Despite his roly-poly physique, Campy was an adept bunter, smart base runner, and graceful fielding catcher. His career ended tragically in January 1958, when his car skidded on a patch of ice and crashed into a telephone pole. He fractured his fifth cervical vertebra and damaged his spinal cord. Left a quadriplegic, he authored a best-selling book entitled *It's Good to Be Alive* and dedicated himself to community relations work with the Dodgers for decades.

On May 7, Jackie flew around the bases in a 10–4 win over the Cubs when Harry Walker fell on his face, allowing Robinson's liner to roll to the right-field wall. The following day Jackie singled twice and doubled as the Dodgers knocked arch-rival St. Louis into the cellar with an 8–7 win. St. Louis manager Eddie Dyer had benched the slumping Enos Slaughter and used nine different lineups in nine days in an attempt to get his team going. Even Musial was hitting only .254.

Robinson singled twice and walloped a homer off Al Brazle, but the Cardinal bats awoke on May 9 to tag the Dodgers, 14–5. The highlight of the win was a grand slam by St. Louis third baseman Eddie Kazak. During World War II, Kazak was bayoneted through the left arm in hand-to-hand fighting in France. His right elbow was smashed by shrapnel and falling mortar in a small town near Brest. Eighteen months of hospitalization and a delicate operation in which plastic was used were necessary to repair the elbow and restore movement to three paralyzed fingers. He was told to forget baseball, yet came back to hit .311 for Rochester in 1948. Through the first half of 1949, Kazak batted .302 and was the only rookie to make the All-Star team.

On May 13, the front-running Braves beat the Dodgers in 10 innings, 6–5, as Eddie Stanky slashed three doubles and two singles. The next day, Robinson tripled in Duke Snider in the top of the twelfth inning to give Brooklyn a 6–5 lead, but the Braves came back with two runs in the bottom of the twelfth to win, 7–6. The Braves lost first baseman Earl Torgeson for the season in the victory. Torgeson suffered a shoulder separation when he tried to take out Robinson and break up a double play with a rolling block.

On May 17, Jackie tripled in a run in the fourth inning, doubled in a run in the eighth frame, ignited a six-run rally with a double in the eleventh, inning and then scored from second on a safe bunt by Gil Hodges. The Bums beat the Cubs, 8–5.

Three days later in St. Louis Jackie singled twice and knocked in a run, but the Cards routed Don Newcombe in his major league debut on the way to a 6–2 win. Newcombe came on in relief in the seventh and yielded successive singles to Red Schoendienst, Musial, and Kazak before Slaughter cleared the bases with a double.

Newcombe would have the last laugh, however. As the third black star on the Dodger's "Newk" led the team with 17 wins against eight losses while compiling a 3.17 ERA in 244 innings. At 6' 4" and 220 pounds, the big right-hander was an intimidating presence to those who sought to throw at Dodger ballplayers. After receiving Rookie of the Year honors in 1949, he became a mainstay on the Dodger staff for seven years, winning 123 games against 60 defeats. In 1956 he compiled a 27–7 record, won the MVP Award and led the Bums to their last pennant in Brooklyn.

The Dodgers turned the tables on the Cards 24 hours later, scoring eight times in the ninth inning to cap a 15–6 win. Robinson singled once, doubled twice, drove in six runs, and scored three times. His double-play partner, Pee Wee Reese, joined in the party with two singles, a double, and a homer while scoring five times and knocking in three runs.

If Robinson was the driving force of the Dodger teams of that era, Harold "Pee Wee" Reese was the team's steadying influence. The Brooklyn captain led NL shortstops in fielding in 1949. No slouch on offense, he hit .279, drew 116 walks, stole 26 bases, and topped the league with 132 runs while batting leadoff. Robinson found an unexpected ally in the white Southerner in his battle against player resentment. Pee Wee told the press a couple of months into the 1947 season, "When I first met Robinson in spring training, I figured, well, let me give this guy a chance. It may be he's just as good as I am. Frankly, I don't think I'd stand up under the kind of thing he's been subjected to as well as he has."[9]

Two days after his rough outing, Newcombe made his first start and blanked the Reds, 3–0. Jackie doubled twice and drove in the first run of the game. On May 24 in Pittsburgh, Jackie connected for a pair of two-run homers off Bob Chesnes and added a single in a 6–1 win. The next day he singled, smacked another two-run homer, reached base four times, and took over the league lead in RBIs with 34. Brooklyn beat the Bucs, 8–6. Robinson was batting .325 and was tied for the league lead in hits with Boston's Alvin Dark.

Back in Brooklyn against the Braves on May 27, Jackie's first-inning RBI ground ball was all Preacher Roe needed en route to his second consecutive shutout. The Braves won the second game of the series, 7–6, on former Dodger Pete Reiser's grand slam. Jackie singled twice, tripled, and chased home two runs in defeat. In the rubber game Robinson's two-run single off Warren Spahn in the seventh was the deciding blow in a 3–2 win that left the Bums in a three-way tie for first place with the Braves and Giants.

The hottest team in the league was the Cardinals, who swept Cincinnati in a Memorial Day doubleheader, 8–6 and 9–2, in St. Louis to move two games from the top. Slaughter ripped a single, three doubles, and a homer and drove in five runs. He had fought his way out of an early slump and on June 2 was batting .310.

Over in the Polo Grounds, the Dodgers and Giants split a Memorial Day doubleheader before a capacity crowd of 53,053. Brooklyn won the first game, 3–1, on Robinson's home run in the thirteenth inning off Dave Koslo. On the last day of the month, Jackie laced three singles and the Dodgers topped the Giants before 43,922 fans in Manhattan, 6–4. A homer by Carl Furillo in the fourteenth inning was the decider.

On June 1 the Cardinals came into Brooklyn and knocked the Dodgers out of first place with a 6–3 win. Musial homered in the first inning off Preacher Roe and tied the game with another homer in the ninth. The Cards scored three more runs in the ninth. In the third inning Robinson swung wide with an elusive slide to score on a Gil Hodges single. The entire Redbird bench stormed umpire Doug Robb to protest the safe call, and catcher Del Rice was ejected.

Musial won the second game of the series with a two-run double in the fourteenth inning, 7–4. Jackie singled and doubled and stole home off Harry Brecheen. The Dodgers salvaged the final game of the series, 5–2, by chasing Gerry Staley with four runs in the seventh inning.

On June 4 Jackie singled and tripled in an 8–6 win over the Pirates. In the eighth inning he banged a base hit, advanced two bases to third on a sacrifice bunt by Hodges, and scored the game-winner on a Furillo single. Robinson laced a two-run single and the Dodgers regained first place with a 7–1 triumph over the Cubs on June 7. The next day Rex Barney threw a two-hitter at the Cubs as Brooklyn won, 3–1. Jackie tripled in a run in the first inning, singled in the Bums' second run in the second inning, and then set up the third marker with a sacrifice bunt. Twenty-four hours later he socked three singles to help pace a 13-hit Brooklyn attack as the Dodgers completed a sweep of the Chicagoans, 9–5. He was leading the league in batting (.348), hits (69), and RBIs (45) as Brooklyn's record stood at 29–20, a half-game ahead of the second-place Cards and Braves.

The Brooklyn offense would lead the NL with 879 runs, far outscoring the second-place Cardinals' 766 runs. Along with Robinson, Campy, and Reese, the Dodgers received good production from such emerging stars as Duke Snider (.292, 23 homers, 92 RBIs), Gil Hodges (.285, 23 homers, 115 RBIs) and Carl Furillo (.322, 18 homers, 106 RBIs). Still, it was Robinson who batted clean-up in this powerful lineup.

Brooklyn's three black stars beat the Reds on June 11, 11–3. Newcombe went the route while striking out nine and yielding just five hits. Campanella homered twice and Robinson singled twice, scored once, and batted in a run. Brooklyn won its seventh straight by a football score of 20–7 over the Reds the succeeding afternoon by combining 13 hits with 11 walks. The Flatbushers scored 10 times in the fifth inning. Robinson torched the explosion with a double, scored three times, and drove in three runs. Hodges knocked out a single and a three-run homer in the fifth inning jamboree and added a grand slam in the seventh to finish with eight RBIs.

Hodges came up as a catcher but with the emergence of Campanella in 1948, he was converted to first base. He remained a mainstay from 1949 to 1959, topping 20 home runs in each of those 11 seasons and driving in more than 100 runs seven times. Reputed to be one of the strongest men in baseball, Hodges possessed large hands and fielded his new position well enough to win three Gold Gloves. The ex-marine managed the "Miracle Mets" to the championship in 1969.

The Bums invaded St. Louis and won their eighth straight on June 14, 7–2. Robinson was caught off first base on a liner by Hodges as part of a first-inning triple play but also singled twice and plated a pair of runs during the game. The Cards came back to win the next two at Sportsman's Park by 9–5 and 6–2 scores, however, and would stay in the pennant hunt to the end.

On June 21 the Dodgers stopped the Reds, 9–4. Robinson singled three times, stole two bases, scored twice, and knocked in a run. Furillo singled twice, doubled twice, and drove home three runs. Furillo was the Dodgers starting right fielder from 1946 to 1958 and became a magician at playing the tricky 40-foot-high wall at Ebbets Field. He averaged .299 lifetime with 1,910 hits and won a batting title in 1953 with a .344 average.

Newcombe pitched 11 innings and suffered his first loss in five decisions, 4–3, the next day in Cincinnati despite two singles and a double by Robinson. Newcombe was interviewed by Peter Golenbock in the 1984 book *Bums*. Newk recalled:

> ... one of the reasons I was as successful as I was had to be Jackie. ... I had a tendency not to bear down all the time with every pitch, especially if I had a big lead. ... One day we were in Pittsburgh, and we were leading the Pirates 11 to 0 in the third inning. I had the bases loaded and no outs and Ralph

Kiner at bat. And Jackie came over to me and said, "Do you know one thing? You should go to the clubhouse and take your uniform off and go home, because you don't want to pitch. You've got no business here in the big leagues, Newk. You ought to go home, because here you are fooling around. You have an 11–0 lead, you're going to fool around and get knocked out of the ballgame, and somebody else is gonna get the win"...And I struck out the side and we beat the Pirates terribly. But that was the kind of thing he would do.[10]

In Pittsburgh the Dodgers out-slugged the Pirates to win a 17–10 game that featured nine homers on June 25. Jackie singled and homered during a nine-run Brooklyn third inning, and for the contest he scored three runs and knocked in four. Hodges smacked five hits, hitting for the cycle plus a second homer. The fun continued for the Bums the next day as they danced home for 10 runs in the seventh inning of a 15–3 rout at Forbes Field. Jackie singled twice, tripled, and scored three times. Furillo banged out three singles, a triple, and a homer. During the seventh inning, Pirate pitcher Hugh Casey fired a fastball at Jackie's legs after Robinson had tried to bunt the previous pitch. Angry words were exchanged but further developments were averted when Casey left the game for a pinch-hitter.

On the Fourth of July, the Dodgers swept the Phils at Ebbets Field, 7–1 and 8–4. Robinson keyed a four-run Brooklyn rally with an RBI triple off Curt Simmons in the morning game then singled twice and stole two bases in the afternoon tilt. Two days later in Boston he scored from first base on a single. On July 10, his three singles plated three runs as the Dodgers bested the Giants, 7–3. At the All-Star break the Dodgers led the Redbirds by a half-game. The main reason was Robinson. He led in batting (.362) and hits (111) and was tied for the RBI lead with Hodges at 65.

Duke Snider came to the Dodgers in 1947. As a rookie he asked Dixie Walker about playing the caroms off the center-field wall at Ebbets Field. Walker replied, "Figure it out for yourself, kid." "The Duke of Flatbush" would do just that. He became baseball's leading home run hitter of the 1950s with 326.

The Dodgers started the second half by topping the Reds, 6–5, in 10 innings. Jackie's RBI single in the ninth inning tied the game and Billy Cox's RBI double in the tenth won it. The next day Brooklyn's three black stars combined to humble the Reds, 11–5. Newcombe went the distance for his seventh win. Campanella clubbed a two-run homer and Jackie banged a solo homer. Cincinnati salvaged the final game of the series, 7–6, in 10 innings. Walker Cooper's second homer of the day, a two-run shot in the top of the tenth, was the winning blow. Jackie led off the bottom of the tenth with a solo homer but Reese flied out with the bases loaded to end the game. Jackie scored a triple steal in the second inning. Cooper was riding a hot streak. On July 6, he had knocked out three singles and three homers in a single game, netting 10 RBIs.

The streaking Redbirds entered Brooklyn for a four-game set on July 22. In the first inning of the opener, Duke Snider tripled and Robinson singled him in. But Musial tied the score with a homer in the bottom of the first, and Cardinal moundsman George Munger yielded just three singles the rest of the way in a 3–1 St. Louis win. In the fourth Redbird center fielder Chuck Diering robbed Jackie of extra bases by coming up with a spectacular grab. The heartwarming story of Ed Kazak ended, however, when he sprained his ankle while sliding into third. He was carried from the field. Hitting .304 through midseason, he never enjoyed much baseball success again.

The second game saw the Redbirds, down to their last strike in the ninth inning, rally for two runs and triumph, 5–4. Robinson singled twice and drove in two runs in defeat. In the seventh he put the Dodgers ahead, 4–3, by scoring Reese on a squeeze bunt. Jackie reached first safely on the play when Gerry Staley's throw hit him in the back. St. Louis skipper Ed Dyer was thrown out of the game for protesting that Jackie ran out of the baseline. Joe Garagiola's RBI single won the contest.

Robinson's play seemed to irritate opposing players. St. Louis shortstop Marty Marion recalled, "Jackie was a challenge to play against ... he was always jumping up and down. He was aggravating. He really was. He kind of got on your nerves. But he was a good ballplayer, no question about that."[11]

Jackie was tough but the Cards were a tough bunch, too. They took over first place on July 24 with a 14–1 shellacking of the Bums. Musial kayoed Newcombe with a two-run triple in the first inning and wound up hitting for the cycle. The fourth game ended in a 4–4 tie when the contest was called by agreement after nine innings to permit both teams to catch trains headed west. Musial singled, doubled, and tripled and went 9-for-15 in the series. Jackie was 6-for-12.

On July 29 it was the Dodgers' turn to travel to St. Louis for another big four-game series. The opener, which was delayed an hour and a half by rain, ended in a 3–3 tie by curfew at 1:09 A.M. Robinson went 2-for-3 with a double and a big eighth-inning RBI single. The Cards opened up a 2½-game lead over Brooklyn in the standings a day later with a 7–6 win before 31,614. Jackie put the Bums ahead, 6–5, in the eighth with a two-run single but the Cards came back with two in the bottom of the inning. The Dodgers managed to break the Cards' nine-game win streak on the last day of July, 4–2. Newcombe went the route for the win and Jackie produced the deciding run with an RBI ground ball. The Bums also won the getaway game, 9–0, behind Branca's four-hitter. Jackie stroked an RBI single in Brooklyn's six-run first inning, tripled in Snider in the second inning, and added another single. The Bums left town one game better off than where they began, a half-game behind St. Louis.

The Cardinals had the edge on Brooklyn in pitching in 1949. St. Louis led the league with a 3.45 ERA while Brooklyn was second at 3.80. Howie Pollet (20–9), George Munger (15–8), Al Brazle (14–8) and Harry Brecheen (14–11) were the starters while Ted Wilks (10–3) and Gerry Staley (10–10, 2.74 ERA in 171 innings) did the bullpen work.

In addition to Newcombe, the Brooklyn staff was led by Preacher Roe (15–8), Ralph Branca (13–5), Joe Hatten (12–8), Jack Banta (10–6), Rex Barney (9–8), Erv Palica (8–9), and young Carl Erskine (8–1). Roe was a hillbilly raconteur who once quipped, "I got three pitches: my change; my change off my change; and my change off my change off my change." From 1951 through 1953 he won 44 games with eight losses. After his retirement he told *Sports Illustrated* that he had another pitch, the spitter. He boasted, "The outlawed pitch was my money pitch."[12]

Branca is most remembered for giving up Bobby Thomson's famous "Shot Heard 'Round the World" home run in 1951, but he also won 21 games at age twenty-one in 1947 to pitch the Dodgers to the pennant. Branca good-naturedly wore number 13 and got a kick out of posing with black cats to dispel notions of superstitions. He changed his number after giving up Thomson's homer.[13]

Brooklyn regained first place with a doubleheader sweep of the Reds in Cincinnati on August 7, winning, 7–0 and 2–1. Jackie slugged a two-run homer in the first inning of the opener off Ken Raffensberger and added a single and double later. Joe Hatten twirled a shutout in the first game and came back in relief to rescue Rex Barney in the second game.

Back home in Flatbush the next day, Newcombe beat the Giants, 2–1, on a three-hitter. Jackie blasted a solo homer in the first inning and contributed a crucial single to the Bums' game-winning rally in the eighth.

With the entrance of Jackie Robinson into the major leagues, attendance rose significantly. New fans of the African American communities began to frequent the games. In Jackie's first year, 1947, the Dodgers drew 1,807,526 fans to Ebbets Field, their all-time record in Brooklyn. Also in 1947 the National League drew a then-record 10,388,470 fans. It took until 1960 for the NL to surpass that number.

In 1949 there was no stopping Jackie Robinson and the Dodgers. In friendly Brooklyn, the Bums kept on winning, sweeping a three-game set from the Phils. Jackie singled, tripled, and scored on a double steal in an 8–1 win of the opener. He won the second game, 7–5, with a two-run homer off Jim Konstanty with two out in the ninth inning. He slapped a two-run single in the third contest, and Reese's three-run homer in the eighth decided a 10–7 win. Jackie was hitting .367 and led the league in hits (153) and RBIs (93). His closest competitor in the batting race was Slaughter at .333.

There was no love lost between Robinson and Slaughter, stemming from a play that occurred in 1947. Slaughter was racing down the line trying to beat out a grounder and clipped the back of Jackie's heel as he crossed first base. Brooklyn radio announcer Red Barber said Jack's career "came within an inch of being ended."[14] Robinson hobbled around for a while in pain but stayed in the game.

Robinson recalled the play in his autobiography: "As I took the throw at first from the infielder, Slaughter deliberately went for my leg instead of the base and spiked me rather severely. It was an act that unified the Dodger team. ... The team had always been close to first place in the pennant race, but the spirit shown after the Slaughter incident strengthened our resolve and made us go on to win the pennant."[15]

In his autobiography, Jackie wrote that several of his teammates ran on the field in anger after the play. Slaughter always denied attempting to injure Robinson. He said he was running down the line trying to beat out the grounder and ran right through the bag hard like he always did. He added that Jackie's foot moved toward the middle of the bag as he tried to catch a low throw. Slaughter wasn't too particular about who he ran into on the paths. In 1946 he knocked Stanky halfway into left field and "the Brat" had to be carried off the field on a stretcher. Also in 1947 he spiked Bill Rigney, giving the Giants second baseman a wound that took 23 stitches to close. Ironically, Robinson's best year, 1949, was arguably Slaughter's best. Enos batted .336 with 92 runs and 96 RBIs.

The Cards came into Brooklyn the next time on August 23 and split a day-night doubleheader. In the matinee Slaughter doubled and tripled and Musial homered. The Cards prevailed, 5–3. Musial got the Cards off to a good start in the nightcap with a two-run homer in the first inning. But the Dodgers fought back with Robinson doubling in Furillo in the fourth and scampering to third on Hodges' fly. Mike McCormick then bounced a grounder to Tommy Glaviano at third. Robinson took off like a shot for the plate and made it when Glaviano's throw hit him in the back, tying the game at 2–2. Brooklyn went up, 3–2, in the fifth on Furillo's RBI double before Slaughter's RBI single tied it in the sixth. Brooklyn finally won, 4–3 on doubles by Campanella and Snider in the eighth. A total of 60,171 fans showed up at Ebbets field for the two games. The Dodgers won the third game easily, 6–0. Newcombe was in command all the way and drove in three runs at the plate.

On August 27 Furillo and Cox homered as the Dodgers broke a team record for home runs that had stood since 1930 in a 6–1 win over the Cubs. In the sixth inning Jackie drove in Reese and Snider with a double. Cub pitcher Warren Hacker fielded the relay to the plate and tried to pick Jackie off second. His throw sailed into center field and Jackie sprinted home. The

Cards were hanging tough, though, as they bested the Giants twice in New York, 5–2 and 11–2. Musial singled, tripled, and walloped two of six Cardinal homers. The next day Newcombe blanked the Pirates on four hits, 9–0, backed by a triple from Jackie and homers from Snider, Hodges, and Campy. But the Cards topped the Braves twice in Boston, 9–7 and 7–1, to open a 2½-game lead. Musial was on fire with a triple and three-run homer in the lidlifter. Nippy Jones was even better, swatting three Redbird homers.

Musial finished second to Jackie in the batting race at .338 and led in hits (207), doubles (41), and triples (13). He scored 128 times with 123 RBIs. He finished second to Jackie in the MVP balloting, receiving 226 points to Robinson's 264 points.

September opened with Robinson plating three runs with a single, double, and homer as the Dodgers outscored the Reds, 11–8. Don Newcombe recorded his third straight shutout and ran his string of scoreless innings to 30 at the Polo Grounds a day later by blanking the Giants, 8–0. Jackie socked two singles and chased home two runs.

On Labor Day, 55,175 showed up at Ebbets Field to see the Dodgers sweep the Braves in a morning-afternoon doubleheader, 7–2 and 13–2. Furillo was the star of the day with two singles, a triple, a home run, and four RBIs. In St. Louis, the Cards routed the Pirates, 9–1, but then lost, 5–4, in ten innings. Slaughter's triple and home run netted five RBIs in the opener. Kazak made his first appearance since his ankle injury with a pinch-hit homer in the second game, but the Bucs won when Danny Murtaugh doubled and scored on Stan Rojek's single.

On September 6, Newcombe won his 15th game, 10–2, over the Braves. It was the Dodgers' 13th win in 17 games. Jackie ignited a five-run second inning with a single, one of his two hits on the day. In the third, he walked, stole second, and dashed home on a single.

Durocher's Giants, who brought up two talented black ballplayers around midseason, Monte Irvin and Hank Thompson, invaded Ebbets Field two days later. Jackie's two-run triple highlighted a six-run second inning as the Dodgers prevailed, 12–7. The game featured 22 walks. The Cards stayed one game up by blanking the Cubs, 8–0. Brecheen tossed a three-hitter and Slaughter netted three RBIs with three singles.

On September 10 the Dodgers beat the Giants, 5–4, as Jackie rapped two more singles, but St. Louis stayed atop by overtaking the Reds, 6–5, on Musial's two-out, ninth-inning three-run homer. Twenty-four hours later Brooklyn beat Durocher's Giants again, 10–5, in a tussle settled by Furillo's seventh-inning grand slam. Robinson singled, doubled, and scored twice. But in Cincinnati, Musial smashed three homers as the Cards swept a doubleheader, 7–5 and 7–4. The Redbird lead was 1½ games.

Durocher remembered Robinson in his autobiography: "I do know that when I went over to the Giants, Jackie and I were always needling each other. And that the more I needled him, the more he killed me. Every time I looked up, it seemed Jackie Robinson was getting the late-inning hit that either tied the game or beat us. Him and Musial. It got to be an obsession with me. I'd run out to the pitcher's box and say, 'Don't let this man beat us again. Anybody but him.'"[16]

The Dodgers followed the Cards into Cincinnati and Robinson's two-run, tenth-inning triple highlighted a 6–3 win. In St. Louis the Cards nipped the Giants, 1–0, on George Munger's one-hitter for their 15th win in 18 games. Munger got the only run he needed on Musial's check-swing RBI double down the third-base line.

Musial was hitting like a fool as he singled twice, tripled, and drove in four runs in a 9–3 victory over New York on September 14. Robinson delivered an RBI single in the seventh inning of a 4–2 Brooklyn win over the Reds. The same day in Pittsburgh, slugger Ralph Kiner hit his 49th homer and tied Robinson for the league lead in RBIs at 117. Kiner finished with 54 homers and 127 RBIs in 1949. He had the misfortune of being a star player on a bad ballclub for his career. The Bucs finished in sixth place at 71–83.

Things looked bad for the Dodgers on September 16 as they were drubbed, 9–2, by Kiner's Bucs. Campanella was struck in the head and knocked unconscious by a pitch from Bill Werle in the second inning. Fortunately, X-rays showed no serious injury. The Cards beat Warren Spahn and the Braves, 7–5, to increase their lead to 2½ games. The Bucs then drubbed the Dodgers again, 7–2. The Dodgers could thank Boston's Bill Voiselle for keeping them in the race by cooling off St. Louis, 4–2. Before that the Cards had won 17 of 20.

Jackie singled in a run after Snider was passed intentionally to help key a four-run rally in the eighth and then plated Reese with a squeeze bunt in the ninth as Brooklyn won in Chicago, 7–1, on September 18. The Cards looked like they had no intention of folding, though, as they humbled the Phils, 15–3, with Musial and Slaughter crashing homers.

But the pennant chase was to take yet one more turn. Rex Barney was at his best on September 19. He beat the Cubs at Wrigley Field with a one-hitter, 4–0. Jackie socked two singles, walked, and scored on Campanella's seventh-inning double. The Phils nipped the Cards in St. Louis, 4–3, and the Redbird lead was 1½ games. The following afternoon Jack Banta shut out the Cubs again, 5–0, and Jackie stole home. It was Robinson's fifth theft of home of the summer. Cub catcher Mickey Owen protested the safe call at home and bumped umpire Artie Gore so hard that the arbitrator fell to the ground. Owen was tossed from the game. Cub manager Frankie Frisch took up the argument and he too was tossed. The Cards woke up to stop the Phils,

7–5. The Dodgers then boarded a train headed west for their final series of the season in St. Louis. To stay in contention, the Bums would have to take two of three on the Redbirds' home turf.

In the first game of a day-night doubleheader on September 21, Max Lanier out-dueled Newcombe, 1–0. Slaughter slashed three hits to overtake Robinson in the batting race. He led off the ninth with his second double of the day. Bill Howerton dumped a bunt down the third-base line. Eddie Miksis let the ball roll, hoping it would go foul, but it stayed fair. Robinson resumed an argument with umpire Bill Stewart over a ball and strike call in his last at-bat. Jackie used a hand to the throat gesture indicating that Stewart had choked, and was thrown out of the game. Garagiola then singled to score Slaughter with the winner. The Cards were 2½ up.

The night game saw Roe help keep the Bums' hopes alive, besting Brecheen with a two-hit shutout, 5–0. Brooklyn pitchers had allowed one run over the last four games. Singles by Furillo and Hodges, a walk to Robinson, a two-run triple by Luis Olmo, and Snider's 21st homer rang up all five Brooklyn runs in the fourth. A total of 63,877 fans witnessed the doubleheader.

In the final game of the series Brooklyn combined 19 hits with 13 walks to bombard the Cards, 19–6. Robinson singled twice, received two intentional passes, and scored four times. Furillo singled twice and doubled three times to knock in seven runs. Snider singled twice, doubled twice, and scored four times while Hodges singled three times for five RBIs. The Cardinal lead had shrunk to a half-game.

An overflow crowd of 34,083 filled Ebbets Field on September 24 for Don Newcombe Night. Newcombe was given an automobile before the game and responded by beating the Phils, 8–1. St. Louis kept the lead by stopping the Cubs, 3–2. Musial doubled and tripled and reliever Ted Wilks quelled a ninth-inning rally in his 56th appearance.

Brooklyn's hopes dimmed the following day, however, as the Phils beat the Bums, 5–3, on the strength of Andy Seminick's two-run homer in the eighth inning. In St. Louis, Harry Brecheen mowed down the Cubs, 6–1. "The Cat" also drove in three runs by slapping four singles. The Cards lead was 1½ games. Brooklyn had four games left; the Cards had five.

The Dodgers were idle the next three days while the Pirates topped the Redbirds, 6–4, on Tom Saffell's grand slam. On September 29 the tide turned. Brooklyn beat the Braves, 9–2 and 8–0, in Boston while Pittsburgh's Murray Dickson beat his former teammates in St. Louis for the fifth time of the season, 7–2. Robinson stroked RBI singles in both wins for the Dodgers, but Furillo and Newcombe were the real stars. Furillo delivered an RBI single and a three-run homer in the opener. Furillo had asked for a rest in early August, much to the outspoken displeasure of manager

Burt Shotton. But since getting back in the lineup on August 7, he batted .425 with 79 hits and 45 RBIs. Newcombe tossed a shutout in the second game, which was called after five innings because of rain. Boston's Connie Ryan was tossed from the game for wearing a raincoat to the on-deck circle in the bottom of the fifth. His teammates lit a fire in the dugout, presumably as a guiding beacon for returning batsmen. Newcombe was unruffled by the antics as he struck out the side to end the game. The Dodgers were in first place by a half-game.

The Bums were idle on the last day of the month but their lead increased to a full game when the last-place Cubs nipped the Cards, 6–5. October opened with the Cubs beating the Cards again, 3–1. Brooklyn had a chance to clinch the pennant by defeating the Phils. The Dodgers knocked out Philadelphia hurler Ken Heintzelman, who had boasted a 5–0 record against them, but lost, 5–3, on Willie Jones' homer in the eighth inning.

The Cards routed the Cubs, 13–5, on the final day of the season. Musial homered twice. In Philadelphia the Dodgers clinched the pennant with a 9–7 victory over the Quakers in ten innings. Jackie singled, stole second, and scored in a five-run third inning, but the Phils knocked out Newcombe and tied the game, 7–7, in the sixth. The Dodgers' winning rally in the tenth started with a base hit by Reese off their nemesis, Heintzelman, who was on in relief. Miksis bunted Reese to second and Snider drove him in with a single. Robinson was walked intentionally and Olmo plated Snider with another single. Jack Banta shut out the Phils for the last four innings and was carried into the dressing room on the shoulders of his teammates.

Robinson won the batting title at .342, with Musial (.339) and Slaughter (.336) right behind. Furillo finished the season with four hits in the 9–7 win and batted .322. Robinson's 203 hits were second to Musial's 207. His 124 RBIs were second to Kiner's 127 and his 122 runs scored ranked third to Reese (132) and Musial (128).

In the first game of the World Series, the Yankees' Allie Reynolds outdueled Newcombe with a sparkling two-hitter, 1–0. The Yanks went on to win in five games. Robinson was just 3-for-16 (.188) in the Series, and the rest of the Dodgers weren't much better. As a team Brooklyn batted .210.

The triumph of Jackie Robinson breaking the color barrier was a triumph for America. Jackie played a significant role in tearing down the walls of segregation. The fact that black players were not allowed in the major leagues for 50 years prior to his arrival is an American tragedy. Two black players in particular, Josh Gibson and Satchel Paige, could have starred for many years. Gibson was a catcher who some estimate hit as many as 950 homers counting the exhibitions he played in. Roy Campanella said, "I couldn't carry Josh's glove. Anything I could do, Josh could do better."[17]

Paige did get a chance to play in the majors at age 41 after logging thousands of innings with his arm. Some say he was the best pitcher ever. Dizzy Dean once declared, "That skinny old Satchel Paige with those long arms is my idea of the pitcher with the greatest stuff I ever saw."[18]

Paige said on many occasions, "If you want to know the truth, I wasn't the onliest one who could pitch in the Negro leagues. ... We had a lot of Satchels. There were a lot of Joshes. We had top pitchers. We had quite a few men could hit the ball like Babe and Josh. Wasn't any mebbe so."[19]

Robinson became a successful business man after leaving baseball. He died at age 53, nearly blind from diabetes. Before dying he scolded major league baseball. Twenty years after 1947, the majors didn't have a single black manager. His words had an effect. Frank Robinson was hired as the first black manager in 1975. Since then there have been many black managers, and some have had great success. Obviously, all they needed was an opportunity.

Chapter Notes

Preface

1. Jack Kavanagh, *Ol' Pete: The Grover Cleveland Alexander Story* (South Bend, IN: Diamond, 1996), p. 71.
2. W. Harrison Daniel, *Jimmie Foxx: The Life and Times of a Baseball Hall of Famer 1907–1967* (Jefferson, NC: McFarland, 1996), p. 138, and William Mead, *Baseball Goes to War* (Washington, DC: Farragut, 1985), p. 99. Also, David Quentin Voigt, *American Baseball*, 3 Volumes (Norman: University of Oklahoma Press, 1966–1983) Volume II, p. 257, and Bruce Kurlick, *To Everything a Season: Shibe Park and Urban Philadelphia, 1909–1976* (Princeton, NJ: Princeton University Press, 1991), p. 96.
3. John Sickels, *Bob Feller: Ace of the Greatest Generation* (Washington, DC: Brassey's, 2004), p. 115.
4. Bob Nightengale, "The Sultans Side by Side," *USA Today Sports Weekly* (April 5–11, 2006), p. 8.
5. John B. Holway, *Josh and Satch: The Life and Times of Josh Gibson and Satchel Paige* (Westport, CT: Meckler, 1991), pp. ix–x.

Chapter 1

1. Tom Simon, ed., *Deadball Stars of the National League* (Washington, DC: Brassey's, 2004), p. 33. From the book's biography of Christy Mathewson, written by Eddie Frierson.
2. Ronald Mayer, *Christy Mathewson: A Game-by-Game Profile of a Legendary Pitcher* (Jefferson, NC: McFarland, 1993), p. xi.
3. Daniel Okrent and Harris Lewine, eds., with historical text by David Nemec, *The Ul-*

timate Book of Baseball (Boston: Houghton Mifflin, 1991), p. 70. From the story "Pitcher: The Real Frank Merriwell," by Jonathan Yardley.
4. *Ibid.*, p. 73.
5. G.H. Fleming, *Unforgettable Season* (New York: Holt, Rinehart and Winston, 1981), pp. 47–48.
6. *Ibid.*, p. 49.
7. *Ibid.*, p. 73.
8. *Ibid.*, p. 98.
9. *Ibid.*, p. 101.
10. *Ibid.*, pp. 103–104.
11. *Ibid.*, p. 125.
12. *Ibid.*, p. 139.
13. Tom Murray, ed., *Sport Magazine's All-Time All Stars* (New York: The New American Library, 1977), p. 410. From "Christy Mathewson: The Immortal 'Big Six,'" Jack Sher, *Sport*, October 1949.
14. *Ibid.*, p. 413.
15. John Carmichael, ed., *My Greatest Day in Baseball* (New York: A.S. Barnes, 1945; Lincoln: University of Nebraska Press, 1996), p. 175.
16. Christy Mathewson, *Pitching in a Pinch* (New York: Putnam, 1912; Lincoln: University of Nebraska Press, 1994), p. 201.
17. Murray, *Sport Magazine's All-Time All Stars*, p. 418.
18. Carmichael, *My Greatest Day in Baseball*, pp. 178–179.
19. Fleming, *Unforgettable Season*, p. 319.

Chapter 2

1. Murray, *Sport Magazine's All-Time All Stars*, p. 122. From "Ty Cobb: The Georgia Peach," Jack Sher, *Sport*, November 1948.

2. *Ibid.*, p. 122.
3. Mark Alvarez, ed., *The Baseball Research Journal #20* (Cleveland, OH: Society for American Baseball Research, 1991), p. 40. From "Cobb on a Rampage," Larry Amman.
4. Al Stump, *Cobb: A Biography* (Chapel Hill, NC: Algonquin, 1994), pp. 72–73.
5. David Jones, ed., *Deadball Stars of the American League* (Dulles, VA: Potomac, 2006), p. 548. From biography on Ty Cobb by Dan Ginsburg.
6. Stump, *Cobb*, p.129.
7. *Sporting News*, April 24, 1911.
8. Lawrence Ritter, *The Glory of Their Times* (New York: Macmillan, 1966), p. 62.
9. *Sporting News*, April 17, 1911.
10. *Sporting News*, April 24, 1911.
11. *Sporting News*, May 8, 1911.
12. *Sporting News*, April 24, 1911.
13. *Sporting News*, June 17, 1911.
14. *Ibid.*
15. *Ibid.*
16. Marc Okkonen, *The Ty Cobb Scrapbook* (New York: Sterling, 2001), p. 63.
17. *Ibid.*
18. Alvarez, *The Baseball Research Journal*, "Cobb on a Rampage," p. 42.
19. F.C. Lane, *Batting* (New York: Baseball Magazine Company, 1925; Lincoln: University of Nebraska Press, 2001), p. 76.
20. Stump, *Cobb*, p. 397.
21. Ty Cobb and Al Stump, *Ty Cobb: My Life in Baseball* (New York: Doubleday, 1961), p. 192.
22. Daniel Okrent and Harris Lewine, eds., and David Nemec, *The Ultimate Book of Baseball* (Boston: Houghton Mifflin, 1991), p. 82.
23. Charles Alexander, *Ty Cobb* (New York: Oxford, 1984), p. 100; *Sporting Life*, August 5, 1911, p. 15.
24. David Fleitz, *Shoeless: The Life and Times of Joe Jackson* (Jefferson, NC: McFarland, 2001), p. 52.
25. Cobb, *Ty Cobb*, p. 176.
26. Stump, *Cobb*, p. 348.
27. *Ibid.*, p. 369.

Chapter 3

1. William Curran, *Big Sticks* (New York: Morrow, 1990), p. 54.
2. Mike Sowell, *The Pitch That Killed* (New York: Macmillan, 1989), p. 236.
3. *Ibid.*, p. 20.
4. John Kuenster, ed., *From Cobb to Catfish* (New York: Rand McNally, 1975), p. 212. From "Carl Mays Recalls That Tragic Pitch," Jack Murphy, *San Diego Union*, 1971.
5. *Ibid.*
6. Okrent and Lewine, *The Ultimate Book of Baseball*, p. 126.
7. Marshall Smelser, *The Life That Ruth Built* (New York: Quadrangle, New York Times Book Company, 1975), p. 149.
8. Paul Gallico, *A Farewell to Sport* (New York: Knopf, 1941), p. 39.
9. Babe Ruth and Bob Considine, *The Babe Ruth Story* (New York: Dutton, 1948), pp. 5–6.
10. Robert Creamer, *Babe: The Legend Comes to Life* (New York: Simon & Schuster, 1974), pp. 229–230.
11. Stump, *Cobb*, p. 330.
12. Fleitz, *Shoeless*, pp. 163–164.
13. Ritter, *The Glory of Their Times*, p. 230.
14. Creamer, *Babe*, p. 242.
15. *Ibid.*
16. *Ibid.*
17. John Mosedale, *The Greatest of All: The 1927 Yankees* (New York: Warner, 1974), p. 193.

Chapter 4

1. Lane, *Batting*, p. 44.
2. *Ibid.*, p. 108.
3. Murray, *Sport Magazine's All-Time All Stars*, from "Rogers Hornsby; The Mighty Rajah," Jack Sher, *Sport*, July 1949, pp. 254–255.
4. *Ibid.*, p. 257.
5. *Ibid.*, p. 244.
6. Lane, *Batting*, p. 37.
7. *Ibid.*, p. 215.
8. Murray, *Sport Magazine's All-Time All Stars*, p. 245.
9. *Ibid.*, p. 248.
10. Peter Golenbock, *The Spirit of St. Louis* (New York: Harper Collins, 2000), p. 93; Donald Honig, *The October Heroes* (New York: Simon & Schuster, 1979), p. 90.
11. Kuenster, *From Cobb to Catfish*, p. 161.
12. *Sporting News*, June 1, 1922, p. 1.
13. Nathan Salant, *Superstars, Stars and Just Plain Heroes* (New York: Stein and Day, 1982), p. 32.
14. *Sporting News*, August 31, 1922, p. 9.
15. Golenbock, *The Spirit of St. Louis*, p. 92.

16. Charles Alexander, *Rogers Hornsby* (New York: Henry Holt, 1995), p. 90.

17. Donald Honig, *Baseball When the Grass Was Real* (New York: Coward, McCann and Geoghegan, 1975), p. 134.

18. Lane, *Batting*, p. 144.

19. Rogers Hornsby and Bill Surface, *My War with Baseball* (New York: Coward-Mc-Cann, 1962), p. 15.

Chapter 5

1. Rick Huhn, *The Sizzler: George Sisler, Baseball's Forgotten Great* (Columbia: University of Missouri Press, 2004), p. 5.

2. Salant, *Superstars, Stars, and Just Plain Heroes*, p. 38.

3. Ken Smith, *Baseball's Hall of Fame* (New York: Grosset and Dunlap, 1952), p. 139.

4. Murray Polner, *Branch Rickey* (New York: Athenaeum, 1982), p. 76.

5. *Ibid.*, p. 77.

6. Mike Shatzkin, ed., *The Ballplayers* (New York: William Morrow, 1990), p. 1177.

7. Curran, *Big Sticks*, p. 152.

8. Roger Godin, *The 1922 St. Louis Browns* (Jefferson, NC: McFarland, 1991), p. 203.

9. *Sporting News*, July 39, 1922, p. 7.

10. *Sporting News*, July 13, 1922, p. 7.

11. *Sporting News*, September 14, 1922, p. 1.

12. James Oscar Lindberg, "Just How Good Was George Sisler?" (unpublished story from the Society For American Baseball Research library), p. 4; quoted from August 30, 1922, edition of *The Outlook* by Frederick M. Davenport.

13. *Sporting News*, September 7, 1922, p. 7.

14. Godin, *The 1922 St. Louis Browns*, p. 157.

15. *Ibid.*

16. *Ibid.*, p. 169.

17. *Sporting News*, September 21, 1922, p. 1.

Chapter 6

1. Clifton Blue Parker, *Fouled Away: The Baseball Tragedy of Hack Wilson* (Jefferson, NC: McFarland, 2000), p. 10.

2. *Ibid.*, pp. 9–10.

3. *Ibid.*, p. 43.

4. Bill Veeck and Ed Linn, *Veeck as in Wreck* (New York: G.P. Putnam's Sons, 1962), p. 32.

5. William Mead, *Two Spectacular Seasons* (New York: Macmillan, 1990), p. 7.

6. *Sporting News*, April 24, 1930, p. 1.

7. *Sporting News*, May 22, 1930, p. 1.

8. Mead, *Two Spectacular Seasons*, p. 74.

9. Parker, *Fouled Away*, p. 94.

10. Mead, *Two Spectacular Seasons*, p. 74.

11. *Ibid.*, p. 85.

12. *Ibid.*, p. 86.

13. *Ibid.*, p. 85.

14. *Sporting News*, August 28, 1930, p. 7.

15. Mead, *Two Spectacular Seasons*, p. 85.

16. Al Stump, "There'll Never Be Another Hack Wilson," *Cavalier*, 1961; *Baseball*, 1962, p. 68.

17. Alan H. Levy, *Joe McCarthy: Architect of the Yankee Dynasty* (Jefferson, NC: McFarland, 2005), p. 143.

18. *Sporting News*, September 25, 1930, p. 1.

19. *Ibid.*

20. Parker, *Fouled Away*, p. 119.

21. *Sporting News*, October 2, 1930, p. 1.

22. Honig, *Baseball When the Grass Was Real*, p. 179.

23. Mead, *Two Spectacular Seasons*, p. 115.

24. Parker, *Fouled Away*, p. 193.

25. *Ibid.*, p. 194.

26. Stump, "There'll Never Be Another Hack Wilson," p. 66.

Chapter 7

1. Mark R. Millikan, *Jimmie Foxx: The Pride of Sudlersville* (Lanham, MD: Scarecrow Press, 1998), p. 141.

2. W. Harrison Daniel, *Jimmie Foxx: The Life and Times of a Baseball Hall of Famer 1907–1967* (Jefferson, NC: McFarland, 1996), p. 11.

3. William Kashatus, *Connie Mack's '29 Triumph* (Jefferson, NC: McFarland, 1999), p. 161.

4. *Ibid.*

5. Charles Einstein, ed., *The Fireside Book of Baseball* (New York: Simon & Schuster, 1958), p. 202. From "Double X: The Brilliant Jimmy Foxx," Bob Holbrook, *Boston Globe*.

6. *Ibid.*, p. 202.

7. Daniel, *Jimmie Foxx*, p. 57.

8. *Sporting News*, May 19, 1932, p. 3.

9. *Sporting News*, May 26, 1932, p. 6.

10. Ray Robinson, *Iron Horse: Lou Gehrig in His Time* (New York: Harper Collins, 1990), p. 165.

11. Jonathan Eig, *The Luckiest Man: The Life and Death of Lou Gehrig* (New York: Simon & Schuster, 2005), p. 156.

12. Daniel, *Jimmie Foxx*, p. 51.

13. Jim Kaplan, *Lefty Grove: American Original* (Cleveland: Society for American Baseball Research, 2000), pp. 256–257.

14. Millikan, *Jimmie Foxx*, p.132.

15. *Ibid.*, pp. 132–133.

Chapter 8

1. Robert Gregory, *Diz: The Story of Dizzy Dean and Baseball During the Great Depression* (New York: Viking Penguin, 1992), p. 126.

2. Vince Staten, *Ol' Diz: A Biography of Dizzy Dean* (New York: Harper Collins, 1992), p. 23.

3. *Ibid.*, pp. 36–37.

4. Salant, *Superstars, Stars and Just Plain Heroes*, p. 185.

5. Frank Graham, *The New York Giants* (New York: G.P. Putnam's Sons, 1952; Carbondale: Southern University Press, 2002), p. 210.

6. Gregory, *Diz*, p. 131.

7. *Sporting News*, May 17, 1934, p. 8.

8. Gregory, *Diz*, p. 138.

9. *Ibid.*, pp. 141–142.

10. *Ibid.*, p. 151.

11. *Ibid.*, pp. 151–152.

12. G.H. Fleming, *The Dizziest Season* (New York: Morrow, 1984), p. 114.

13. *Ibid.*, p. 132.

14. Gregory, *Diz*, p. 155.

15. *Ibid.*, pp. 161–162.

16. *Ibid.*, p. 171.

17. Salant, *Superstars, Stars and Just Plain Heroes*, p. 187.

18. Gregory, *Diz*, p. 180.

19. Staten, *Ol' Diz*, pp. 130–131.

20. *Ibid.*, p. 131.

21. Leo Durocher and Ed Linn, *Nice Guys Finish Last* (New York: Simon & Schuster, 1975), p. 98.

22. Gregory, *Diz*, p. 206.

23. Durocher and Linn, *Nice Guys Finish Last*, p. 101.

24. Gregory, *Diz*, p. 229.

25. Durocher and Linn, *Nice Guys Finish Last*, pp. 102–103.

Chapter 9

1. Mosedale, *The Greatest of All*, p. 108.

2. *Sporting News*, June 25, 1936, p. 3.

3. Eig, *Luckiest Man*, p. 317.

4. Robinson, *Iron Horse*, p. 278.

5. *Ibid.*, p. 32.

6. *Ibid.*, p. 58.

7. *Ibid.*, p. 59.

8. *Ibid.*, p. 74.

9. Eig, *Luckiest Man*, p. 102.

10. Robinson, *Iron Horse*, p. 141.

11. *Ibid.*

12. Murray, *Sport Magazine's All-Time All Stars*, p. 7. From "Lou Gehrig, The Man and the Legend," by Jack Sher, October 1948.

13. Mosedale, *The Greatest of All*, p. 108.

14. Murray, *Sport Magazine's All-Time All Stars*, p. 27.

15. *Ibid.*, p. 32.

16. *Ibid.*, p. 15.

17. *Ibid.*, p. 28.

18. Joe DiMaggio, *Lucky to Be a Yankee* (New York: Greenberg Publishers), 1943, p. 96.

19. *Sporting News*, July 2, 1936, p. 2.

20. Murray, *Sport Magazine's All-Time All Stars*, p. 11.

21. Eig, *Luckiest Man*, p. 109.

22. *Sporting News*, August 20, 1936, p. 6.

23. *Sporting News*, August 27, 1936, p. 6.

24. *Sporting News*, September 10, 1936, p. 3.

25. *Sporting News*, September 24, 1936, p. 1.

26. Robinson, *The Iron Horse*, p. 222.

Chapter 10

1. Hank Greenberg and Ira Berkow, *Hank Greenberg: The Story of My Life* (New York: Random House, 1989), p. 94.

2. *Ibid.*, p. 103.

3. *Ibid.*

4. *Ibid.*, pp. 41–42.

5. *Ibid.*, p. 17.

6. *Ibid.*, p. 22.

7. Mike Blake, *Baseball Chronicles* (Cincinnati: Betterway Books, 1994), p. 59.

8. *Ibid.*

9. Greenberg and Berkow, *Hank Greenberg*, pp. 61–62.

10. *Sporting News*, May 27, 1937, p. 8.

11. Greenberg and Berkow, *Hank Greenberg*, p. 51.

12. Donald Honig, *The Greatest First Basemen of All Time* (New York: Crown, 1988), p. 61.

13. *Sporting News*, June 24, 1937, p. 1.

14. Greenberg and Berkow, *Hank Greenberg*, pp. 55–56.

15. *Sporting News*, August 26, 1937, p. 10.

16. Honig, *The Greatest First Basemen*, p. 62.

17. *Sporting News*, September 9, 1937, p. 1.

18. *Ibid.*, p. 6.

19. *Sporting News*, September 23, 1937, p. 5.

20. Greenberg and Berkow, *Hank Greenberg*, p. 45.

21. *Sporting News*, September 23, 1937, p. 6.

22. Shatkin, *The Ballplayers*, p. 383.

23. Greenberg and Berkow, *Hank Greenberg*, p. 121.

24. *Ibid.*, p. 120.

25. *Ibid.*, p. 131.

26. *Ibid.*, p. 149.

Chapter 11

1. Ted Williams and John Underwood, *My Turn at Bat: The Story of My Life* (New York: Simon & Schuster, 1969), pp. 7–8.

2. *Ibid.*, p. 29.

3. *Sporting News*, June 19, 1941, p. 7.

4. Williams and Underwood, *My Turn at Bat*, p. 81.

5. *Ibid.*

6. Ed Linn, *Hitter: The Life and Turmoils of Ted Williams* (New York: Harcourt Brace, 1993), p. 146.

7. *Ibid.*

8. *Ibid.*

9. *Sporting News*, June 5, 1941, p. 5.

10. *Sporting News*, June 19, 1941, p. 1.

11. *Ibid.*

12. *Ibid.*

13. DiMaggio, *Lucky to Be a Yankee*, p. 130.

14. *Sporting News*, July 10, 1941, p. 10.

15. Williams and Underwood, *My Turn at Bat*, p. 89.

16. Kaplan, *Lefty Grove*, p. 245.

17. *Sporting News*, July 31, 1941, p. 14.

18. *Sporting News*, September 5, 1941, p. 5.

19. Linn, *Hitter*, p. 155.

20. *Sporting News*, September 18, 1941, p. 8.

21. *Ibid.*, p. 2.

22. Williams and Underwood, *My Turn at Bat*, p. 85.

23. *Ibid.*, p. 90.

24. *Ibid.*

Chapter 12

1. Bob Feller and Bill Gilbert, *Now Pitching Bob Feller* (New York: Harper Collins, 1991), p. 35.

2. John Sickels, *Bob Feller: Ace of the Greatest Generation* (Washington, DC: Brassey's, 2004), p. 15; Bob Feller and Burton Rocks, *Bob Feller's Little Black Book of Baseball Wisdom* (Chicago: Contemporary, 2001), p. 5.

3. Sickels, *Bob Feller*, p. 125; Bob Feller, *Bob Feller's Strikeout Story* (New York: Grosset and Dunlap, 1947), p. 213.

4. Sickels, *Bob Feller*, p. 115.

5. *Ibid.*, p. 140; Feller, *Bob Feller's Strikeout Story*, p. 226.

6. *Sporting News*, May 9, 1946, p. 6.

7. *Ibid.*

8. *Ibid.*

9. *Ibid.*

10. *Ibid.*

11. *Ibid.*, p. 13.

12. Sickels, *Bob Feller*, p. 132.

13. *Sporting News*, May 23, 1946, p. 13.

14. *Sporting News*, July 10, 1946, p. 19.

15. Greenberg and Berkow, *Hank Greenberg*, p. 166.

16. Feller and Gilbert, *Now Pitching Bob Feller*, p. 30.

17. *Sporting News*, July 31, 1946, p. 11.

18. *Sporting News*, August 21, 1946, p. 14.

19. *Sporting News*, September 25, 1946, p. 9.

20. *Ibid.*

21. Sickels, *Bob Feller*, p. 143.

22. *Sporting News*, October 9, 1946, p. 11.

Chapter 13

1. Stan Musial and Bob Broeg, *Stan Musial: The Man's Own Story* (Garden City, NY: Doubleday, 1964), p. 9.

2. *Ibid.*, p. 104.
3. *Ibid.*, p. 109.
4. *Ibid.*, p. 110.
5. *Ibid.*, p. 111.
6. *Ibid.*, p. 112.
7. Jerry Lansche, *Stan "The Man" Musial: Born to Be a Ballplayer* (Dallas: Taylor, 1994), p. 75.
8. Musial and Broeg, *Stan Musial*, p. 112.
9. Durocher and Linn, *Nice Guys Finish Last*, p. 208.
10. Musial and Broeg, *Stan Musial*, p. 113.
11. *Ibid.*
12. Lansche, *Stan "The Man" Musial*, p. 109.
13. Enos Slaughter and Ken Reid, *Country Hardball: The Autobiography of Enos "Country" Slaughter* (Greensboro, NC: Tudor, 1991), p. 115.
14. *Ibid.*, p. 15.
15. *Ibid.*
16. Musial and Broeg, *Stan Musial*, p. 115.
17. *Ibid.*, pp. 114–115.
18. *Ibid.*, p. 116.
19. Golenbock, *The Spirit of St. Louis*, p. 392.
20. Lansche, *Stan "The Man" Musial*, pp. 123–124.

Chapter 14

1. George DeGregorio, *Joe DiMaggio: An Informal Biography* (New York: Stein and Day, 1981), p. 113. The lyrics to the song "Joltin' Joe DiMaggio" were written by Alan Courtney and the music was written by Ben Homer. It became a hit when played by Les Brown's Band.
2. Mark Alvarez, ed., *The National Pastime #19* (Cleveland: Society for American Baseball Research, 1999), p. 3. From "The Last Yankee," written by Tommy Henrich and Richard Nikas.
3. Richard Ben Cramer, *Joe DiMaggio: The Hero's Life* (New York: Simon & Schuster, 2000), p. 63.
4. DeGregorio, *Joe DiMaggio*, p. 44.
5. *Ibid.*, p. 54.
6. *Ibid.*, p. 163.
7. *Ibid.*, p. 168.
8. *Ibid.*, p. 169.
9. Alvarez, Henrich and Nikas, *The National Pastime #19*, p. 3.
10. Murray, *Sport Magazine's All-Time All Stars*, p. 155. From "The Joe DiMaggio I Remember," Jimmy Cannon, *Sport*, September 1956.
11. *Ibid.*, p. 159.
12. *Sporting News*, June 9, 1948, p. 16.
13. Okrent, Lewine and Nemec, *The Ultimate Book of Baseball*, p. 230.
14. *Sporting News*, June 30, 1948, p. 17.
15. David Kaiser, *The Epic Season: The 1948 American League Pennant Race* (Amherst: University of Massachusetts Press, 1998), p. 83.
16. *Sporting News*, July 14, 1948, p. 34.
17. Bill Koenig, "Farewell Joe," *USA Today's Baseball Weekly*, (March 10–16, 1999), p. 8.
18. DeGregorio, *Joe DiMaggio*, p. 174.
19. *Ibid.*, p. 175.
20. *Ibid.*, p. 181.

Chapter 15

1. Arnold Rampersad and Rachel Robinson, *Jackie Robinson* (New York: Ballantine, 1997), p. 219.
2. *Ibid.*, p. 109. The complete record of Robinson's court-martial trial, August 2, 1944, including a transcript of the trial and a copy of all depositions are in U.S. Army Records, Jackie Robinson Papers, Jackie Robinson Foundation, New York City.
3. Jackie Robinson and Alfred Duckett, *I Never Had It Made* (New York: Putnam, 1972), p. 34.
4. *Ibid.*
5. *Ibid.*, p. 78.
6. *Ibid.*, p. 79.
7. *Ibid.*, p. 80.
8. *Ibid.*, pp. 80–81.
9. *Ibid.*, p. 65
10. Peter Golenbock, *Bums: An Oral History of the Brooklyn Dodgers* (New York: G.P. Putnam's Sons, 1984), p. 239.
11. Golenbock, *The Spirit of St. Louis*, p. 387.
12. Shatkin, *The Ballplayers*, p. 932.
13. *Ibid.*, p. 106.
14. Rampersad and Robinson, *Jackie Robinson*, p. 184.
15. Robinson and Duckett, *I Never Had It Made*, p. 68.
16. Durocher and Linn, *Nice Guys Finish Last*, pp. 208–209.

17. John B. Holway, *Josh and Satch: The Life and Times of Josh Gibson and Satchel Paige* (Westport, CT: Meckler, 1991), p. 192.

18. John Thorn and Pete Palmer, eds., *Total Baseball* (New York: Warner Books, 1989), p. 523. From "Black Ball" by Jules Tygiel.

19. Holway, *Josh and Satch*, p. ix.

Bibliography

Books

Alexander, Charles. *John McGraw*. New York: Viking Penguin, 1988.
_____. *Rogers Hornsby*. New York: Henry Holt, 1995.
_____. *Ty Cobb*. New York: Oxford University Press, 1984.
Anderson, David W. *More Than Merkle*. Lincoln: University of Nebraska Press, 2000.
Blake, Mike. *Baseball Chronicles*. Cincinnati: Betterway Books, 1994.
Bucek, Jennine, ed. *The Baseball Encyclopedia,* 10th Edition. New York: Macmillan, 1996.
Carmichael, John. *My Greatest Day in Baseball*. New York: A.S. Barnes, 1945. Reprinted Lincoln: University of Nebraska Press, 2000.
Charlton, James, ed. *The Baseball Chronology*. New York: Macmillan, 1991.
Cobb, Ty, and Al Stump. *Ty Cobb: My Life in Baseball*. New York: Doubleday, 1961.
Cramer, Richard Ben. *Joe DiMaggio: The Hero's Life*. New York: Simon & Schuster, 2000.
Creamer, Robert. *Babe: The Legend Comes to Life*. New York: Simon & Schuster, 1974.
_____. *Baseball in '41*. New York: Viking Penguin, 1991.
Curran, William. *Big Sticks*. New York: Morrow, 1990.
Daniel, W. Harrison. *Jimmie Foxx: The Life and Times of a Baseball Hall of Famer 1907–1967*. Jefferson, NC: McFarland, 1996.
DeGregorio, George. *Joe DiMaggio: An Informal Biography*. New York: Stein and Day, 1981.
DiMaggio, Joe. *Lucky to Be a Yankee*. New York: Greenberg, 1943.
Durocher, Leo, and Ed Linn. *Nice Guys Finish Last*. New York: Simon & Schuster, 1975.
Eig, Jonathan. *Luckiest Man: The Life and Death of Lou Gehrig*. New York: Simon & Schuster, 2005.
Einstein, Charles. *The Fireside Book of Baseball*. New York: Simon & Schuster, 1958. From the story *Double X: The Brilliant Jimmy Foxx,* by Bob Holbrook of the *Boston Globe*.
Feller, Bob, and Bill Gilbert. *Now Pitching Bob Feller*. New York: Harper Collins, 1991.
_____, and Burton Rocks. *Bob Feller's Little Black Book of Baseball Wisdom*. Chicago: Contemporary Books, 2001.
Fleitz, David. *Shoeless: The Life and Times of Joe Jackson*. Jefferson, NC: McFarland, 2001.
Fleming, G.H. *The Dizziest Season*. New York: Morrow, 1984.
_____. *Unforgettable Season*. New York: Holt, Rinehart and Winston, 1981.
Gallico, Paul. *Farewell to Sport*. New York: Knopf, 1938.
Godin, Roger A. *The 1922 St. Louis Browns*. Jefferson, NC: McFarland, 1991.
Golenbock, Peter. *Bums*. New York: G.P. Putnam's Sons, 1984.
_____. *Dynasty*. Englewood Cliffs, NJ: Prentice-Hall, 1975.
_____. *The Spirit of St. Louis*. New York: Harper Collins, 2000.
_____. *Wrigleyville*. New York: St. Martin's, 1996.
Graham, Frank. *The New York Giants*. New York: G.P. Putnam's Sons, 1952. Reprinted Carbondale: Southern Illinois University Press, 2002.
Greenberg, Hank, and Ira Berkow. *Hank Greenberg: The Story of My Life*. New York: Random House, 1989.

Gregory, Robert. *Diz: The Story of Dizzy Dean and Baseball During the Great Depression.* New York: Viking Penguin, 1992.

Holway, John B. *Josh and Satch: The Life and Times of Josh Gibson and Satchel Paige.* Westport, CT: Meckler, 1991.

Honig, Donald. *Baseball When the Grass Was Real.* New York: Coward, McCann and Geoghegan, 1975.

_____. *The Greatest First Basemen of All Time.* New York: Crown, 1988.

_____. *The Man in the Dugout.* Chicago: Follett, 1977.

_____. *The October Heroes.* New York: Simon & Schuster, 1979.

Hood, Bob. *The Gashouse Gang.* New York: Morrow, 1975.

Hornsby, Rogers, and Bill Surface. *My War with Baseball.* New York: Coward-McCann, 1962.

Huhn, Rick. *The Sizzler: George Sisler, Baseball's Forgotten Great.* Columbia: University of Missouri Press, 2004.

Jones, David. *Deadball Stars of the American League.* Dulles, VA: Potomac, 2006. Includes biography of Ty Cobb by Dan Ginsburg and biography of Sam Crawford by Bill Lamberty.

Kahn, Roger. *The Boys of Summer.* New York: Harper and Row, 1971.

Kaiser, David. *The Epic Season: The 1948 American League Pennant Race.* Amherst: University of Massachusetts Press, 1998.

Kaplan, Jim. *Lefty Grove: American Original.* Cleveland: Society for American Baseball Research, 2000.

Kashatus, William. *Connie Mack's '29 Triumph.* Jefferson, NC: McFarland, 1999.

Kavanagh, Jack. *Ol' Pete: The Grover Cleveland Alexander Story.* South Bend, IN: Diamond, 1996.

_____. *Rogers Hornsby.* New York: Chelsea House, 1991.

_____. *Walter Johnson: A Life.* South Bend, IN: Diamond, 1995.

Kuenster, John, ed. *From Cobb to Catfish.* New York: Rand McNally, 1975. Includes "Carl Mays Recalls That Tragic Pitch" by Jack Murphy, *San Diego Union,* 1971; "Rogers Hornsby's Five Fabulous Years" by Tom Meany, condensed from the book *Baseball's Greatest Hitters*; and "Hack Wilson: The Tragic End of a Great Hitter" by Al Drooz, *Cincinnati Enquirer,* 1974.

Lane, F.C. *Batting.* New York: Baseball Magazine Co., 1925. Reprinted 2001 by Society for American Baseball Research, Cleveland, OH.

Lansche, Jeffrey. *Stan the Man Musial: Born to Be a Ballplayer.* Dallas: Taylor, 1994.

Levy, Alan H. *Joe McCarthy: Architect of the Yankee Dynasty.* Jefferson, NC: McFarland, 2005.

Linn, Ed. *The Great Rivalry: The Yankees and Red Sox 1901–1990.* New York: Houghton Mifflin, 1991.

_____. *Hitter: The Life and Turmoils of Ted Williams.* New York: Harcourt Brace, 1993.

Lowry, Philip J. *Green Cathedrals.* New York: Walker, 2006.

Mathewson, Christy. *Pitching in a Pinch.* New York: Putnam, 1912. Reprinted 1994, University of Nebraska Press, Lincoln.

Mayer, Ronald. *Christy Mathewson: A Game-by-Game Profile of a Legendary Pitcher.* Jefferson, NC: McFarland, 1993.

Mead, William. *Two Spectacular Seasons.* New York: Macmillan, 1990.

Millikin, Mark R. *Jimmie Foxx: The Pride of Sudlersville.* Lanham, MD: Scarecrow Press, 1998.

Mosedale, John. *The Greatest of All: The 1927 Yankees.* New York: Warner, 1974.

Murray, Tom, ed. *Sport Magazine's All-Time All Stars.* New York: New American Library, 1977.

Musial, Stan, and Bob Broeg. *Stan Musial: "The Man's" Own Story.* New York: Doubleday, 1964.

Neff, David S., Richard Cohen, and Micheal Neft, eds. *The Sports Encyclopedia: Baseball,* 21st Edition. New York: St. Martin's, 2001.

Okkonen, Marc. *The Ty Cobb Scrapbook.* New York: Sterling, 2001.

Okrent, Daniel, and Harris Lewine, eds., with historical text by David Nemec. *The Ultimate Book of Baseball.* Boston: Houghton Mifflin, 1991.

Parker, Clifton Blue. *Fouled Away: The Baseball Tragedy of Hack Wilson.* Jefferson, NC: McFarland, 2000.

Polner, Murray. *Branch Rickey.* New York: Athenaeum, 1982.

Rampersad, Arnold, and Rachel Robinson. *Jackie Robinson.* New York: Ballantine, 1997.

Ritter, Lawrence. *The Glory of Their Times.* New York: Macmillan, 1966.

_____. *Lost Ballparks.* New York: Viking, 1992. Reprinted New York: Penguin, 1994.

Robinson, Jackie, and Alfred Duckett. *I Never Had It Made*. New York: Putnam, 1972.
Robinson, Ray. *Iron Horse: Lou Gehrig in His Time*. New York: Harper Collins, 1990.
Ruth, Babe, and Bob Considine. *The Babe Ruth Story*. New York: Dutton, 1948.
Salant, Nathan. *Superstars, Stars and Just Plain Heroes*. New York: Stein and Day, 1982.
Shatzkin, Mike, ed. *The Ballplayers*. New York: Morrow, 1990.
Sickels, John. *Bob Feller: Ace of the Greatest Generation*. Washington, DC: Brassey's, 2004.
Silverman, Al. *Warren Spahn: Immortal Southpaw*. New York: Bartholomew House, 1961.
Simon, Tom. *Deadball Stars of the National League*. Washington, DC: Brassey's, 2004. Includes biography of Christy Mathewson by Eddie Frierson and biography of Hooks Wiltse by Gabriel Schechter.
Skipper, John. *Charlie Gehringer: A Biography of the Hall of Fame Tigers Second Baseman*. Jefferson, NC: McFarland, 1993.
Slaughter, Enos, and Ken Reid. *Country Hardball: The Autobiography of Enos "Country" Slaughter*. Greensboro, NC: Tudor Publishers, 1991.
Smelser, Marshall. *The Life That Ruth Built*. New York: New York Times Book Company, 1975.
Smiles, Jack. *Big Ed Walsh*. Jefferson, NC: McFarland, 2008.
Smith, Curt. *Voices of the Game*. South Bend, IN: Diamond, 1987.
Smith, Ken. *Baseball's Hall of Fame*. New York: Grosett and Dunlop, 1952.
Snider, Duke, and Bill Gilbert. *The Duke of Flatbush*. New York: Zebra Books, 1988.
Sowell, Mike. *The Pitch That Killed*. New York: Macmillan, 1989.
Staten, Vince. *Ol' Diz: A Biography of Dizzy Dean*. New York: Harper Collins, 1992.
Stump, Al. *Cobb: A Biography*. Chapel Hill, NC: Algonquin, 1994.
Thorn, John, and Pete Palmer, eds. *Total Baseball*. New York: Warner Books, 1989.
Veeck, Bill, and Ed Linn. *Veeck as in Wreck*. New York: G.P. Putnam's Sons, 1969.
Williams, Ted, and John Underwood. *My Turn at Bat: The Story of My Life*. New York: Simon & Schuster, 1969.

Articles

Anman, Larry. "Cobb on a Rampage." *The Baseball Research Journal,* 1994.
Cannon, Jimmy. "The Joe DiMaggio I Remember." *Sport,* September 1956.
Henrich, Tommy, and Richard Nikas. "The Last Yankee." *The National Pastime,* 1999.
Keonig, Bill. "Farewell Joe." *USA Today's Baseball Weekly,* March 10–16, 1999.
Lindberg, James Oscar. "Just How Good Was George Sisler?" Unpublished story from the library of the Society for American Baseball Research.
Nightengale, Bob. "The Sultans Side by Side." *USA Today Sports Weekly,* April 15–11, 2006.
Sher, Jack. "Christy Mathewson: The Immortal 'Big Six.'" *Sport,* October 1949.
_____. "Lou Gehrig, The Man and the Legend." *Sport,* October 1948.
_____. "Rogers Hornsby: The Mighty Rajah." *Sport,* July 1949.
_____. "Ty Cobb: The Georgia Peach." *Sport,* November 1948.
Stump, Al. "There'll Never Be Another Hack Wilson." *Cavalier,* 1961. Reprinted in *Baseball,* 1962.
Warburton, Paul. "George Sisler." *The National Pastime,* 2000.
_____. "The 1921 A.L. Race." *The National Pastime,* 1998.
_____. "Rogers Hornsby." *The Baseball Research Journal,* 1999.
_____. "Stan Musial's Spectacular 1848 Season." *The Baseball Research Journal,* 2001.
_____. "Ted Williams in 1941." *The National Pastime,* 2003.

Newspapers

New York Times
Sporting News
USA Today Baseball Weekly
USA Today Sports Weekly

Index

Aaron, Henry 67, 184, 187
Abbatichio, Ed 21
USS *Alabama* 3, 174
Alexander, Dale 97
Alexander, Grover Cleveland 2, 59, 65
All America All-Star team in Tokyo 101
All-American Girls Professional Baseball League 110
Allen, Johnny 104, 109, 136, 154
American Association 151, 160
Ames Leon 8, 10, 18
Amman, Larry 27, 34
Amyotrophic Lateral Sclerosis 130
Appling, Luke 138–139
USS *Arkansas* 76
Arnold, Dorothy 203
Asheville, North Carolina 53
Associated Press 28
Augusta, Georgia 27
Auker, Eldon 125–126, 136, 148, 151
Aulick. W.W. 12
Averill, Earl 127

Bacharach Giants 218
Baer, Max 137
Bagby, Jim 46
Baker, Del 148–149, 151, 153
Baker, Frank 27, 32, 42, 48–49, 75, 98
Baker Bowl: right field wall 91; Rogers Hornsby's hitting stats at (1922) 62
Baldwin Locomotive Works 82
Baltimore Elite Giants 218

Baltimore Orioles (International League) 45
Bancroft, Dave 51
Banta, Jack 224, 227, 299
Barber, Red 225
Barney, Rex 220, 224, 227
Barrett, Charles 117–118, 197
Barrow, Bonnie and Clyde 116
Barrow, Ed 40, 131
Barry, Chad 16
Barry, Jack 32–33
Baseball Hall of Fame 7, 24–25, 30, 63, 86, 183
Baseball Magazine 42
The Baseball Research Journal 34
Basie, Count 151
Battle of the Bulge 162
Battle of the Philippine Sea 174
Bauer, Hank 24
Bay Parkways 145
Bearden, Gene 206, 212
Beaumont, Texas 145
"Begin the Beguine" 151
Bell, Les 61
Bender, Chief 32, 35
Bennett, Dr. George 203
Bennett Park: last game 37
Berger, Wally 92
Berra, Yogi 207, 210
Bevens, Bill 175, 177
Bigbe, Carson 62
Bishop, Max 104–105, 109
Bissonette, Del 90
Black Sox Scandal 40
Blackstone Valley League 145
Blair, "Footsie" 87
Blake, "Sheriff" 92
Blue Ridge League 82

Bob Feller: Ace of the Greatest Generation 174
Bob Feller's Little Black Book of Baseball Wisdom 173
Bodie, Ping 23
Bofors antiaircraft mount 174
Boley, Joe 101
Bonds, Barry 3, 40, 67, 157, 159
Bonham, Ernie 169, 181
Bonura, Zeke 139, 149
Boston University 106
Bottomley, Jim 63, 87
Boudreau, Lou 174–176, 180, 182, 204–205, 208, 210–212
Bowerman, Frank 9
Boyle, Buzz 123
Braddock, James J. 137
Branca, Ralph. 189, 217, 223–224
Braves Field: location and prevailing winds 196; record attendance for season (1948) 193; Rogers Hornsby's batting average at (1928) 61
Brazle, Al 224
Breadon, Sam 66, 117, 121–122
Brecheen, Harry 190–191, 193–196, 220, 224, 226, 228
Brennan, Mike 98
Bresnahan, Roger 9, 12–13, 16–17, 22
Brett, George 157
Bridges, Tommy 105, 107, 124–126
Bridwell, Al 9, 12, 15, 18–19, 23
Briggs Stadium: Ted Williams' stats at 162

Brissie, Lou 209
Broaca, Johnny 134
Brock, Lou 27
Broeg, Bob 96, 188–189, 196
Brooklyn Daily Eagle 34, 119, 124
Brooklyn Times-Union 119
"Brother Can You Spare a Dime" 105
Brought, James 113–114
Brown, Bobby 205
Brown, Lloyd 138
Brown, Mordecai 6, 13–17, 19, 21–24
Brown, Tommy 196
Browne, George 9
Bucknell College 5
"Bums" 221
Bunning, Jim 162
Burnett, Johnny 106
Burns, Jack 136
Burns, George (Giants) 52
Burns, George (Indians) 47
Busch Stadium: statue of Stan Musial 198
Bush, Donie 31, 36, 46
Bush, Guy 84, 90, 92
Bush, Joe 44, 75, 78–79
Byrne, Tommy 206

Cain, Pat 138, 147
Caldwell, Earl 211
Caldwell, Ray 36
"Caliban" 85
Camnitz, Howie 11
Camp, Walter 5
Campanella, Roy 218, 221–222, 225–227, 229
Capone, Al 89
Carens, George C. 106
Carew, Rod 157
Carleton, Tex 115–116, 120, 123
Carlson, Hal 87, 93
Carpentier, Georges 48
Carter, Craig 27
Case, George 174, 176, 180–181
Casey, Hugh 189, 222
CBS Game of the Week 127
Chalmers, Hugh 28–29
Chance, Frank 8, 12–14, 22–24
Chandler, "Happy" 192, 217
Chapman, Ben 104–105, 134, 148
Chapman, Ray 42–43, 71

Chase, Hal 36
"Checkbook Champions" 75
Chemical Warfare Division 2, 70
Chesbro, Jack 25
Chesnes, Bob 194, 219
Chester, Pennsylvania 81
Chicago's Municipal Tuberculosis Hospital 92
"The Cinderella Man" 137
Civil War 26, 28, 30
Clarke, Fred 11–12, 19
Clarke, Nig 30
Coakley, Andy 14, 131
Cobb, Amanda 27
Cobb, Florence 39
Cobb, Shirley Marion 33
Cobb, Ty 2, 26, 31–32, 33, 36, 46–48, 55–56, 59, 67–68, 74–78, 138, 159, 169, 194, 197, 217; batting race with Joe Jackson (1911) 37–38; built hospital 39; career stats 25; death 27–28; educational fund 39; end of 40-game hitting streak 33–34; family 27; first Major League at bat 25; fist fights 28; foot speed timed 27; Gas and Flame division in World War I 38; Hall of Fame 25; hazing by Tiger teammates 28; Hollywood movie 39; on Hughie Jennings 35; idolization of Confederacy 28; on integration 28; managing Tigers 38, 39; on place hitting 34; racist remarks 28; recovering stolen automobile 31; Sam Crawford quote on 30; steals of home 27; winning Chalmers automobile 28–29
Cobb, William Hershel 27
Cobb Educational Fund 39
"Cobb on a Rampage" 34
Coca-Cola 33
Cochrane, Mickey 98, 100, 102–103, 105–106, 109–110, 124–127, 134, 148–149, 151, 154
Coleman, Ed 101
Collins, Eddie 32–33, 35, 158–161
Collins, James "Ripper" 116–118, 120, 122–124

Columbia University 42, 130–131; Columbia's South Field 131
Columbus, Ohio 69, 192–193
Combs, Earle 104, 165
Comiskey Park: Bob Feller's Opening Day no-hitter (1940) 173; record night game crowd for "Satchel" Paige's shutout (1948) 210
Commerce High School 130
Confederacy 28, 39,
Connery, Bob 57
Coogan's Bluff 10, 22
Coombs, Jack 32
Cooper, Gary 130
Cooper, Walker 222
Cooperstown 4, 24, 86, 190
Corriden, John 28
Coveleski, Harry 20–21
Coveleski, Stan 49–51
Cox, Billy 222, 225
Cramer, Doc 101, 105, 108, 154
Crandall, Otis 10, 12, 14, 17
Cravath, Gaavy 63
Crawford, Sam 30–31, 33, 35–37, 43
Cronin, Joe 110, 119, 140, 161, 170
Crosetti, Frank 104, 134–137, 142
Crotona Park 145, 152
Crowder, Alvin 109, 124
Curtis, Don 114
Cunningham, Bill 65
Cuyler, Kiki 84, 87–88, 121

Dahlen, Bill 9
Daniel, Dan 133, 206
Dark, Alvin 219
Dascoli, Frank 197
Davids, Bob 27
Davis, Curt 123, 137
Davis, Frank 78
Davis, Virgil 116
Daytona Beach, Florida 185
Dead Ball era 8, 27, 29, 37, 48
Dean, Albert 112
Dean, Chubby 140
Dean, Dizzy 118, 120, 123, 126, 230; All-Star Game (1934) 119; All-Star Game injury (1937) 127; August holdout (1934) 121; bought out of army 113–114; childhood 113; death 127;

engagement and marriage 114; Houston Buffaloes 114; May holdout (1934) 116–117; opening day win (1934) 114–115; origin of nickname Dizzy 113; pitched shutout in seventh game World Series (1934) 126; pitching skills discovered 113; prediction (1934) 112; radio announcer for St. Louis Browns 127; St. Joseph 114; stats (1934) 112; stories on location of birth 119; suspension and fine (1934) 121–122; television announcer for CBS Game of the Week 127; thirtieth win (1934) 124; traded to Cubs 127; won World Series opener (1934) 124

Dean, Patricia 114, 127
Dean, Paul 112–113, 115–125
Delahanty, "Big Ed" 34
Delahanty, Jim 34–36
Delancey, Bill 116, 118, 122, 124–125
Dempsey, Jack 48
Denison, Texas 57
The Depression 101–102, 105, 118, 121, 137, 151, 159
Derringer, Paul 119, 124
Des Moines, Iowa 173
Detroit Times 152
Devlin, Art 9, 12, 15, 18–20, 23, 131
Dewey, Governor Thomas 204
Dickey, Bill 104, 106, 134–135, 137, 139–141, 151, 175, 177–178
Dickson, Murray 188, 228
Diering, Charles 223
Dillinger, John 120
DiMaggio, Dom 162, 208–209, 212
DiMaggio, Giuseppe 199, 201
DiMaggio, Joe, 3, 60, 128–129, 134–137, 139, 141–143, 155, 157, 161, 169–170, 175–177, 204, 208, 211; accused of using loaded bat 206; batting success against Bob Feller 205; benched (1950) 213; bone spur in right heel (1948) 207; cartilage in knee (1934) 201; childhood 200–

201; enlisted in Army Air Force 203; fifty-six game hitting streak 157, 162–163, 165–166, 202; great return series against Red Sox (1949) 213; hit tune "Joltin' Joe DiMaggio" 199; holdout (1938) 202, (1942) 202; honorary pallbearer at Babe Ruth's funeral 210; infected eye 202; injuries late in (1948) 209; *Life* magazine 213; made fortune 213; marriage to Dorothy Arnold 202–203; marriage to and divorce with Marilyn Monroe 213; muscles in leg (1939) 202; rookie season with Yankees 201–202; San Francisco Seals 201; sandlot ball 201; sixty-one game hitting streak 201; surgery on elbow 203; surgery to remove bone spurs (1946) 203, (1948) 212; Tommy Henrich quote on 199; ulcers 203; Yankees signed him 201
DiMaggio, Vince 199–201
discolored baseballs 71
the "Dixie Demon" 27
Dobson, Joe 208
Doby, Larry 210
Doerr, Bobby 161, 177, 179–181
Donahue, Pete 85, 90
Donald, Atley 168
Donlin, Mike 9–10, 15–16, 18–20, 22–23
Donovan, Bill 32, 34
Donovan, Patsy 10
Donura, Pennsylvania 185
Douglas, Phil 52
Doyle, Larry 9, 12, 17–18, 23
Dreyfuss, Barney 70
Duffy, Hugh 79, 164
Dugan, Joe 44, 55, 75, 78
Dunn, Jack 45
Durocher, Leo 117, 120, 122–123, 125–126, 186, 189–190, 192–195, 215, 226–227
Dust Bowl 118
Dyer, Eddie 186, 188, 190, 192, 218, 223

Earnshaw, George 101–104, 110
Easterly, Ted 37

Eastern League 132
Eastern Shore League 98
Easton, Maryland 98
Ebbets Field: record attendance (1947) 224; Stan Musial batting stats at (1948) 189
Eckhardt, Oscar 201
Edwards, Hank 174
Edystone Print Works 81
Egan, Dave 160, 206
Ellerbe, Frank 71
Ellington, Duke 151
Elliott, Jumbo 90
Ellwood City, Pennsylvania 81
Emslie, Bob 19
English, Woody 88, 91
Erskine, Carl 196, 224
Essick, Bill 201
Etten, Nick 175, 180
Evans, Russell 139
Evers, Johnny 13, 16, 19, 21, 23
Ewing, Bob 14
Exposition Park 14, 17

Faber, Red 46, 71, 79
Factoryville, Pennsylvania 8
Fain, Ferris 209
Felker, Carl 164
Feller, Bill 172–174, 204
Feller, Bob 3, 150, 153, 163, 165–167, 178, 204–206, 208, 211; breaks strikeout record 179; broke Rube Waddell's strikeout record 172, 182; built ballpark 172; built house 173; childhood 172–173; co–record with Nolan Ryan 183; enlisted in navy 174; father 172–174; games on farm 172–173; no-hitter against Yankees (1946) 175–176; one hitter against Boston (1946) 179; one hitter against Chicago (1946) 179; opening day no-hitter (1940) 173; possible stats 183; reveals diet 180; return from the war (1945) 174; rivalry with Hal Newhouser 177; stats (1941) 173, (1946) 172; test of speed of fast ball 181; on throwing curve ball at an early age 178; on USS

Alabama 174; visiting wounded soldiers 176; war action in the Pacific 174; on war heroes 174
Fenway Park: Ted Williams career and stats at (1941) 169
Ferguson, Alex 79
Ferguson, George 9
Ferrell, Wes 102, 135
Ferriss, David "Boo" 177, 181–182
Fewster, Chick 42, 45–46, 50
Finney, Lou 110, 163
Fisherman's Wharf 200
Fitzsimmons, Fred 90, 92, 94, 119–120, 122–123, 142
Fleming, Les 176
Florida State League 185
Fohl, Lee 78
"Forgotten Man" speech 107
Fort Hood, Texas 216
Fort Wayne Daisies 110
Fort Worth, Texas 56–57, 67
Foster, Eddie 76, 78
Fournier, Jack 61, 63
Fowler, Dick 170, 209
Fox, Pete 149
Foxx, Helen 108
Foxx, Jimmie 68, 98, 99, 102, 104–105, 109, 119, 134–135, 137, 140, 150, 160, 167; and Babe Ruth's home run record 97; bad health and death 111; chronic sinus condition 110; Connie Mack quote on 108; cut in salary (1933) 103; Easton 98; Fort Wayne Daisies 110; golf course venture 110; high school 98; Lefty Gomez quote on 100; longest homer 101; personality 107; Providence 98; raise in salary 110; screens erected in ballparks 97; sold to Boston 110; sprained wrist (1932) 108; stats (1929–1931) 100, (1932) 97; three homers and a double 106; in *Time* magazine 100; took fewer pitches in (1932) 103; underpaid salary 100; use of lighter bat (1932) 101; in World War II 110
Frazee, Harry 40, 44, 79
French, Larry 122–123

Frey, Bennie 123
Frick, Ford 96
Frisch, Frankie 51–52, 66, 87, 115–118, 120–126, 227
Furillo, Carl 220–222, 225–226, 228–229

Gainor, Del 32, 34
Galbreath, John 155
Gallico, Paul 45
Garagiola, Joe 223, 228
Garcia, Mike 171
Gardner, Larry 47
Gas and Flame Division 24, 38
Gas House Gang 112, 126
Gehrig, Christina 130–133
Gehrig, Eleanor Twitchell 130, 133
Gehrig Lou 45, 68, 89, 94, 102, 104–105, 119, 134–135, 138–140, 145, 149–150, 153–155, 163, 165, 169, 202; acting 137; All-Star Game homer (1936) 137; American League RBI record (1931) 133; back injury (1936) 141; career record for RBIs per game 128; career world series stats 142; childhood 130; chipped bone in hands 130–131; at Columbia 131; consecutive game streak 132; death from amyotrophic lateral sclerosis 130; discovered by Paul Kritchell 131; Eleanor Gehrig quote on 133; farewell speech at Yankee Stadium 130; four home runs in one game 104–105, 143; at Hartford 131–132; high school 130; highest salary 128; home run off Carl Hubbell (1936 World Series) 142; home run race with Ruth (1927) 132; Joe DiMaggio quote on 129, 136; marriage to Eleanor Twitchell 133; on Miler Huggins 132; parents 130; post nineteenth century record for runs scored per game 128; "Pride of the Yankees" 130; stats (1936) 129; Tarzan 129–130
Gehringer, Charlie 107, 124–125, 146, 148, 150–152, 154

General Motors 33
Gerber, Wally 77
Gharrity, Patsy 41
Gibson, Josh 4, 229–230
Gillespie, Ray 74
Gionfriddo, Al 203
Glaviano, Tommy 225
The Glory of Their Times 30
Golenbock, Peter 221
Gomez, Vernon "Lefty" 61, 100–106, 109, 134, 148, 151, 165, 168
Goodman, Benny 151
Goodman, Billy 204
Gordon, Joe 175, 205, 211
Gore, Artie 227
Gorsica, Johnny 162
Goslin, Leon "Goose" 124–126
Gotham Theatre 17
Gould, James M. 65
Grants Pass, Oregon 72
Greenberg, Hank 2, 3, 68, 110, 124–126, 134, 149, 151, 178, 182; anti-Semitic abuse 144–145; at Beaumont 145; on best season (1937) 144; Bud Shaver quote on 152; Charlie Gehringer quote on 146, 148; childhood 145; dilemma on Rosh Hashanah (1934) 146–147; disappointment on not breaking Gehrig's RBI record (1937) 155; at Hartford 145; last game of season(1937) 154; last season in Pittsburgh 155–156; on Mickey Cochrane 148; NYU 145; offer to sign with Yankees 145; on opposition 154; parents 145; at Raleigh 145; refusal to play in All-Star Game (1938) 150; refusal to play on Yom Kippur 147, 153; run into by Jake Powell 147; second all-time career RBIs per game 144; self made ballplayer 152; sign stealing 152–153; switch to outfield (1940) 155; in World War II 155
Griffith, Clark 180–181
Grimes, Burleigh 60, 65
Grimm, Charlie 67, 88–91, 93
Groh, Heinie 61
Grove, Robert "Lefty" 86,

98, 101–103, 106–109, 134, 140, 147, 164–167

Haas, Mule 84, 102, 109
Hackenschmidt, George 82
Hacker, Warren 225
Hadley, Bump 134, 142, 148, 151
Hafey, Chick 87, 123
Haines, Jesse 65, 121
Hallahan, "Wild Bill" 85, 93, 116, 125–126
Hamner, Granny 192
Haney, Fred 38
Hank Greenberg: The Story of My Life 144
Harder, Mel 107–108, 136, 147, 154, 165
Harper, Harry 50
Harris, Bob 160, 163
Harris, Bucky 204, 208–209, 212
Harris, Mickey 204
Hartford, Connecticut 131, 140, 145
Hartnett, Gabby 88, 90, 92, 137
Hatten, Joe 150, 195, 224
Hayes, Frankie 170, 176–177, 180
Hayes, Jack 139
Haynes, Joe 181
Hayworth, Ray 149
Hegan, Jim 182, 208
Heilmann, Harry 48, 59, 73, 75
Heintzelman, Ken 229
Helton, Todd 157
Henderson, Rickey 25, 27
Henrich, Tommy 175–176, 199, 205–206, 208, 212
Henry Ford Hospital 180
Herman, Babe 86, 88, 121
Herman, Billy 121, 137, 166
Herman, Woody 151
Herrmann, Gary 70
Herzog, Buck 9, 16, 19, 22–23
Hesse, Harry 131
Heydler, John 62, 117
Hildebrand, Oral 151
Hine, Jeanette Pennington 64
Hite, Mabel 9–10
Hoag, Myril 134, 139
Hodges, Gil 219–222, 225–226, 228
Hodgin, Ralph 177

Hoffman, Danny 30
Hoffman, Solly 19
Hogan, Shanty 88
Hogsett, "Chief" 126
"Hole in the Wall" 84
Holiday, Billie 151
Hollywood 39, 127, 130
Holmes, Tommy 119
Honig, Donald 64, 95
Hoover, President Hubert 107
Hornsby, Ed 57
Hornsby, Mary 57
Hornsby, Rogers 54, 58, 62, 84–88, 90, 94–95, 157, 184, 197–198; affair with and marriage to Jeanette Pennington Hine 64; batting average of .402 56; batting stance 29; batting stats at Sportsman's Park 60; at Braves Field 61; broke existing NL single season home run record 64; California fall league (1921) 59; Clyde Sukeforth quote on 64; discovered by Cardinals 57; dispute over salary 66; divorce from Sarah Hornsby 64; fielding ability 62; final game (1922) 65–66; foot speed 60–61; Giants 59, 66; Grover Cleveland Alexander quote on 59; hitting stats against Giants 63; John McGraw quote on 59; Les Bell quote on 61; manager of Braves, Browns, Cubs and Reds 66–67; manager of Cardinals 66; *My War with Baseball* 67; parents 57; on reading, drinking and smoking 56; stats in (1922) 56; stock in Cardinals 66; surgery to right heel 67; theory on hitting 56–57; thirty-three game hitting streak 64–65; trade to Giants 66; Ty Cobb quote on 59; youth in Fort Worth 56
Hornsby, Rogers, Jr. 64
Hornsby, Sarah 64
Hotel Elysée 212
Houdini, Harry 124
Houston Buffaloes 114
Howerton, Bill 228

Hoyt, Waite 43, 46, 50–52, 74, 78–79, 124
Hubbell, Carl 88, 94, 112, 114, 116, 119, 122–123, 129, 141–142
Hudlin, Willis 138
Hudson, Sid 210
Huggins, Miller 43, 46, 51–54, 57, 59, 75, 98, 132
Hughson, Tex 177
Huston, Cap 40, 42, 51
Hutchinson, Fred 211
Hyland, Dr. Robert 77, 186

"I Want a Girl Just Like the Girl that Married Dear Old Dad" 124
International League 45, 98
"The Iron Horse" 130, 143
Irvin, Monte 226
It's Good to Be Alive 218

Jackson, Joe 29, 33, 35, 37–38, 48, 71
Jackson, Travis 118
Jacksonville, Florida 168
Jacobson, William 72, 73, 77
Jamieson, Charlie 47, 50
Jansen, Larry 193, 217
Jennings, Hughie 28, 32, 35–37
Jersey City, New Jersey 48
Jimmy Fund 171
"John Henry" 82
Johnson, Ban 28
Johnson, Billy 208, 211
Johnson, Charles 138
Johnson, Jack 28
Johnson, Walter 31–32, 44, 70, 79, 177
"Joltin' Joe DiMaggio" 199
Jones, Davy 30
Jones, Jake 174
Jones, Nippy 188, 193 226
Jones, Sam 44, 49, 75
Jones, Sheldon 193
Jones, Tex 29
Jones, Willie 229
Joost, Eddie 209, 211
Joss, Addie 179–180
Judge, Joe 73

Kaese, Harold 160
Kansas City Monarchs 216
Kaugn, Jennie 81
Kazak, Eddie 218–219, 223, 226

Keeler, Wee Willie 34, 165–166
Keener, Sid 122
Kell, George 210
Keller, Charlie 157, 168–169, 175–176, 181
Kelley, Dave 27
Kelley, George "Highpockets" 51, 53
Keltner, Ken 174, 176, 179, 206, 211
Kerr, Dickie 185
Kinder, Ellis 211
Kiner, Ralph 155, 184, 187, 194, 197, 221–222, 227, 229
King, Clyde 198
Kirk, William P. 12
Klein, Chuck 86, 89, 91–93
Klem, Bill 118
Kling, Johnny 13, 22, 23
Knickerbockers, Bill 135
"Knot Hole Gang" 60
Kolp, Ray 85
Konstanty, John 224
Korean War 3, 159, 170–171
Koslo, Dave 220
Koufax, Sandy 172, 181
Kramer, Jack 178, 212
Krause, Lou 107
Kritchell, Paul 131–132, 145
Kuhel, Joe 206–207
Kurowski, Whitey 189, 191

Laabs, Chet 150
La Guardia, Mayor 141
Lajoie, Napoleon 28–29
Lake, Eddie 175
Land, Grover 30
Landis, Judge Kenesaw Mountain 61, 71, 96, 122, 126, 139
Lane, F.C. 42
Lanier, Max 228
Lanigan, Ernest 183
Lary, Frank 162
Lary, Lyn 102, 150
Lavagetto, Cookie 115
Lawrence, Frank 82
Lazzeri, Tony 104, 134–135, 139, 142
Leach, Tommy 14
League of Nations 44
A League of Their Own 21
League Park: Babe Ruth home run at (1921) 46; Tris Speaker's 42 doubles at (1921) 47

Leever, Sam 11–12
Leiber, Hank 122
Leifield, Lefty 11
Lemon, Bob 174–175, 180–181, 204–205, 208
Les Brown and His Band of Renown 199
Lewis, Lou 131
Lieb, Fred 97, 132
Life magazine 213
Lindstrom, Fred 86
Liscombe, Gerald 151
Livingston, Paddy 34
Lockhardt, Texas 57
Lolich, Mickey 172
Lopat, Ed 206–207
Lord, Bris 32
Lou Gehrig's Disease 130
Louis, Joe 207
Lucas, Arkansas 112, 119
Lumber Leagues 201
lumiline chronograph 181
Luque, Dolf 88, 90, 93
Lyons, Al 197
Lyons, Ted 106, 108–109, 137, 164

Mack, Connie 8, 29, 35, 84, 97–98, 100–101, 103–104, 106–109, 140, 170, 205, 207, 209
Mack, Ray 175–176
MacPhail, Lee 203
Madison Square Garden 17
Maddox, Nick 11–12, 17
Magee, Sherry 20
Mahaffey, Roy 103–104
Mails, Duster 72
Majaeski, Hank 209
Malone, Pat 84, 86, 88, 94–96, 134, 138–139
Mancuso, Gus 124
Mantle, Mickey 2
Manush, Heinie 38, 100, 102
Marberry, Firpo 102
Marcum, Johhny 110
Marion, Marty 223
Marquard, Rube 20, 63
Martin, John "Pepper" 114, 117–118, 123–126, 217
Martinez, California 200
Martinsburg, West Virginia 82, 96
Marx Brothers 139
Masi, Phil 195
Mathewson, Christy 2, 7, 11–13, 15–17, 19–21, 61, 69, 77;

basketball center 5; at Bucknell 5; career pitching stats 6; checkers and chess 5; control stats in pitching 6; death 24; fade-away pitch 6; football 5; golf 5; Merkle game 22–24; opening day at Polo Grounds (1908) 9–10; parents 8; Pitching in a Pinch 5; quote from Larry Doyle on 18; refusal to play on Sundays 5; tuberculosis 24; twenty-two-game win streak 14; World Series (1905) 8; World Series stats 6; in World War I 24
Mathewson, Gilbert 8
Mathewson, Jane 23
Mathewson, Minerva 8
Matthias, Brother 45
Mauer, Joe 135
Mayo, Eddie 175
Mayo Clinic 130
Mayor's Trophy Game 212
Mays, Carl 42–44, 46–47, 49–52, 75
Mays, Willie 67
McAfee, Bill 109
McCarthy, Joe 67, 82, 85, 87, 90–91, 93–95, 105, 133–137, 143–144, 150, 202–204
McConnell, Andy 29
McCormick, Frank 166
McCormick, Mike 197, 225
McCormick, "Moose" 9, 18–19, 23
McCullough, Bill 119
McGann, Dan 9
McGinnity, Joe 8–10, 12–15, 17–19, 22
McGovern, Artie 54
McGowan, Roscoe 115, 119
McGraw, John 6, 8–18, 20–23, 51, 53, 59, 66, 82, 120, 143
McHenry, Austin 60, 63
McInnis, Stuffy 32
McManus, Marty 77–78
McNair, Eric 101, 109, 135
McNally, Mike 42
McQuillan, George 9, 14, 18
"Meal Ticket" 129
"the Mechanical Man" 154
Medwick, Joe 114–117, 120, 124, 126, 137
Meer, Johnny Vander 194
Mele, Sam 207

Merkle, Fred 6, 10, 19–23
Meusel, Bob 42–44, 46, 50, 52, 71, 73
Meusel, Emil 52
Miami Marlins 110
Miami University 110
Michigan University 69–70, 154
Miksis, Eddie 229
Miles, John 31
Miller, Bing 74, 101, 108
Miller, Eddie 166
Miller, Elmer 42, 51–52
Milwaukee Brewers (minor league team) 98
Minneapolis Millers 110, 160, 168
Minner, Paul 191
"Miracle Mets" 221
"Mister Average Fan — Joe Early Night" 211
Mitchell Report 1
Mize, Johnny 184, 187, 193, 195, 197
Monroe, Marilyn 223
Montreal Royals 216–217
Moore, Jo Jo 118–119, 122
Moore, Terry 191
Moran, Bugs 89
Moriarty, George 36
Moses, Wally 179
Mountain States League 185
Mullin, George 37
Mullin, William 186
Muncrief, Bob 205
Munger, George 223–224, 227
Mungo, Van Lingle 119
Municipal Stadium: attendance 89, 179, 204, 206, 284; first game 108; record attendance (1946) 179; Satchel Paige shutout 210; single game attendance record (1948) 206; single season record (1948) 204
"Murderers' Row" 133, 135, 141, 176
Murphy, Jack 42
Murphy, Johnny 134, 148
Murphy, Sam 84–85
Murtaugh, Danny 194, 226
Musial, Ed 185
Musial, Lukasz 185
Musial, Mary Lancos 185
Musial, Stan, 3, 186–88, 190–191, 193, 195, 218–220,

223, 225–229; All-Star Game homer (1946) 192; All-Star Game records 192; appendicitis (1947) 186; arm injury 185; career stats 184; career total bases 184; childhood 185; consecutive game streak of 896 games 197; at Daytona Beach 185; on fielding 196; on Leo Durocher 194; on *Newsweek* 197; origin of nickname "Stan The Man" 189; parents 185; at Pearl Harbor 186; at Rochester 185–186; *Sporting News* Player of the Decade 197; at Springfield 185; stats at Ebbets Field (1948) 189; stats (1948) 184; on road in (1948) 189; statue of 198; third world championship (1946) 186; tied Ty Cobb's record (1948) 196–197; unusual batting stance 184–185; at Williamson 185
My Greatest Day in Baseball 22
My War with Baseball 67
Myers, Elmer 48

Narrows, Georgia 28
National City Bank 54
National Commission 70
National Vaudeville Association 73
Needham, Tom 9, 12, 20
Negro Leagues 4, 207, 230; Negro American League 216; Negro National League 218
Nehf, Art 52, 63
New York American 12, 24–25
New York Evening Journal 10, 118
New York Sun 53
New York Times 11–12, 115, 119
New York Tribune 9–10, 22
New York University 145
Newark, New Jersey 134
Newcombe, Don 219, 221–229
Newhouser, Hal 162, 177–182, 204, 206, 212, 220–221
Newsom, Bobo 134, 149–150, 153, 166, 179
Newsweek magazine 197

Niarhos, Gus 210
Nice Guys Finish Last 189
Niggeling, Johnny 164
No! No! Nanette 44

O'Connor, Jack 28
O'Connor, Paddy 131
O'Day, Hank 19–21
O'Doul, Lefty 91, 93–94, 119, 201
Ohio Penn League 69
Okkonen, Marc 34
Olmo, Luis 228–229
Olson, Ivy 37
O'Malley, Walter 193
"One O'Clock Jump" 151
O'Neill, Steve 47, 50,-51, 138
Order of the Elks 96
Orlando, Johnny 170
Ott, Mel 86, 116, 118–120, 192–193
Outlaw, Johnny 182, 212
Outlook 77
Overall, Orval 13, 16, 19
Overmire, Stubby 175
Owen, Marv 126, 149
Owen, Mickey 227
Owens, Jesse 181, 216

Pacific Coast Conference 216
Pacific Coast League 160, 201
Page, Joe 204
Paige, Leroy "Satchel" 4, 113, 172, 207, 210, 229–230
Palace Theater 43
Palica, Erv 225
Panama Canal 174
Park Plaza Hotel 122
Parmelee, Roy 120
Pasadena, California 216
Pasadena Junior College 216
Passarello, Art 205
Passeau, Claude 166
Patkin, Max 179
Pearl Harbor 3, 155, 174, 176, 186, 202
Pearson, Monte 134, 140, 142
Peckinpaugh, Roger 42, 46–47, 52, 73, 165
Pennock, Herb 44, 79
Pesky, Johnny 179
Pfeister, Jack 12–13, 16–17, 19, 22–23
Pfirman, Charles 62
Phelps, Babe 88, 93
Philadelphia Inquirer 107–108
Picinich, Val 66

"the Picture Player" 68
Pipgras, George 104
Pipp, Wally 42, 52, 78, 132
Pitching in a Pinch 5, 22
Pitler, Jack 214
Plank, Eddie 32
Poffenberger, Cletus 150
Pollet, Howie 224
Polo Grounds: Babe Ruth at 47–48, 73; Babe Ruth's stats at (1920, 1921) 41; Christy Mathewson's entrance 6; enlargement (1908) 17; George Wiltse at 14; Giants' major league record attendance season at (1908) 6; Giants' NL record attendance at (1921) 51; Merkle at 19; National League game record crowd in (1934) 123; record opening day crowd in (1908) 9; replayed Merkle game 22–24; World Series (1921) 52–53, (1936) 141–142; Yankees and Indians at (1921) 50–51; Yankees' major league record attendance at (1920) 41
"Pop Bottle Incident" 79
Portsmouth, New Hampshire 110
Portsmouth Truckers 82
Potter, Nelson 155
Powell, Jake 134, 147, 150
Pratt, Del 44
Price, Jackie 179
Pride of St. Louis 127
Pride of the Yankees 130
Providence Grays 98
Pruett, Hubert 74, 78
Pulliam, Harry 20–22

Quinn, John Picus 51, 79

Radcliffe, Rip 138
Raffensberger, Ken 224
Raschi, Vic 206, 208
Rawhide 137
Reese, Harold "Pee Wee" 196, 219, 221–223–225, 227, 229
Reiser, Pete 195–196, 220
Remagen Bridge 191
Reulbach, Ed 13, 20
Reynolds, Allie 204–206, 229
Reynolds, Carl 89, 106
Rhodes, Gordon 102, 140, 147

Rice, Del 189, 220
Rice, Grantland 96
Rickey, Branch 59, 66, 69–70, 114, 117, 121, 122, 216–217
Rigler, Charles 14, 21, 117
Rigney, Bill 225
Rigney, Johnny 162, 164, 167, 169
Ring, Johnny 66
Ritter, Lawrence 30, 49
Rixey, Eppa 65
Rizzuto, Phil 175–176, 206, 210
Robb, Doug 220
Robinson, Aaron 179
Robinson, Bill "Bojangles" 209
Robinson, Eddie 208, 211
Robinson, Frank 3, 230
Robinson, Jackie 3–4, 71, 80, 144, 189–190, 195–196, 215, 216, 218, 220, 226, 228–229; America's opposition to integration of baseball 214; with Branch Rickey 216, 217; businessman 230; childhood 216; court martial trial 216; on cover of *Time* magazine 217; death from diabetes 230; Don Newcombe quote on 221–222; Enos Slaughter spiking incident 225; fifth steal of home (1949) 227; Kansas City Monarchs 216; Leo Durocher quote on 227; Marty Marion quote on 223; Montreal Royals 217; NCAA title in broad jump 216; officer in army 216; older brother Mack 216; parents 216; at Pasadena Junior College 216; with Pee Wee Reese against player resentment 219; rise in attendance due to integration 224; Rookie of the Year (1947) 214, 217; scolded major league baseball 230; stats (1949) 214, 216; stole home 20 times 214; threats 217; at UCLA 216
Robinson, Jerry 216
Robinson, Mack 216
Robinson, Mallie 216
Robinson, Rachel 217

Robinson, Wilbert 89
Rochester Red Wings 186, 218
Roe, Preacher 190–191, 220, 224
Rojek, Stan 226
Rolfe, Red 134, 136–137, 139–140, 151
Rommel, Ed 46, 104, 107, 206
Roosevelt, President Franklin D. 107, 134
Root, Charlie 55, 84, 87, 90, 93
Rose, Pete 25, 138
Rosh Hashanah 146
Roth, Braggo 42, 46–47
Rothrock, Jack 125–126
Rowe, Lynwood "Schoolboy" 124–126, 149
Royston, Georgia 27, 39
Rucker, Napoleon 12, 18
Ruffing, Red 104–105, 109, 134, 136–137, 141
Rutgers University 131
Ruth, Babe 3, 6, 25, 27, 38, 41, 44, 46, 52, 54, 56, 59, 66–67, 69, 71, 73–75, 77–78, 81, 89, 93, 97, 99–101, 103–104, 107–108, 119, 128–129, 132–134, 137–138, 142–144, 151, 154–155, 157, 159, 162, 169, 185, 199, 203–205, 210, 214, 230; all or nothing swing 48; altercation with Cobb 48; arrested for speeding (1921) 47; called home run (1932) 55; career stats 55; collapse in North Carolina 53; Columbia University testing 42; compassion for sick kids 45; death of first wife Helen 54; elbow injury in World Series (1921) 52–53; five hits on Opening Day in (1921) 43; funeral 210; impressed by Brother Matthias 45; Joe Dugan quote on 55; Johnny Sylvester story 54–55; marriage to Claire Hodgson 54; nicknames 42; with Red Sox 40; at St. Mary's Industrial School for Boys 45; Sam Jones quote on 49; showdown series with Cleveland 50–51; sold to Yankees 40; stats in (1921) 40, at Polo Grounds 41; surgery

for intestinal abcess 53; sus-
pensions (1922) 53; World
Series (1921) 52–53; with
Yankees 51
Ruth, Claire Hodgson 54
Ruth, Dorothy 54
Ruth, Helen 54
Ruth, Julia 54
Ryan, Connie 229
Ryan, Nolan 172, 183

Saffell, Tom 228
Sain, Johhny 190–191, 193–
195
St. Elizabeth Hospital 135,
148
St. Joseph, Missouri 114
St. Louis Post Dispatch 65,
123, 188
St. Louis Star 74
"St. Louis Swifties" 186
St. Mary's Industrial School
for Boys 40, 45
St. Patrick's Cathedral 210
Sallee, Harry 15
Salvation Army 159
"Salvation May" 160
San Antonio Public Service
Company 112
San Diego Padres (minor
league team) 160
San Diego Union 42
San Fransico Seals 201
Sandburg, Carl 84
Saranac Lakes, New York 24
Sauer, Hank 188
Scarborough, Ray 182
Schang, Wally 42–43
Schmidt, Charles 28
Schoendienst, Red 190–191,
197, 219
Schulte, Frank 21, 23
Schumacher, Gary 118, 123
Schumacher, Hal 120, 122–
123, 142
Scott, Everett 44, 75, 78
Scourby, Alexander 6
Seery, Pat 174, 177, 180
Selkirk, George 134–137, 139
Seminick, Andy 228
Severeid, Hank 73, 78
Sewell, Joe 47, 51
Seymour, Cy 9, 12, 16–18, 23
Shakespeare, William 85
Shannon, Spike 10
Shaver, Bud 152
Shaw, Artie 151

Shawkey, Bob 43, 76, 78–
79
Sheckard, Jimmy 16, 23–24
"She'll Be Coming 'Round the
Mountain" 126
Sher, Jack 18, 25, 133, 137
Sherdel, Wee Willie 142
Shibe, John 153
Shibe Park: attendance (1929–
1932) 103; fans turned away
from game (1948) 207;
opening (1909) 97; over-
flow crowd (1911) 35; reno-
vations cost 103
shine ball (banned) 8, 71
Shocker, Urban 50, 71, 74,
76, 78–79
"Shot Heard 'Round the
World" 224
Shotton Burt 73, 192–195,
229
Shoun, Clyde 190, 197
Sickels, John 3, 174, 176
Simmons, Al 98, 100, 102–
107, 109, 119, 140–141, 143,
209
Simmons, Curt 222
"Sing, Sing, Sing" 151
Sisler, Dave 80
Sisler, Dick 80
Sisler, George 2, 49, 50, 59,
61, 72, 75–76, 78, 165; All-
American with University
of Michigan 69; batting
coach for Brooklyn 80;
Branch Rickey quote on 69;
with Browns 70, 80;
Christy Mathewson quote
on 77; end of 40-game hitting streak 79; eye problems
68; injury to right shoulder
77; fielding prowess 73;
friendship with Branch
Rickey 70; mi-nor league
contract dispute 69–70;
Ray Gillespie quote on 74;
sons Dick and Dave Sisler
80; stats (1922) 68, (1920)
71; Ty Cobb quote on 68;
in World War I 70; Yankees
offer 71
Sisti, Sibby 193
Slaughter, Enos 2, 188–189,
191–192, 194, 219–220,
224–227, 229
Slocum, Bill 45
Smith, Ed 162

Smith, Elmer 47, 75
Smith, Red 208
Snider, Duke 218, 221–223,
225, 227–229
Society of Baseball Research's
Ad Hoc Committee of
Steals of Home 27
Sothoron, Allan 49
Souchock, Steve 212
South End Grounds 10
South Field at Columbia 131
Southworth, Billy 168, 190–
191, 193, 195
Spahn, Warren 190–191, 193–
196, 220, 227
Speaker, Tris 34, 43, 46–47,
51, 55
Spence, Stan 167
spitball (banned) 8, 71
Sport Magazine 25
Sporting Life 36
Sporting News 12, 30–31, 59,
61, 63, 74–77, 79, 84, 87,
92, 94–95, 97, 103, 113, 116,
129–130, 135, 140–141, 147,
152–153, 163–164, 168–169,
175–177, 180, 183, 197,
205–207
Sports Illustrated 224
Sportsman's Park: Browns' at-
tendance (1923) 80; Browns'
Labor Day crowd in (1922)
76; Browns' showdown
series with Yankees (1922)
77–79; Cardinals atten-
dance 121; Cardinals' attendance record (1922) 60;
Cardinals' showdown series
with Brooklyn in (1949)
228; Rogers Hornsby's
(1922) and (1924) batting
average at 60
Springfield, Missouri 185
Staley, Gerry 220, 223–224
"Stan the Man" 186, 198
Stanky, Eddie 218, 225
Steinfeldt, Harry 12, 23
Stengel, Casey 35, 61, 65, 197,
212–213
Stephens, Vern 208
Stephenson, Riggs 47, 84,
87–88, 93
Stevens, Ed 194
Stewart, Bill 228
Stirnweiss, Snuffy 175–176,
210
Stock, Milton 61

Stockton, J. Roy 95, 213
Stoneham, Charles 66
Stovall, George 29
"Strikeout City" 79
Strikeout Story 175
Stump, Al 28
Sudbury, Massachusetts 54
Sudlersville, Maryland 98
Suhr, Gus 93, 115, 122
Summers, Bill 138–139
Summers, Ed 35
Sukeforth, Clyde 64, 95
Suzuki, Ichiro 71, 138
"Swing It Brother Swing" 151
Sylvester, Johnny 54–55

Tabor, Jim 167
Taft, President William Howard 32
"Take the A Train" 151
Talmud 146
Tarzan movies 130
Taylor, Danny 92
Taylor, Luther "Dummy" 8, 10, 13–14, 17
Teachout, Bud 95
Tebbetts, Birdie 144, 149, 160, 166
Tempest 85
Tenney, Fred 9–10, 12, 18, 22–23
Terry, Bill 86, 91, 115, 118, 120, 142
Texas League 145, 151
Texas Rangers 116
Thomas, Ira 32, 35
Thompson, Hank 226
Thomson, Bobby 224
Time magazine 110, 129, 217
Tinker, Joe 13, 15–16, 23–24
Tobin, Jack 72–73, 79
Toledo, Ohio 82, 149
Toot's Shors 207
Topping, Dan 207
Torgeson, Earl 219
Torporcer, George 60
Travis, Cecil 162
Traynor, Pie 93, 115
Trosky, Hal 138, 150, 163
Trout, Dizzy 162, 170
Trucks, Virgil 175, 180
Truman, President Harry 204
Tucson, Arizona 201
The Ty Cobb Scrapbook 34

UCLA 216
Uhle, George 46, 49–50, 79

"Uncle Robbie" 62, 90
U.S.A. Today Sports Weekly 3

Valo, Elmer 209
Van Meter, Iowa 172, 173
"Van Meter Meteor" 177
Vance, Dazzy 62, 86, 88, 93, 121
Vangilder, Elam 71, 73, 77
Vaughn, Arky 123, 195
Vaughn, Porter 170
Veach, Bobby 76, 154
Veeck, Bill 84, 178–179, 182, 204
Veeck, William, Sr. 84, 94, 178
Vernon, Mickey 204
Vila Joe 12, 53
Virginia League 82
Voiselle, Bill 227

Waddell, Rube 172, 179–180, 182, 183
Wade, Jake 154
Wagner, Honus 11–12-, 15, 17, 20–21, 25
Wakefield, Dick 182
Walberg, Rube 102–103, 109
Walker, Bill 121–123
Walker, "Dixie" 186, 222
Walker, Gee 147–148
Walker, Harry 218
Walkup, Jim 152
Walsh, Ed 29, 33
Walter Reed Hospital 176
Waner, Lloyd 92
Waner, Paul 184
Wanninger, Pee Wee 132
Ward, Aaron 42, 44, 77–78
Ward, Leo 189
Warneke, Lon 117, 119–120
Warsaw, Poland 185
Washington Park: opening day (1908) 9
Wehmeier, Herb 191
Weiss, George 203
Weissmuller, Johnny 130
Werle, Bill 227
Wesleyan College 131
West Side Grounds 17
Western Association 114
White, Guy "Doc" 30
Wilber, Del 188
Wilks, Ed 91
Wilks, Ted 224, 228
Williams, Billy 197
Williams, Danny 160

Williams, Joe 125
Williams, Ken 61, 72–73, 76, 78
Williams, Ted 3, 56–57, 67, 163, 167, 176, 178–179, 182, 184, 205–208; All-Star game (1941) 166; ankle injury 161–162, 166; batted .388 at age thirty-nine 171; batting average if sacrifice flies counted (1941) 157; career on-base percentage 157; career stats at Briggs Stadium 162; career stats at Yankee Stadium 168–169; Carl Felker interview with The Sporting News 164; childhood 159–160; on DiMaggio 165; efforts on behalf of Jimmy Fund 171; feud with Boston writers 160–161; games missed due to wars 159; hitting at Fenway 169; Korean War 159, 170; last game (1941) 170; Minneapolis Millers 160; parents 159–160; San Diego Padres in Pacific Coast League 160; signed by Eddie Collins 160; stats (1941) 157; total average in batting 157–159; walks (1941) 167–168; World War II 159
Williams College 131
Williamson, Ned 64
Willis, Vic 11–12, 14–15, 17, 19, 21
Wilson, Hack 83, 86–88, 90, 94; at Baldwin Locomotive Works 81–82; bought by John McGraw 82; carousing 84; Charlie Grimm quote on 91; childhood 81–82; clerical error story 82; colorful mannerisms at plate 89; death and funeral 96; divorce and second marriage 96; early stardom with Cubs 82–84; goat of World Series (1929) 84–85; Grantland Rice quote on 96; Hall of Fame induction 96; Joe McCarthy quote on 91; Joe McCarthy's handling of 91; at Martinsburg 82; met future wife Virginia

Riddleburger 82; on New York Giants 82; origin of nickname Hack 82; physique 81; at Portsmouth 82; Rogers Hornsby's berating and fining of 95; stats at Wrigley Field (1930) 91; stats (1929) 84, (1930) 81; suspension (1931) 95; target of bench jockeying 85; at Toledo 82; William Veeck quote on 84; Woody English quote on 91
Wilson, Hazel 96
Wilson, Jack 149
Wilson, Owen 15
Wilson, Robert 81, 85, 96
Wilson, Virginia Riddleburger 82, 84
Wilson, President Woodrow 44
Wiltse, George 10, 12–20
Winters, Texas 57
Witt, Lawton "Whitey" 75, 78
Wolff, Roger 170
Wood, Joe 31, 35–36, 47, 50

Wood, Wilbur 172
"Woodchopper's Ball" 151
Woodling, Gene 178
World Telegram 126
World War I 2, 24, 70, 87
World War II 2–3, 110, 130, 144, 151, 159, 162, 172, 186, 209, 216, 218
Wright, Taft 174
Wrigley, William K., Jr. 67, 89, 94
Wrigley Field: attendance (1930) 89; Cubs win-loss record at (1930) 91; Hack Wilson's stats at (1930) 91; Ruth's called shot 55; major league season record attendance (1929) 84; upkeep and cleanliness of park 89
Wyatt, Whitlow 107, 154
Wynn, Early 204, 206
Wyrostek, Johnny 188

Yager, Abe 34
Yankee Stadium: Babe Ruth's batting stats at (1923) 41; Bob Feller's no-hitter (1946) 175–176; crowd of 85,264 in doubleheader against A's (1928) 98; Hank Greenberg hit first homer into center field beachers 153; Jimmie Foxx's legendary home run (1932) 105; Joe DiMaggio's batting at 199; subway series (1936) 141–142; Lou Gehrig's farewell speech 130; Ted Williams' career batting stats at 169; record world series crowd (1936) 142
Yardley, Jonathan 6
Yawkey, Tom 110, 207
Yom Kippur 147, 153
York, Rudy 149–153, 155, 166, 179
Young, Irving 17
Youngs, Ross 52

Zieder, Rollie 29
Zimmerman, Heinie 15–16
Zoldak, Sam 206
Zuber, Bill 168